Global Social Economy

The term "global economy" is associated with international trade and finance, investment and development, and the political economy of the international market economy. This book addresses "global *social* economy" which addresses the relation of capitalism to human flourishing, the role of international governance in the world economy, the transformation of work and use of time in internationalizing economies, cross-country developments in gender, poverty, and ageing, and ethics economic policy issues in the international economy.

This edited collection examines the social nature of capitalism today, the possibilities for social and economic development in the world under the democratic leadership of the United Nations, and the middle ground between market and hierarchy occupied by gift exchange as a means of coordinating economic value creation and the creation of knowledge. It considers long term issues in the global social economy concerning gender and discrimination, intergenerational poverty transmission, and the role of ageing.

From a variety of internationally acclaimed contributors, this collection introduces new social economic perspectives on the global economy that contest the neoliberal Washington Consensus view dominant until recent financial crises. They emphasize the issue of well-being in economic life, and how cooperative relationships are finding new roles in the global economy. The book also examines important changes in the advanced economies with respect to work, pensions, and the impact of technological change.

Global Social Economy will be of interest to social economists, institutional economists, public policy makers as well as students of economics and sociology.

John B. Davis is Professor of Economics at Marquette University, USA, and Professor of History and Philosophy of Economics at the University of Amsterdam, Netherlands.

Routledge advances in social economics
Edited by John B. Davis
Marquette University

This series presents new advances and developments in social economics think-ing on a variety of subjects that concern the link between social values and eco-nomics. Need, justice and equity, gender, cooperation, work poverty, the environment, class, institutions, public policy and methodology are some of the most important themes. Among the orientations of the authors are social econo-mist, institutionalist, humanist, solidarist, cooperatist, radical and Marxist, femi-nist, post-Keynesian, behavioralist, and environmentalist. The series offers new contributions from today's foremost thinkers on the social character of the economy. Published in conjunction with the Association of Social Economics.
Previous books published in the series include:

1 **Social Economics**
   Premises, findings and policies
   Edited by Edward J. O'Boyle

2 **The Environmental Consequences of Growth**
   Steady-state economics as an alternative to ecological decline
   Douglas Booth

3 **The Human Firm**
   A socio-economic analysis of its behaviour and potential in a new
   economic age
   John Tomer

4 **Economics for the Common Good**
   Two centuries of economic thought in the humanist tradition
   Mark A. Lutz

5 **Working Time**
   International trends, theory and policy perspectives
   Edited by Lonnie Golden and Deborah M. Figart

6 **The Social Economics of Health Care**
John Davis

7 **Reclaiming Evolution**
A Marxist institutionalist dialogue on social change
William M. Dugger and Howard J. Sherman

8 **The Theory of the Individual in Economics**
Identity and value
John Davis

9 **Boundaries of Clan and Color**
Transnational comparisons of inter-group disparity
Edited by William Darity Jr. and Ashwini Deshpande

10 **Living Wage Movements**
Global perspectives
Edited by Deborah M. Figart

11 **Ethics and the Market**
Insights from social economics
Edited by Betsy Jane Clary, Wilfred Dolfsma, and Deborah M. Figart

12 **Political Economy of Consumer Behaviour**
Contesting consumption
Bruce Pietrykowski

13 **Socio-Economic Mobility and Low-Status Minorities**
Slow roads to progress
Jacob Meerman

14 **Global Social Economy**
Development, work and policy
Edited by John B. Davis

Global Social Economy

Development, work and policy

Edited by John B. Davis

Routledge
Taylor & Francis Group

LONDON AND NEW YORK

First published 2010
by Routledge
4 Park Square, Milton Park, Abingdon, Oxon OX14 4RN

Simultaneously published in the USA and Canada
by Routledge
605 Third Avenue, New York, NY 10017

Routledge is an imprint of the Taylor & Francis Group, an informa business

Typeset in Times by Wearset Ltd, Boldon, Tyne and Wear

First issued in paperback in 2013

British Library Cataloguing in Publication Data
A catalogue record for this book is available from the British Library

Library of Congress Cataloging in Publication Data
Global social economy: development, work, and policy/edited by John B. Davis.
p. cm.
Includes bibliographical references and index.
1. Economic development–Social aspects. 2. International cooperation.
3. Globalization–Social aspects. I. Davis, John B.
HD75.G5524 2009
338.9–dc22   2009009798

ISBN13: 978-0-415-74663-2 (pbk)
ISBN13: 978-0-415-77809-1 (hbk)
ISBN13: 978-0-203-87098-3 (ebk)

Contents

List of illustrations   ix
Notes on contributors   xi

1 **Global social economy: an introduction**   1
  JOHN B. DAVIS

PART I
Capitalism, human development and knowledge   11

2 **Capitalism and human flourishing? the strange story of**
  the bias to activity and the neglect of work   13
  DES GASPER

3 **The United Nations and democratic globalization: a**
  reconnaissance of the issues   42
  KEITH COWLING, SILVIA SACCHETTI, ROGER SUGDEN
  AND JAMES R. WILSON

4 **Knowledge development and coordination via market,**
  hierarchy and gift exchange   58
  WILFRED DOLFSMA AND RENE VAN DER EIJK

PART II
Time and work   79

5 **"Time sovereignty": its meaning and externalities**   81
  FRANÇOIS-XAVIER DEVETTER

6 **Age differences in the consequences of overwork**   97
  BETH A. RUBIN AND CHARLES J. BRODY

7 The implications of happiness research for work time
reform 115
ROBERT M. LAJEUNESSE

8 Social time in international work environments 136
ESTHER RUIZ BEN

PART III
Gender, poverty transmission and ageing 147

9 The rise of the adult worker model: balancing work and
family life in Europe 149
JANNEKE PLANTENGA

10 Redistribution, intergenerational inequality and poverty
transmission: Germany and the United States compared 164
VERONIKA V. EBERHARTER

11 Pension reform and household financial position 182
GIANDEMETRIO MARANGONI, CHIARA MARCOMINI AND
STEFANO SOLARI

PART IV
Ethics and social economics 211

12 Market operation and distributive justice: an evaluation
of the ACCRA confession 213
JOHAN GRAAFLAND

13 The social economics of corporate social responsibility:
informational abundance and collective action 234
MARTHA A. STARR

14 A proper choice 256
JAN DE JONGE

15 Toward an ethical economics of planning horizons and
complementarity 275
FREDERIC B. JENNINGS, JR.

Index 292

Illustrations

Figures

2.1	The puzzle triangle	24
9.1	Total employment rate 2007	151
9.2	Employment rate of women 2007	152
9.3	Employment gender gap 2007	153
9.4	Employment impact of parenthood on men and women 2006	154
9.5	Use of formal childcare arrangements, age 0–2	155
9.6	Use of formal childcare arrangements, three years old to mandatory school age	156
9.7	Months of (paid) maternity and parental leave, 2005	159
10.1	Income inequality in Germany and the USA	172
10.2	Contribution of income source to total income inequality	173
10.3	Poverty intensity, poverty gap for different age cohorts	174
11.1	Household debts	204
11.2	The contribution to household financialization	204
13.1	Stakeholders in the world gold industry	243

Tables

2.1	Political and economic arguments for and against markets	21
4.1	Coordinate mechanisms	65
4.2	Coordination dissected	66
5.1	Length offered according to the situation of colleagues	87
6.1	Moderating effects of age on relationship between anger and overwork	107
6.2	Moderating effects of age on relationship between stress and overwork	108
8.1	Typology	141
10.1	Intergenerational income mobility, Germany 2000–2005, USA 1999–2005	175
10.2a	Intergenerational income transition Germany 1984/1999	177
10.2b	Intergenerational income transition Germany 1984/2002	177

10.2c	Intergenerational income transition Germany 1980/1994	178
10.2d	Intergenerational income transition Germany 1980/1997	178
10.3	Determinants of intergenerational poverty transmission	179
11.1	Pension reforms	191–197
11.2a	Net acquisition of PFs and life insurance as percentage of net financial assets	198
11.2b	Net acquisition of PFs and life insurance as percentage of GDP	198
11.3	Share ownership as percentage of total in value	200–201
11.4a	Different measures of household financial wealth, percentage GDP	202
11.4b	Net financial wealth GDP net of pension funds, percentage GDP	203
11.5	Details of household assets, 2000–2004, percentage GDP	205–206
12.1	Ten alternative standards of distributive justice	215
12.2	Aspects of economic freedom according to the Fraser Institute	222
12.3	Poverty (less than $1.09 per day, as percentage of population)	223
12.4	Income distribution, government share and economic freedom	227
12.5	Trends in worldwide income relations	228
12.6	The contributions of trade openness to economic growth	229
13.1	Retail jewelers: probability of adopting the "Golden Rules"	245
13.2	Retail jewelers: estimated effects on stock prices of the NDG campaign	247
13.3	Major gold mining companies: effect on stock prices of the NDG campaign	248

Contributors

Charles J. Brody is Professor of Sociology at University of North Carolina at Charlotte where he is also affiliated with the doctoral programs in Public Policy and Organizational Science. From 2001–2008, he chaired the sociology department at UNC-Charlotte. He held prior faculty appointments at Tulane University and the University of South Carolina. His current research focuses on generational differences in workplace attitudes and behaviors and gender differences in the expression of political attitudes.

Keith Cowling is Professor of Economics, University of Warwick. He is the author of many books and articles including *Monopoly Capitalism* (Macmillan, 1982) and *Beyond Capitalism: Towards a New World Economic Order*, with Roger Sugden (Pinter, 1994). Currently his research interests revolve around the deficiencies of monopoly capitalism and the formation of appropriate industrial strategies for addressing this world.

John B. Davis is Professor of History and Philosophy of Economics at the University of Amsterdam and Professor of Economics at Marquette University. He is author of *Keynes's Philosophical Development* (Cambridge, 1994) and *The Theory of the Individual in Economics* (Routledge, 2003), is the former editor of the *Review of Social Economy*, and currently co-editor of the *Journal of Economic Methodology*.

François-Xavier Devetter is Assistant Professor of Economics at the University of Lille 1 (France) and member of the Lille Centre of Sociological and Economic Studies (CLERSE). Most of his recent work on labor economics has been on the question of the quality of employment mainly in services sectors (working time, wages, and dignity at work).

Wilfred Dolfsma, economist and philosopher, is Professor of Strategy and Innovation at the University of Groningen School of Economics and Business. In his main fields of social, institutional and evolutionary economics, he has published *Institutional Economics and the Formation of Preferences* (Edward Elgar, 2004), *Knowledge Economies* (Routledge, 2008), *The Elgar Companion to Social Economics*, edited with John B. Davis (Edward Elgar, 2008), and *Institutions, Communication and Values* (Palgrave, 2009). He is the corresponding editor for the *Review of Social Economy.*

Veronika V. Eberharter is Associate Professor in Economics at the University of Innsbruck, Austria. Her main areas of interest are personal income distribution, poverty, and intergenerational income and social mobility. Her work bridges theoretical concepts, empirical analysis, and policy implications.

Rene van der Eijk is an economist at the Rotterdam School of Management, Erasmus University. Key research interests include knowledge sharing, social networks and innovation. He has written and published articles on these topics and has spoken at various international conferences.

Des Gasper studied economics and international development at the universities of Cambridge and East Anglia, and worked through the 1980s in Southern Africa. He now teaches public policy analysis and discourse analysis at the Institute of Social Studies in The Hague, and was Visiting Professor in 2005–2008 for the Research Centre on Well-being in Developing Countries at the University of Bath. His publications include *Arguing Development Policy* (co-editor R. Apthorpe; Frank Cass, 1996), *The Ethics of Development* (Edinburgh University Press, 2004; Sage India, 2005), *Trans-local Livelihoods and Connections* (co-editor T.-D. Truong; Sage 2009), and *Development Ethics* (co-editor, A. Lera St Clair; Ashgate, 2009).

Johan Graafland is Professor of Economics, Business and Ethics at Tilburg University in the Netherlands. He studied economics at Erasmus University Rotterdam and theology at Utrecht University. He works in the fields of philosophy of economics, economic ethics, business ethics, corporate social responsibility and the relationship between economics and religion. His most recent books are *Economics, Ethics and the Market: Introduction and Applications* (Routledge, 2007) and *The Eye of the Needle: About the Market, Happiness and Solidarity* (Ten Have, in Dutch).

Frederic B. Jennings Jr. has taught in the economics departments at Tufts University in Medford, MA and Bentley College in Waltham, MA, and worked as an economic consultant in the litigation group at Charles River Associates in Boston, MA and in the Office of Federal Tax Services at Arthur Andersen in Washington, DC. He has his own economic consulting firm, EconoLogistics in Ipswich, MA, which focuses on economic analyses mostly related to litigation. He is also president of the Center for Ecological Economic and Ethical Education in Ipswich, MA which he founded in 1998.

Jan de Jonge has worked on labor market issues, in particular on youth unemployment and on the effects of the concentration of unemployment in inner cities. He has recently finished a thesis on rational choice theory at the University of Amsterdam titled: "Rational and Moral Actions."

Robert M. LaJeunesse is Senior Lecturer in Economics at the University of Newcastle, Australia. His research interests are in labor economics, history of economic thought, and macroeconomics. He combines his knowledge and research in these areas in his book *Work Time Regulation as a Sustainable Full Employment Policy* (Routledge, 2009). His professional background includes work in the US Peace Corps, the US Treasury, and the AFL-CIO.

GianDemetrio Marangoni is Professor of Political Economy in the Faculty of Education, University of Verona, and in the Faculty of Law, University of Padua, Italy. He also holds teaching positions in Quantitative Methods for Business Economics in the Faculty of Economics, University of Lugano, Switzerland. His research interests include the theory of production and income distribution, technological change, the economics of production sectors, infrastructure, the provision of services to business, and decision theory.

Chiara Marcomini is a PhD student in the Doctoral School in Business Governance and Administration of the University of Siena (Italy). She has an MA in healthcare management (University of Ferrara). Her interests include welfare and health economics.

Janneke Plantenga works at the Utrecht University School of Economics. She received her PhD in Economics from the University of Groningen in 1993. Her research interest focuses on labor market flexibilization, the reconciliation of work and family and (European) social policy. She is the Dutch member and coordinator of the European Experts Group on Gender and Employment (EGGE). She has written widely on (the redistribution of) unpaid work, changing working time patterns, childcare issues and modernizing social security.

Beth A. Rubin is Professor of Sociology and Organizational Science and Adjunct Professor of Management at UNC-Charlotte. She served as Sociology Program Director at the National Science Foundation, 2004–2006. She has published numerous articles in leading academic journals on economic and workplace transformation on the re-employment of displaced workers, labor unions, homelessness and social policy and social theory. She has also published three books: *Research in the Sociology of Work: Workplace Temporalities* (2007); *Beside the Golden Door: Policy, Politics and the Homeless*, with James Wright and Joel Devine (1998), and *Shifts in the Social Contract* (1996). Rubin's current research is on time in organizations, organizational commitment, work–family balance, organizational and workplace restructuring and inequality and gender differences in the expression of political attitudes.

Esther Ruiz Ben is Assistant Professor at the Institute of Sociology of the Technical University of Berlin. Her main areas of interest include the sociology of professions, economic sociology, sociology of science and technology, and social inequality and gender. Her most recent research focuses on the impact of internationalization dynamics on tasks and knowledge transformation in the German IT industry. She has previously published: *Professionalisierung der Informatik* (2005).

Silvia Sacchetti is Lecturer at the Birmingham Business School and Coordinator of the Institute for Economic Development Policy at the University of Birmingham (UK). Her research interests are in the organization of production, theory of the firm, knowledge and creativity, economic democracy and local development. She addresses these issues from an institutionalist perspective, focusing on the relationships between: the governance of production systems and networks; learning and the production of knowledge; the unfolding of creativity and critical thinking across local economic systems; the development of economic systems based on deliberative democracy.

Stefano Solari is Associate Professor of Political Economy in the Department of Economics and Faculty of Law of the University of Padua (Italy). His interests include the history of economic thought (particularly of the social economy) and the evolution of institutional arrangements in the Western economies, with particular attention on the financial and welfare regimes.

Martha A. Starr is a member of the economics faculty at American University in Washington, DC. Previously she was a Senior Economist at the Federal Reserve Board of Governors. Her research is centrally concerned with consumption, saving, and the role of social values in economic life, including consumption and lifestyle norms, identity, socially responsible investment and consumption, corporate social responsibility, and social enterprise. She is a co-editor of the *Review of Social Economy*.

Roger Sugden is Professor of Socio-economic Development and Director of the Stirling Management School at the University of Stirling (UK). His research interests concentrate on local economic development viewed in the context of globalization, and are centered on the prospects for public initiatives that might stimulate economic democracy. His general research preoccupation is not with disciplinary boundaries, hence not per se with any one notion of "economics" but rather with the scientific analysis of (aspects of) economies. This has led most recently to a particular concern with creativity and critical thinking, the subject of his ongoing agenda of action research and the focal point of a framework that encompasses analysis of different ways of organizing production – through varied forms of enterprise and entrepreneurship, including particular types of (multi-locality) networking – and analysis of education, health and communication.

James R. Wilson is Senior Researcher in Clusters, Regional Development and Innovation at the Basque Institute of Competitiveness (Orkestra), and Lecturer in Economics at the University of Deusto (Spain). His main research interests are in the areas of economic development and competitiveness policy, in particular analysis of the governance of the interface between business, policy and economic development processes. He has published conceptual analysis of themes such as globalization, privatization, competitiveness and firm networking/clustering, as well as applied analysis in specific industry and country contexts.

1 Global social economy

An introduction

John B. Davis

Social economics investigates the social economy. The term "social economy" originated as a way of referring to the third sector in mixed market economies seen as distinct from the more familiar private and public sectors. With the development of national market economies in the eighteenth and nineteenth centuries, along with the development of capitalist market economies, it became apparent that there existed a significant amount of economic activity that neither reflected the standard logic of markets, nor that was part of the activities of the state. As there already existed an understanding of the institutions and economic functions of the market and the state, much of the early interest in this third sector was directed toward explaining the nature of its distinctive institutions and the social-economic structures. The principal forms originally identified remain those generally emphasized today, albeit in terms of a more contemporary vocabulary: cooperatives, not-for profit organizations, mutual associations, and voluntary activities and community organizations of various kinds. These institutions were argued to also possess their own distinctive set of motivating principles understood as a specific set of social values. These are less easy to summarize, but can perhaps be best associated with community, democracy, cooperation, equality, and the dignity and autonomy of individuals and social groups. These twin foundations – the institutions and social values of the social economy – constitute the primary basis on which social economics has developed to the present.

One might suppose, then, that as the market and the state dominate economic activity in the world today that social economic values and institutions play a subordinate role in modern economies. Yet we find at the beginning of the twenty-first century that they have in fact come to play a surprisingly important role in the global economy. Consider two quite different ways in which this has occurred. First, key supra-national economic organizations in the world today, such as the European Union, the North American Free Trade Association, the Asia-Pacific Economic Cooperation organization, the World Trade Organization, and many other regional economic associations, clearly function as cooperative associations that create shared rules for trade and investment for member countries. Indeed it is now widely agreed that the remarkable extension of trade and investment links between countries over the last quarter-century is very much due to a long record of post-war success in establishing these supra-national economic communities. In effect, the ideals of community as developed on a small scale basis within national economies in the past have been transferred in new form to the larger stage of the global economy. Of course, the principles of the market and state economic development still obtain, but they are now increasingly framed by international and regional cooperative agreements. Second, a key new actor in the post-war economy is the international non-governmental organization (NGO). These not-for-profit organizations are not only transnational in scope and mission, but they also explicitly value individuals and social groups for themselves; that is, they invest all individuals and social groups with an inherent dignity and the right to a relative autonomy simply as members of the world community. This goes beyond both the more traditional emphasis on freedom associated with market social values and the citizenship values of the state. Indeed, in keeping with their respective missions, NGOs value people irrespective of whether their nations do and whether or not they are successful in the marketplace.

Thus social economics today is in the process of acquiring a new subject of investigation: the global social economy. A little post-war history offers us clues as to why social economic values have come to have this new meaning. Consider what has brought about our globalized economy. The post-war global economy was effectively inaugurated in 1973 with the collapse of the Bretton Woods exchange rate system, the United States' abandonment of the dollar-gold exchange system, and the world's adoption of free floating exchange rates. One very important consequence of these developments was the opening of nations' capital accounts, the resulting free flow of capital across national boundaries, the migration of multinational firms to all parts of the world, and the attendant emergence of international banking as a dominant form of cross-country finance. Until the Asian Crisis of 1998, then, the dominant values associated with this quarter-century of development were those of the free market neoliberal "Washington Consensus" which called for privatizing public property and liberalizing markets everywhere (Williamson 1989). However, the Asian Crisis created serious doubts about the stability of a global economy developed on this basis, and this in turn led to further doubts about the desirability of neoliberal values. In fact these doubts had been building for many years. The World Bank estimates that from the 1970s to the end of the century there were more than 100 important national financial crises with significant impact on economies and people's well-being and livelihoods (World Bank 2001). But it was only in the aftermath of 1998, that many began to search for alternatives to the Washington Consensus world view and its social values.

Thus the world-wide crisis that began in late 2008 is now widely seen as confirming evidence that the institutions and values of free markets are inadequate to the needs of people and nations. At the same time, it is also now widely believed that nations will be unable to address the crisis each on their own. Accordingly as policy-makers struggle to deal with the financial crisis and the economic downturn, it seems to have become consensus opinion that the way forward depends on devising new forms of cooperation and joint burden-sharing across countries that respects the interests and traditions of people everywhere as members of one world community. Remarkably, then, social economic values have emerged as an alternative foundation for thinking about the global economy. The sense many have today is that people all have an inherent dignity and equality irrespective of their economic prosperity and material success in life. This conviction is often defended under the banner of human rights. But why have human rights become so visibly important in the thinking of so many at this time in history? Prior to globalization, individual rights were mostly believed to be the liberal democratic rights of speech, political participation, religion, and thought – that is, essentially national citizenship rights. But globalization not only made these traditional rights the ambition of people everywhere, but with many countries' tremendous development needs, it has also put social and economic rights on the agenda as the necessary concomitant of the former. Yet social and economic human rights, not having national foundations, have as their ultimate rationale simply that all people are members of a single world community. That is, they are human rights and indeed social economic values *par excellence* in virtue of valuing the inherent dignity of people irrespective of their locations, cultures, origins, or goals.

Nonetheless, these universal social values, despite their immense appeal in the world today, must still be seen as having a very fragile place in the global economy, particularly in the face of an increasingly disordered economic process that puts so many people at risk and threatens the whole idea of shared community. Indeed, whereas the social values of the Washington Consensus were paired with established economic institutions of open markets and free movement of capital, the social values of cooperation and community lack a comparable institutional basis in the international economy. A special difficulty they face is that historically these social values arose in national settings within the interstices of mixed capitalist economies, and were consequently generally local in nature with limited cross-national reach. Indeed one of the foundations of the idea of community is the sense of personal connection, as made possible by local proximity and ease of contact, in contrast to the sense of impersonal ties that operate in global markets that has motivated neoliberal social values. This makes the recent emergence of social economic values in the global economy all the more paradoxical. Why should people feel a sense of community and a desire to cooperate with people with whom they not only have no personalized contact but who are also likely to be dramatically different in background, culture, and experience? The answer can only be that these social values are more versatile than we have had reason to believe in that they are able to root in institutional settings far different from those in which they historically developed in modern market economies.

But there is still much to understand about how this new vision of the world economy is coming about. If the values of cooperation and human dignity are being adopted as the basis for an emerging global social economy, what institutional forms and arrangements exist that provide a basis for their development?

The chapters in this volume are in search of answers to this question. They presuppose the social values of a global social economy, and ask what supports them, and how are they to be extended. In this respect, these chapters are exceptionally forward-looking. They are in search of the global social economy that frames private and the public. They are in search of how the third way becomes the main way forward.

Capitalism, human development and knowledge

The three chapters in this section of the book respectively appraise three overarching concerns facing the global social economy: the social nature of capitalism today, the possibilities for social and economic development in the world under the democratic leadership of the United Nations, and the middle ground between market and hierarchy occupied by gift exchange as a means of coordinating economic value creation and the creation of knowledge.

In the opening chapter, "Capitalism and human flourishing?: the strange story of the bias to activity and the neglect of work," Des Gasper provides a broad overview of capitalism as a social economic system at the beginning of the twenty-first century. He focuses on a fundamental question: what sort of conception of human flourishing does capitalism promote? Most discussions of the relationships between capitalism and human flourishing, he notes, concern capitalism as a means or as an instrument. They consider how efficacious or not this instrument is with respect to some conception or conceptions of human flourishing. Capitalism is also defended as being, amongst other things, a field of freedom; a forcing ground of innovation; a system for widespread opportunity for involvement in decision making and hence for the growth of skills, knowledge and experience; a mechanism to reward effort and creativity; and a stable basis for political democracy. Each of these lines of defense carries a potential for critical assessment and for motivating reform and redesign. Most of these lines of thought also have implications for the conceptions of human flourishing that are associated with capitalism. But what conception of human flourishing does capitalism promote? While multiple conceptions of flourishing may exist under capitalism, he asks whether certain types of human flourishing are promoted by capitalism and are more in harmony with it, rather than simply able to co-exist with it. With reference to current conceptions of well-being – pleasure or satisfaction, preference fulfillment or fulfillment of substantive needs, and so on – he also suggests that capitalism does not fit any of them very well. Instead, its motor of unending restless expansion and destruction may fit an activist conception of well-being.

Keith Cowling *et al.* in "The United Nations and Democratic Globalization: A Reconnaissance of the Issues" are concerned with the direction of contemporary capitalism and the role the United Nations has in influencing the democratic development of economies. They seek to contribute to economic and political debate about the organization's role in the modern world, and their chapter gives an initial reconnaissance of the issues. Without attempting to provide a detailed history or analysis of the current situation within the organization, and maintaining a distance from the baggage of its internal politics, their objective is to present and consider a perspective based upon a particular analysis of processes of economic development. The analysis focuses on the social economic goal of including all peoples in the realization of the economic development goals that they themselves would democratically identify and seek, given the opportunity. They suggest that this is an approach that is consistent with many of the principles of the United Nations. Most notably, it has the realization of the aspirations of peoples at its heart and to that degree is in line with Kofi Annan's vision for the United Nations in the twenty-first century. If that vision is meant to be real and realizable, the issues they identify and discuss represent economic and political challenges that must be overcome.

In "Knowledge development and coordination via market, hierarchy and gift exchange," Wilfred Dolfsma and Rene van der Eijk ask us to consider how economic value creation in general and knowledge creation in particular require coordination, and that coordination can take several forms. In addition to markets, where prices coordinate, and hierarchy, where authority coordinates, there are networks that coordinate activities. This chapter suggests that the idea of gift exchange allows for the middle ground between market and hierarchy to be explored more fruitfully. The three coordination mechanisms are assessed in the context of knowledge creation and diffusion. Each has particular advantages, but those offered by gift exchange make it an effective and sometimes preferred alternative.

Time and work

The second section of the book is devoted to one of the most fundamental issues in social economics, the nature of work. Perhaps no other issue is of greater concern than how people earn their livelihoods in interaction with one another. The particular focus of the four chapters here is the changing nature of the relationships between time and work in modern economies and the impact of work time arrangements on well-being, all in the context of changing technologies of work in the global economy.

François-Xavier Devetter, in "'Time sovereignty': Its meaning and externalities," begins with an examination of changes post-1980 in the meaning of working time. From the 1930s until the 1980s the Fordist wage-earner relationship remained relatively stable, and applied to a large majority of salaried workers. However, this organization of time, which can be called a Fordist regime of temporal availability, seems to have been disputed since. This challenge is partially visible from a statistical point of view, but seems more pronounced when examined from the point of view of its legitimacy. The Fordist organization of working time is criticized both from the points of view of the wage-earner and the employer. For the wage-earner the criticism is based largely on the desire for greater flexibility or "choice" in working hours. Requests from the employer for greater flexibility are equally numerous and have intensified over the past 20 years. These two positions seem to merge in the writings of various observers to clear the way for a new compromise based around the concept of "time sovereignty." It is this kind of time sovereignty – the freedom to work more to earn more – that is the subject of this chapter. The issue is particularly important today in France, but could come to concern other countries such as the United Kingdom or the United States where managerial autonomy to shape the organization of work is less restricted. The situation is slightly different elsewhere in Western Europe, particularly in the Nordic countries. Nevertheless, the French case could be important for understanding larger trends. After describing what is currently meant by time sovereignty in France and highlighting the role it plays in an eventual new "post-Fordist" compromise, the chapter demonstrates how this mechanism favors long working hours and entails important externalities.

In "Age differences in the consequences of overwork," Beth A. Rubin and Charles J. Brody begin by noting that feeling "overworked" is a frequent experience of work in the contemporary economic life. Its negative consequences for employees are also increasingly well documented. The non-profit Families and Work Institute has issued two reports, one in 2001 and one in 2004 that demonstrate the prevalence of feeling overworked and its personal costs to employees of increased stress, depression, and anger. This chapter asks if these negative effects differ by age group. Using the 2004 "Overwork in America" data, and building on their previous research, the authors examine the impact of feeling overworked on employees by age group since their prior research, as well as anecdotal accounts, that suggest that younger workers differ fundamentally from older workers in their expectations about the labor force experience. They test competing hypotheses from the perspective of normative social contract theory and life course theory, and find minimal support for life course explanations of the moderating effect of age on the negative consequences of overwork.

Robert M. LaJeunesse, then, in "The implications of happiness research for work time reform," inquires about how people view work from the perspective of their self-perceived happiness. Recent psychological research on the impact of economic growth on well-being has challenged the efficacy of traditional Keynesian macroeconomic policies to foster improved well-being. The findings are that, beyond an adequate subsistence level, relationships and social engagement are more important to life satisfaction than income. This has important implications for socio-economic policy. In particular, achieving the goal of full employment will require significant labor market reform if the outcome is to be welfare enhancing. This chapter reviews the recent research on happiness in the context of work time reform, and seeks to identify a role for work time reorganization in improving lives and well-being.

Finally, Esther Ruiz Ben's "Social time in international work environments" looks at the impact that new information technologies have on the nature of working time in international work environments. Different time dimensions and temporality meanings are interwoven in international work environments through these new information technologies. In this chapter, she advances a theoretical model to analyze the relation between social temporalities and information technologies in international work environments using Lewis and Weigert's typology of social time and Orlikowski's structurational model of technology. Ruiz Ben suggests that institutional properties situated in distinctly located organizations influence the use, appropriation and development of the new information technologies, while at the same time these information technologies serve to synchronize different social time dimensions and contribute a temporal embeddedness to working time.

Gender, poverty transmission and ageing

In this section of the book we look at long run issues that cross social groups in the global social economy. The focus is on the state of development in the advanced economies on concerns targeted by social policies. Have policies that address gender inequality, poverty and intergenerational mobility, and pension protection for retired workers been successful? The three chapters in this section take stock.

In "The Rise of the Adult Worker Model: Actual Policies and the Implications for Gender Equality," Janneke Plantenga explains the adult worker model, and argues that a gender equality point of view implies a rethinking of the usual division of responsibilities and entitlements between women and men, especially with regard to the organization of care. The concept of the adult worker model is especially strong at the level of the European Union, both for social and economic reasons. Within the European employment strategy, growing labor force participation is favored as a means of promoting gender equality and social inclusion, as well as to increase economic competitiveness and to increase the tax base of the European welfare states. The rise of the adult worker model also necessitates a rethinking of the principles of social welfare systems, especially with regard to the provision of services and the organization of time. In this chapter Plantenga assesses the developments in the European member states on this issue and seeks to answer the question whether actual developments are in line with the gender equality challenge.

Veronika V. Eberharter, in "Redistribution, intergenerational inequality, and poverty transmission: Germany and the United States compared," examines the determinants and the extent of intergenerational income mobility and poverty persistence in two large economies representative of world's advanced countries. Using GSOEP-PSID (German Socio-Economic Panel–Panel Study of Income Dynamics) data and employing the common inequality measures and poverty indices, she compares the intergenerational effects of redistribution policy on income inequality and poverty. The key findings are: in Germany younger age groups tend to face lower income inequality in post-government income suggesting that redistribution policies become more progressive in the life course; in both the countries, labor income contributes the largest part to total income inequality; intergenerational income and poverty persistence is more strongly expressed in the United States; and gender, educational attainment, and employment hours significantly contribute to the intergenerational income mobility and determine the extent of intergenerational poverty persistence in the United States.

"Pension reform and household financial position," by GianDemetrio Marangoni *et al.* examines recent pension reforms that have been implemented in many countries oriented toward introducing or expanding pension funds or insurance. The main reason for these reforms is to reinforce the sustainability of intergenerational redistribution due to the ageing of society. However, a secondary aim has also been to help the development of financial markets and expand the role of the stock exchanges. The authors focus on developed countries and more specifically on European pension reforms. A number of questions arise concerning the impact of such reforms. In particular, they deal with the change in household savings investment and with the impact that these reforms have on the financialization of the economy. Their chapter provides a broad comprehensive account of the state of old age protection, and points toward further policies to be undertaken in the future.

Ethics and social economics

The last section of the book is devoted to four chapters that address the place of ethics in economic life. The first two by Johan Graafland and Martha Starr look at efforts to establish normative criteria to influence economic life: justice criteria vis-à-vis neoliberal globalization and broadly-held social values for corporate social responsibility. The latter two chapters, by Jan de Jonge and Frederic B. Jennings respectively, probe the meaning of ethical thinking itself as it applies to economic life: the first in regard to the nature of ethical choice and the second in regard to the intersection of economics and ethics.

Johan Graafland's "Market operation and distributive justice: an evaluation of the ACCRA confession" examines the so-called ACCRA declaration of 2004 of the World Alliance of Reformed Churches (WARC) that condemned neoliberal globalization on grounds of lack of justice. His chapter outlines ten alternative criteria for distributive justice. He shows that biblical ethics supports a variety of these criteria, including distribution in accordance to needs, the capability approach of Sen, reward of productivity, and procedural justice in transactions. Then Graafland presents an overview of empirical research on the impact of international market effects on distributive justice, and closes by evaluating the conclusion of the WARC that market operation is opposed to Christian faith.

In "The social economics of corporate social responsibility: informational abundance and collective action," Martha Starr argues that that over the past 15 years the idea of "corporate social responsibility" (CSR) has become an important part of the business world. Her chapter looks at CSR through a social economics lens by examining the role of broadly-held social values in shaping CSR objectives, identifying the source of market pressures on firms to bring their operations into better conformity with these values, in particular in connection with how this occurred in the "No Dirty Gold" campaign. Starr argues that an important part of the effectiveness of CSR rests on informational abundance.

Because information and communication technologies like the Internet make it much easier to publicize ethically problematic behavior of firms, it is easier to get mainstream consumers and investors (whose behavior is not systematically shaped by ethical concerns) to participate in efforts to sanction them. Her case study points to both the promise and limitations of relying on CSR to improve social responsibility in the profit system.

Jan de Jonge's "A proper choice" raises a number of important questions regarding ethical choices. How do we know whether the reasons for an action justify that action? Was there a good reason to act in the way a person did? Was it rational for the agent to do it and was it good that she did it? How can we decide on the goodness of actions? And how can we take account of them? The last two questions are taken to be central to the problem of valuation. A valuation is meant to establish the (natural) properties of the object or the state of affairs under consideration, to assess their (intrinsic) value and to qualify the object/event or state of affairs ("X is good/bad"). By way of introduction, de Jonge first discusses the question of how agents come to formulate their preferences. This concerns the question: what is it that makes an action desirable? This is explained in terms of an answer to the question: what attracts an agent, and why does she prefer this object or this action above an alternative? The formulation of preferences is from this point of view not different from the task of valuing objects, actions, or the states of affairs that result from our actions.

Finally, Frederic B. Jennings' chapter, "Toward an ethical economics of planning horizons and complementarity," aims to explore the relation of planning horizons and their property of complementarity to the role of ethics in economic society. Orthodox substitution assumptions stand on nothing more than assertion of a decreasing return to production. The whole argument for competition as an efficiency standard depends on a hard core of indefensible – but well-defended – traditions. The chapter begins with a case for realism, and for the value of theory as a guide to action in its structuring of imagined projections on which all decisions are based. The claims for decreasing returns and substitution are rejected in favor of falling cost and complementarity. Then the pricing and growth effects of planning horizons are used to reinforce the importance of complementarity in the economy, and to develop an argument that competition – in making us short-sighted – harms ecologies, educational learning, information transmission, and the fabric of social cultures. The chapter concludes by emphasizing the need for revision in our economic conceptions in favor of a "horizontal" emphasis on complementary interdependence, suggesting the need for institutional change from competition to cooperation as the source of efficiency.

Together, the chapters in this volume seek to map out a new vision of the world economic system as a global social economy. All were originally presented at the Twelfth World Congress of Social Economics – "Social Values and Economic Life" – in Amsterdam in June 2007, along with many other valuable papers. This volume is intended to convey the insights and thinking of the many contributors at that congress.

10   *J.B. Davis*

References

World Bank (2001) *Finance for Growth: Policy Choices in a Volatile World*, Washington, DC: World Bank.

Williamson, John (1989) "What Washington Means by Policy Reform," in Williamson, John (ed.) *Latin American Readjustment: How Much has Happened*, Washington, DC: Institute for International Economics.

Part I

Capitalism, human development and knowledge

2 Capitalism and human flourishing?

The strange story of the bias to activity and the neglect of work

Des Gasper[*]

1 Clarifying and distinguishing the debates

What sort of conception of human flourishing does capitalism promote? This question is less familiar than its popular sister "Does capitalism promote human flourishing?" and also less popular than "Is capitalism desirable?" and than the policy variant "Is capitalism better than the alternatives?" The last two questions here are bigger than the questions about human flourishing, because human flourishing is not the only relevant evaluation criterion.

Deirdre McCloskey's grand project on "the bourgeois virtues" and her recent book of the same title ask whether capitalism is desirable, in process and in outcome. In this opening book in her series she primarily considers two questions: "What are the virtues?" and "Does capitalist society recognize, practice and promote them?" However, she declares at the outset that her overall destination is a vindication that capitalist society, indeed specifically American capitalist society, is desirable. In contrast, my main question in this chapter is: "What ideas of the desirable does the real practice of capitalism represent and encourage?"

Most discussion on the relationships between capitalism and human flourishing concerns capitalism as a means, an instrument. It considers how efficacious or not the instrument is, with respect to some conception or conceptions of human flourishing. Peter Saunders (1995), for example, measures capitalism against Abraham Maslow's posited fundamental human needs. As we will see in the second section of the chapter, the existing defenses of capitalism are, in terms of its instrumentality, for far more than economic growth. It is also defended as being, amongst other things: a field of freedom; a forcing ground of innovation; a system for widespread opportunity for involvement in decision making and hence for the growth of skills, knowledge and experience; a mechanism to reward effort and creativity; and a stable basis for political democracy. A writer like McCloskey looks at a wide range of possible effects. Each of these lines of defense carries a potential for critical assessment too, and for motivating reform and redesign. Most of the lines of thought have implications also for the conceptions of human flourishing that are associated with capitalism.

This question of "What conception of human flourishing does capitalism promote?" has received less attention. While multiple conceptions of flourishing may *exist* under capitalism – and sometimes claims are even made that capitalism provides space for whatever conception of flourishing people happen to hold – we should ask whether certain types of conception are *promoted* by capitalism and more in harmony with it, rather than simply able to co-exist with it. For, with reference to conceptions of well-being as pleasure or satisfaction or fulfillment of substantive needs, the third section of this chapter will suggest that capitalism does not fit any of them very well. Instead, its unending drives for expansion and destruction may fit an activist conception of well-being. The fourth section examines this further.

Yet paradoxically, the typical conception of work under capitalism is as a cost, for the capitalist must pay for it. We should reflect on the categorization of costs and benefits under capitalism. There are fundamental implications of extending capitalist accounting categories from the level of the individual capitalist enterprise to that of an entire society. The highly questionable results which this extension produces in the case of discounting of future costs and benefits have been extensively discussed. The comparable extension of capitalist categories for the treatment of paid work time may produce major distortions in policy evaluation, given the considerable evidence that for many people work is one of the major sources of fulfillment. The chapter's fifth section raises this issue. It ends by asking how alternative conceptualizations of work might contribute to a more adequate treatment of human flourishing.

I have framed the issues in terms of a pair of vast and vague general notions: capitalism and human flourishing. I should explain why, and what I mean by them.

What is human flourishing?

I have chosen to use the category of human flourishing, more than welfare or well-being, for two reasons. First, welfare and well-being are too easily seen as nouns, presumed unitary and ready for measurement, rather than as verbs; and they are thus, second, too readily subsumed into the utilitarian mindset of mainstream economics.

Martha Nussbaum points out that while most eighteenth-century to nineteenth-century English translations of the classical concept of "eudaimonia" reduced it to mean happiness, it refers to "a complete and flourishing human life" (1997: 118–119), "activity in accordance with excellence" (2005: 175), "a specific plurality of valuable activities" (2005: 171) that reflect our human specificity, including, not least, love and friendship. The term "human flourishing" represents "eudaimonia" far more revealingly. While the concept of "well-being" that has revived in the past generation is a great improvement over the notions of "utility" or "economic welfare," it too is more prone to hypostatization than is the concept of human flourishing. Well-being should be conceived of as a verb, or a verb noun (gerund) – well-*being* – more than as a thing noun, in order to match the fluid, elusive and ongoing character of life. Life, the noun, really consists of living, the verb. As Nussbaum notes: "Most [ancient] Greeks would understand *eudaimonia* to be something essentially active, of which praiseworthy activities are not just productive means, but actual constituent parts" (1986: 6). Pleasure was seen as "so closely linked to the relevant activities that it cannot be pursued on its own" (2005: 176).

Second, there is a danger that this well-being becomes thought of as a quantity of something relatively straightforward, that we can weigh or otherwise measure, a sum of mental money or some quasi-biological variable that can be read-off by the appropriate technical apparatus. This is the path that was followed in reducing the concept of utility, perceived usefulness, into a concept of ophelimity (Pareto's term), a supposed measure of satisfaction.[1] I will still sometimes use the term "well-being," which is standard now both in scientific and everyday language, but we should use "human flourishing" when we need to emphasize that we are talking about processes of be-ing, as valued in processes of reflection and discussion, and not about quantities of a mental money nor some counterpart to mental temperature which we could adequately measure by deft use of a well-being thermometer (Gasper 2008).

What is capitalism?

The concept of capitalism contains various elements. Typically highlighted are:

- first, the commodity form;
- second, the habitat for commodities, namely, markets (a system of resource allocation through buying and selling, using prices for monetized exchange);
- third, private property.

Much discussion in the Weberian tradition concentrates on markets – capitalism is "production for a market by enterprising individuals or combines with the purpose of making a profit" (Berger 1987: 19) – not other features of capitalism. But markets are found also outside capitalist societies; as in market socialism, for example. Similarly, John Douglas Bishop's survey of issues in the ethics of capitalism defines capitalism as the combination of private property and free markets (Bishop 2000: 4). This is problematic in both what it highlights and what it leaves out. The idea that capitalism by definition involves *free* markets – meaning that prices are determined in markets – implies that monopoly capitalism cannot exist. Adam Smith was more realistic, noting that nothing was more typical of capitalism than collusion to restrict free competition. Attempts to define capitalism by the freedom of markets lead to the exclusion of misdemeanours, by definition, as well as to diversion of attention from more central aspects. Thus in addition the definition does not go far enough. Essential to capitalism are two further features:

- fourth, particular forms of property and enterprise law and accounting practice, which assign all net surpluses to the owners of capital. The default setting for the allocation of net surplus is that it goes to the capitalists, and not (also) to the workers or the community. We can call this "the prerogative of capital" (see, e.g. Ellerman 1982);
- fifth, the combination of the first four features – markets, monetization, private property, the prerogative of capital – can gradually generate something more than the sum of the parts: stupendous accumulated holdings of capital, transferable monetized claims over resources that constitute the greatest source of power in their societies and in the whole world.

The fourth feature, missing from Bishop's characterization and even from the fuller one by Saunders (1995: 9), deserves special attention. The prerogative of capital takes us beyond merely private property, to distinctively capitalist property arrangements and categories and their implications. It is more fundamental than "the systematic and self-interested pursuit of profit" (Saunders 1995: 5), for capitalism is still capitalism when pursuit of profit is half-hearted. Fundamental is the category of profit itself, seen as net earnings to the enterprise owner, the capitalist, after payment for all other inputs, including for labour treated as merely a commodity. One of the implications can be called "the perspective of capital," wherein work is presumed to be a cost and human flourishing becomes presumed to be measured by net present value.

We can then note two further features:

- sixth, an apparatus of supportive systems (including of state power) that defend and extend the commodity form, private property, market transactions free from non-profit obligations, and the capitalist prerogative; and
- seventh, and more broadly, the types of politics, culture and society that may be symbiotic with capitalist economy and its supportive apparatus.

There is obviously not just one type of capitalist society. Capitalist societies are not totally integrated mega-systems with a unitary rationale. They contain far more than capitalism, even if we defined that to cover all seven features above, not only the first five. Capitalist societies also contain families, religions, arts, sciences, other cultural forms (such as, typically, nationalism), and non-capitalist elements of civil society in many fields. So we can distinguish: capitalist economic arrangements and activity, namely the first four features above, and their eventual product (the fifth feature); capitalist theory and ideology, which can differ from the actual behaviour, for example by downplaying the negative features; and capitalist societies, which include much more than just capitalist economy and capitalist theory.

Mainstream economics emphasizes only the first three features we alluded to: the circulation of commodities in a private property system of markets – "the market system." McCloskey has a richer conceptualization of capitalism, yet one that is still fundamentally incomplete. She sees capitalism as "merely private property and free labor without central planning, regulated by the rule of law and by an ethical consensus" (2006: 14). This touches on or implies most of the features we mentioned, but the definition has become moralized, as if there cannot be capitalism unregulated by the rule of law, such as we have seen in contemporary Russia and much of the global South. McCloskey does not consider that to be true capitalism. And, critically, her definition excludes the essential capitalist prerogative, or smuggles it in via particular interpretations of private property and free labor. Implicitly, "free labor" here means labor as a commodity that is free from having a share in surplus. Toward the end of the book McCloskey provides a yet more reduced and idealized definition of capitalism, close to Bishop's: "a market-oriented, free-trade, private property, enterprising, and energetic economy, [just as] in the Lower Galilee of Jesus' time" (2006: 462). In the relatively self-enclosed, abstracted, intellectual world of much market theory the same fundamental verities apply for all times (cf. 2006: 508). This sort of notion from neo-classical economic theory is insufficient for thinking about twenty-first-century forms of capitalism, in which the principles of commoditization, private property rights and the capitalist prerogative are being extended and modified in attempts like those to patent the neem leaf and the human genome, and in an international trade in trafficked persons and in human body parts.

McCloskey's definition of capitalism serves to insulate it from criticism. Problems are due to other systems – notably statism – and not due to capitalism; and/or they are due not to too much capitalism, but to too little. Thus McCloskey has little to say on the natural environment, except that "the absence of property rights brought the ecological endangerment" (2006: 32) – not capitalism but the absence of capitalism. The capitalist system becomes judged by its results, except where they are bad, when it is said that the problem is not the system, but instead too little of it. Yet private property does not always lead to resource conservation; it can lead to resource-mining, with the profits then switched into other sectors. Elsewhere McCloskey urges us to understand and evaluate the system as a system, an overall culture that is reinforced by and reinforces its legal and economic arrangements; but sometimes it seems that we are required to close our eyes to the fact that the system is not only a set of abstracted textbook arrangements but a rich composite of consequences and causes. One such consequence is that property rights are often *not* yet introduced when the rich and rapacious think that they can get more for themselves individually by using their powers to seize wealth and privileges.

Real capitalism cannot be discussed with all the disliked bits and interconnections left out – such as that an economic system requires a state, or that superwealth spreads and buys political power, or that rich producers inevitably seek to capture a regulatory apparatus. For McCloskey capitalist capture of the state is seen as part of statism, not capitalism (2006: 35); the supposed mistake is to have created a regulatory apparatus. Likewise for cases of the feeding of corporations with public money (ibid.: 44ff.), even though these cases are driven by corporate power. McCloskey recognizes that the robber barons "corrupted politics. But when have the rich not done so?" (ibid.: 493). Her advice is to mini-mize the state apparatus that is available for them to corrupt and capture. Even the disastrous imposition of capitalist ideology on Africa in the 1980s and 1990s spearheaded by the IMF and World Bank is presented by her as a failing of statism – the misdeeds of two intergovernmental organizations, not of capitalism.[2]

We must keep in mind the dangers of essentializing capitalism, in whichever direction: as pure and timeless good, or pure and timeless evil. Capitalism has many operationalizations possible at a given time, and is additionally flexible over time. Consider for example the emergence of a "shared capitalism" in some corners, as described by Jeff Gates (1998). We need to think about possible potentials for the evolution and mutation of capitalist categories and practice, in more humane directions.

2 Is capitalism desirable?

Amongst mainstream economics arguments for capitalism – seen only as "the market system," with the other features overlooked or tacitly assumed – come first the familiar pictures of markets as fine-tuned machines for making margin-alist calculations about benefits and opportunity costs: the neo-classical, equilibrium-focused, emphasis. We must of course here ask: *whose* benefits and costs? Markets are also then looked at as sensitive mechanisms which can go wrong in many ways. Second, come the pictures of markets as eco-systems that are strong in generating learning, adaptation, and innovation: the longer-run emphasis given by the evolutionary and Austrian schools. I see overall a set of four conventional themes asserted in pro-market economics:

1   markets as relatively efficient *transmitters* of information and incentives (but having significant transaction costs);
2   markets as ways of *mobilizing* the energies and information of myriads of diverse agents in diverse situations across a whole economy, indeed the whole world;
3   markets as flexible *adjusters* to changes in conditions; and
4   markets as efficient a*llocation* mechanisms, a proposition that tacitly rests on the previous three features.

The fourth theme has received the lion's share of attention in academic eco-nomics textbooks, though they rarely adequately specify the assumptions required to sustain the conclusion that a market equilibrium is socially efficient (in some sense of the term). The assumptions concern the absence or unimportance of each of the following: externalities and "public goods"; (other) information fail-ures (producers and consumers must be well-informed on the nature of products, on available present and future alternatives, on costs and benefits, etc.); and of monopoly power (prices and quantities must respond well to excess supply or demand). Required in addition are the absence or unimportance of incompetence or irrationality, and of improper interference with free exchange and price movements, whether by criminals or by the State.

The potential failings of markets in terms of economic efficiency arise from the presence, to a significant degree, of one or more of the factors just listed. The potential failings concern also matters beyond economic efficiency: distributive equity and the acceptability of preferences.

- Markets are *liberal* institutions in the sense that they allow anything to be bought and sold as long as that is not prohibited *and* prevented. For good and/or ill, markets have no views or guarantees about the content and outcomes of the process. Where consumer preferences are judged ethically unacceptable then so too will be market outcomes (consider, say, preferences for hurting other people, and in some cases, ironically, preferences about exactly how other people should live).
- Distributive equity concerns a morally acceptable *distribution* of income, tasks, duties and risks. Markets only respect effective demand. Sen's entitlements approach highlights the possibility of disastrous market outcomes – through to famine, starvation, and death – caused not by technical market failures but by the structural blindness of markets to people without money, those who lack or lose sufficient money-backed title to benefits. In 2008 newspapers reported that some people in Haiti were reduced to filling their stomachs with "pies" made from mud, as food prices had soared worldwide.

These considerations lead us further beyond economic arguments, including to social and political themes such as that:

- Markets are presented as avenues of *free choice*; thus whether or not the preferences pursued are considered good or not, their free pursuit is itself considered a good. The freedom argument for markets still applies to some extent even when agents are incompetent and irrational, within certain limits. Merely formal freedom is clearly insufficient, though, as Sen for one reminds us.
- Markets are presented also as a *decentralized* way of organizing societal decision-making, in the sense that they do not require (*a*) consensus on societal objectives or (*b*) a central decision-making authority; thus, they offer allocation without a (centralized) allocator. In reality, the decentralization seen in modern capitalism is far from that in a dream of village-green democracy; it is the interaction of vastly diverse and mutually remote agents, some of them immensely resourced, some with almost nothing – the latter being free of resources, free of enforceable claims, and free of rights to a part of social surplus.

Extending the purview of evaluation beyond economics arguments reveals that externalities concern also, and perhaps more importantly, matters of *cultural and political side-effects*. As we saw, market proponents claim that markets provide a multi-polar source of power independent of the State, which helps to counterbalance it. Market critics argue to the contrary that markets generate concentrations of wealth which can be converted in a commodity-based society into other types of *power*, via political campaign funds, bribery, "favors," threats, mass media ownership, selective funding of research and education, and so on (cf. Walzer 1983). Markets tend to spread, both because money often tries to buy other types of power, and because a market-mentality can spread.

Similarly, market proponents stress that markets can and do build skills, independence, self-reliance and initiative, whereas market critics stress that uncontrolled markets do not promote altruism and community, and can in some circumstances undermine them, as seen currently in certain countries. By promoting narrowly self-interested behavior and ignoring side-effects, markets can weaken institutions that keep societies coherent and humane (see e.g. Stretton and Orchard 1994).

The entry on "market" in the *Oxford Dictionary of Sociology* sums up that there are both political and economic arguments for and against markets. Table 2.1 provides an overview of such arguments.

This sort of evaluation is a major advance over looking only or overwhelmingly at the bottom left quadrant in the table: the potential economic virtues of a market system. It still has several major limitations. First, regarding what it looks at: we noted that capitalism is more than "the market system." It is a particular sort of market system, centered on the prerogative of capital, and in practice marked by the power of vast accumulations of privately held capital. Some of the implications of this begin to emerge in the table's assessment of weaknesses. Second, however, regarding how the table treats what it does look at: the table centers on proposed strengths and presents weaknesses mostly as counterarguments that set limits to the claimed strengths, rather than as independent primary considerations. Third, and central to this chapter, regarding what the table fails to look at – by unthinking restriction within the categories of capitalism – it does not take up two key issues in the evaluation of capitalist systems and in understanding how capitalist systems evaluate: how is work treated? and is money income – even if maximized in a market system – the predominant or even a major source of well-being?

The *Oxford Dictionary of Sociology*, to its credit, proceeds to consider this third set of issues. Drawing on Robert Lane's massive survey *The Market Experience* (1991), it remarks that welfare economics and economic policy arguments typically make two fundamental questionable assumptions: that work is always a cost; and that money income is a major source of well-being. How much the mainstream economics themes above have to do with human flourishing depends on these two factors:

- First, the connections between human welfare and the maximization of the value of commodity production. Such connections are shaky (Easterlin 2001; Gasper 2005; 2007a), as we touch on in the next part of the chapter

Table 2.1 Political and economic arguments for and against markets

	Asserted strengths	*Asserted weaknesses*
POLITICAL	Freedom	Freedom 'to sleep under bridges' is not enough
		Free choice is not always wise or good choice
	Decentralization	Great concentrations of wealth distort politics and administration, information generation, dissemination and interpretation, and opinion formation
	Rewards effort and skill	Private property system also rewards luck, and accidents of birth. It ignores some other aspects of equity
ECONOMIC	Prices cheaply coordinate agents by transmitting information	Information is not shared by all
	…that reflects both supply conditions and demand conditions, the information needed for efficiency;	Markets only use information of certain types, and only on things that can be related to money. They ignore external effects or respond to them in unreliable and inequitable ways, considered in the Coase theorem
	…and they provide incentives for effort, adjustment, and innovation	Competition and its rewards and penalties lead to concentration of economic power
	Markets allow and encourage specialization	Markets can be risky and unstable (not least financial markets). They leave many people vulnerable
	Markets train in decision-making and self-reliance	They train in selfishness and decadence?

(Section 3). In contrast, political arguments for markets need not make strong assumptions about such connections; they stress markets instead as channels for freedom, and as spaces to use one's energies and ideas.

- Second, the significance of work for our well-being. The standard economics literature makes relatively little reference to the status of work, and much of the literature implicitly focuses on markets rather than on capitalism in its entirety. Yet work is central to people's lives. Given an activity-conscious conception of well-being, seen as well-living rather than as a mental-profit output category (but also without equating well-being to sheer activity, a conception we critically probe in Section 4), work should be central in discussion of capitalism and human flourishing. We will look at this further in Section 5.

3 Capitalism and the conception of human flourishing

What sort of human flourishing does capitalism in reality further?

The most summary and critical view that one encounters in response to this question is that under capitalism the meaning given to flourishing becomes: to flourish one's possessions. Under this lies something deeper though: to flourish one's possessions is to assert one's importance, one's success, one's quality; even if at the same time this assertion sometimes aims and succeeds in diminishing other people's importance.

The most extensive and laudatory view is presented by Deirdre McCloskey – that capitalism can and generally does represent and fulfill the classical virtues. In between these extremes lie many more qualified positions, including historically specific positions, in the spirit of Albert Hirschman. Hirschman concluded in his *Rival Views of Market Society* – a work surprisingly not cited by McCloskey – that market activity both conduces to peace and order (the so-called *doux-commerce* thesis) and to undermining its own moral foundations (the self-destruction thesis); and that where the balance lies in particular cases depends on many factors which require case-specific investigation. We find such investigation in parts of the literature of social history. Given the constraints of space and of my own knowledge, I will present some more generalized ideas that require historically specific exploration.

Capitalist society may allow space for expression of all sorts of criteria, but which criteria predominantly drive or steer the system? For business decision makers, profit, and for present-day government decision makers, economic growth, are clearly major criteria. In both cases, forces of competition often punish much divergence from the paths laid down by these criteria. Other criteria may be honored in speech, but the racing train of capitalist society proceeds along tracks that may not allow them much weight in practice. In contrast to McCloskey, her sparring partner Arjo Klamer stresses in his book *In Hemelsnaam!* (In Heaven's Name!) how the most important aspects of life, the most important criteria of life quality – such as family relations, friendship, mutual respect, "quality time" – are typically not measured in the ruling calculations in our capitalist societies.

In terms of existing conceptions of well-being – pleasure or contentment, preference fulfillment, the fulfillment of substantive needs, and so on – it can be argued that capitalism does not fit any of them very well; for only preferences backed by money are referred to, and only in proportion to purchasing power. Capitalism's motor of restless expansion and destruction may best fit an activist, productivist conception of well-being, or perhaps a Darwinist model. I will outline the arguments here, and then extend them to look more deeply at the activist conception and at its paradoxical counterpart, the low status of work in capitalist calculations.

A huge body of research indicates that the domain of economic inputs to life which economics has studied in detail – resource holdings, income, expenditure

– is relatively weakly connected to the domains of valued ends, whether we look at the domain of universally or authoritatively valued life-functionings (such as longevity, mobility, low morbidity, autonomy and agency), which we may call objective well-being (OWB), or at the domain of felt satisfactions, which we may call subjective well-being (SWB). Sometimes subjective well-being and objective well-being are not strongly connected to each other either. They clearly have partly different determinants, and both also depend in large part on factors other than economic inputs (Gasper 2005).

Does income promote subjective well-being? There are different dimensions of subjective well-being. At minimum we must distinguish pleasure, contentment, and negative affect (cf. Lane 2000: 15), for the three do not always move in line. Even so, it reportedly appears workable in many contexts to use a composite of the three, or to prioritize the second, contentment. There are some disputes over what the evidence shows, inevitably, but also a remarkable degree of consensus about some main lines of what we know. The so-called Easterlin paradox is now widely accepted as a first approximation, even if there is dispute over the details: average subjective well-being increases markedly with income to annual income levels per capita around $10K–$15K, markedly slows down thereabouts and thereafter and is virtually flat from $20K per capita or so. Some authors stress that certain studies show a still slight upslope at the higher income levels, while some others stress how slight is the upslope or find that it does not exist.

Richard Easterlin himself, who highlighted the paradox back in the early 1970s, is now even more skeptical (2005a; 2005b). He warns that typically "the diminishing returns generalization is based on data for a single point of time and on a simple bivariate comparison of happiness or life satisfaction with income without controls for other possible variables" (2005a). His deeper reading of the data, including time-series data, proposes that, at least from lower middle income levels, income has on average no significant correlation with subjective well-being, let alone a significant causal contribution. Significance here means socio-economic significance, size of effect, and not statistical significance, closeness of correlation.

Next, does income growth promote the components of objective well-being? The evidence is sometimes yes, sometimes the reverse – for example because income-getting can compete attention and resources away from more important things – and sometimes that income is irrelevant. Life expectancy, health, and family relationships – core elements in most public specifications of "objective well-being" and core determinants of most people's subjective feelings of contentment – are as good or better in middle-income country Costa Rica than in top-income country the United States.

I present the overall problematique in a "puzzle triangle." The Easterlin paradox concerns the right side of the triangle and the very weak or negligible (time-series and cross-country) relation of income to subjective well-being after middle- or high-middle income levels. Easterlin himself holds, as we saw, that there is no reliable relation even at low-middle income levels. There are other

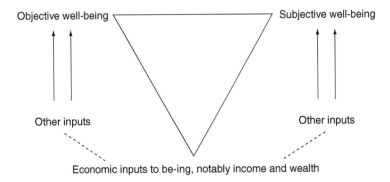

Figure 2.1 The puzzle triangle (source: Gasper 2005).

factors which have notably more substantial favorable impacts on subjective well-being, including friendship, good family relationships and work felt as meaningful.

The Sen paradox, if I may coin a term, concerns the weak relation in many cases between income and objective well-being. Expectations have not been met for the impact of income and consumption on many objective well-being dimensions, such as mental health; this concerns the left side of the triangle. Yet there are other factors which have substantial favorable impacts on aspects of objective well-being like physical and mental health, including again friendship, family relationships and work felt as meaningful.

The Easterbrook paradox (Easterbrook 2004), to coin a further term, concerns the weak relation of objective well-being to subjective well-being, at the top of the triangle, as presented in Greg Easterbrook's book *The Progress Paradox*. Contributing to all the other paradoxes, the Schwartz paradox concerns the stresses and discomforts brought by ever widening ranges of required (or promoted) consumer choice, brilliantly explored in Barry Schwartz's *The Paradox of Choice: Why More Is Less* (2005).

To explain this diverse and worldwide set of observations, one strategy is to look at the other inputs to well-being, besides income and wealth, and to see their degree of independent importance and the extent to which they may be competitive with market-mediated aspects. Many major aspects or determinants of well-being pass outside markets – family, friends, health, recreation, feelings of dignity. Non-market sources appear more important in general for happiness than do market sources. These non-market sources of well-being can be competitive with the market-mediated aspects. Jerome Segal and Robert Lane amongst others summarize much evidence that obtaining extra income and consumption can undermine or replace more rewarding routes, by undermining some aspects of objective well-being which contribute to subjective well-being, or some of the "other inputs" in Figure 2.1; for example by undermining the quality (and quantity) of family life and other personal relationships (Gasper 2005). Lane hypothesizes, for example, that materialism contributes to impoverishment of personal relationships, which in turn leaves people more emotionally vulnerable when they face difficulties. Amongst the market sources of subjective well-being, experiences during work hours or unemployment appear typically more determinant of personal satisfaction than is the level of income or consumption (see Gasper 2007b and literature cited there).

The diagram represents paradoxes that arise with respect to the expectations of the "material welfare" mainstream in economics (see Cooter and Rappaport 1984). The findings about sources of well-being oblige us to go back to reconsider conceptions of well-being that are conventionally applied as criteria of performance: the allocation of attention toward the outcomes of production and consumption, and away from the processes of work and the ongoing relationships to persons not only to things.

The conceptions of well-being or flourishing

Systematic thinking about conceptions of well-being intensified in the 1980s, partly in response to the lived experience of, and theoretical puzzlement around, these emergent paradoxes. The philosopher Derek Parfit's book *Reasons and Persons* (1984) highlighted three conceptions, and facilitated discussion amongst economists and analytical philosophers:

1 well-being as pleasure (and as avoidance of pain); this is a subjective well-being conception, of hedonistic form;
2 well-being as preference fulfillment; and
3 "objective list" conceptions of well-being, which specify the components of or for a flourishing life.

Psychologists refine or extend the first conception. Hedonic psychologists distinguish contentment/satisfaction from pleasure, as an empirically distinguishable and independently varying form of subjective well-being (Kahneman *et al.* 1999). Some other psychologists go further and present a eudaimonic interpretation of subjective well-being, which emphasises autonomy, competence and relatedness (Ryan and Deci 2001). For our purposes here we can remain with Parfit's three headings, for the evidence reported on pleasure and contentment is apparently not widely different, and because the varieties of eudaimonic well-being conception appear to converge substantially with most objective-list conceptions, such as that for example by Martha Nussbaum.

Amartya Sen extended Parfit's list with three other conceptions:

4 Opulence. In reality, instead of measuring pleasure, economists imputed it from the acquisition and control of commodities.
5 Choice. Similarly, instead of measuring preference fulfillment, economists imputed that too, from choices: by the axiom of revealed preference whatever one chose was deemed to be what one preferred. Since the axiom is demonstrably wrong, it is better reinterpreted as representing a commitment

to the priority of free choice: one's well-being consists here in choosing freely, including freely making one's own mistakes.

6   Considered freedom. There is then space for a conception of well-being as informed free choice, or better, as in Sen's own position, of well-being as access to outcomes which one has reason to value (the "one" can also refer to a group). "Reason" here implies decision that is wise as well as informed.

So, many different ideas of well-being or human flourishing are present and advocated under capitalism. Which of these sets of ideas are promoted and encouraged by the operations of capitalism? Which of them then predominate under capitalism? And which variants of human flourishing are actually furthered by the operations of capitalism? These questions could well have different answers. There may be a discrepancy between capitalist ideology – what it says it does, what it says it values: freedom or utility or whatever – and capitalist reality, what it actually furthers and implicitly prioritises, which might be activity.

Mainstream economists have typically treated well-being as pleasure, but operationalized as opulence; or secondly, as desire/preference fulfillment, but operationalized as free choice, and in practice, thanks to a series of assumptions, further operationalized as income or, for a collectivity, as national income; and thus, implicitly, thirdly, well-being has been in effect interpreted as sheer activity – Gross National Product (GNP) was created as a measure of market activity not of human well-being. Activity must then be added as a seventh member of the list.

Yet where does work figure in the list of conceptions of well-being and/or flourishing? It is prominent in many "objective lists" and in the eudaimonic understanding of subjective well-being. Remarkably, it is little considered in some of the modern analytical philosophy literature on well-being. If we take two of the most highly used and praised books from the 1980s and 1990s, James Griffin's *Well-Being* (1986) and L.W. Sumner's *Welfare, Happiness and Ethics* (1996), their indexes make no mention of the topic of work. Much of the analytical philosophy literature grows out of a conversation with welfare economists and is as prone to consumer bias as is mainstream economics literature. Where does work enter in the puzzle diagram? In one interpretation it is implicit, as negative income, with quality of work treated as an "other input"; or work as a whole is an "other input."

4   The lust for activity: when costs become benefits

The bourgeois believed in the virtue of work, as against the aristocratic idealization of (genteel) leisure.

(Berger 1987: 98)

If activism is something we do not see in economic theory, but induce from economic practice, do we find it expounded and explored in other theory? Yes. We may have to look outside economics in order to explain the functioning of economies, and to use a historically aware conceptualization of capitalism that incorporates non-capitalist elements, rather than only theories about capitalism as an abstracted ideal type.

Many authors, such as Max Weber, have argued that Reformation Europe adopted "the revaluation of work as something worthwhile in itself" (Hughes 2007: 37). The primacy given earlier to *vita contemplativa* over *vita activa* was removed and reversed; absence from productive work became seen as idleness and failure to fulfill one's duty. This applied to both the capitalist, and to the propertyless laborer obliged to work for the capitalist. The paradox built into the system is that while it extols (putting people to) work, the felt content of the worker's work time is of no independent significance – to the capitalist, whose perspective dominates. Only the output of the worker is accorded independent value, and "output" here means market value – there is no other value seen in the process of production or the particular content of what is produced, whether pushpin or poetry or pornography. Unlike in a eudaimonic perspective which highlights a range of particular substantive excellences, the pure capitalist takes joy in one thing alone: endless monetary gain, even far beyond his ability to spend. Why? Weber, amongst others, considered that this could not be understood only in terms of the structural imperatives of competition, but required reference to factors beyond reason and calculation. For example, in

> Victorious capitalism … [in] the field of its highest development, in the United States, the pursuit of wealth, stripped of its religious and ethical meaning, tends to become associated with purely mundane passions, which often actually gives it the character of sport.
> (Weber 2001: 123–124; cited by Hughes 2007: 60)

The de facto preoccupation with activity arises for diverse reasons, for diverse groups. First, activity levels were easier to measure than were well-being levels. Indeed well-being levels are not at all the same sort of entity, but are, despite the reified name, in fact evaluative judgments of a state of being. Their assessment requires valuation not only measurement.

Second, typically it is politically safer to leave that door closed. To think of well-being levels in another way than as levels of monetized activity can open the door on the contentious processes of valuation that are implied. For politicians, activity levels are also easier to point to and influence.

Third, capitalist property relations and accounting mean that the capitalist reaps more profit from incessant turnover than from contented and replete customers: from built-in obsolescence of particular products, designed to break down after some years and to have spare parts no longer available, and from the cultural obsolescence of generic product-lines, displaced by continually generated novelty. Alfred Sloan of General Motors gave explicit formulation to the strategy of built-in obsolescence during the 1930s Great Depression. If instead capitalists owned all consumer durables and rented them to consumers they might have more financial incentive to ensure that the products do not break down or become unserviceable after a few years; but this would be effective only if they could earn more than by incessant generation of demand for new types of product. The tactics go hand-in-hand: the consumer is forced to buy not merely a replacement item but often a new "improved" product-type, since the old one is no longer available or deemed respectable.

These first three reasons all concern incentives for influential actors in capitalist society to focus on activity levels rather than any deeper notion of well-being. A fourth explanation is systemic: if competition is built in to capitalist markets then it drives new activity.

A fifth reason, however, concerns a strand of thought and emotion that extols activity as indeed the relevant criterion of well-being. It connects to explaining capitalism's frenetic activity by arguing that capitalism channels a range of deeper motives – an insight which is well understood and intensively used by business marketers. Adam Smith himself stressed that money's frequent strength as a motivator rests not merely on its offering generalized command over commodities, but in addition because commodities are desired in major part as sources of identity, status, novelty, security and other forms of meaning (Hirschman 1977; Gasper 2004). In a more atavistic subset of this line of explanation, humans are considered to have a lust for activity. The drive can have either safe or destructive outlets. Hirschman shows how this view was prominent in eighteenth-century writings: capitalism was considered to re-channel the angry passions, the passions that had devastated Europe in the sixteenth- and seventeenth-century wars of religion and other civil and international wars.

Probably all these explanations are needed, but the fifth is perhaps now least familiar and deserves further attention. It spans a variety of forms, many of which use a biological imagery that can fit better with the energy of the term "flourishing" than with the term "*well*-being": people's fulfillment and destiny is seen to lie in the furies of endeavor, for species, nation, or race. Nietzsche combined these sentiments in his dismissal of utilitarianism: "Man does *not* strive for happiness; only the English do that" (1998: section 1.9). Man, real Man, strove for mastery, even world mastery.

Not long after Nietzsche, and at around the same time as Max Weber lauded a similar arduous ethic of the quest for national supremacy (cited and discussed in Lichtheim 1972), an American leader spoke in these tones:

> I wish to preach, not the doctrine of ignoble ease, but the doctrine of the strenuous life, the life of toil and effort, of labor and strife; to preach that highest form of success which comes, not to the man who desires mere easy peace, but to the man who does not shrink from danger, from hardship, or from bitter toil.

This was Theodore Roosevelt, in the opening paragraph of an astonishing speech given in 1899 entitled *The Strenuous Life*. He continued:

A life of slothful ease, a life of that peace which springs merely from lack either of desire or of power to strive after great things, is as little worthy of a nation as of an individual ... [If a man] treats this period of freedom from the need of actual labor as a period, not of preparation, but of mere enjoyment, even though perhaps not of vicious enjoyment, he shows that he is simply a cumberer of the earth's surface, and he surely unfits himself to hold his own with his fellows if the need to do so should again arise. A mere life of ease is not in the end a very satisfactory life, and, above all, it is a life which ultimately unfits those who follow it for serious work in the world.

(Roosevelt 1900: para. 2)

Roosevelt was happy with a capitalism allied to militarism that pursued gain through non-market means too. He rejected the type of capitalism that replaced the passions by the interests and diverted men from war. He attacked as weaklings those who shrank from military intervention abroad because they preferred quiet money making – "that base spirit of gain and greed which recognizes in commercialism the be-all and end-all of national life" – but he explicitly welcomed a strenuous capitalism as "one of the many elements that go to make up true national greatness" (ibid.: para. 3). The more strenuous the better, indeed, for great effort keeps one prepared for the great national and global challenges. By these he referred directly to matters such as the conquest of the Americas, contemporary challenges of seizing the Philippines and other remnants of Spanish empire, and ultimately "the domination of the world" (para. 18). In this extreme variant of activism, acclaim for striving becomes acclaim for strife: "for it is only through strife, through hard and dangerous endeavor, that we shall ultimately win the goal of true national greatness" (ibid.: para. 18).

One of Joseph Schumpeter's insights from historically sensitive examination of capitalist societies was that they incorporate major residues of pre-capitalist formations and cultures, and, further, that these can be centrally important. Like Deirdre McCloskey he tended to blame non-capitalist strands for the problematic aspects of capitalist societies, but he was strongly analytically attentive to their presence. Raymond Apthorpe and I have described his views as follows:

In Schumpeter's (1927; 1942; 1951) analyses of capitalist development, "true" capitalism always tended to efficiency, prosperity and the reform and rationalization of its environment. The travail and conflict of early capitalism was due in part [he thought] to the presence of powerful groups derived from precapitalist eras. Likewise, the association of mature capitalism with imperialism and protectionism was not "from any tendencies of the competitive system," i.e. not from "true" capitalism in his opinion, but from its "distortion" by these entrenched precapitalist groups to serve their own financial interests and atavistic ideologies. For Schumpeter this was "an historical observation, to his critics it seems a childish trick of definition" (Stretton; 1969: 119–120). Finally, his predicted decline of capitalism, to be replaced by perhaps less rational and efficient forms of organization, was held again to imply no failing on capitalism's part but in fact to indicate the magnitude of its successes, such that its inheritors could indulge themselves in some novel and less demanding form of social organization.

(Apthorpe and Gasper 1982: 655)[3]

The theme of incorporation of powerful pre-capitalist forces in capitalism is strong in Hirschman's work too, though in a different way. The market, believed Adam Smith and his contemporaries, had helped to control and replace the angrier passions by more reasoned, calmer siblings – "the interests" (Hirschman 1977: 28–43; Gasper 2004). Underlying capitalists' storms of creative destruction were drives for meanings – for status, novelty and more – that gave the search for economic gain its never-ending, never-satisfied impetus (Hirschman 1977: 108ff.).

Romantic and Counter-Enlightenment thinkers were not satisfied with this bottling up of the genie of passion in the engine-rooms of the capitalist system. By the late nineteenth and early twentieth centuries, as we saw, various theorists and leaders had produced a Romantic stance now often fortified with Darwinist philosophy. Georges Sorel, Nietzsche's near contemporary, was one who gave such leanings eloquent expression. He did so in ways partly similar to Nietzsche and Roosevelt, partly distinctive. In Isaiah Berlin's words:

> Sorel was dominated by one *idée maitresse*: that man is a creator, fulfilled only when he creates ... He is, for Sorel, in the first place, a producer who expresses himself in and through his work, an innovator whose activity alters the material provided by nature ... History shows that men are essentially seekers not of happiness or peace or knowledge or power over others, or salvation in another life – at least these are not men's primary purposes.
>
> (Berlin 1981: 298–299)

Man seeks to fulfil himself:

> In the imposition of his personality on a recalcitrant environment.... Man lives fully only in and by his works, not by passive enjoyment or the peace or security that he might find by surrender to external pressures, or habit, or convention ... [T]he true end of human life ... [is] the effort to be and do something.
>
> (ibid.: 299–300)

"Sorel, like Nietzsche, preached the need for a new civilisation of makers and doers" (ibid.: 327).

Sorel shared the image of Promethean capitalism drawn by Marx and Engels in *The Communist Manifesto*.[4] From Marx he drew the conception of "man as an active being, born to work and create" (Berlin 1981: 308). "Men['s] essence, for Sorel, is to be active beings" (ibid.: 303). Action is all: not reasoned prediction, which is impossible and in addition unnecessary since we have an evolved (or experience-gained) intuition; Sorel shared the Bergsonian belief in *élan vital*. Thus unlike Marx, Sorel demanded permanent revolution: we need unending activity, and revolution cleanses. Ironically, it is capitalism, history shows, which provides the permanent revolution. Sorel himself was anti-capitalist, opposed to the alienations of commodity society. He had, says Berlin, "a Jansenist hatred of the twin evils of hedonism and materialism" (ibid.: 300). Yet he admired the quest for riches as opposed to passivity and contentedness, and as exemplified by robust American business barons. His ideal was a heroic class of producers, steeled in the furnace of conflict. This form of insurgent, vitalist, doer mentality can be part of various ideological stances. Its cult of action, of doers, of rooted men, as opposed to cosmopolitan administrators and manipulators, contained a Fascist potential, reflected in Sorel's final enthusiasm for Mussolini. One of modern capitalism's triumphs has been to harness to the games of consumerism the angry avant-garde passions of minds like Sorel's.

As highlighted by Keynes, Hirschman and McCloskey, much of the actual operation of capitalist businessmen and even consumers can be described not as prudence but as animal spirits (McCloskey 2006: 433). It is strewn with errors, real or apparent. Cost underestimation is endemic.[5] Some of the underestimation is deliberate, for market society generates incentives to manipulate its own categories, and some of it can be seen as an outgrowth of activism, as explored for example in Hirschman's theory of the "Hiding Hand" (Hirschman 1967; Gasper 1986). The active "sinking" of project costs is one noteworthy aspect. More boldly, in higher levels of policy discourse, costs can become reclassified as benefits, badges of heroic commitment and identity, proof of the indisputable rightness of a commitment; the stigmata of struggle.

The thrust for profits and economic growth under capitalism promotes, for sure, the personal goals of the rich and powerful. Part of GDP's attraction to national elites is that it also reflects power over others: power of governments to acquire military capability; power of elites to acquire property; some people's power to be heard and to communicate, to manage the generation of information and steer the evolution of opinion (Gasper 2007c). However, to explain the sheer force of this thrust and the way it holds sway across internally diverse societies, we need also the previously mentioned explanations of capitalism's frenetic activity: that apart from the element of competition built into the system which spurs ongoing effort, capitalist accounting categories mean that the controlling agent's profit comes from continual turnover and permanently generated dissatisfaction and obsolescence rather than from contentment and repose; and that the energy for the system relies on channeling and harnessing a range of deep motives, including some of the angry passions and lust for activity. For vitalist thinkers such as Theodore Roosevelt, Nietzsche or Weber, influenced by Darwinist conceptions of unending struggles for superiority, this frenetic activity could be seen as both inevitable and desirable.

5 The paradoxes of work

Is work a cost? When and for whom?

We should compare the activist strand in capitalist practice, and in corners of
capitalist theory, with the normal presumption in capitalist society that work is a
cost. This was highlighted and queried, we saw, by Robert Lane. The capitalist
hires other people's time, and that time must therefore be considered, by the capitalist, a cost. Indeed, if the work is alienated work it will probably feel like a
cost, to the worker. The capitalist's own time is, in contrast, typically treated as
expression of exuberant animal spirits, creative and enriching, as befits a master.
So, built-in to capitalist social relations is the treatment of most work as a cost
and, says Lane in *The Market Experience*, a subordination of the quality of work
experience to the priorities of purchasers. When those market priorities are
served by job enrichment, so be it; but when they are served by job impoverishment, job insecurity, and in the extreme by human trafficking and bondage, so be
it too. Saunders' apologia for capitalism acknowledges this structural weakness.
In mitigation he argues that advanced capitalism's high productivity and innova-
tive technologies have increased opportunities for self-fulfillment outside of paid
employment, in increased and enriched leisure time, and notably in do-it-your-
self *work*. This line of argument offers more consolation to a harried formal
sector employee than it does to a dependent informal sector worker or a trafficked "illegal."

Yet well-being research, as we saw, indicates that employment is potentially
and even frequently a major source of fulfillment. Csikszentmihalyi reports that
on average, the people in various studies of American workers and managers in
the 1980s had more rewarding experiences at their work than in their leisure.
Work provided more occasions where people faced challenges, focused their
attention, reached targets, matched their activities with their abilities, and grew
as persons (2002, chapter 7; Csikszentmihalyi and LeFevre 1989).

"The Paradox of Work," Csikszentmihalyi reports, is that, despite this, people
want more leisure rather than more work (2002: 157ff). He examines first the
possible explanation that people are near their limit of energies, but is skeptical.
Instead, the issue is that work is felt "as an imposition, a constraint, an infringe-
ment of their freedom, and therefore something to be avoided as much as possible." So even if "the momentary on-the-job experience may be positive, they
tend to discount it" (ibid.: 160).

A sister paradox arises, concerning allocation of attention within the scientific
literature. Quality-Of-Life studies consistently show that work and relations with
other people are the key determinants of well-being (Csikszentmihalyi 2002:
164). "Love and work," remarked Freud (as cited in Csikszentmihalyi 2002).
Despite this, work remains relatively neglected in economics, and what we
called the capitalist perspective is thoughtlessly spread to new contexts. Saunders (1995: 90) suggests, for example, that putting "all the emphasis ... on the
goal of monetary success while insufficient attention was paid to the normatively

approved means for achieving it" contributed to the major growth in crime rates in rich countries in the second half of the last century.

McCloskey's *The Bourgeois Virtues* makes an early affirmation of the bourgeois work ethic: "the common element in any bourgeoisie [is] the honoring of work apart from manual drudgery or heroic daring … bourgeois humans [are] self-defining workers." Work is the path to autonomy, identity, and adulthood (McCloskey 2006: 75). But after these emphatic statements near the beginning of her systematic exposition, McCloskey leaves the subject of work as such untouched for nearly four hundred pages. She perhaps has relatively so little to say on work and workers because her book is in reality more about markets than about capitalism as a whole social order.[6]

The tyranny of capitalist accounting categories

> If consumption were the only end, and if production and exchange were only means to its achievement, certain rules about the optimum conditions of production and exchange could be laid down. The formulation of these rules has been the aim of an important branch of traditional welfare economics. But the disturbing fact is that neither the conditions in which production is carried on, nor the relationships generated by exchange are purely instrumental. They are *human* conditions, and *human* relations, which are valued as much as, and in some cases more strongly than, the end of consumption.
>
> (Streeten 1954: 365)

Capitalist accounting categories have both virtues and dangers. The capitalist prerogative allocates surplus to a relatively cohesive and capable entity that is typically focused on investment and capital growth. On the other hand, these categories have led us into the lunacies of built-in obsolescence, for example. And capitalist market categories and formats have been, and increasingly are, extended from the level of the individual capitalist enterprise into other arenas, including the evaluation of community programmes and the evaluation of the performance and welfare of entire societies. Life worlds become invaded by a relatively primitive calculus from the world of business. The principle of discounting, for example, established to order the profit calculations of investors in impersonal markets, has become mindlessly extended to determine the fundamental societal issue of the relationship between the present generation and future generations.

Let us take a related example. In evaluations of community programs, the treatment of volunteer time can be decisive. Howard Richards's book *The Evaluation of Cultural Action: An Evaluative Study of The Parents and Children Program (PPH)* provides a case study of the central significance of how volunteer time is considered. In the PPH program in rural southern Chile, parents taught their own small children at home, after group meetings in which they themselves learned with the help of a volunteer coordinator and sometimes a paid coordinator. The program used a hypothesis of synergy between the three sets of activities: child education, adult education, and community development. The adult education component had to be left somewhat tacit, in order not to jeopardize parents' self-respect and the children's respect for them. The program was "in order to show our children that we are people" said a program participant (Richards 1985: 19). But viewed from a market perspective, the program was deplorably profligate with its use of parents' time. They were put to work in enormous numbers to produce very little, as measured in market terms.

Richards asked: Is the PPH program more expensive or less expensive, per child taught, than kindergartens? The comparison was between PPH and a kindergarten in which a group of children receive basic instruction and supervision from a paid instructor. The key question was: Is volunteers' time a cost? Everything hung on this. Using a very modest estimate of the money value of volunteers' time, "PPH costs approximately four and a half times as much as kindergarten.... [Whereas] [m]aking the same assumptions except for disregarding the money value of the time of volunteers, kindergartens cost nearly five times as much as PPH" (Richards 1985: 46).

Richards argued that volunteer time should not be considered as a monetized cost, and suggested that costing it monetarily – as some representatives of large international funding agencies insisted on – is "a metaphysical error" (ibid.: 64), an error arising from the basic way one sees the world. As we noted, from employers' perspective paid work is a cost; whereas some workers may feel work as a cost and others may feel it as a benefit. The choice can make an enormous difference in evaluation. Market-dominated thinking, imported into public policy and evaluation, assumes – often without argument – that public discourse must use the perspective of the capitalist employer.

It may be argued by economists that volunteer time has an opportunity cost, in terms of efforts withheld from activities that would contribute more directly to economic production; or that, simply, work is pain. But sometimes the work is not viewed merely or primarily as pain but instead as personal growth, as opposed to economic growth; and the foregone economic production may be of little significance – to the people concerned – compared to the use of their time for interacting with their friends and loved ones. Work and love, said Freud. We should not presume that economic growth is the objective, nor automatically adopt the classification of costs and benefits that would be used by private sector business.

Is perhaps the volunteer's case a "special" one, whereas in the "normal" case of waged work there would be no danger of overestimating cost, given the expectation that if you enjoy, or cherish, your work you will accept less pay to do it, so that money costs will be lower? This is true in some vocations, including academe and the priesthoods. In places such as Kerala, educated young people certainly accept much lower pay in order to avoid the dishonor and disutility of manual labor in the rice field or the brick field as opposed to in the shop or the office.

However, pay is not so flexible: remuneration is in large part to cover socially-determined subsistence needs, and pay levels are partly set to convey a social status. Work enjoyment, or lack of it, is not the only determinant of reward. An academic who might willingly work for relatively little is still paid fairly handsomely. More generally, the "decision utility" expectations about work, in advance of doing it, may in various instances fall below the "experienced utility" from doing it, for reasons similar to in Csikszentmihalyi's "Paradox of Work." Public expenditure choices could sometimes be distorted by underestimation of the benefits in work, as well as by the subsequent attempts to massage calculations so as to compensate for the depressing effect on the benefit–cost ratio of the overestimation of social costs (as opposed to market costs).

Rethinking work

How can we build-in alternative conceptualizations of work, as part of more adequate approaches to human flourishing? Let me suggest a few agenda points, around the general theme that work has to be rethought within the framework of well-living: as central to living and central to human flourishing, rather than as a tedious prelude to frenetic consumption.

Two sectors of "work" that are centrally important for thinking about human well-being and flourishing are domestic work and caring work. Yet such activity, key to human fulfillment as well as social reproduction, is liable to be ignored when not commodified. There are vibrant literatures, research programs and social movements that attempt to redirect and restructure our attention to and in these two areas, as well as related broader thinking within feminist and Green circles, querying the categories of exchange economics.[7]

While those areas are vibrant, within the literature on "human development" the issue of work seems still relatively neglected. The potential is there. Manfred Max-Neef in his theory of "Human-Scale Development" requires attention, in each of a series of life spheres, to dimensions of: Having, *Doing*, and Interacting – and not only of Being. His ideas are used by some environmentalist and community development groups, but remain marginal in influence compared to the work of Amartya Sen. Sen has criticized several major aspects of the conventional economics conceptualization of welfare, but he does not appear to have directly queried the transplantation of market categories into societal decision-making, including the equation of work with cost. His elaboration of the case for a shadow wage, for instance, was based rather on the instrumentality for increasing net economic product of using lower-than-market wages in public expenditure decision-making. His subsequent discussions of the personal value of employment focus on the increased range of options a person has, in the context of intra-family and intra-group negotiations, more than on the effects of employment on a person's skills, self-image or character. This latter direction of analysis provides a basis for a more adequate critique and for an alternative based on developing people rather than capital.

Grounding the discussion of "human development" more solidly in the rich and growing work on well-being should be the way ahead. From the empirically based well-being literature Mihaly Csikszentmihalyi's *Flow*, for example, examines how fulfillment can be promoted in each area of human endeavor. He argues that well-being means making experience rewardingly meaningful, whether through restructuring the external situation or restructuring how we experience it. The important elements are: an ordered mind (through the mobilization, steering and focusing of attention), a feeling of control, and a feeling of meaningfulness. Each of these requires skills, and in turn they build an enriched self. Lack of such autonomy is exploited by others, not least by the marketing divisions of capitalist corporations. The presence of such autonomy allows one, to use Csikszentmihalyi's term, to achieve "flow" – sustained flow of energies in furtherance of one's goals without distraction or psychic disorder. Changed external conditions alone will not suffice for peace of mind. "Enjoyment," in the sense of more than merely pleasure from fulfillment of biological needs or social expectations, comes through exercise of one's skills in an activity that well matches and stretches one's skills; that thereby fully absorbs one, through providing a real challenge that is yet manageable; and that involves definite goals and direct feedback on progress toward them. The activity should be one that is perceived as independently valuable, not only instrumentally useful. Unfortunately some "flow activities" – not least, war – can be instrumentally damaging activities. A focus on activity and work alone carries dangers, as the impending environmental crisis of industrialism shows.

Contemporary capitalism requires a value transition, environmentalists warn. In the terms used by the *Great Transition Initiative* and the Earth Charter (see Kates *et al.* 2006), we must move from the values of consumerism – salvation through buying – to a focus instead on quality of life; from individualism to human solidarity; and from domination of nature to ecological sensitivity and stewardship. This adds further dimensions to the historical scenario presented by Keynes, who sketched the transition required beyond the material chase once that era has completed its work in establishing a comfortable basis for living. We must move on to a greater concern with the contents of living. The same transition is expounded by Deirdre McCloskey's associate and critic, Arjo Klamer (2005). In effect these authors advise that once we have reached the Easterlin plateau, upon which income growth brings no longer any significant benefit in terms of well-being, we need to reorient our societies away from the material chase. People are misled by "hedonistic disconnect," the belief that we can get sustained happiness directly from things, with affluence not understood as a platform that allows experiences that can take us well beyond it, but instead assumed to be the end itself, where more is always better and never enough. Motivating such a move away from the material chase will require more than Csikszentmihalyi's extension of the spirit of the master craftsman into all the activities of living. It will require connecting to the driving passions for action which have powered capitalism; including – a final agenda point for future examination – by linking also to the spirit of play. Work as discussed in this chapter covers far more than paid work; family work, community work, work for a cause, are the stuff of meaningful and fulfilling living.

6 Conclusion

> There is perhaps nothing more urgent, in a world increasingly driven by multinational corporations and the power motive that is built into their operations, than to articulate a set of humanly rich goals for development.
>
> (Nussbaum 2006: 306)

I proposed that besides asking what is the impact of capitalism in terms of our preferred notions of well-being and human flourishing, we should consider what ideas of the desirable the real practice of capitalism represents and encourages. To address this question well requires further historically specific examination, but I have suggested two important possible patterns: capitalism undervalues work and yet overemphasizes activity, monetized throughput. These biases apply at levels both of theory and practice. We noticed for example how economics arguments for markets typically questionably assume that money income is a reliable major source of well-being, and that work is always a cost.

First, the undervaluation of work. Capitalism consists of much more than private property and a market system. It contains what we called "the prerogative of capital," in which surplus remains with the owners of capital, and "the perspective of capital," in which hired work is defined as a cost. This perspective is widely and often inappropriately extended into public policy discourse in capitalist societies.

Well-being research shows us how central is interesting and respected work, both for felt well-being and, through its contributions to physical and mental health and capability, as a socially recognized component of "objective well-being." This theme is evident in the hedonic strand of research on subjective well-being, but is examined more deeply in the eudaimonic tradition of thinking about well-being, which gives more attention to meanings. Thus while the modern concept of well-being provides a great advance over notions of "utility" and "economic welfare," the concept of "human flourishing" is better: it is more activity- and process-oriented, and less prone to being reduced to a single supposed essence.

Second, preoccupation with monetized activity arises as a different effect of capitalist categories of social accounting. Ongoing profit relies on unending turnover, which is further fanned by competition. Modern capitalism's mechanisms of built-in obsolescence and engineered dissatisfaction drive the never-ending activity. This preoccupation with increasing the supply of commodity inputs to being does not fit well any of the conventional academic conceptions of well-being, and implies instead an activist conception and perhaps a Darwinist model. It is an aspect of the particular ways in which capitalism channels deeper human motives and has incorporated pre-capitalist forces. Non-abstracted views of capitalism recognize that capitalist systems are always mixed with other social and cultural patterns.

Does the activist strand in capitalist practice and in corners of capitalist theory compensate for the ruling presumption in capitalist society that work is a cost, and thus in effect respect the evidence from well-being research that work can frequently be a major source of fulfillment? Perhaps to some extent. But it is an unsatisfactory, accidental and incomplete type of respect for work, smuggled in via waste and obsolescence, the constant generation of dissatisfaction and new vanities, encased in concern only with the saleable, and too readily married to ideologies of struggle and strife.

We need instead to consider and use implications of the well-being literature more fully and directly, in (re)conceptualization of work, reform of our categories of societal accounting, and deepening of the work on "human development." We must resist the transfer of capitalist accounting categories, including the automatic assumption that work is a cost, from the level of the individual capitalist enterprise across to evaluations of the performance of community programs and of the welfare of entire societies. The great transition that is required must, however, absolutely still find connections to the sorts of driving passions for action and meaning which capitalism has long managed to powerfully engage.

Notes

* My thanks go to John B. Davis and Ian Gough for careful commentary which helped to strengthen the arguments at several points.
1 See Fisher (1918), Cooter and Rappaport (1984).
2 McCloskey's comments on Africa at various points show considerable ignorance, e.g. "The Afrikaners of 1910 had no experience of work and no respect for it" (2006: 471).)
3 For an analysis of Schumpeter's arguments, see Apthorpe and Gasper (1979: section 6).
4 I follow in this paragraph the account provided by Isaiah Berlin.
5 McCloskey cites Bent Flyvbjerg's study of cost overruns in transportation projects (2006: 434) and some similar studies (2006: 435). For a parallel study of cost overruns in large dams in India, see Singh (1990).
6 She returns to the theme, claiming extraordinarily that: "only the bourgeoisie thinks of work as a calling," and that "until the quickening of commerce in bourgeois societies, work except praying and fighting was despised" (McCloskey 2006: 461, 470). Yet on the next page she cites Lester K. Little as saying

> The ideals of Christian society as formulated in earlier centuries [pre-thirteenth] had come to include high regard for creative work, and so the problem of the legitimacy of the merchant's activities generally, as well as of the profit he made, turned largely on the question of whether what he did could properly be considered creative work.
>
> (cited in McCloskey 2006: 462)

7 An interesting example is the work of Genevieve Vaughan; see e.g. Vaughan (1999).

References

Apthorpe, R. and D. Gasper (1979), "Public Policy and Essentialism: the case of Rural Cooperatives," Occasional Paper no. 75, Institute of Social Studies, The Hague.
—— (1982), "Policy Evaluation and Meta-evaluation," *World Development*, 10(8), 651–668.
Berger, P. (1987), *The Capitalist Revolution*, Aldershot: Wildwood House (Gower).

Berlin, I. (1981), "Georges Sorel," in *Against the Current – Essays in the History of Ideas*, Oxford: Oxford University Press, 296–332.

Bishop, J.D. (2000), "Ethics and Capitalism: A Guide to the Issues," in J.D. Bishop (ed.) *Ethics and Capitalism*, Toronto: University of Toronto Press, 3–48.

Cooter, Robert and Peter Rappaport (1984), "Were the Ordinalists Wrong about Welfare Economics?," *Journal of Economic Literature*, XXII, 507–530.

Csikszentmihalyi, M. (2002), *Flow*, London: Random House.

Csikszentmihalyi, M. and J. LeFevre (1989), "Optimal Experience in Work and Leisure," *Journal of Personality and Social Psychology*, 56(5): 815–822.

Easterbrook, G. (2004), *The Progress Paradox*, New York: Random House.

Easterlin, R.A. (2001), "Income and Happiness: Towards a Unified Theory," *Economic Journal*, 111 July: 465–484.

—— (2005a), "Diminishing Marginal Utility of Income? Caveat Emptor," *Social Indicators Research*, 70(3): 243–255.

—— (2005b), "Feeding the Illusion of Growth and Happiness: A Reply to Hagerty and Veenhoven," *Social Indicators Research*, 74(3): 429–443.

Ellerman, D. (1982), *Economics, Accounting, and Property Theory*, Lexington, MA: Lexington Books.

Fisher, I. (1918), "Is 'Utility' the Most Suitable Term for the Concept It is Used to Denote?," *American Economic Review* (8): 335–337. Online, available at: www.efm.bris.ac.uk/het/fisher/utility.htm.

Gasper, D. (1986), "Programme Appraisal and Evaluation: The Hiding Hand and Other Stories," *Public Administration and Development* (6): 467–474.

—— (2004), *The Ethics of Development*, Edinburgh: Edinburgh University Press.

—— (2005), "Subjective and Objective Well-being in Relation to Economic Inputs," *Review of Social Economy*, LXIII (2): 177–206.

—— (2007a), "Human Well-being: Concepts and Conceptualizations," in M. McGillivray (ed.) *Human Well-being: Concept and Measurement*, Basingstoke: Palgrave, 23–64.

—— (2007b), "Uncounted or Illusory Blessings? Competing Responses to the Easterlin, Easterbrook and Schwartz Paradoxes of Well-being," *Journal of International Development*, 19(4): 473–492.

—— (2007c), "Human Rights, Human Needs, Human Development, Human Security – Relationships between Four International 'Human' Discourses," *Forum for Development Studies* (NUPI, Oslo), 2007/1: 9–43.

—— (2008), "Understanding the Diversity of Conceptions of Well-being and Quality of Life," plenary address, conference on Happiness and Capability, Ravenstein, Radboud University of Nijmegen.

Gates, J. (1998), *The Ownership Solution: Towards a Shared Capitalism for the 21st Century*, London: Penguin.

Griffin, J. (1986), *Well-Being*, Oxford: Clarendon Press.

Hirschman, Albert (1967), *Development Projects Observed*, Washington, DC: Brookings Institution Press.

—— (1977), *The Passions and the Interests*, Princeton: Princeton University Press.

—— (1986), *Rival Views of Market Society*, New York: Viking.

Hughes, J. (2007), *The End of Work: Theological Critiques of Capitalism*, Oxford: Blackwell.

Kahneman, D., E. Diener and N. Schwartz (eds.) (1999), *Well-Being: The Foundations of Hedonic Psychology*, New York: Russell Sage Foundation.

Kates, R., A. Leiserowitz and T. Parris (2006), *Great Transition Values: Present Attitudes, Future Changes*, Great Transition Initiative. Online, available at: www.gtinitiative.org/documents/PDFFINALS/9Values.pdf.

Klamer, A. (2005), *In hemelsnaam! Over de economie van overvloed en onbehagen*, Kampen: Uitgeverij ten Have.

Lane, R. (1991), *The Market Experience*, Cambridge, UK: Cambridge University Press.

—— (2000), *The Loss of Happiness in Market Democracies*, New Haven: Yale University Press.

Lichtheim, G. (1972), *Europe in the Twentieth Century*, London: Weidenfeld and Nicholson.

Marshall, G. (1998), *Oxford Dictionary of Sociology*, Oxford: Oxford University Press.

Max-Neef, M. (1989), "Human-scale Development," *Development Dialogue*, 1989(1): 5–81. Expanded as *Human-scale Development* (1991), New York and London: Apex Press.

McCloskey, D.N. (2006), *The Bourgeois Virtues: Ethics for an Age of Commerce*, Chicago: Chicago University Press.

Nietzsche, F. (1998), *Twilight of the Idols*, translated by Duncan Large, Oxford: Oxford University Press.

Nussbaum, M. (1986), *The Fragility of Goodness*, Cambridge, UK: Cambridge University Press.

—— (1997), *Cultivating Humanity*, Cambridge, MA: Harvard University Press.

—— (2005), "Mill Between Aristotle and Bentham," in L. Bruni and P.L. Porta (eds.) *Economics and Happiness*, Oxford: Oxford University Press, 170–183.

—— (2006), *Frontiers Of Justice*. Cambridge, MA: Harvard University Press/Belknap.

Parfit, D. (1984), *Reasons and Persons*, Oxford: Oxford University Press.

Richards, H. (1985), *The Evaluation of Cultural Action: An Evaluative Study of The Parents and Children Program (PPH)*, London: Macmillan.

Roosevelt, T. (1900), *The Strenuous Life*. Online, available at: www.bartleby.com/58/.

Ryan, R.M. and E.L. Deci (2001), "On Happiness and Human Potentials: A Review of Research on Hedonic and Eudaimonic Well-being," *Annual Review of Psychology*, 52: 141–166.

Saunders, P. (1995), *Capitalism: A Social Audit*, Buckingham: Open University Press.

Schumpeter, J. (1927), "Social Classes in an Ethnically Homogeneous Environment," Reproduced in Schumpeter (1951).

—— (1942), *Capitalism, Socialism and Democracy*, London: George Allen & Unwin.

—— (1951), *Imperialism and Social Classes*, P. Sweezy (ed.) Oxford: Blackwell.

Schwartz, B. (2005), *The Paradox of Choice: Why More is Less*, New York: Harper Perennial.

Singh, Satyajit K. (1990), "Evaluating Large Dams in India," *Economic and Political Weekly*, 25(11): 561–574.

Streeten, P.P. (1954), Programs and Prognoses. *Quarterly Journal of Economics*, 68(3): 355–376.

Stretton, Hugh and Lionel Orchard (1994), *Public Goods, Public Enterprise, Public Choice: Theoretical Foundations of the Contemporary Attack on Government*, Basingstoke: Macmillan.

Sumner, L.W. (1996), *Welfare, Happiness and Ethics*, Oxford: Oxford University Press.

Vaughan, Genevieve (1999), "Mothering, Co-muni-cation and the Gifts of Language." Online, available at: www.gift-economy.com/articlesAndEssays.html.

—— (n.d.), *For-giving: A Feminist Criticism of Exchange*. Online, available at: www.for-giving.com/.

Walzer, M. (1983), *Spheres of Justice*, Oxford: Blackwell.

Weber, M. (2001 [1904]), *The Protestant Ethic and the Spirit of Capitalism*, London: Routledge.

3 The United Nations and democratic globalization

A reconnaissance of the issues

Keith Cowling, Silvia Sacchetti, Roger Sugden and James R. Wilson[*]

> For the United Nations, success in meeting the challenges of globalization ultimately comes down to meeting the needs of peoples. It is in their name that the Charter was written; realizing their aspirations remains our vision for the twenty-first century.
>
> (Kofi A. Annan (2000: 14))

1 Introduction

The concern of this chapter is to discuss some ideas on the role of the United Nations in influencing the democratic development of economies, thereby to contribute to economic and political debate about the organization's role in the modern world. It is an initial reconnaissance of the issues. Without attempting to provide a detailed history or analysis of the current situation within the organization, and maintaining a distance from the baggage of its internal politics, the objective is to present and consider a perspective based upon a particular analysis of processes of economic development. The analysis focuses on the inclusion of all peoples in the realization of the economic development goals that they themselves would democratically identify and seek, given the opportunity. We suggest that it is an approach that is apparently consistent with many of the principles of the United Nations. Most notably, it has the realization of the aspirations of peoples at its heart and to that degree is in line with Annan's (2000) vision for the United Nations in the twenty-first century; if that vision is meant to be real and realizable, the issues we identify and discuss represent the economic and political challenges that must be overcome.

The chapter echoes aspects of Stutzer and Frey (2005) in their discussion of democracy in international organizations, and in appraising the economic and political relevance of our approach we draw on their concluding words (ibid.: 324–325): the proposal we offer

> Is certainly in a preliminary stage and many aspects need further consideration. But one thing can be predicted with certainty: the decision-makers in international organizations and national governments will reject it. While

the basic thrust of an increased democratic element is difficult to deny, the proposal will be labeled naïve and impossible to realize. But such a reaction would correspond exactly to the interests of these decision-makers ... It would therefore be in their interests to find as many arguments against the proposal as possible. Quite another strategy would be to simply ignore the proposal. In any case, the entrenched persons and groups will not support it. But this does not necessarily mean that it will never be put into practice [at least in certain respects and with significant consequences amongst some peoples and in some parts of the world economy].

Specifically, our approach is centered on the governance of economic activity; on who determines the strategic direction of production, and on what basis. As argued in some detail by Branston *et al.* (2006a), such a governance-centric approach to policy is at odds with current and previous practice, certainly in Anglo-US economies. Insofar as this practice has a theoretical rationale in economics, its foundation is essentially market failure; see, for example, Pitelis (1994) on the British case. Such market-centered approaches give little or no direct importance to strategy; they emphasize the benefits of markets and most especially market competition, in contrast to our focus on strategic choice. The governance-centric and market failure analyses are also markedly different in their treatment of policy objectives. For example, whilst Pitelis (1994: 4) observes that the literature on market failure has "no clear consensus on, or even discussion of" industrial policy objectives, he sees increases in the per-capita incomes of consumers as a typical concern. See also Coates (1996) and Wren (2001) on, for instance, the desire for increased productivity. However, the prime policy objective in the governance-centric approach is not reducible to rises in per-capita incomes or productivity. Rather, the objective would need to be determined through a democratic process (that goes beyond nation states and that entails far more than elections) involving everyone affected by the economic activity. Dewey (1927) is especially interesting for a provocative consideration of how this might be achieved in practice, and his approach has been taken up in recent literature exploring specific challenges in greater detail; see, for instance, Branston *et al.* (2006a) on the public interest in corporate governance, and Branston *et al.* (2006c) on the health industry.

The chapter is organized as follows. Section 2 uses a series of illustrations to outline a particular analysis of processes of economic development and of globalization. More specifically, its focus is the strategic decision-making analysis of the development of economies (as explored in, for example, Cowling and Sugden (1998a; 1998b; 1999), Bailey *et al.* (2000), Cowling and Tomlinson (2000), Sugden and Wilson (2002a) and Sacchetti and Sugden (2003)). Section 3 observes that international institutions are well-placed to stimulate and nurture processes of globalization, but identifies possibilities with widely differing outcomes for peoples' welfare: on the one hand there is the potential to promote a process that is elitist and exclusionary, and on the other to catalyze democracy and inclusion. We remark on the impact in practice of the World Bank and the

International Monetary Fund, consider the founding charter of the United Nations and comment on the future role of the organization. We argue that the attainment of inclusive development processes necessitates public initiatives to which the United Nations is uniquely placed to contribute. A short summary of the argument is included in the concluding Section 4.

2 Processes of economic development

Governance

Imagine that you live in a locality within a city in Argentina, the harbor area – El Puerto – of Mar del Plata, for example. What does the term "economic development" mean to you? Perhaps it encapsulates a desire that your children have higher standards of education and/or healthcare. It might mean the opportunity to earn a higher income than at present. If you have a job, maybe you desire the creation of more jobs, or of better quality jobs, so as to alleviate poverty and social problems around you. "Economic development" might also incorporate a wish to build on the traditions and cultures of your community. Perhaps its meaning to you is founded on an attachment to certain activities and ways of doing things; for example, the history and culture of El Puerto is deeply rooted in fishing (Allen 2001). However, while we can analyze the meaning of economic development for you, as "outsiders" we cannot hope to be totally accurate.[1]

Within El Puerto itself, while each person will have different views, there are likely to be common concerns and desires. Each person is related through their direct and immediate stake in the development of their locality. More fundamentally, they are linked through their everyday relationships and communications, through the common firms and institutions that impact on their daily lives. Many will have lived through the locality's recent history, and been brought up within its cultures and traditions. Consequently, there are likely to be common threads and a potential for the emergence of broad consensus on what is desired, albeit one that is evolving and at times contested. We suggest that the specification of development in El Puerto be taken from these aims and objectives, and that "development" by other criteria lacks meaning for the people of El Puerto.

Now consider what development of the locality means for those who make the key decisions impacting on its future. At a national level motivations and desired outcomes may differ to those found in El Puerto. Certain policies formulated in Buenos Aires, Argentina's capital city, might reflect the interests of groups or individuals that are successful at lobbying. What constitutes "development" for such a group might at times cut across the objectives of those in El Puerto. Allen (2001), for example, demonstrates how the nationally determined restructuring of the Argentinean fishing industry has impacted on Mar del Plata; while the expansion of fishing rights during the 1990s no doubt constitutes "development" for the Argentinean and European companies involved, Allen argues that it has brought to Mar del Plata "not only negative social and natural impacts but ... the deterioration of the city's environment, particularly the harbor area" (ibid.: 162).

Moreover, given the physical and cultural distance between people in El Puerto and the decision-making apparatus in Buenos Aires, the degree of transparency and accountability in such decisions is likely to be low. This is compounded by the general suspicion of "spectacular corruption" in Argentina (Pastor and Wise 2001: 61). During the financial crisis of the late 1990s, for example, the people of El Puerto would have had virtually no recourse to impact on or call to question the policy changes that seemed to arrive daily from Buenos Aires, but that critically affected their lives.

Similarly, some important decisions are made outside of Argentina. Many key choices are taken within international institutions such as the World Bank and the International Monetary Fund (IMF). The impact of strategy formed in Washington (for example) is felt in places such as El Puerto both directly, through externally directed programmes, and indirectly, through the concept of aid conditionality applied to national governments. Again, there are likely to be differences between the outcomes that constitute "development" for those making decisions in Washington, and outcomes that are meaningful for the people of El Puerto. Once more there are few, if any, channels for the people of that locality to have an influence.

The significance of decision-making processes has also been identified in other contexts relevant to an understanding of the development process; see, for example, Cowling and Sugden (1998b) on international trade; Bailey *et al.* (2000) on the accountability of transnational corporations; Cowling and Tomlinson (2000) on strategic failure in Japan; and Sacchetti and Sugden (2003) on different types of network.

Consider, more particularly, the governance of firms and most especially of modern transnational corporations (Cowling and Sugden 1998a; 1999; Branston *et al.* 2006a). To take one of many illustrations, the South African economy is heavily reliant on the activities of a small number of large transnationals, including Anglo American, BHP Billiton (formerly Billiton), Old Mutual and SABMiller (formerly South African Breweries). Yet these firms are governed by only a subset of those with an interest in their activities. This subset determines the corporations' strategies and therefore their impacts. During the late 1990s each took the key decision to move their primary stock exchange listings and relocate their headquarters to London.[2] The impact of this, while determined by a narrow elite of shareholders and directors, is ultimately felt among wider groups in South African society, where considerable concern at the moves has been registered.[3] The result is strategic failure; concentration of strategic decision-making power in the hands of a few implies a failure to govern production in the interests of the community at large (Cowling and Sugden 1999). To avoid such failure, the democratization of governance is required, to reflect the concerns of everyone interested in a corporation's activities. More generally, a similar argument for democratization applies to all aspects of economies, and to economies as a whole.

In line with this analysis, Sugden and Wilson (2002a) present a theoretical approach centering on the key argument that "economic development" is only meaningful to the people seeking to develop when that development reflects their own aims and objectives. Moreover, it rejects the currently prevalent, largely "external" definitions and evaluations of development as inappropriately biased, given their potential to influence and skew the development priorities of specific localities, and to undermine the possibility of development solutions that are rooted in localities' own histories, cultures, aims and desires. The idea is that "external" criteria inevitably reflect external interests, to that extent yielding inefficient outcomes with respect to the aims of the communities seeking to develop.

This focus signals a need for people and peoples to be involved in the planning for their development, and thus in the decision-making processes affecting the societies where they live. In other words, the governance of economic development is crucial.

Knowledge and learning

Linked to the importance of governance is a concern with knowledge and learning, the foundations on which engagement in governance can be built.

The emphasis that we have in mind as regards knowledge and learning differs fundamentally from a conventional economists' concern with tangible skills and training, and the static transfer of codified information. Consider, for example, the analysis of mainstream development economics. Given movement toward a "new" economy, where knowledge is seen to be the key to realizing returns, it has become widely accepted that education and the generation and diffusion of knowledge are vital components of development processes. The 1998/99 "World Development Report" (World Bank 1998), for example, was dedicated to knowledge, a focus that has since taken on ever more importance in the analysis of development. The standard approach is to see knowledge as important in terms of the value it can add to production processes, and crucially, therefore, the ability to attract investment. A primary concern is with bridging knowledge gaps so that localities can "compete" on a more equal footing, or extending knowledge gaps so that localities can enhance their "competitive advantage" (see the discussion in Sacchetti (2004)).

While we recognize the importance of this "competitive" imperative for knowledge, our focus is different. We see knowledge and learning as especially important when they afford people the opportunity to engage effectively in the decision-making processes that govern development. We suggest that appropriate knowledge and learning processes can free people to become suitably involved in formal and informal networks for the governance of firms, institutions, government and other economic actors. This is, in part, knowledge about how to govern democratically; a process of learning about how to form opinions and express them, and in doing so to impact on development. Where effective governance networks do not exist, knowledge and learning about governance, obtained through participation in the process itself, can lead to their establishment.

Again, let us illustrate with an example. Ocotal is a small city in Nicaragua. It is close to the northern border with Honduras and suffers from many of the problems that characterize cities in Central America. At the end of the 1990s, 55 percent of its population was under 20, creating a high degree of dependency. Yet even before Hurricane Mitch hit Nicaragua in 1998, 60 percent of the economically active population of Ocotal was unemployed (Rocha 1999). With figures such as these it is clear that Ocotal faced significant economic and social problems. However, the way in which these problems were approached provides an indication of the sorts of learning and knowledge that can underpin the democratic governance of development.

According to Ocotal's mayor, Marta Adriana Peralta:

> At the end of 1997 we began a process of strategic planning for sustainable development that includes the participation of Ocotal's citizens. We had round-table discussions on five issues: the economy, the environment, tourism as an employment generator, social and urban planning, and social factors.
>
> (cited in Rocha 1999: 1)

While this process was not what is commonly thought of as learning or transferring knowledge in a formal sense, it was nevertheless a process of learning and knowledge generation. In particular, knowledge was being developed not through explicit skills and training, but through interaction and participation, through communication across interested parties. The process allowed people to learn what they sought from development, and to learn what each other sought. It also allowed people to learn how to represent, reconcile and achieve those aims in a democratic fashion (Walker 1997).

The experiences of Ocotal, or indeed any number of similar examples, show that active citizenship can yield significant economic benefits. Such citizenship does not require specific skills such as engineering or information technology qualifications, although it can benefit from different types of knowledge, and not only in the physical sciences but also the arts, humanities and social sciences. Within this, certain forms of static knowledge are important; information about decisions being made by firms or government is necessary if people are to develop views on and govern what happens in their societies (see for example Bailey *et al.* (1998; 2000) on monitoring large corporations). But vital for success is a dynamic process of learning to develop and communicate ideas, and, in so doing, learning to determine democratically the development of a locality.

While learning to be democratic may sound a simple notion, it is an emphasis that is typically lost in debate and policy.[4] In line with Branston *et al.* (2006a), it entails each person learning to think about, and learning to engage in, the governance process; learning to be alert to the need for certain types of knowledge; learning to exercise their voice in the pursuit of that knowledge; and learning to use that knowledge in expressing their voice on strategic ways forward.

It is in this sense that we see knowledge and learning as cornerstones of development. Moreover, following the approach to globalization elaborated in Sugden and Wilson (2003; 2005), knowledge and learning are especially pertinent in today's world because they determine how people are able to respond to and shape the changes that are occurring as borders assume different importance (see also Sacchetti (2004)). Globalization of its essence implies changes in activity and behavior associated with new geography and new technology. Within this, knowledge and learning, and their impact on governance, are fundamental to economic well-being. However, our perspective on development suggests that who governs and how implies that globalization can take two broad forms. It can be "elite globalization" or "democratic globalization," one a process harnessed to further the prosperity of exclusive interests and the other a process harnessed to further the prosperity of all. If knowledge and learning are fundamental in the governance process, they are accordingly fundamental to the choice between elite and democratic globalization.

3 International institutions

It is in this context of different possibilities for globalization that we see a significant role for international institutions in influencing economic development, albeit with outcomes that might vary considerably in their desirability. On the one hand there is the potential to promote a process that is elitist and exclusionary, and on the other to catalyze democracy and inclusion.

The possibility of influence is illustrated by the impact of the World Bank and IMF in many countries over recent years. For example, they have had a telling effect in Argentina, as we have already hinted. Under their influence, the experience of the Argentinean economy over the last 15 years or so characterizes a particular form of globalization, more specifically a form of "elite globalization." In the late 1980s the country was in one of its periodic crises, characterized by what Romero (2002: 285) describes as "a bankrupt state, the national currency in shambles, wages that did not meet basic necessities, and social violence." In 1989 inflation was 4,923 percent, GDP having shrunk by 1.5 percent since 1980 (Schirm 2002). The response of the incoming administration was to ally political and economic populism in embracing the "general recipe" provided by the Washington consensus, in doing so aiming "to make possible an appropriate insertion into the global economy" (Romero 2002: 285–286). The consensus advocates "free markets," containing corporations largely unfettered by regulatory requirements and state constraints, thus free to trade and invest in and across all countries throughout the world (Williamson 1990; 1993). The spread of these characteristics is seen as the route to economic development; they are argued to result in closer cross-country integration, increased trade and investment ties, and the generation of more wealth.

So successful were these attempts that Argentina became what Stiglitz (2002: 79) calls the "star student" of the IMF; it was the exemplar for Washington consensus policies, in terms of both what to do and what success to expect.

However, Romero (2002: 334) argues that by 1999 "no one could ignore the economic dead-end" that the country faced. At the start of the twenty-first century it was once more plagued by acute economic and political turmoil. For the people of Argentina, seeking this form of globalization brought unemployment, poverty – 40 percent of the population was below the poverty line by 2001 (ibid.) – civil unrest and near pariah status amongst the world's economies.

There has been often-fierce debate over where things went wrong in Argentina (see Pastor and Wise (2001) and IMF (2002) for discussion). According to Bianchi (2002), the neo-liberal path of privatization, trade liberalization and deregulation resulted in the emergence and invasion of a small number of family groups governing key parts of the productive system. Nochteff and Abeles (2000) also suggest that the deregulation led to economic and social fragmentation. They note that the concentration of economic and political power has resulted, on the one hand, in abuses of dominant positions and extraordinary profits, and on the other in unemployment, poverty and increasing income inequality. In addition, it seems that the neo-liberal approach to (lack of) regulation in the Argentinean social, cultural and institutional context has nurtured a vacuum in which corruption and malpractice have flourished. In short, in the case of Argentina, globalization according to the overview and approval of the international institutions at the heart of the Washington consensus was elitist and exclusionary, benefiting some but failing to overcome problems of poverty and underdevelopment (Sugden and Wilson 2002b).[5]

More generally, a common criticism of the Washington institutions in their dealings with less developed countries is that development professionals arrive, stay in top hotels, and then return after a few weeks or months to their career paths in Washington; they are distant from the actual process of development. Stiglitz (2002) discusses this in the context of the IMF, and Taylor (1997: 151) draws an interesting parallel with the criticism by Von Mises (1935) of socialism

> On the grounds that "as if" planners could never improve upon capitalism because they would just "play" a market game without being disciplined for their mistakes. The same doubts apply to bureaucrats "playing" at running national economies with their attention focused on career advancement in the institutions back in the United States.

When combined with the charge that the Washington institutions are highly prescriptive in their advice (Palast 2002; Stiglitz 2002), a one-way rather than two-way flow, it becomes clear why they are often viewed as "outsiders." Indeed, they are often seen as having a stake or interest in the local development process that differs markedly from that of the local people. In this sense we suggest that a problem with the Washington institutions is that they forge "international" but not "multinational" development relationships. In other words, they operate across nations, but they do not do so in a manner that is rooted in and respectful of the constituent interests of each nation.

While the Washington institutions facilitate a form of elite globalization, however, this is not the only option. A different form of international institution might play a different and more positive role in stimulating alternative forms of globalization. More specifically, we would advocate a role for the United Nations as regards the attainment of democratic globalization.

The United Nations

The Preamble to the Charter of the United Nations (United Nations 1945) identifies as an objective the "promotion of the economic and social advancement of all peoples," based (amongst other things) on the "dignity and worth of the human person." Article 1 refers to "respect for the principle of *equal rights* and *self determination of peoples*" alongside "international *cooperation* in solving international problems of an economic, social, cultural or humanitarian character" (our emphasis). It calls for the United Nations "to be a centre for *harmonising the actions of nations* in the attainment of these common ends" (our emphasis). Chapter IX focuses on international economic and social co-operation, reaffirming "respect for the principle of equal rights and self determination of peoples." Members "pledge" to cooperate so as to promote: "higher standards of living, full employment, and conditions of economic and social progress and development"; "solutions of international economic, social, health, and related problems"; and "universal respect for, and observance of human rights and fundamental freedoms for all without distinction as to race, sex, language, or religion."

These principles and aims have been stressed by the Secretary General of the United Nations in his reflections on its role in a modern world (Annan 2000). Because "it is the only body of its kind with universal membership and comprehensive scope, and encompassing so many areas of human endeavour," he sees the organization as "a uniquely useful forum – for sharing information, conducting negotiations, elaborating norms and voicing expectations, coordinating the behaviour of states and other actors, and pursuing common plans of action" (ibid.: 5–6). He explicitly identifies this unique role as also being rooted in "the shared values embodied in our Charter" (ibid.: 13). Furthermore, according to Annan, the United Nations "exists for, and must serve, the needs and hopes of people everywhere" (ibid.: 6). He goes on to assert that

> The central challenge we face today is to ensure that globalization becomes a positive force for all the world's people, instead of leaving billions of them behind in squalor. *Inclusive globalization* must be built on the great enabling force of the market, but market forces alone will not achieve it. It *requires a broader effort to create a shared future, based upon our common humanity and its diversity.*
>
> (Ibid.: 6, our emphasis)

We see these principles, aims and sentiments as in line with a desire to stimulate and nurture throughout the world processes in which each interested person is able to think about and participate fully in the governance of economic development; they point to a role for the United Nations and its constituent agencies in shifting the development focus to localities and to democratic relationships within and between localities, in line with the theoretical arguments of the previous section.[6] Such a shift would be radical, and for some commentators might seem a vain ideal in the modern world. But the economic and political reality implied by the United Nations Charter and by Kofi Annan's reflections necessitates its contemplation.

This chapter has argued that currently typical processes of economic development and correspondingly of globalization are characterized by strategic failure, a concentration of strategic decision-making power amongst exclusive interests that implies a failure to govern production in the interests of communities at large. Avoiding this failure necessitates the democratization of governance within and across all economic organizations and institutions. Success in this regard would deliver what Annan (2000) refers to as inclusive globalization, and could not be achieved through the market alone. Whilst the existing literature on the democratizing of strategic choice in economic development is far from clear about *all* that is needed to achieve desirable outcomes, there is *no* doubt about its conclusion that a free market characterized by a concentration of power yields exclusive governance and elite globalization.

To achieve democratic outcomes the literature lays stress on various factors, including the significance of appropriate public policy that serves the public interest. For example, Cowling and Sugden (1998a) conclude their analysis of the theory of the firm with the observation that the emergence of a democratic form necessitates purposive public policy.[7] It cannot rely on a natural evolution in a process of free competition between alternative possibilities, because of the power of currently incumbent forces. This points to the need for policy organizations that stimulates and catalyzes democratic outcomes, and at the international level it would seem to us that this suggests a pivotal opportunity for the United Nations. Its unique position resulting from global membership and, in particular, the common values of the Charter indicate a concern with economic democracy, whilst comments about its focus on voice, coordination, plans of action and so on reflect an explicit concern with policy.

Annan's (2000) mentioning of voice is also especially interesting because it prompts reference to ideas about the relative importance of voice and "exit" in democratic development and globalization (see in particular Branston *et al.* 2006a). Following Hirschman (1970), exit is central to market processes and voice to democracy. He argues that exit is "neat," "impersonal" and "indirect," respects in which

> Voice is just the opposite of exit. It is a far more "messy" concept because it can be graduated, all the way from faint grumbling to violent protest; it implies articulation of one's critical opinions rather than a private, "secret" vote in the anonymity of the supermarket; and finally, it is direct and straightforward rather than roundabout.

(Ibid.: 15–16)

The conclusion of Hirschman (1970: 17 and 43) is that the democratic process of its essence entails "the digging, the use, and hopefully the slow improvement" of channels of voice, "essentially an *art* constantly evolving in new directions." Consistent with this, we see the policy challenge as the design of a set of initiatives that recognize and nurture this constantly evolving art.

Exactly what the initiatives might entail in practice is partially explored in existing literature. They might include, for example, experimentation with different forms and processes of direct democracy, discussed in some depth by Stutzer and Frey (2005). Their focus is on all citizens having democratic participation rights; they advocate mechanisms of random citizen selection to make democracy realizable. It also seems likely that practical economic democracy would necessitate the promotion of novel forms of organizations based on participatory governance processes. These might include social enterprises which have social objectives, as discussed in Borzaga and Defourny (2001). Similarly pertinent are the specific suggestions for evolving democracy in large corporations analyzed in Branston *et al.* (2006a); these suggestions encompass new company laws and suitably designed regulatory environments. Moreover, such proposals are extended to the sphere of democracy across productive sectors by Branston *et al.* (2006b), discussing privatization and in particular the electricity sector, and by Branston *et al.* (2006c), on the health industry. These contributions are consistent with the guiding principle for realizable democratic development suggested by Sugden and Wilson (2002): to design and implement a dual approach, on the one hand perforce accepting certain requirements as laid down by currently powerful decision-makers, on the other hand using any room for maneuver to focus on possibilities for democratic development, according to the aims and objectives of the people seeking to develop.

We would emphasize very strongly that meeting the policy challenge places a stress on understanding the needs and desires of people, and on the nurturing of relationships amongst people. This would include recognition of peoples having numerous concerns and dimensions, an argument suggested by Sunstein (2001b). He contrasts consumer and political sovereignty, arguing that the latter requires something other than unfettered pursuit of consumer interests. The key point is that people are not merely consumers; rather, they are multi-dimensional. We would highlight something similar in the search for an economic democracy. In issue are the interests of people in all of their dimensions (Branston *et al.* 2006a). Such recognition would seem to be entirely consistent with the principles of the United Nations, for example with the focus of the Charter on "the dignity and worth of the human person" (United Nations 1945: Article 1).

More generally, we see an effective democracy as founded upon mutual respect amongst its participants, upon their listening to each other and upon their searching for some form of mutual understanding. There is a need to provide arenas for discussion and conflict resolution, for eliciting compromise and negotiating agreements (Branston *et al.* 2006a). These are precisely the sorts of issues with which there is considerable and unique experience in the United Nations. Accordingly it is well placed to help to enable preferences to evolve within the choice process as relationships develop between all of the different interested parties.[8] Doing this, the United Nations might then be able to advance the evolution of economic democracy based on public deliberation, discussion and reason-giving, an approach that we see as deserving special attention when analyzing the possibilities for democratic governance, rather than concentrating on, for instance, what Dewey (1927) might refer to as foolish majority rule.[9]

4 Concluding remarks

This chapter has focused on different processes of economic development. Illustrations are used to depict the currently typical situation in which exclusive interests determine the aims of economic activity, and more generally to consider the significance of governance; it is argued that appreciating who makes strategic decisions, and on what basis, is central to an understanding of economic development. The chapter suggests a need for people to be involved in the planning for their development, and thus in the decision-making processes affecting the societies where they live. More particularly, we advocate the democratization of governance and favor democratic globalization.

Effective democratic processes need to be rooted in and respectful of the constituent interests of each nation. They are accordingly difficult to realize because they imply the need for relationships to emerge over time. This necessitates a lengthy process of learning, and an evolution of trust and knowledge amongst participants so as to yield productive co-operation. Achieving this on a global basis would require significant input from one or a set of organizations that are active in nations throughout the world, and that carry the respect of people from different parts of the world. In that regard we suggest that the unique position of the United Nations implies a pivotal opportunity for it to stimulate and catalyze desirable outcomes.

We would also emphasize that if development is to be based on the aims, objectives and actions of the people of a locality, and if those outside a locality might be able to contribute ideas and suggestions in a co-operative process, then the ways in which the outsiders conduct themselves is crucial. That is a lesson from the experiences of the World Bank and IMF. There needs to be conscious awareness of sensitivities and concerns, and of the economic, political and social characteristics of the locality. Related to this requirement, there needs to be sensitivity on the part of local people; for example a refusal to jump to the depiction of interfering outsiders when that is not accurate. Both insiders and outsiders need to be aware of each other's roles, respectful of each other, and willing to learn together as the process unfolds.[10]

Such an approach would seem to be in line with the principles, aims and sentiments of the Charter of the United Nations, and the same can be said for the democratization of processes of economic development more generally. Whether or not the approach is realizable in practice is an open question. For example, Ryan (2000) argues that the United Nations is a body that has been shaped by states, and that the domination of states will likely be maintained. For the future, he sees it as a forum in which the world's poor may continue to exercise their voice, seeking to pressure rich countries into dealing with problems of poverty and hunger, but he also suggests that the rich countries might choose not to listen. Gareis and Varwick (2005) make a related argument. In suggesting that Annan saw the UN as tailored to an "inter-national world," while we in fact live in a "global world," they argue that the "fundamental institutional challenge of this century" lies "in the effective reaction to this transition" (Gareis and Varwick 2005: 243). Within this they see three future scenarios for UN development: "Marginalization," "World Government," and "Muddling Through" (ibid.: 252). Ryan's comments on the domination of states could be seen to infer that "world government" is unlikely, which in this scheme would imply "marginalization" or "muddling through." However, our analysis suggests that this array of alternatives is too limited.

In particular, we identify a fourth, and more desirable, alternative to aim for: "A Democratic Multinational Agency for Development in a Global World." This would not be "marginal," nor "world government," nor "muddling through," but "active, multilateral, democratic and central," in the way we have described. Indeed, we would argue that the Charter implies the appropriateness of democratizing processes of economic development, and that its sentiments are a positive force to build upon. Our advocated approach is focused on meeting the needs of peoples, all peoples in all lands without discrimination and with respect for their dignity. Moreover, for the United Nations to champion such development successfully would be for it to realize peoples' aspirations and – echoing the words of Kofi Annan with which we opened this chapter – fulfill its vision for the twenty-first century.

Notes

* Acknowledgment: The authors are grateful for the comments of participants on earlier drafts at the conference on *Regionalisation and the Taming of Globalisation? Economic, Political, Security, Social and Governance Issues*, University of Warwick, October 2005, and the *Twelfth World Congress of Social Economics*, University of Amsterdam, June 2007.
1 According to Annan (2000), a poll of 57,000 adults in 60 countries in 1999 for the United Nations revealed that "people everywhere valued good health and a happy family life more highly than anything else. Where economic performance was poor, they also stressed jobs" (ibid.: 16).
2 See, for example, "South African Companies Head for the Open Door: Groups are Seeking Overseas Listings to Raise their Profile and Gain Access to Hard Cash," *Financial Times*, March 22, 1999.
3 This concern is reflected in the reported hesitancy of the South African government in sanctioning the moves, and was evident in vocal disquiet by groups such as the South African Congress of Trade Unions (COSATU) who felt at the time that South African employment would suffer ("SA Breweries: No Longer a Home Brew," *Mail* and *Guardian*, December 11, 1998; "Manuel Gives Green Light to Big SA Firms Wanting Offshore Listings," *Business Day*, November 9, 1998).
4 In considering the potential weaknesses of a democratic approach, one issue stressed by Stutzer and Frey (2005) focuses on education – more specifically, on its being

inadequate to equip citizens to play an appropriate role in a democratic economy. In contrast, the stress on learning in our approach is not merely an issue of education.

5 It is argued, however, that Argentina did not conform to the strict principles of the Washington consensus. Romero (2002: 288) refers to the "careless" privatizations "at odds with other declared objectives, such as encouraging competition." Further detailed discussion can be found in Williamson (2003).

6 We would argue that it is the people in those localities, not their agents (e.g. consultants), who need to be the objects of the relationships that might be catalyzed by the United Nations.

7 See also Sunstein (2001a) on political democracy and in particular the role of constitutions.

8 On the notion that individual values can change in a decision-making process, see Buchanan (1954).

9 Sunstein (2001a: 6) comments that "the ideal of democracy can be understood in many different ways. Some people think that democracy calls simply for majority rule; other people think that a democratic system qualifies as such if it is highly responsive to popular will." He rejects these approaches, instead favoring "*deliberative democracy*, an idea that is meant to combine political accountability with a high degree of reflectiveness and a general commitment to reason-giving" (ibid.: 6–7). See also Stutzer and Frey (2005) on the factors that mean citizens "could start to feel an incentive and obligation to participate in the joint effort" (ibid.: 316); general discussion among citizens on aspects of the democratic process is identified as important.

10 For a discussion of related points in the context of the participation of academics in local economic development processes, see Branston *et al.* (2003).

References

Allen, Adriana (2001), "Urban Sustainability under Threat: The Restructuring of the Fishing Industry in Mar del Plata, Argentina," *Development in Practice*, 11(2–3): 152–173.

Annan, Kofi A. (2000), "'We the Peoples': The Role of the United Nations in the 21st Century," New York: United Nations.

Bailey, David, Harte, George and Sugden, Roger (1998), "The Case for a Monitoring Policy across Europe," *New Political Economy*, 3(2): 296–300.

—— (2000), "Deregulation of Industrial Development: A Multilateral Framework on Investment and the Need for Regulated Corporate Accountability," *Accounting, Auditing and Accountability Journal*, 13(2): 197–218.

Bianchi, Patrizio (2002), "Che Cosa Impariamo dalla Crisi Argentina," *L'industria – Revista di Economia e Política Industriale*, XXIII(1): 5–28.

Borzaga, Carlo and Defourny, Jacques (eds.) (2001), *The Emergence of Social Enterprise*, London: Routledge.

Branston, J. Robert, Sugden, Roger and Wilson, James R. (2003), "International Perspectives on the Prosperity of a Region: A Personal Reflection," in Roger Sugden, Rita Hartung Cheng and G. Richard Meadows (eds.) *Urban and Regional Prosperity in a Globalised, New Economy*, Cheltenham: Edward Elgar.

Branston, J. Robert, Cowling, Keith and Sugden, Roger (2006a), "Corporate Governance and the Public Interest," *International Review of Applied Economics*, 20(2): 189–212.

Branston, J. Robert, Sugden, Roger, Valdez, Pedro and Wilson, James R. (2006b), "Generating Participation and Democracy: An Illustration from Electricity Reform in Mexico," *International Review of Applied Economics*, 20(1): 47–68.

Branston, J. Robert, Rubini, Lauretta, Sugden, Roger and Wilson, James R. (2006c), "The

Healthy Development of Economies: A Strategic Framework for Competitiveness in the Health Industry," *Review of Social Economy*, LXIV(3): 301–329.

Buchanan, J. (1954), "Social Choice, Democracy, and Free Markets," *Journal of Political Economy*, 62: 114–123.

Coates, David (ed.) (1996), *Industrial Policy in Britain*, London: Macmillan.

Cowling, Keith and Sugden, Roger (1998a), "The Essence of the Modern Corporation: Markets, Strategic Decision-Making and the Theory of the Firm," *Manchester School*, 66(1): 59–86.

—— (1998b), "Strategic Trade Policy Reconsidered: National Rivalry vs Free Trade vs International Cooperation," *Kyklos*,51(3): 339–357.

—— (1999), "The Wealth of Localities, Regions and Nations: Developing Multinational Economies," *New Political Economy*, 4(3): 361–378.

Cowling, Keith and Tomlinson, Philip R. (2000), "The Japanese Crisis – A Case of Strategic Failure," *Economic Journal*, 110(464): F358–381.

Dewey, J. (1927), *The Public and its Problems*, Denver, CO: Holt.

Gareis, Sven Bernhard and Varwick, Johannes (2005), *The United Nations: An Introduction*, London: Palgrave Macmillan.

Hirschman, Albert O. (1970), *Exit, Voice, and Loyalty: Responses to Decline in Firms, Organizations, and States*, Cambridge, MA: Harvard University Press.

IMF (International Monetary Fund) (2002), "Dornbusch on Global Economy, Argentina, Russia, and Much More," *IMFsurvey*, March 25: 93–96.

Mises, Ludwig von (1935), "Economic Calculation in the Socialist Commonwealth," in Freidrich Hayek (ed.) *Collectivist Economic Planning*, London: Routledge.

Nochteff, H. and Abeles, M. (2000), *Economic Shocks without Vision: Neoliberalism in the Transition of Socio-Economic System: Lessons from the Argentine Case*, Madrid: Iberoamericana.

Palast, Greg (2002), *The Best Democracy Money Can Buy: An Investigative Reporter Exposes the Truth about Globalization, Corporate Cons, and High Finance Fraudsters*, London: Pluto Press.

Pastor, Manuel and Wise, Carol (2001), "From Poster Child to Basket Case," *Foreign Affairs*, November/December: 60–72.

Pitelis, Christos N. (1994), "Industrial Strategy – For Britain, in Europe and the World," *Journal of Economic Studies*, 21(5): 3–92.

Rocha, José Luis (1999), "Ocotal: Urban Planning for People," *Envio Revista*, September.

Romero, Luis Alberto (2002), *A History of Argentina in the Twentieth Century*, Pennsylvania: Pennsylvania State University Press.

Ryan, Stephen (2000), *The United Nations and International Politics*, London: Macmillan.

Sacchetti, Silvia (2004), "Knowledge Caps in Industrial Development," *New Political Economy*, 9: 389–412.

Sacchetti, Silvia and Sugden, Roger (2003), "The Governance of Networks and Economic Power: The Nature and Impact of Subcontracting Relationships," *Journal of Economic Surveys*, 17(5): 669–691.

Schirm, Stefan A. (2002), *Globalization and the New Regionalism*, Cambridge, UK: Polity Press.

Stiglitz, Joseph E (2002), *Globalization and its Discontents*, New York: Norton.

Stutzer, Alois and Frey, Bruno S. (2005), "Making International Organisations More Democratic," *Review of Law and Economics*, 1(3): 305–330.

Sugden, Roger and Wilson, James R. (2002a), "Development in the Shadow of the Consensus: A Strategic Decision-Making Approach," *Contributions to Political Economy*, 21: 111–134.

—— (2002b), "Cambiando Attitudini alla Cooperazione: Il Fondamento per una Nuova Struttura Industriale in Argentina," *L'industria – Rivista di Economia e Politica Industriale*, XXIII(3): 529–538.

—— (2003), "Urban and Regional Prosperity in a Globalised, 'New' Economy: An Agenda and Perspective," in Roger Sugden, Rita Hartung Cheng and G. Richard Meadows (eds.) *Urban and Regional Prosperity in a Globalised, New Economy*, Cheltenham: Edward Elgar.

—— (2005), "Economic Globalisation: Dialectics, Conceptualisation and Choice," *Contributions to Political Economy*, 24: 1–20.

Sunstein, Cass R. (2001a), *Designing Democracy. What Constitutions Do*, Oxford: Oxford University Press.

—— (2001b), *Republic.com*, Princeton: Princeton University Press.

Taylor, Lance (1997), "Editorial: The Revival of the Liberal Creed – the IMF and the World Bank in a Globalized Economy," *World Development*, 25(2): 145–152.

United Nations (1945), "Charter of the United Nations," New York: United Nations. Online, available at: www.un.org/aboutun/charter/.

Walker, Thomas W. (1997), "Introduction: Historical Setting and Important Issues," in Thomas W. Walker (ed.) *Nicaragua Without Illusions: Regime Transition and Structural Adjustment in the 1990s*, Wilmington, DE: Scholarly Resources.

Williamson, John (1990), "The Progress of Policy Reform in Latin America," in J. Williamson (ed.) *Latin American Adjustment: How Much Has Happened*, Washington, DC: Institute for International Economics.

—— (1993), "The Meaning of the Washington Consensus," *World Development*, 21(8): 1329–1336.

—— (2003), *An Agenda for Restoring Growth and Reform*, Washington, DC: Institute for International Economics.

World Bank (1998), *World Development Report 1998/99*, Oxford: Oxford University Press.

Wren, C. (2001), "The Industrial Policy of Competitiveness: A Review of Recent Developments in the UK," *Regional Studies*, 35: 847–860.

4 Knowledge development and coordination via market, hierarchy and gift exchange

Wilfred Dolfsma and Rene van der Eijk

From hunter-gatherer society onwards people in society have experienced the need to cooperate. The need for cooperation, where individuals become dependent on one another, has increased over time as a result of increased ongoing division of labor and specialization. Indeed, as Adam Smith claims, the division of labor and specialization have been an important source of economic development. Individuals no longer master the totality of available knowledge and skills and so the need for exchange of resources and cooperation has increased. This is acknowledged broadly in economics (Hayek 1945; Schumpeter 1934; Nahapiet and Ghosal 1998), but ill understood in that discipline (Lopes and Caldas 2008). As individuals only have partially overlapping goals and interests, exchange and cooperation needs coordination of some sort (Barnard 1968). By necessity, coordination, be it through the market, in a hierarchy or through some other means of cooperation, requires that not only self interest is relied on, but that shared goals and moral convictions are assumed to exist and play a role (Akerlof 1982; Dolfsma 1998; Le Grand 2003; Lopes and Caldas 2008).

In a world characterized by emerging knowledge economies, intangible assets such as knowledge and information have become increasingly important for economic dynamics (OECD 2001). Where the conceptualization of coordination of economic activities is problematic even in case of tangibles, in case of a discussion of knowledge creation and diffusion this problem is enhanced. Knowledge has specific properties as a commodity that need to be taken into account when discussing coordination in this context.

This chapter will discuss the three different mechanisms of coordination between actors that have been acknowledged in the literature. A first coordination mechanism is market exchange. Well known among economists, market exchange can be defined as voluntary agreement involving the offer of any sort of present, continuing, or future utility in exchange for utilities of any sort offered in return (Weber 1978). Secondly we can identify hierarchies or bureaucracies, well established as a coordination mechanism at least since Williamson (1975). Here authority, derived from a person's position in an organization, can be used to coordinate. A third coordination mechanism is not as well established. In the literature different terms are used: social relations (Adler and Kwon 2002), communities (Adler 2001; Bowles and Gintis 1998), clans (Ouchi 1979; 1980), (social) networks (Powell 1990; Miles and Snow 1986; Thorelli 1986). Despite the different terms and descriptions almost all of these concepts have in common that they describe situations where the coordination between individuals is based on socio-cultural mechanisms instead of market or hierarchy.

The existing literature has examined the merits of market and hierarchy as a means of coordination, but not in the context of knowledge development and diffusion. Given the relevance of innovation in the current economic context, this is a major concern. Social economics is well positioned to address this issue, as it is able to analyze not just the two coordination mechanisms most often analyzed – market and hierarchy – but also to conceptually grasp the middle ground where social relations and social values play a role. Notwithstanding the ideal typical approach that a conceptual discussion takes almost by necessity, these exchange mechanisms may not necessarily be substitutes but can be complements (Akerlof 1982, Bradach and Eccles 1989).

Ways of coordinating

In market exchange the presumption is that economic order will emerge from independent, egoistic acts of autonomous individuals in pursuit of their own gain. Hierarchy assumes that the best economic outcome will result from standardization and following the chain of command. A third way, one we shall describe as gift exchange, generally refers to a type of exchange conducted between parties that are characterized by social properties and particularistic ties, the nature of which influences the exchange. In a world with zero transaction costs one may argue that markets as a way of coordinating behavior might be preferable (Coase 1937, Williamson 1975). When transaction costs are present, hierarchy might work better (Hennart 1993; Kreps 1990; Williamson 1975). The literature that has developed to understand hierarchy from an economic perspective may be able to deal conceptually with situations where individuals are boundedly rational, have only partially overlapping goals, and are opportunistic (Williamson 1975). Certainly when discussing knowledge development, and diffusion, however, trust and social norms may play a role too. Understanding how this plays a role may require one to look for ways of coordination where the parties involved are not legally obliged to behave in a certain way because a labor contract specifies it, nor are they involved in a quid pro quo where all relevant goods traded are specified (Arrow 1972). We will briefly present the different ways of coordinating – markets (*A*), hierarchy (*B*), and social relations or gift exchange (*C*) – and discuss the extent to which they help understand the process of knowledge development and diffusion.

A Markets

For economists, a perfect market is not an empirical reality but, rather, a set of assumptions: a large number of firms compete in a market for homogeneous commodities to cater to the demand of a large number of consumers. No producing firm or consumer is able to influence the price; all parties have complete knowledge (Stigler 1968). Markets are where demand and supply meet to set an equilibrium price; all necessary information is summarized in the prices quoted in a market. Modern economics view the market as a price-setting mechanism and have left its workings implied rather than explicitly discussed (see Barber 1977; Coase 1937; Rangan 2000; Stigler 1968). Cooperation between actors can take place anonymously; rules of the game are clear to all participants. As Williamson (1975: 5) puts it "The marvel of the economic system is that prices serve as sufficient statistics, thereby economizing on bounded rationality." In this ideal type of market exchange, the exchange that takes place is de-socialized in nature, it is not "embedded" in a larger social context (Granovetter 1985). In addition it is assumed that exchanges are freely consented to by opportunistic economic actors (Williamson 1975). Exchange takes place within the context of complete contracts, marginal pricing assures optimized production and allocation and, last, property rights are protected by the state and the appropriate legal institutions. A Pareto efficient situation will result from free and unfettered working of the market; exchange in competitive markets assures that the exchange is equitable.

In the "pure" market model it is assumed that risk but no fundamental uncertainty is present. If not all possible future states of the world and the likelihood of their occurrence are known, there is a situation of fundamental uncertainty. Certainly in such a situation complete contracting is impossible. Prices are likely not to reflect the true value of the commodity exchanged and/or prices do not contain all relevant information (Hennart 1993). One may characterize such situations as market failure, and economists do so. The term implies that markets may be made to work in these situations. One may also claim that a different mechanism is at work.

Knowledge and the market

Many firms make use of the market mechanism to develop and procure relevant knowledge. In the year 2000, $142 billion was paid internationally by users to parties that owned intellectual property rights (IPRs) in order to make use of knowledge that was legally protected under IPR Law (Dolfsma 2006).[1] The IPR system thus allows for a market that coordinates the exchange of knowledge. Knowledge as a commodity to be exchanged on the market is no ordinary good. It is non-rivalrous: it is not consumed by their use (Adler 2001; Arrow 1984), and non-exclusive: consumption or use by non-payers cannot be excluded. Knowledge is a (quasi) public good – reliance on the market creates a trade-off between production and allocation. The market may not stimulate the creation of new knowledge in amounts that are beneficial for society (Alder 2001; Stiglitz 1994; Nelson 1959; Romer 2002). If knowledge is available in an explicit form, and possibly digitized too, it can be very easily copied by others (Soete and ter Weel 2005; Cowan *et al.* 2000).

Knowledge development is cumulative, though the extent to which this is true differs across fields. New knowledge is for the most part based on (related) work done by others (in the past): we stand on the shoulders of giants (and dwarfs). One of the conditions conducive to scientific progress thus is "open research" or the full and free dissemination of research results (Nelson 1959). However, from the perspective of the party that invested in the generation of new knowledge, the notion of "open research" may be unappealing since it increases the risk of not recouping initial investment.

Furthermore, Grant (1996) points out that for knowledge creation, but less so for knowledge diffusion, due to the far-reaching extent of specialization, the coordinated effort of many individual specialists and organizations of different kinds is needed. Markets are at a significant disadvantage when it comes to performing this coordinating role. Because they address actors as motivated by extrinsic benefits, markets may actually increase the risk of opportunistic behavior (Le Grand 2003; Grant 1996). Thus, while markets as a means of coordinating behavior for knowledge development and diffusion are not to be dismissed, neither are they to be relied on exclusively.

B Hierarchy

Transaction cost theory (Coase 1937; Williamson 1975) stresses that to transact actors involved incur costs – transaction costs – other than those needed for the good or service exchanged. These transaction costs are costs of coordination, and include costs of contract drafting and contract enforcement. According to transaction cost theory, transactions may take place either in the market or in a hierarchy (firm, organization) – these are the two alternatives. Given the type of transaction (for instance its frequency, investments required, number of competitors faced, duration of the contract), and the characteristics of the good involved, transaction costs will differ (Hennart 1993; Kreps 1990; Williamson 1975).

By seeking to explain what type of activities need to be left to the market, and which need to be brought within the domain of the firm, transaction costs theory endogenizes the boundaries of the firm. Hierarchies coordinate the activities of individuals through the use of authority (legitimate power) aiming at some organizational goal (Williamson 1975; Ouchi 1979; 1980; Adler 2001; Adler and Kwon 2002). The organization uses authority to set rules and issue directives with regard to processes completed or standards of output or quality (Grant 1996; Ouchi 1979). Members must abide by the rules and directives. Surveillance and direction of subordinates are employed by hierarchy to ensure that rules are followed, which involves a cost on its own (Hennart 1993; Ouchi 1980). A perception of equity about the coordination in a hierarchy is the result of social agreement that the hierarchy has the ability and the right to value each contribution and reward it fairly (Ouchi 1980). Hierarchy may be efficient especially in case of a complex situation where the activities of multiple specialized units and large numbers of people need to be coordinated (Grant 1996; Jacques 1990; Romme 1996).

Hierarchy's costs are associated with measuring performance. When "tasks become highly unique, completely integrated or ambiguous for other reasons" performance may be impossible to measure (Ouchi 1980; Adler 2001). Certainly when the counterfactual – the outcome that could have resulted had someone acted in line with the interests of the hierarchy rather than her own – is impossible to determine, performance of hierarchy members cannot be determined. This is obviously the case when new knowledge is (not) created or diffused. Hierarchies may offset performance measurement problems when an incomplete employment contract allows for providing directions on a day-to-day basis and almost casual monitoring as a by-product.

As Homans (1950) has argued, however, when people work closely together within an organization an atmosphere of trust and goal congruence results. Opportunistic behavior and therefore the need for monitoring are reduced. Hierarchies can create an "atmosphere of trust" since they not only provide the stability of long-term cooperative relationships but also employ socialization to create goal congruence and a sense of shared destiny and belonging (Ouchi 1979; 1980; Adler 2001; Grant 1996). Thus, hierarchies permit parties to deal with uncertainty/complexity in an adaptive sequential fashion. While it may be argued that an atmosphere of trust is more likely to grow within hierarchy than in the market, trust may be established between parties in the market as well (Van der Eijk *et al.* 2006). What is more important to observe, conceptually, is that the emergence of trust within hierarchy is not taken into account in transaction costs theory.

Knowledge and hierarchy

To coordinate, hierarchies create horizontally and vertically differentiated units to divide labor. Such organizational structuring may be especially efficient when performing routine tasks but encounters difficulty in case of creation of new knowledge (e.g. Mintzberg 1979; Scott 1992; Adler 2001). Hierarchy coordinates by centralizing information. However, centralizing information functions effectively only if information is "characterized by a high degree of confirmation and little novelty" (Romme 1996) and is not tacit in nature (Grant 1996). Managers may not be able to coordinate and absorb the knowledge their experts have mastered. Knowledge also gives rise to performance measurement difficulties (Adler 2001). According to Adler (2001) vertical differentiation performs well in facilitating downward communication of explicit knowledge and commands, but is less effective in facilitating upward communication of new ideas and knowledge. Hierarchy may thus be an obstacle to learning. Learning might instead require team-like, non-hierarchical structures (Iannello 1992; Levinthal and March 1993; Peters 1987; Senge 1990; Romme 1996). As Powell *et al.* (1996: 118) point out "Knowledge creation occurs in the context of a community, one that is fluid and evolving rather than tightly bound or static. The canonical formal organization, with its bureaucratic rigidities, is a poor vehicle for learning."

Direct horizontal communication between the relevant experts in different units might compensate for hierarchy's difficulty in facilitating upward communication of new ideas and knowledge needed for coordination. However, horizontal differentiations within hierarchies makes cooperation with regard to knowledge creation between units difficult, because units oftentimes have different goals, priorities, working procedures or even locations depending on the needs and circumstances they face that make direct, horizontal (informal) contact between experts difficult. What is more, even though formal structure is able to stimulate knowledge development and diffusion, imposing directives to be creative is not likely to work well. Coordination of knowledge development activities often requires a more "personal" kind of interaction between experts rather than managers than can be achieved by means of rules and directives (Galbraith 1973; Grant 1996; Hansen 1999; Kogut and Zander 1992).

Galbraith (1973) points out that information processing within the hierarchy besides the formal vertical linkages oftentimes takes place via informal horizontal linkages. In this connection, Romme (1996) points toward the importance of teams for knowledge production. Brown and Duguid (1991) emphasize that knowledge creation takes place within the context of an informal community which generally spans departmental and even organizational boundaries. Given the informal nature of many of these horizontal linkages and exchanges, the employment of authority as hierarchy's central coordination mechanism is impaired. This, however, does not prevent horizontal knowledge exchanges from taking place. What in the absence of hierarchy and the market mechanism, whose rigidities are considered a poor vehicle for learning, coordinates these exchanges?

C Social relations: gifts

A number of scholars have proposed alternative ways of coordinating the behavior of actors. Sometimes these are presented as "in-between" markets and hierarchies to be analyzed in similar terms; sometimes they are posed as alternatives in their own right. Terms such as social relations (Adler and Kwon 2002), communities (Adler 2001; Bowles and Gintis 1998), clans (Ouchi 1980) and networks (Powell 1990; Miles and Snow 1986; Thorelli 1986) have been introduced. Most of these conceptions have a common aim to coordinate by curbing the effects of opportunism and goal incongruence using social and/or cultural mechanisms such as trust (Adler 2001; Bradach and Eccles 1989; Nooteboom 2002), common values and beliefs (Ouchi 1980; Granovetter 1985) or network and reputation effects (Powell 1990; Nooteboom 2002).

Coordination through both hierarchy as well as through the market can fail, especially as we have argued in the context of knowledge development and diffusion (innovation). Coordination does not need to be formal either in terms of (labor) contracts and directives, however (Ouchi 1980; Scott 1992), as informal mechanisms of coordination can provide an alternative. Trust, the expectation that the exchange partner will act honestly and in good faith (Ring and Van de Ven 1992), can alleviate fears of opportunistic behavior and as such has been compared to a lubricant to both social and economic activity (Arrow 1974). Economic transactions that might otherwise prove extremely costly and time consuming to arrange, or involving extensive use of bureaucratic procedures to supervise, are undertaken in informal settings. Values and beliefs held in common – a "culture" in the anthropological sense of the term – by a community will allow for and support such informal dealings. A national context, social stratification as well as a group or organizational culture can be involved, even when each can prevent trust from emerging in the informal setting. Common values and beliefs become internalized via socialization and habituation partly in the form of tacit knowledge (Hofstede 1991; Schein 1992; Rousseau 1990), and are associated with shared representation and systems of meaning among parties (Cicourel 1973; Rousseau 1990; Schein 1992; Allaire and Firsirotu 1984). Common agreement between individuals about what constitutes proper behavior and a sense of solidarity or common destiny reduces goal incongruence. While usually not explicitly for that purpose[2] the tendency for opportunistic behavior and thus the need for monitoring are thereby reduced, sometimes reduced significantly. While Ouchi (1980) emphasizes the ability of the organization to employ common values and beliefs as a result of socialization, coordination on the basis of informal and socio-cultural mechanisms can also take place across organizational borders (e.g. Allen 1977; Allen and Cohen 1968; Kreiner and Schultz 1993; Von Hippel 1987; Agrawal *et al.* 2003).

Social relations and gift exchange as a third coordination mechanism beside market or hierarchy is not as much explored even when there are some suggestions (Ouchi 1980; Powell 1990; Van der Eijk *et al.* 2006). Table 4.1 summarizes some of the main features of each of these three coordination mechanisms. We will elaborate on this further below in the context of knowledge development and diffusion. What need to be acknowledged, however, are the interconnections and interactions between mechanisms discussed as ideal types here (Williams 1988; Nooteboom 2000; 2002; Parsons 1951; Shapiro 1987).

Thus, individuals may be motivated by, or addressed as having, egoistic or other-oriented considerations. Other-oriented considerations might be altruistic ones, but need not be solely directed at the well-being of others. Similarly, coordination of the actions of individuals might be through concrete persons or take an impersonal route through directives and rules developed explicitly. Coordination through the market as well as through hierarchy has been conceptualized generally as involving actors that are egoistically motivated where coordination takes the route of impersonal interaction. In Table 4.2, both market and hierarchy are to be found in cell I only. It should be noted that also social and personal interaction can be egoistically motivated. As has been argued by social scientists since the classical anthropologists Mauss and Malinowsky, social interaction and gift exchange involves egoism and power struggles, as well as altruism (see also Bugental 2000; Williams 1988; Sherry 1983; Komter 1996; Vandevelde 2000)[3]; it can be highly personal involving strong ties but also impersonal as in cases where immediate personal relations are absent and actors address (unknown) others. Social relations and gift exchange thus encompasses cells II through IV.

Table 4.1 Coordination mechanisms

Dimension	Coordination mechanism		
	Market	*Hierarchy*	*Social relations/gift exchange*
What is exchanged?	Goods and services for money or barter	Obedience to authority for material and spiritual security; time in return for some type of monetary compensation	Favors/gifts: tangible (goods/money) and intangible (information/services/love/status) (Foa and Foa 1980)
Specific or (deliberately) unclear terms of exchange	Specific	Unspecified, open (employee will follow directives within general limits of law and of morality)	Deliberately unclear (A gift/favor creates an obligation to reciprocate; however, the value, form and timing of the counter gift is left open to discretion) (van der Eijk *et al.* 2006)
Expected individual orientation	Self-interest	Subordination to directives and rules	Reciprocity, social obligations (vertical and horizontal)
System regulation	Self-regulation; contract law, property rights	Organizational procedures; third party arbiters; labor law	Reputation effect; benefits of continued cooperation; hostages; moral norm of reciprocity; norms and social solidarity; network closure

Sources: Adapted from Adler and Kwon (2002), Biggart and Delbridge (2004), Bugental (2000), Fiske (1992), Ouchi (1980) and Powell (1990).

Coordination through gift exchange can thus complement the market and hierarchy as a means of coordination. For instance, in a context where the value and belief system emphasizes the moral significance of reciprocity, gift exchange may need to depend less on calculative self-interest to coordinate.

Gift exchange is known for its role in establishing social ties or maintaining relationships (Cheal 1986; Darr 2003; Mauss 1954; Gouldner 1960; Larsen and Watson 2001; Belk 1979; Van der Eijk *et al.* 2006), despite the presence of possible ulterior motives (Sherry 1983).[4] As exchange continues, positive emotions are generated and uncertainty is reduced which, in turn, generates cohesion and commitment to the exchange relation (Lawler *et al.* 2000; Homans 1958). As both Granovetter (1985) and Homans (1950) argue: what may have started out as a purely goal-oriented interaction tends to become embedded over time in social trust relations. These relations of affect can act as a source of cooperation and exchange (Coleman 1988; Ingram and Robert 2000). Altruistic behavior can result from routines and habituation, as can be argued even from a behaviorist psychological point of view. Operant conditioning in exchange, i.e. behaviors that are reinforced by rewards, are more likely to be repeated over time (Homans 1958; 1974). Behavior that becomes a routine, or non-reflective and tacit in nature, can continue even when the behavior is no longer reinforced by (immediate) rewards (Homans 1958; 1974).

Some social mechanisms such as expected benefits of continued future cooperation, hostage and reputation effect emphasize the egoistic element to social interaction by focusing on the incentive structure participants face when deciding to honor their obligations. The latter of these is one of the less egoistic mech-

Table 4.2 Coordination dissected

Motivation	Sources	
	Impersonal	*Personal*
Egoistic	I – Sanctions imposed by authority; contractual obligation	II – Calculative self-interest; benefits of continued cooperation (Abreu 1998; Telser 1980; Axelrod 1984; Hill 1990; Heide and Miner 1992; Parkhe 1993); reputation (Weigelt and Camerer 1988; Kreps 1990; Coleman 1990); hostages (Williamson 1985)
Other-oriented	III – Norms, value and belief systems, ethics (Porter and Sensenbrenner 1998; Nye 1979; Hofstede 1991; Schein 1992)	IV – Relations of affect; routines, habituation; empathy

Sources: Adapted from Willliams (1988) and Nooteboom (2002).

anisms, and may be on the boundary of self-interested and other-oriented, indicating the difficulty of distinguishing them conceptually or empirically. In a situation where the focal actor and the recipient are part of a triad[5] (Simmel 1964), given that the reputation[6] effect is sufficiently strong, the incentive structure can be structured in such a way that calculative self-interest makes honoring debts rational (Kreps 1990; Ostrom and Ahn 2003; Coleman 1988; Sherry 1983; Ferrary 2003; Gouldner 1960). As Williamson (1975: 107) formulates it in a rare instance where he acknowledges the social in the economic realm: "Individual aggressiveness is curbed by the prospect of ostracism among peers, in both trade and social circumstances." By the same token if one has a reputation for generously compensating those who have helped you, one will induce others to do you favors ([Barney and Hansen 1994] taken from Rose-Ackerman 1998). In the literature on gifts, this is known as the Matthew Effect: those who have shall be given to. This may lead to a situation where those who do not have are excommunicated. Nevertheless, as the value of a gift is defined within a specific context, the deleterious effects may be more limited than in cases where action is coordinated by the market or by hierarchy. In any case the Matthew Effect is an effect that is well-documented in how science develops as well (Merton 1968).

Knowledge and gift exchange

We submit that exchange outside of market and hierarchy is predicated on gift exchange (e.g. Akerlof 1982; Blau 1964; Boulding 1981; Heath 1976; Homans 1974; Mauss 1954; Sherry 1983), and involves actors, resources and structures (Molm 2003). Gift exchange is omnipresent and not just limited to charitable ("altruistic") gifts. It is a significant economic phenomenon (*The Economist* 2006). Gift exchange allows for the exchange of both tangible goods as well as intangible goods.

Gift exchange has a number of properties that differentiate it from other forms of coordination. First, according to the norm of reciprocity[7] an individual is obliged to give, to receive[8] and to reciprocate (Gouldner 1960; Levi-Strauss 1996; Malinowski 1996; Mauss 1954; Sahlins 1996; Schwartz 1996; Simmel 1996). The imperative nature of this three-fold obligation derives from its cultural embeddedness (Sherry 1983). Gift exchange is carried out without a legal contract, even in business settings (Darr 2003; Ferrary 2003), but does create strong obligation to reciprocate (Gouldner 1960; Levi-Strauss 1996; Malinowski 1996; Mauss 1954; Sahlins 1996; Schwartz 1996; Simmel 1996). Those who cannot or will not reciprocate are no longer part of the community or are subordinated. Gift exchange gives rise to a psychological contract between the giver and givee (Schein 1965). Acceptance of the gift is, to a certain extent, acceptance of the giver and the relationship between the parties (Larsen and Watson 2001; Carrier 1991). Gifts valued highest tend to be those where a personal element is involved – it is for this reason that the material value of a gift is often hidden from direct view, though not unappreciated, especially between actors that know each other and are close. By the same token the refusal of the initial gift marks the refusal to initiate the dynamic of exchange, thus to refuse a gift is to refuse a relationship (Ferrary 2003; Mauss 1954).

Second, the nature of the countergift is not specified beforehand – reciprocity is open to discretion as to the value, the form and the moment of occurrence of the countergift (Bourdieu 1977; Gouldner 1960; Mauss 1954; Deckop *et al.* 2003). Schwartz (1996) states that it is even prohibited to make an equal-return "payment" (homeomorphic reciprocity) in gift exchange since this is tantamount to returning the offered gift to the donor – in the context of knowledge development returning the same good makes no sense as knowledge has public goods characteristics; at the same time paying for a gift of knowledge in a social context of trust negates the personal element and symbolically ends the relation. Many scholars emphasize that the return gift should ultimately, over the longer term be of roughly equal value, even when equivalence is context dependent and defined by the actors involved (Gouldner 1960).

Third, the diachronous nature of the exchange means that the gift is not reciprocated by immediate compensation, but instead by a deferred form of return (Mauss 1954; Bourdieu 1977; Ferrary 2003; Deckop *et al.* 2003). A deferred return obligates one individual to another, and thus creates a social debt. As a coordination mechanism it thus operates through time, making it particularly useful for knowledge development and the circumstances in which it flourishes.

Gift exchange coordinates exchange by interlocking personal and impersonal sources of coordination based on both egoistic and altruistic motivation, enabling exchange in circumstances where the market and hierarchy cannot (Ferrary 2003; Smart 1993). Some have argued that gift exchange may be the only type of exchange to develop specific commercial products – open source software being a case in point (Zeitlyn 2003). The literature generally stresses that there is a propensity to give, yet there also is a need for equity (Adams 1965; Deckop *et al.* 2003; Gouldner 1960; Maitland 2002; Walster *et al.* 1973). Reciprocity is essential to this conceptualization, since an initial gift creates an informal obligation to reciprocate in due time or when needed (Gouldner 1960; Levi-Strauss 1996; Malinowski 1996; Mauss 1954; Sahlins 1996; Schwartz 1996; Simmel 1996) and has been characterized as short-term altruism for long-term self-interest (Putnam 2000: 134). Much of gift exchange's effectiveness hinges on the force of the felt need to reciprocate, internalized or socially imposed, considering that the value, form and moment of the countergift is not specified beforehand.

It has been argued that intellectual objects more often than physical ones are the result of cooperation (Bowles and Gintis 1998; Dolfsma 2008). Some consider knowledge creation as equivalent to combination, exchange and recombination of existing knowledge (Schumpeter 1934). In that sense knowledge development is a cumulative process (Nelson 1959; Nelson 2004) where scientists must necessarily draw on the work of others. Moreover it oftentimes requires the integration of the specialized knowledge of multiple individuals (Grant 1996), and as such collaborative teamwork, cooperation and knowledge sharing become essential (Adler 2001; Moran and Ghosal 1996; Nahapiet and Ghosal 1998; Tsai and Ghosal 1998). At the same time, coordination via the market and hierarchy was shown to be difficult when dealing with knowledge. Partly because the outcome of the innovation process is fundamentally uncertain, the viability of use of contracts is limited: detailed rights and obligations for all possible future scenarios is prohibitively difficult and thus costly (Nooteboom 2002). Even when drafting elaborate contracts is still just feasible technically, such contracts may undermine the trust necessary for knowledge development (Woolthuis *et al.* 2005). Monitoring activities during the process of knowledge development may be difficult too; indeed, establishing the quality of the knowledge developed after it has been created may be difficult, even *ex post*. The linear model of developing knowledge, where a separate group of individuals is to develop knowledge until it is ready and then to pass it on for design of a product that will be sold in the market, is obsolete. Knowledge development is a perpetual process, and the market does not offer definitive tests *ex post* of the usefulness of what is developed. There is more involved, thus, than a situation of asymmetric information and a problem of determining what is the individual contribution to a group outcome.

For anything more that the very minor adaptations of existing goods and processes, actors will resort to an alternative coordination mechanism, at least in part. The generation and diffusion of knowledge depends to a very large extent upon "communities" (Brown and Duguid 1991; Cohendet *et al.* 2004). These communities are made up of (oftentimes) informal networks and ties (Freeman 1991; Cross *et al.* 2002; Madhaven and Grover 1998). Gift exchange provides such an alternative perspective on coordination.

A number of features of gift exchange are especially relevant when dealing with and engaging in the exchange of knowledge based assets: decentralization of monitoring, provision of incentives for knowledge sharing on an individual level, and a guide to knowledge exchange within and across organizational boundaries.

MONITORING

One striking feature of gift exchange is that coordination occurs in the absence of a centralized structure capable of making decisions binding on its members. When "tasks become exceedingly unique, fully integrated, or ambiguous for other reasons, then even bureaucratic mechanisms fail" (Ouchi 1980: 134). However, performance ambiguity on an organizational level does not necessarily equate to performance ambiguity on an individual level. As coordination via gift exchange generally takes place on an individual level, the need to monitor is effectively decentralized to that individual level. Given that actors are generally more capable of monitoring and valuing one another's performance, gift exchange can coordinate in the face of extensive performance measurement difficulties.

MOTIVATION

For coordination of behavior to be effective, the willingness of the actors involved to engage is required. This is especially relevant within the context of innovation since "knowledge sharing cannot be forced; people will only share knowledge if there is a personal reason to do so" (Huysman and De Wit 2004). For coordination between individuals in the context of innovation to be effective there must thus be an intent or willingness, in addition to the ability, to share relevant knowledge (Hansen 1999). The willingness issue is especially relevant, though infrequently analyzed, considering the costs and uncertainty associated with sharing knowledge in terms of time, energy, and vulnerability on the part of the donor (Reagens and McEvily 2003). The actor's position is vulnerable as redundancy increases, competition from the givee may result and a countergift may not materialize (Davenport 1997; Reagens and McEvily 2003).

Yet, despite the possible costs from the donor's perspective, knowledge continues to be shared (e.g. Wenger and Snyder 2000; Wenger 1998; Brown and Duguid 1991; 2001). Why do individuals, in the absence of clearly defined, formal, enforceable obligations or contracts, continue to provide recipients with knowledge? Gift exchange provides the parties involved with a context for the exchange of resources, as well as a socially embedded informal sanctioning or enforcement mechanism. Gift exchange incorporates altruistic as well as more self-interested motives, of which the latter are generally emphasized. The act of giving creates obligations, which the giver can draw on in the future (Coleman 1988; Mauss 1954; Bourdieu 1977). The givee owes the giver, at some point in the future, something of similar value, depending on the rituals for giving within the relevant group (Avner 1997; Blau 1964; Bourdieu 1977; 1986; Humphrey and Hugh-Jones 1992; Darr 2003). At the same time, through giving, a reputation can be established and accumulate which can provide prestige and standing as well as ease of access to resources held by others. A reputation for generosity or trustworthiness can be a valuable asset (Bourdieu 1977).

ACCESS TO KNOWLEDGE WITHIN AND BETWEEN ORGANIZATIONS

Horizontal differentiations or departmentalization within hierarchies makes cooperation with regard to knowledge creation between units difficult, first because units have different knowledge bases, and second, because units often have different priorities (Adler 2001). Cooperation required for knowledge development requires participation of specialists, not merely as a result of the tacit nature of much knowledge (Burt 2004; Grant 1996; Hansen 1999; Kogut and Zander 1992). Coordination of tasks related to knowledge development requires a more "personal" interaction than can be achieved by means of rules and directives (Galbraith 1973), even when the formalized interaction should not be underestimated (Aalbers *et al.* 2006). Galbraith (1973) argues that information processing within the hierarchy often bypasses vertical linkages, taking place via informal (horizontal) ties. Romme (1996) points to teams for knowledge production. Brown and Duguid (1991) emphasize that knowledge creation takes place within (informal) communities of practice which may span across departmental and even organizational boundaries. Given the informal nature of many of these linkages, the use of authority as the central coordination mechanism within a hierarchy is impaired.

Gift exchange can enable knowledge exchange in circumstances where the market and hierarchy cannot (Ferrary 2003; Smart 1993) since it allows actors to forge and personalize relationships and to develop personal ties that can act as a "guarantee" that their initial gift will not be abused and will also be returned (Zucker 1986; Shapiro 1987). Knowledge that is classified and highly sensitive is exchanged between individuals from different firms, even if the giver and their firms may be at risk when the givee abuses the trust placed in him. Bouty (2000) shows that despite the risks, giving and favor exchange of this kind ends up helping giver, givee, and both their firms. In such circumstances the risks and costs of knowledge development and diffusion can be considerably reduced when gift exchange is used as a coordination mechanism. Knowledge is thus exchanged via informal routes and personal networks, possibly transcending organizational borders (Allen 1977; Kreiner and Schultz 1993; Von Hippel 1987) as communities-of-practice may extend beyond them (Wenger and Snyder 2000; Wenger 1998; Brown and Duguid 1991; 2001). Gift exchange both relies on and establishes a shared frame of reference that allow the parties involved to determine what the risks and costs are of using this mechanism as opposed to another mechanism (cf. Van der Eijk *et al.* 2006). Gift exchange allows people to establish and maintain social relations[9] that can help actors gain access to relevant individuals and communities while allowing at the same time some "guarantee" to prevent abuse.

Conclusion

In addition to market and hierarchy there is a third coordination mechanism, one that is not much discussed: gift exchange in social relations. Some have argued that gift exchange is conceptually of the same order as market or hierarchy; we argue that it is of a different order, requiring additional concepts to understand (Biggart and Delbridge 2004). In this chapter we argue that in the context of knowledge development and diffusion gift exchange has often been the preferred alternative. We discuss this coordination mechanism conceptually, especially focusing on the context of knowledge development. Depending on the circumstances, one mechanism may be better suited to provide coordination; in some circumstances coordination mechanisms work in tandem (Adler 2001; Bradach and Eccles 1989). Gift exchange offers an understanding of how social relations develop and are maintained allowing for the trust required under the circumstances of uncertainty that characterize knowledge development.

Gift exchange allows actors to forge and personalize relationships and to develop guarantees through personal bonding (Zucker 1986; Shapiro 1987). As anthropologists in line with Mauss have argued: there is a need to give, receive, and reciprocate. If one does not adhere to this, one may be ex-communicated and barred from exchanges that are both socially and economically meaningful. This certainly holds for non-standard situations where technological and market uncertainty and the possibility of opportunism are high, such as for venture capital provision in Silicon Valley (Ferrary 2003), as well as in markets that are mature (Darr 2003). Contrary to the dictum of the New Institutional (Neoclassical) Economics that "in the beginning there were markets," Boulding (1981) has even claimed that gift exchange is the quintessential kind of exchange. In the context of knowledge development he certainly is correct.

Notes

1 IPRs include patents, copyrights and trademarks.
2 In line with Bourdieu's (1980) argument about the "production of belief" (Bourdieu and Nice 1980).
3 Classically, literature has emphasized that the exchange of gifts in many cases is motivated by calculative self-interest (e.g. Blau 1964; Heath 1976; Homans 1974; Mauss 1954). A gift, however, *can* represent a free gift, "a completely disinterest gesture without expectation of reciprocity" (Malinowski 1996). According to Vandevelde (2000: 15): "the logic of the gift thus can be reduced neither to disinterestedness or altruisms, nor to strict calculative egotism."
4 The book Proverbs in the Bible, which is said to contain the wisdom of King Solomon, says that: "A man's gift makes room for him and brings him before great men" (Prov. 18: 16).
5 A triad is a relationship between at least three actors who either are directly or indirectly connected with one another resulting in a closure of the network where specific norms are created and enforced (Simmel 1964). Coleman (1990) also indicates that in such a situation of redundancy the costs of punishment of norm-transgressing behavior by one party can be split between the other two, making norm-following behavior more likely.
6 Reputation is information on past behavior that the focal actor has, communicated by a third party, about the supposed trustworthiness of a party. An actor's reputation – even if incorrect, if sufficient alternatives exist for the focal actor – will decrease the uncertainty associated with potential future coordination of the focal actor with the actor (Kreps 1990). Particularly in case of genuine uncertainty, such as in cases of newly established firms or in case of knowledge development, this is important (Ferrary 2003).
7 Although the norm of reciprocity may be seen as a universal moral norm, the norm may operate differently in different contexts and is not unconditional. According to Noonan ([1984], taken from Steidlmeier 1999: 4): "Reciprocity is in any society a rule of life, and in some societies at least it is *the* rule of life."
8 A social reality captured by the proverb "never look a gift horse in the mouth." Which can be translated as "never criticize or express displeasure at a gift" (Seidl and McMordie 1978).
9 Put differently: "The reciprocity domain involves the management of costs and benefits between functional equals" (Bugental 2000).

References

Aalbers, R., W. Dolfsma and O. Koppius (2006), "Not Just with your Friends: Knowledge Transfer in Organizations," Working Paper, Erasmus University Rotterdam.

Abreu, D. (1988), "On the Theory of Infinitely Repeated Games with Discounting," *Econometrica*, 56(2): 383–396.

Adams, J.S. (1965), "Inequity in Social Exchange," in J. Berkowitz (ed.) *Advances in Experimental Social Psychology*, New York: Academic Press.

Adler, P.S. (2001), "Market, Hierarchy, and Trust: The Knowledge Economy, and the Future of Capitalism," *Organization Science*, 12(2): 215–234.

Adler, P.S. and S.W. Kwon (2002), "Social Capital: Prospects for a New Concept," *Academy of Management Review*, 27(1): 17–40.

Agrawal, A.K., Cockburn, I.M. and J. McHale (2003), "Gone but not Forgotten: Labor Flows, Knowledge Spillovers and Enduring Social Capital," Working Paper 9950.

Akerlof, G.A. (1982), "Labor Contracts as Partial Gift Exchange' *Quarterly Journal of Economics*, 97: 543–569.

Allaire, Y. and M.E. Firsirotu (1984), "Theories of Organizational Culture," *Organization Studies*, 5(3): 193–226.

Allen, T.J. (1977), *Managing the Flow of Technology: Technology Transfer and the Dissemination of Technological Information within the R&D Organization*, Cambridge, MA: The MIT Press.

Allen, T.J. and S.I. Cohen (1969), "Information Flow in Research and Development Laboratories," *Administrative Science Quarterly*, 14: 12–19.

Arrow, K.J. (1972), "Gifts and Exchanges," *Philosophy and Public Affairs*, 1: 343–362.

—— (1974), *The Limits of Organization*, New York: Norton.

—— (1984), "Information and economic behavior," in *Collected Papers of Kenneth J. Arrow*, 4.

Avner, O. (1997), "Between the Gift and the Market: The Economy of Regard," *Economic History Review*, 50(3): 450–476.

Axelrod, R. (1984), *The Evolution of Cooperation*, New York: Basic Books.

Barber, B. (1977), "Absolutization of the Market," in G. Bermant (ed.) *Markets and Morals*, Washington, DC: Hemisphere.

Barnard, C.I. (1968), *The functions of the Executive, 30th anniversary edition*, Cambridge, MA: Harvard University Press.

Belk, R. (1979), "Gift-giving Behavior," in J. Sheth (ed.) *Research in Marketing Volume 2*, Greenwich, CT: JAI Press.

Biggart, N.W. and R. Delbridge (2004), "Systems of Exchange," *Academy of Management Review*, 29(1): 28–49.

Blau, P. (1964), *Exchange and Power in Social Life*, New York: Wiley.

Boulding, K.E. (1981), *A Preface to Grants Economics: The Economics of Love and Fear*, New York: Praeger.

Bourdieu, P. (1977), *Outline of a Theory in Practice*, Cambridge, UK: Cambridge University Press.

—— (1986), "Forms of Capital," in J.G. Richardson (ed.) *Handbook of Theory and Research for the Sociology of Education*, New York: Greenwood Press.

Bourdieu, P. and R. Nice (1980), "The Production of Belief: Contribution to an Economy of Symbolic Goods," *Media, Culture and Society*, 2: 261–293.

Bouty, I. (2000), "Interpersonal and Interaction Influences on Informal Resource Exchanges between R&D Researchers across Organizational Boundaries," *Academy of Management Journal*, 43(1): 50–65.

Bowles, S. and H. Gintis (1998), "The Moral Economy of Communities: Structured Populations and the Evolution of Pro-social Norms," *Evolution and Human Behavior*, 19: 3–25.

Bradach, J.L. and R.G. Eccles (1989), "Price, Authority, and Trust: From Ideal Types to Plural Forms," *Annual Review of Sociology*, 15: 97–118.

Brown, J.S. and P. Duguid (1991), "Organizational Learning and Communities of Practice: Towards a Unified View of Working Learning and Organizing," *Organization Science*, 2(1): 40–57.

—— (2001), "Knowledge and Organization: A Social Practice Perspective," *Organization Science*, 12(2): 198–213.

Bugental, D.B. (2000), "Acquisition of the Algorithms of Social Life: A Domain-based Approach," *Psychological Bulletin*, 126(2): 187–219.

Burt, R.S. (2004), "Structural Holes and Good Ideas," *American Journal of Sociology*, 110: 442–455.

Carrier, J. (1991), "Gifts, Commodities, and Social Relations: A Maussian View of Exchange," *Sociological Forum* 6(1): 119–136.

Cheal, D. (1986), "The Social Dimensions of Gift Behaviour," *Journal of Social and Personal Relationships*, 3: 423–439.

Cicourel, A. (1973), *Cognitive Sociology: Language and Meaning in Social Interaction*, Harmondsworth, UK: Penguin Books.

Coase, R.H. (1937), "The Nature of the Firm," *Economica*, 4: 386–405.

Cohendet, P., Creplet, F., Diani, M., Dupouet, O. and E. Schenk (2004), "Matching Communities and Hierarchies within the Firm," *Journal of Management and Governance*, 8: 27–48.

Coleman, J.S. (1988), "Social Capital: In the Creation of Human Capital," *American Journal of Sociology*, 94 Supplement: S95–S120.

—— (1990), *"Foundations of Social Theory,"* Cambridge, MA: Belknap Press.

Cowan, R., David, P.A. and D. Foray (2000), "The Explicit Economics of Knowledge Codification and Tacitness," *Industrial and Corporate Change*, 9(2): 211–253.

Cross, R., Borgatti, S. and A. Parker (2002), "Making Invisible Work Visible: Using Social Network Analysis to support Human Networks," *California Management Review*, 44(2): 25–46.

Darr, A. (2003), "Gifting Practices and Inter-organizational Relations: Constructing Obligations Networks in the Electronics Sector," *Sociological Forum*, 18(1): 31–51.

Davenport, T.H. (1997), "Ten Principles of Knowledge Management and Four Case Studies," *Knowledge and Process Management*, 4(3): 187–208.

Deckop, J.R., Cirka, C.C. and L.M. Andersson (2003), "Doing Unto Others: The Reciprocity of Helping Behavior in Organizations," *Journal of Business Ethics*, 47: 101–113.

Dolfsma, W. (1998), "Labor Relations in Changing Capitalist Economies: The Meaning of Gifts in Social Relations," *Journal of Economic Issues*, 32(2): 631–638.

—— (2006), "IPR's, Technical Development, and Economic Development," *Journal of Economic Issues*, 40(2): 333–342.

—— (2008), *Knowledge Economies: Innovation, Organization and Location*, London: Routledge.

Eijk, R. van der, W. Dolfsma and A. Jolink (2006), "No Black Box and No Black Hole: From Social Capital to Gift Exchange," Working Paper Erasmus University Rotterdam.

Ferrary, M. (2003), "The Gift Exchange in the Social Networks of Silicon Valley," *California Management Review*, 45(4): 120–138.

Fiske, A.P. (1992), "The Four Elementary Forms of Sociality: Framework for a Unified Theory of Social Relations," *Psychological Review*, 99(4): 689–723.

Foa, E. and U.G. Foa (1980), "Resource theory: Interpersonal behavior as exchange," in K. Gergen, Greenberg, M. and Willis, R. (eds.) *Social Exchange: Advances in Theory and Research*, New York: Plenum.

Freeman, C. (1991), "Networks of Innovators: A Synthesis of Research Issues," *Research Policy*, 20: 499–514.

Galbraith, J.R. (1973), *Designing Complex Organizations*, Reading, MA: Addison-Wesley.

Gouldner, A.W. (1960), "The Norm of Reciprocity: A Preliminary Statement," *American Sociological Review*, 25: 161–178.

Grand, J. le (2003), *Motivation, Agency, and Public Policy: Of Knights and Knaves, Pawns and Queens*, Oxford, UK: Oxford University Press.

Granovetter, M.S. (1985), "Economic Action and Social Structure: The Problem of Embeddedness," *American Journal of Sociology*, 91: 481–510.

Grant, R.M. (1996), "Towards a Knowledge-based Theory of the Firm," *Strategic Management Journal*, 17: 109–122.

Hansen, M.T. (1999), "The Search-transfer Problem: The Role of Weak Ties in Sharing Knowledge," *Administrative Science Quarterly*, 44(1): 82–111.

Hayek, F. (1945), "The use of Knowledge in Society," *American Economic Review*, 35: 519–530.

Heath, A.F. (1976), *Rational Choice and Social Exchange: A Critique of Exchange Theory*, Cambridge, UK: Cambridge University Press.

Heide, J.B. and A.S. Miner (1992), "The Shadow of the Future: Effects of Anticipated Interaction and Frequency of Contact on Buyer–Seller Cooperation," *Academy of Management Review*, 35: 265–291.

Hennart, J. (1993), "Explaining the Swollen Middle: Why Most Transactions Are a Mix of 'Market' and 'Hierarchy'," *Organization Science*, 4(4): 529–547.

Hill, C.W.L. (1990), Cooperation, Opportunism and the Invisible Hand: Implications for Transaction Cost Theory," *Academy of Management Review*, 15(3): 500–513.

Hippel, E. von (1987), "Corporation between Rivals: Informal Know-how Trading," *Research Policy*, 16: 291–302.

Hofstede, G. (1991), *Cultures and Organizations: Software of the Mind*, London: Harper-Collins Business.

Homans, G.C. (1950), *The Human Group*, New York: Harcourt, Brace.

—— (1958), "Social Behavior as Exchange," *American Journal of Sociology*, 63: 597–606.

—— (1974), *Social Behavior: Its Elementary Forms*, New York: Harcourt Brace Jovanoviech.

Humphrey, C. and S. Hugh-Jones (1992): *Barter, Exchange and Value*, Cambridge, UK: Cambridge University Press.

Huysman, M. and D. de Wit (2004): "Practices of Managing Knowledge Sharing: Towards a Second Wave of Knowledge Management," *Knowledge and Process Management*, 11(2): 81–92.

Iannello, K.P. (1992), *Decisions without Hierarchy*, New York: Routledge.

Ingram, P. and P. Roberts (2000), "Friendship among Competitors in the Sydney Hotel Industry," *American Journal of Sociology*, 106(2): 387–423.

Jacques, E. (1990), "In Praise of Hierarchy," *Harvard Business Review*, 68: 127–133.

Katz, L.M. and H.S. Rosen (1994), *Microeconomics*, Boston, MA: Irwin.

Kogut, B. and U. Zander (1992), "Knowledge of the Firm, Combinative Capabilities, and the Replication of Technology," *Management of Technology*, 3(2): 383–397.

Komter, A.E. (1996), *The Gift: An Interdisciplinary Approach*, Amsterdam: Amsterdam University Press.

Kreiner, K. and M. Schultz (1993), "Informal Collaboration in R&D: The Formation of Networks across Organizations," *Organization Studies*, 14(2): 189–209.

Kreps, D.M. (1990), "Corporate culture and economic theory," in J. Alt and Shepsel, K. (eds.) *Perspectives on Political Economy*, Cambridge, UK: Cambridge University Press.

Larsen, D. and J.J. Watson (2001), "A Guide Map to the Terrain of Gift Value," *Psychology and Marketing*, 18(8): 889–906.

Lawler, E., Thye, S. and J. Yoon (2000), "Emotion and Group Cohesion in Productive Exchange," *American Journal of Sociology*, 106: 616–657.

Levinthal, D.A. and J.C. March (1993), "The Myopia of Learning," *Strategic Management Journal*, winter special issue, 14: 95–112.

Levi-Strauss, C. (1996), "The Principle of Reciprocity," in A.E. Komter (ed.) *The Gift: An Interdisciplinary Perspective*, Amsterdam: Amsterdam University Press.

Lopes, H. and J.C. Caldas (2008) "Firms: Collective Action and its Supportive Values" in J. Davis and W. Dolfsma (eds.) *Companion to Social Economics*, Cheltenham: Edward Elgar.

Madhaven, R. and Grover, R. (1998), "From Embedded Knowledge to Embodied Knowledge: New Product Development as Knowledge Management," *Journal of Marketing*, 62: 1–12.

Maitland, I. (2002), "The Human Face of Self-interest," *Journal of Business Ethics*, 38: 3–17.

Malinowski, B. (1996), "The Principle of Give and Take," in A.E. Komter (ed.) *The Gift: An Interdisciplinary Perspective*, Amsterdam: Amsterdam University Press.

Mauss, M. (1954 [2000]), *The Gift: Forms and Functions of Exchange in Archaic Societies*, New York: Norton.

Merton, R.K. (1968), "The Matthew Effect in Science: The Reward and Communication Systems of Science are Considered," *Science*, 159: 56–63.

Miles, R. and C. Snow (1986), "Organizations New Concepts for New Forms," *California Management Review*, 28: 62–73.

Mintzberg, H. (1979), *The Structuring of Organizations*, Englewood Cliffs, NJ: Prentice-Hall.

Molm, L.D. (2003), "Theoretical Comparisons of Forms of Exchange," *Sociological Theory*, 21(1): 1–17.

Moran, P. and S. Ghosal (1996), "Value Creation by Firms," *Academy of Management Proceedings*: 35–39.

Nahapiet, J. and S. Ghosal (1998), "Social Capital, Intellectual Capital, and the Organizational Advantage," *Academy of Management Review*, 23(20), 242–266.

Nelson, R.R. (1959), "The Simple Economics of Basic Scientific Research," *Journal of Political Economy*, 57: 297–306.

—— (2004), "The Market Economy and the Scientific Commons," *Research Policy*, 33(3): 455–471.

Nooteboom, B. (2000), *Learning and Innovation in Organizations and Economies*, Oxford, UK: Oxford University Press.

—— (2002), *Trust: Forms, Foundations, Functions, Failures and Figures*, Cheltenham: Edward Elgar.

Nye, F.I. (1979), "Choice, Exchange and the Family," in W.R Burr, R. Hill, F.I. Nye and I.R. Reiss (eds.) *Contemporary Theories about the Family*, New York: Free Press.

Organization for Economic Co-operation and Development (OECD) (2001), *Science, Technology and Industry Outlook 2001*, Paris: OECD.

Ostrom, E. and T.K. Ahn (2003), *Foundations of Social Capital*, Northampton: Edward Elgar Publishing Limited.

Ouchi, W.G. (1980), "Markets, Bureaucracies, and Clans," *Administrative Science Quarterly*, 25(1): 129–141.

—— (1979), "A Conceptual Framework for the Design of Organizational Control," *Management Science*, 25(9): 833–848.

Parkhe, A. (1993), "Strategic Alliance Structuring: A Game Theoretic and Transaction Cost Examination of Inter-firm Cooperation," *Academy of Management Journal*, 36: 794–829.

Parsons, T. (1951), *The Social System*, London: Routledge and Kegan Paul.

Peters, T. (1987), *Thriving on Chaos*, London: Pan Books.

Portes, A. and J. Sensenbrenner (1993), "Embeddedness and Immigration: Notes on the Social Determinants of Economic Action," *American Journal of Sociology*, 98: 1320–1350.

Powell, W. (1990), "Neither Market nor Hierarchy: Network Forms of Organization," *Research in Organization Behavior*, 12: 295–336.

Powell, W.W., Koput, K.K. and L. Smith-Doerr (1996), "Inter-organizational Collaboration and the Locus of Innovation" *Administrative Science Quarterly*, 41: 116–145.

Putnam, R.D. (2000), *Bowling Alone: The Collapse and Revival of American Community*, New York: Simon & Schuster.

Rangan, S. (2000), "The Problem of Search and Deliberation in Economic Action: When Social Networks Really Matter," *The Academy of Management Review*, 25(4): 813–828.

Reagans, R. and B. McEvily (2003), "Network Structure and Knowledge Transfer: The Effects of Cohesion and Range," *Organization Science*, 13(3): 232–248.

Ring, P.S. and A. van de Ven (1992), "Structuring Cooperative Relationships between Organizations," *Strategic Management Journal*, 13: 483–498.

Romer, P. (2002), "When Should We Use Intellectual Property Rights," *American Economic Review*, 92(2): 213–216.

Romme, A.G.L. (1996), "A Note on the Hierarchy–Team Debate," *Strategic Management Journal*, 17(5): 411–417.

Rose-Ackerman, S. (1998), "Bribes and Gifts," in A. Ben-ner and Putterman, L. (eds.) *Economics, Values and Organization*, Cambridge, UK: Cambridge University Press.

Rousseau, D.M. (1990), "Assessing Organizational Culture: The Case for Multiple Methods," in B. Schneider (ed.) *Organizational Climate and Culture*, San Francisco: Josey-Bass.

Sahlins, M.D. (1996), "On the Sociology of Primitive Exchange," in A.E. Komter (ed.) *The Gift: An Interdisciplinary Perspective*, Amsterdam: Amsterdam University Press.

Schein, E.H. (1965), *Organization Psychology*, New York: Prentice-Hall, Englewood Cliffs.

—— (1992), *Organizational Culture and Leadership, 2nd edition*, San Francisco: Josey Bass.

Schumpeter, J. (1934 [1978]), *The Theory of Economic Development*, London: Oxford University Press.

Schwartz, B. (1996), "The Social Psychology of the Gift," in A.E. Komter (ed.) *The Gift: An Interdisciplinary Perspective*, Amsterdam: Amsterdam University Press.

Scott, W.R. (1992), *Organizations: Rational, Natural and Open Systems*, New York: Harper.

Seidl, J. and W. McMordie (1978), *English Idioms and How to Use Them*, Oxford: Oxford University Press.

Senge, P.M. (1990), *The Fifth Discipline*, New York: Doubleday Currency.

Shapiro, S.P. (1987), "The Social Control of Impersonal Trust," *American Journal of Sociology*, 93: 623–658.

Sherry, J.F. (1983), "Gift Giving in Anthropological Perspective," *Journal of Consumer Research*, 10(2): 157–168.

Simmel, G. (1996), "Faithfulness and Gratitude," in A.E. Komter (ed.) *The Gift: An Interdisciplinary Perspective*, Amsterdam: Amsterdam University Press.

Smart, A. (1993), "Gifts, Bribes, and Guanxi: A Reconsideration of Bourdieu's Social Capital," *Cultural Anthropology*, 8(3): 388–408.

Soete, L. and B. ter Weel (2005), *The Economics of the Digital Society*, Cheltenham: Edward Elgar.

Steidlmeier, P. (1999), "Gift Giving, Bribery and Corruption: Ethical Management of Business Relationships in China," *Journal of Business Ethics*, 20: 121–132.

Stigler, G. (1968), "Competition," in D.L. Sills (ed.) *International Encyclopedia of the Social Sciences*, volume 3, New York: Macmillan.

Stiglitz, J.E. (1994), *Wither Socialism?*, Cambridge, MA: MIT Press.

Telser, L.G. (1980), "A Theory of Self-enforcing Agreements," *Journal of Business*, 53: 27–44.

The Economist (2006), *The Business Of Giving: A Survey Of Wealth And Philanthropy*, February 25.

Thorelli, H.B. (1986), "Networks: Between Markets and Hierarchies," *Strategic Management Journal*, 7(1): 37–51.

Tsai, W. and S. Ghosal (1998), "Social Capital and Value Creation: The Role of Intra Firm Networks," *Academy of Management Journal*, 41(4): 464–476.

Vandevelde, A. (2000), "Reciprocity and Trust as Social Capital" (in Dutch), in Vandevelde, A. (ed.) *Over Vertrouwen en Bedrijf*, Leuven: Acco: 133–142.

Walster, E., Berscheid, E. and G.W. Walster (1973), "New Directions in Equity Research," *Journal of Personality and Social Psychology*, 25(2): 151–176.

Weber, M. (1978), *Economy and Society*, Berkeley: University of California Press.

Weigelt, K. and C. Camerer (1988), "Reputation and Corporate Strategy: A Review of Recent Theory and Applications," *Strategic Management Journal*, 9: 443–454.

Wenger, E.C. (1998), *Communities of Practice: Learning, Meaning and Identity*, Cambridge, UK: Cambridge University Press.

Wenger, E.C. and Snyder, W. (2000), "Communities of Practice the Organizational Frontier," *Harvard Business Review*: 139–145.

Williams, B. (1988), "Formal Structures and Social Reality," in D. Gambette (ed.) *Trust: Making and Breaking of Cooperative Relations*, Oxford: Blackwell.

Williamson, O.E. (1985), *The Economic Institutions of Capitalism: Firm Markets, Relational Contracting*, New York: Free Press.

—— (1975), *Markets and Hierarchies: Analysis and Antitrust Implications*, New York: Free Press.

Woolthuis, R.K., Hillebrand, B. and B. Nooteboom (2005), "Trust, Contract and Relationship Development," *Organization Studies*, 26(6): 813–840.

Zeitlyn, D. (2003), "Gift Economies in the Development of Open Source Software," *Research Policy*, 32(7): 1287–1291.

Zucker, L.G. (1986), "Production of Trust: Institutional Sources of Economic Structure, 1840–1920," *Research in Organizational Behavior*, 8: 53–111.

Part II
Time and work

5 "Time sovereignty"

Its meaning and externalities

François-Xavier Devetter

From the 1930s until the 1980s the Fordist wage-earner relationship remained relatively stable. The various aspects of working time remained constant and were imposed on a large majority of salaried workers. This organization of time, which can be called a Fordist regime of temporal availability, is based on three complementary aspects:

- reduced hours in relation to the previous era and regrouped overwhelmingly around 40 to 42 hours per week;
- a locally standardized working day (08.00–16.00) and week (Monday–Friday);
- an increase in the foreseeable nature of working hours, but with working hours to be determined unilaterally by the employer.

This working time regime, however, seems to have been disputed since the 1980s. This challenge is, indeed, partially visible from a statistical point of view but seems more pronounced when examined from the point of view of its legitimacy. The Fordist organisation of working time is criticised both from the point of view of the wage-earner and the employer. For the wage-earner the criticism is based largely on the desire for greater flexibility or "choice" in working hours (Golden 2001). Requests from the employer for greater flexibility are equally numerous and have intensified over the past 20 years. These two positions seem to merge in the writings of various observers (e.g. Godet 2006; Salin 1995) to clear the way for a new compromise based around the concept of "time sovereignty." More recently, the speeches of the new French President, Nicolas Sarkozy, stress the "freedom of working time": choosing to do overtime should be a right for workers to enable them to earn more. It is this kind of time sovereignty that will be examined in this chapter: the freedom to work more to earn more.[1] This question is particularly important today in France, but could concern other countries such as the United Kingdom or the United States of America where managerial autonomy to shape the organisation of work is less restricted. The situation is slightly different elsewhere in Western Europe, particularly in the Nordic countries. Nevertheless, the French case could be important to understand larger trends.

After describing what is currently meant by time sovereignty in France and highlighting the role it plays in an eventual new "post Fordist" compromise (section 1), this chapter will demonstrate how this mechanism favors long working hours and thus entails important externalities (section 2). A short conclusion ends the chapter.

1   Time sovereignty: a new possible compromise...

Time sovereignty at first seems to be at the heart of a symbolic representation of the post-Fordist worker, but this theoretical (and rhetorical) vision also attempts to manifest itself as a new compromise between employers and wage-earners.

Time sovereignty within the symbolic and theoretical representation of the post-Fordist worker

The workman whose working hours are fixed and foreseeable has long been the archetypal image of the worker. This figure, as a representation of the dominant wage-earner relationship, is now out-of-date. It has been replaced by the "flexible worker of informal capitalism" (Lojkine and Malétras 2002), a veritable "consumer-entrepreneur" (Rochefort 1997) at the head of his own small business, his "Me Ltd" Rose (1989) or du Gay (1996), with the notion of "enterprising selves," have emphasized how post-Fordist restructuring of the workplace has created a need for employees who can be self-developing, self-motivating and self-regulating. This is the image of the post-Fordist worker as the ideal or dominant representation (or a rhetorical figure in the case of "Me Ltd"), and not of the necessarily diverse and less clear-cut reality of currently observable forms of working[2] (see below).

What are the main features of this "new worker" (as a symbolic representation)?

In simple terms, he enjoys less security than his Fordist predecessor: he must change jobs (if not his profession), attend training courses throughout his life, and there is a strong possibility that he may be unemployed for a time. He is clearly affected by the influence of the model of the independent worker, or may even become like the skilled workmen of the nineteenth century.

Within his workplace he is evaluated on the basis of his "competencies" and no longer on the skills required by his job. His more subjective skills (flexibility, availability, etc.) have to be mobilized. The remuneration is tailored to suit and is more flexible in order to follow the fluctuations of the business, and also to increase the incentive nature of the wage.

It is the third dominant aspect, however, which interests us here: the radical modification of how workers view time. Fixed working hours determined by the company long in advance are no longer the norm: working hours must be flexible. In the optimistic version of the model, the key words are chosen hours, or even time sovereignty. Pascal Salin summarized this ideal: "Imagine a world where working hours can be determined exactly as desired. Some would prefer to work longer by using their abilities to their best advantage.... Time sovereignty should be restored" (Salin 1995). In a more pessimistic version, time becomes the "stake" in a game of stress and conflict between family and work, where the actors must acquire new skills. The community must provide the actors with the means to manage their time, but the time must be chosen by the individual. It clearly becomes a resource which the individual manages in order to maximize his interest. Here, this image of the post-Fordist worker is similar to the Beckerian model, one of whose fundamental tenets is the interplay between time and money.

The traditional model of labor supply is in fact based on this principle of the reconciliation of two largely interchangeable commodities: time and money. Neo-classical studies have "refined" the model by considering, for example, the fact that consumption itself uses time (which complicates this reconciliation, especially as services take up an ever-increasing portion of the household budget). In the equations derived by Gary Becker (1965) to summarize the behavior of the economic agent, time and material resources thus explicitly become comparable. In this context, time sovereignty is a prerequisite to maximize the individual's well-being: it allows the diversity of preferences to be expressed, and introduces a specialization (work more to earn more, for example) which is of benefit to everyone. This theoretical vision fits perfectly with the idea of the emblematic (supposedly) flexible worker of post-Fordism. When speaking of the "consumer-entrepreneur" in a chapter called "The price of time," Robert Rochefort (1997) thus maintains "that time is becoming a commodity. It is becoming exchangeable. ... The marginal hour can be very highly valued."

Toward a new legal compromise?

The law has partly kept pace with these developments and has tried to satisfy both the wage-earners' desire for greater choice in their working hours, and the employers' request for flexibility. These reforms have produced more of a "patchwork" (Gardin 2002) than a truly coherent whole: the measures relating to part-time work, for example, run alongside those on personalized working hours and overtime. Similarly, expectations of flexibility have been introduced into labor laws as symbolic measures, such as the adjustments to annualized working hours or part-time work introduced in France in the 1990s.

These two kinds of evolution thus challenge the Fordist compromise based on the trade-off between limited working hours and control of the business by the employer.[3] They do not appear to have been able, however, to result in a new stable compromise as witnessed by the difficulties encountered by researchers in describing a stable post-Fordist wage-earner relationship, and not least by the conflictuality of the issue of working hours over the past 15 years. On the contrary – flexibility has become a veritable bugbear for trade unions, whilst employers firmly oppose a reduction in working hours. The major clashes over the Aubry Law in France, and the to-ing and fro-ing over reduced working hours

(RTT) in Germany are evidence of this situation which has reached a stalemate in some areas.

For several years another basis for compromise seems to have been emerging: the desire for working hours which are more flexible and adaptable to the expectations of the actors could find common ground with employers and wage-earners. The aim is thus to allow greater freedom in working hours which respects individual preferences. Criticism of the RTT laws in France have thus been concentrated on the idea that they were "imposed," insufficiently negotiated and without respect for individual choice. Since 1995, Pascal Salin has defended the principle of time sovereignty, saying that it is to the advantage of everyone, but it was not until the 2000s that this sovereignty came to the fore. Choosing one's working hours, or deciding whether or not to work on Sundays would become essential "freedoms" for the workers. This situation becomes emblematic in Sarkozy's speeches with the slogan of "work more to earn more."

Worker sovereignty must thus complement consumer sovereignty to allow the individual to make his choices fully and improve his well-being. This assertion is conveyed in political demands and in the development of employment law: restrictions on the right to work during certain periods are widely disputed, such as an end to the ban on women working at night, challenges to the Sunday rest day, etc. In France, the issue of time sovereignty is widely debated and is being set down in certain legislative developments, such as the recent publication of the "chosen hours" purview or the discussion of the new overtime law. At a European level this debate is at the heart of renegotiations of the Working Time Directive: far beyond the determination of an actual limit (48 or 60 hours), it is the very existence of a limit which is causing problems and even more so its rigidity. Some countries such as Great Britain are asking for opt-out clauses to be retained to allow the choice of the individual wage-earner to be respected.

Despite recent developments, working hours are still a matter of great concern with regard to employers' power within the law. This is particularly the case in France where "decisions relating to timetables and work developments are imposed on the wage-earners who know to challenge potential changes justified by reasons of good management" (Le Goff 2001: 536). The 1998 and 2000 Aubry Laws did nothing whatsoever to change this situation, as reaffirmed regularly by the courts of appeal. With regard to hourly volume, the main issue revolves around overtime, which in turn depends on the power of the employer who can impose it on his workers. The workers can neither escape overtime nor ask for it, as its suppression entails no modification in the work contract. Working hours are likewise regulated by the joint timetable drawn up by the employer. The wage-earner's requirement to work is thus confirmation of the employer's discipline over the planning of working hours, as shown in the work of various historians such as E.P. Thompson (1967).

For all this, the employer's prerogatives have been partially reduced by legislative developments since the 1970s, for example individually-tailored timetables or guarantees for part-time workers. Finally, however, recent changes concerning the possibility to work longer, such as "relaxing" the 35-hour working week, have introduced factors, potentially increasing the worker's room to maneuver vis-à-vis his supply of work, through the "chosen hours" purview introduced in 2005, which allows voluntary workers to work overtime above the legal quota. More recently, the new government has decided to encourage overtime by reducing taxes.

The law, however, has not just increased the worker's prerogatives over his working hours. The employer's room for maneuver has also been strengthened, mainly by the change from a weekly definition of working hours to an annual regulation.

Thus, the growth in working hours' flexibility seems real but limited; furthermore, it is highly inegalitarian. Indeed, in France, if certain workers have effectively won a certain kind of sovereignty over their working hours, a majority of them continues to have no room for maneuver over their timetable. Jobs offered are still for the most part "packages" combining a length of time and a salary with no real possibility of negotiating the volume of work: employers retain control of the hours offered, i.e. "take it or leave it" (Schor 2005). Managers seem to be the only real beneficiaries of having the ability to control their own working hours. If the working week and year are long, they allow the managers concerned to receive relatively high remuneration and not least to control part of their working hours (of which an increasing portion is worked at home). For other workers, however, the methods of controlling working hours are slow to evolve and the power of the employer is still very much in evidence. Thus, if 60 percent of managers and professionals can choose a part of their working time, over 80 percent of employees and workmen are still subject to timetables drawn up exclusively by the company.

Nevertheless, even if time sovereignty was not a reality for all workers, it would thus appear that a coherent theoretical vision of the economic actor is emerging, based on two key principles: a symbolic figure born of observations of the development of Fordism (corresponding in some way to an ideal), and the formalization of the behavior of *homo oeconomicus*. This vision is, however, struggling to find form in a new compromise between employers and wage-earners, despite considerable developments in the regulation of working hours. If the English speaking countries offer a large diversity of negotiated working hours, the Continental European countries retain more rigid temporal norms (Messenger 2004). Time sovereignty is more widely debated there and is struggling to produce a new stable compromise, but could this compromise be useful for workers (namely managers or professionals who are already partially affected)?

2 A dangerous compromise for wage-earners?

As currently viewed in France, time sovereignty first of all favors long working hours. It comes across as an incentive mechanism aiming to increase working hours, but this increase does not come without creating important negative externalities.

Time sovereignty favors long working hours

Working time choices cannot be made without any external influences. The first of these concerns decisions made by colleagues. This situation is valid both with regard to time (as will be demonstrated below) and with regard to the voluntary acceptance of work during certain periods, such as Sundays. In fact, several studies (Eastman 1998; Landers *et al.* 1996) show that an individual's supply of work is very closely related to that of his colleagues. This notion was tested during a survey of engineering students. A survey of post A-level engineering students was carried out in October and November 2006 on the basis of a written questionnaire filled in at the beginning of a lecture. Every level and all classes at the college were represented in the sample (about 200 students). All claimed to have had at least one period of professional experience, or attended at least one training course in a company. 196 questionnaires on working time preferences were exploited. I complete this first exploitation by means of semi-directed interviews with about ten students. These interviews were done inside the college for about half an hour each, mainly in December 2006. The small size of the sample obviously does not allow complex analysis, and great care must be exercised when manipulating the results. The trends which emerged from the questions which are of interest here are, however, sufficiently strong to support analysis.

The aim of the questionnaire was to answer the following question: do people's working hours correlate to those of their immediate colleagues? Several questions were asked to this end. The first question asked what would be the desired length of the working week, stressing that remuneration would be directly proportional to the number of hours worked (i.e. the hourly rate would remain absolutely constant). The question was then put again, but this time the average length of working week quoted by other staff in the company was quoted (successively 35, 40, 50 and 60 hours). Finally, if one could be certain that everyone would make exactly the same choice, the sample was asked what the desired length would be.

The first result concerns the very high homogeneity of the initial preferences expressed by the individuals. With no reference to the length desired by colleagues, the desired number of working hours was on average identical for men and women (around 39 hours). Notably, the spread of time quoted was very narrow: all those questioned expressed a desired total working week of between 35 and 40 hours.

The preferences diverge considerably, however, as soon as the desired number of hours expressed by colleagues is known: in every case the "selected" times correlate with those of colleagues, but the correlation is much more clear-cut with men than women (see Table 5.1 below).

It can be seen that the number of hours offered clearly follows the number offered by colleagues, and the gap between the number offered and the number desired increases accordingly as the latter increase their offer.

This clear correlation between an individual's supply of work and that of his colleagues can easily be explained by two complementary phenomena: "compe-

Table 5.1 Length offered according to the situation of colleagues

	Length offered by colleagues 35 hours	Length offered by colleagues 40 hours	Length offered by colleagues 50 hours	Length offered by colleagues 60 hours	No reference to colleagues	Choice made when certain that colleagues would make the same choice
Male	40.7	41.2	45.7	49.3	38.8	40.0
Female	40.8	39.9	44.1	46.1	38.9	40.0

tition for promotion," and the development of an ostentatious form of work among the skilled professions.

Ruth Simpson (1998) thus talks of "competitive presenteeism" between managers. Given the lack of accurate methods of measuring productivity or efficiency, the amount of time spent at work can appear to be a simple indicator of performance; it can also be used as a basis for selection during restructuring, or for promotion. The link between the probability of promotion and working hours is being demonstrated with ever increasing frequency, as in the works of Marco Francesconi (2001) for Great Britain and Markus Pannenberg (2005) for Germany. The principle is indeed largely shared by the future engineers who were interviewed. In France this link between long working hours and promotion criteria is just as clear-cut: the fact that individual performance is regarded as a central criterion for promotion has a very marked positive effect on the incidence of long working hours among managers and within the Technicians and Associates Professionals category.[4]

The desire to work longer (or at least more than one's colleagues) however, is not just linked to the logic of "contest." More subjective or symbolic factors can also intervene: the value attributed to work (indeed to the idea of being snowed under and thus feeling irreplaceable) can be a determining factor. This hypothesis is developed by Gershuny (2005): being engaged in one's work is regarded in a positive light by one's peers, and having shorter working hours than one's colleagues can have a negative effect on the individual's reputation. In such a framework, individual time sovereignty does not allow for the cooperation required to offer shorter hours – a situation akin to the classic "Prisoner's Dilemma."

In such a framework the strategy of working longer hours is clearly dominant. In other words, in the absence of cooperation both workers risk going home late and gain absolutely nothing (with regard to their lifestyle). The employer thus gets longer working hours without having to bear the burden of control costs. Time sovereignty and the more or less direct competition of workers are very strong incentives for offering longer working hours.

Alongside the microeconomic argument of freedom to motivate effort, time sovereignty seems equally preferable for employers to increase consumption and working-time in a work and spend cycle (Schor 2005; George 2001). Various studies such as those by Galbraith on the role of artificial demand, have highlighted the influence exercised by producers on consumption, and have thus relativized the sovereignty of the latter. The historian Gary Cross (1993; 2000) has also highlighted this consumerist pressure which comes across as a strong preference for revenue over free time, and thus a decision in favor of long working hours where they can be chosen (George 2001; Hamermesh and Slemrod 2005). These mechanisms challenge consumer sovereignty and stress the fact that time sovereignty could be contrary to the individual's "meta preferences" (what they hope to prefer). Time sovereignty provides consumerist pressure with a greater voice as it "opens a door" to revenue constraints. Pressure in favor of market consumption being much greater than that in favor of "convivial" activities (as described by Gorz or Illich), individual choice is partly skewed.

Furthermore, the preference for earnings (and therefore the mechanisms which encourage it) plays an even greater role in that it enters a context where satisfaction linked to consumption has some connection to the way of life of other agents, in particular the individual's immediate entourage. Indeed, if one were in a situation where satisfaction and choice were influenced by one's relative position in society and not just by the individual's absolute position, fear of a fall in status (see the works of Eric Maurin (2004) on choice of housing) would push one to do one's utmost to improve one's revenue. This is the logic of positional goods as developed by Fred Hirsch (1976) who sets the "material" sector (which gathers together goods and services desired for their straightforward utility value) against the positional sector (goods and services whose consumption gives even greater satisfaction in that they allow their beneficiary to "stand out" from other members of society).

If it is difficult to provide statistical proof for this view, the international studies by Bowles and Park (2005) provide interesting perspective: there is a greater correlation between working hours and global social inequality than inequality in any given economic sector. Similarly, statistical analyses carried out in the "Enquête sur les conditions de vie des ménages [Study on household living conditions]" (see Devetter 2006) show that the incidence of longer working hours (more than 41 hours per week) is greater when the average neighborhood income is high, and that independent of the revenue of the person himself.

The increase in couples' working hours by way of an increase in female activity is demonstrated by a large increase in purchasing power, and by a rapid rise in a "decent" or "desirable" standard of living. The basket of goods deemed necessary becomes greater as the standard of living rises. Time sovereignty feeds this race toward material consumption. More generally, the link between time sovereignty and the valuation of work is very strong (Jefferys 2007).

Thus, the manner in which time sovereignty is viewed in France today (as in most English speaking countries) favors the offer of long working hours (work more to earn more) rather than the option of reduced hours, which is the aim of

Dutch and Scandinavian policies. This desire to favor a long working week can thus involve numerous externalities.

Time sovereignty and externalities

The costs associated with longer working hours are diverse in their nature: medical; environmental; social; and family.

1 The medical argument is the longest-standing, and historically is at the origin of the movement to reduce working hours (see, for example, Marx's *Das Kapital*, chapter X). Despite the tertiarization of jobs, this aspect is still largely relevant today – in fact, research is united in stressing the real impact of heavy workloads. In a recent report for the International Labour Organization, however, Spurgeon (2003) demonstrates the harm caused by long working days or weeks: a working week of over 48 hours is an important contributing factor for stress and issues of mental health, and increases the risk of depression (Shields 1999). In addition to the purely medical aspects, the impact of long working hours on stress, on the "feeling of being snowed under" etc. and on the conciliation between different paces of life is equally well established.

   Spurgeon's report also states that "important epidemiological studies carried out since the 1950s highlight a direct link between cardiovascular diseases and long working hours." It is also known that the incidence of premature births clearly increases with an increase in working hours (3.6 percent of births to women with shorter working hours, and 10 percent for women who work more than 45 hours per week). Complaints such as headaches, muscular pain and insomnia are cited as "secondary effects" of long working hours. A heavy workload (and even more so the switch to longer hours) also accentuates "risky" behavior, such as alcohol and tobacco consumption,[5] reduced physical activity among women and a corresponding increase in weight among men (Shields 1999). Last, studies of household medical expenditure (Devetter 2006) show a link between the presence of one person working more than 45 hours per week and higher than average medical expenses. The impact of long working hours is certainly much weaker than the presence of children, or being over 60 years of age, but it nevertheless plays a significant role.

2 The second important externality of long working hours relates to environmental costs. Two different kinds are involved: direct costs on the one hand, and, more importantly, indirect costs linked to a decision made in favor of revenue over free time on the other. Although it is difficult to establish a direct link, an analysis of consumer budget as a function of working hours (and by neutralizing the effect of revenue thanks to a regressive logic of "other things being equal") produces some interesting points: when one person in a household works more than 45 hours, certain developments in consumption can be observed which can be grouped into

three areas which are particularly important in terms of environmental degradation:

* public transport use falls;
* package tours (usually including a flight) increase considerably as do leisure services;
* more is spent on "eating out"; such costs entail an ecological footprint which, per ton consumed, is 4 times greater than that for meals eaten at home (Wiedmann *et al.* 2006: 40). Jalas (2002) obtained the same results from his calculations on the material and energy intensity of consumption.

Similarly, the works of Wiedmann, *et al.* (2006) and Lenzen and Murray (2001) highlight the important differences in ecological footprint between the different socio-economic groups. In the case of Great Britain, Australia and New Zealand, the socio-economic profile with the strongest ecological footprint is that of "company managers living in suburbia" – a group which is clearly over-represented among those with long working hours (Schief 2005). In fact, the option (more or less forced upon) of longer working hours favors a choice of consumption that is more demanding in terms of money, and less demanding in terms of time (see also Jalas 2005).

Regarding indirect costs, the main link between longer working hours and environmental externalities is earnings. The preference for revenue inevitably manifests itself by increased consumption and hence increased environmental costs: although environmental polices often focus on the direct production or economics of energy, research on the concept of "sustainable consumption" largely highlights the impact consumption has on the environment (e.g. Ropke 1999). The links between revenue and ecological footprint are thus evidenced both on a macroeconomic level (strong correlation between GDP and the national ecological footprint), and on a personal consumption level. This correlation thus affects the links between working hours and ecological footprint (Schor 2005, Wiedmann *et al.* 2006; Lenzen and Murray 2001.

The reduction of working hours as a privileged mechanism for transforming the benefits of productivity thus appears to be an essential condition for the introduction of sustainable development.

3   Long working hours also entail significant social costs. Longer working hours mainly reduce the determinants of social capital (group support networks which can be mobilized for socially useful ends), notably sociability time and time for associational commitments (Putman 2000). Various empirical and statistical studies stress that there is a correlation between participation in associational activities and working hours. According to Prouteau and Wolff (2002), the probability of participating in associational activities falls from 48 percent for those working 35 hours per week, to 30 percent for those working 48 hours or more; similarly, wage-earners whose working hours have fallen tend to participate more. In dynamic terms, wage-

earners benefiting from RTT tend to get more involved in the associations of which they are members (Prouteau and Wolff 2005). According to Putman (2000), the increase in working hours witnessed over the past two decades could explain as much as a 10 percent reduction in social relations and civic participation in the United States of America.

Similarly, an increase in working hours tends to weaken the quality of free time by reducing the proportion of relational leisure in favor of purely individual leisure. Thus Corneo (2005), using an international comparison between OECD countries as a basis, believes that an increase in working hours leads to an increase in the amount of time spent in front of the television to the detriment of other leisure activities, particularly relational leisure. Osberg (2003) shares this opinion, and demonstrates that longer working hours increase the costs of synchronization and thus reduce the probability of easily finding "somebody to play with."

Last, long working hours have a further impact on social cohesion via the inequality they convey, i.e. it seems that extended working hours intensify social inequality (Messenger 2004). The inequalities between men and women are particularly intensified; first, because longer working hours affect men disproportionately and impede the equal division of domestic tasks; and last, because in companies, promotion is often awarded on the basis of easily observable factors, and time spent at work is the most commonly used of these. This mechanism is a major contributing factor in denying women access to managerial positions (Francesconi 2001).

4   Family relations constitute a different important "social time" which is particularly influenced by long working days. Conciliation policies between the family sphere and the professional sphere are incompatible with increased working hours. According to the international studies cited by Spurgeon (2003), conflicts between private life and work life are more frequent for wage-earners who have a working week of more than 44 hours. Numerous British studies highlight the instance of dissatisfaction linked to long working hours (see Kodz *et al.* 2003: 209–210 for various examples of opinion polls and surveys). American and Australian research also emphasizes the difficulties that families experience (including the parents' personal relationship), when both parents work more than 40 hours per week (Pocock 2001). According to a British survey into long working hours, 42 percent of those surveyed felt that their working hours had a negative impact on their friendships and social life, and 19 percent on relations with their children, whilst 83 percent of spouses felt the same (Kodz *et al.* 2003).

Most of these data are based on subjective perceptions, and little time is devoted to the study of the impact of long working hours on the pace of family life. Nevertheless, it seems that professional timetables partly dictate the timetables of children. In a study of the schedules of 10–11-year-old children (Devetter 2003), it appeared that a significant area of differentiation concerned sleeping patterns: children with both parents working full time get up earlier than their friends –

the differences in terms of bedtime and getting-up time combine to create differences in terms of length of time [spent in bed]: children whose parents are not in active employment are more likely to sleep more then ten hours per day (approximately 70 percent, against 58 percent of children with both parents working). Similarly, professional working hours influence both the time children go home and the time evening meals are taken. These two aspects combine to shorten the amount of free time children have at the end of the school day: barely one-third of children with both parents working have more than 2.5 hours between getting home from school and meal time, as against more than half of all other children. Time spent with parents and for joint activities is also greatly reduced by longer working hours. From a more subjective point of view, these children claimed much more frequently than other children that they "do not have enough time" or are even "snowed under." The production and reproduction of social inequalities within a family also involves time management and the conveyance of a particular conception of the management of social time.

Thus, long working hours, even "opted for," involve increased costs, and it would seem that the development of "excessively" long hours has a negative impact on individual well-being, and even more so on collective well-being. Loss of free time thus likely exceeds the benefits in terms of purchasing power (Osberg 2003).

Conclusion

Thus, insistence on time sovereignty is not neutral and involves a broad prescriptive dimension. This sovereignty seems risky for wage-earners: various aspects (competition resulting from the hours offered, marketing pressure, positional consumption, fear of losing status, the ostentatious aspect of work) create a gap between the actors' ideal "meta preferences" and the "preferences" they clearly express in their decision to supply work.

Given such a context, expression of choice in favor of reduced working hours seems difficult and only a referee can "force" agents to act in the common interest. As stated by Nick Donovan and David Halpern in a report for the British government on "life satisfaction": "leisure take up may suffer from a collective action problem – if I work fewer but my colleagues don't then I will suffer. This argument has been used to support stronger regulation on work life balance" (2002: 38).

For all that, the call for greater control of working hours, mainly so that professional constraints and constraints on family life can be more clearly accommodated, is widespread in OECD countries. Certain types of flexibility can, in fact, be regarded in a positive light by the agents concerned (Golden 2001) and do not necessarily lead to a strengthening of the employer's position. Highlighting the perverse effects of working time sovereignty does not solve the problem and does not suppress the legitimate expectations of the actors.

In an attempt to overcome this contradiction, two very different ways of reasoning will be introduced, as described by Michael Walzer (2004). He opposes the reasoning of "holiday" where free time is shared out on a market basis (voluntary renunciation of paid working hours) to the reasoning of the collectively imposed "public holiday." The main characteristic of the latter is that it is "not free" in that possible activities are more regulated. Converting these periods into money is rejected, and conversely this type of time cannot be acquired for money or any other material goods: "it is something that money cannot buy" (Walzer op. cit.). Thus, more often than not, the convention defining these periods requires coercion: without a mechanism for forcing it to be respected, "compulsory rest" cannot exist. In this sense, this type of non-worked time is not free in the strict sense of the word. It is similar to taxation in the sense that it involves a "levy on productive time or wage earner for the benefit of the common good" (Walzer op. cit.). Banning Sunday working falls into this reasoning.

From this perspective, a reduction in working hours would not be based on individual choice but on the granting of "rights to reduce one's working hours" based on jointly established criteria. Such is the reasoning, for example, behind training leave or even parental leave in the Nordic countries. The case of Sweden is interesting in the sense that part of this "right" to leave is reserved for fathers and that specific incentives have been introduced to "force" them to exercise their rights. The fully free choice, in fact, led to women being disadvantaged on the labor market. This second reasoning is in line with the will to pursue the decommodification of work (Esping-Andersen 1990) and stands opposite working time "sovereignty" as it has been described for the past few years.

Notes

1 We agree there are others ways to consider "time sovereignty" (more autonomy of the schedules or choice of duration for part time work for example) but we would like to concentrate our reflection on the recent issues in France.
2 It is important to note that in numerous texts on the evolution of work, the boundary between the description of on-going developments and that of desired tendencies is not always very clear.
3 Here a broader tendency of the "deal" supposed to characterize post-Fordism is encountered: the wage-earner becomes an actor in the business in exchange for greater individualization in appraisal and remuneration (Postel *et al.* 2006).
4 The working week of managers and intermediary professions for whom personal performance is taken into consideration for promotion is on average almost four hours longer than other managers and intermediary professions (source: Enquêtes permanentes sur les conditions de vie des ménages 1996–2003 [Permanent studies on household living conditions 1996–2003], see Devetter 2008).
5 The consumption of tobacco, alcohol, and particularly medication and coffee, are strategies frequently used by Australian lorry-drivers to deal with a lack of sleep (Arnold 1997).

References

Arnold, P.K., L.R. Hartley, A. Corry, D. Hochstadt, F. Penna, A.-M. Feyer (1997), "Hours of Work and Perceptions of Fatigue among Truck Drivers," *Accident Analysis and Prevention*, 29(4), July: 471–447.

Becker, G. (1965), "A Theory of Allocation of Time," *Economic Journal*, 299 September: 493–517.

Bowles, S. and Park, Y. (2005), "Emulation, Inequality, and Work Hours: Was Thorstein Veblen Right?," *Economic Journal*, 115(507), November: F397–F412.

Boyer, R. and Saillard, Y. (2002), *Regulation Theory, the State of the Art*, London: Routledge: 352.

Corneo, G. (2005), "Work and Television," IZA Discussion Paper 376, Institute for the Study of Labor (IZA).

Cross, G. (1993), *Time and Money*, London: Routledge.

—— (2000), *An All Consuming Century*, New York: Colombia University Press: 320.

Devetter, F.-X. (2003), *Approche socio-economique des relations entre temps de travail et temps des enfants*, rapport pour la DARES, March 2003.

—— (2006), "Temps de Travail et Externalités," in C. Bourreau-Dubois and B. Jean-didider, *Economie Sociale et Droit*, Paris: Harmattan.

—— (2008), "Travailler au-delà de 48 heures par semaines," *Travail et Emploi*, 114 April–June: 59–68.

Donovan, N. and Halpern, D. (2002), *Life Satisfaction: The State of Knowledge and Implications for Government*, London: Strategy Unit, December 2002.

Gay, P. du (1996), *Consumption and Identity at Work*, London: Sage.

Eastman, C. (1998), "Working for Position: Women, Men and Managerial Work Hours," *Industrial Relations*, 37(1): 51–65.

Esping-Andersen, G. (1990), *The Three World of Welfare Capitalism*, Cambridge, UK: Polity Press: 248.

Franscesconi, M. (2001), "Determinants and Consequences of Promotion in Britain," *Oxford Bulletin of Economics and Statistics*, 63(3): 279–310.

Gardin, A. (2002), "La prise en compte de la vie familiale du salarié dans les normes légales et conventionnelles du travail," *Droit Social*, 9–10: 854–861.

George, D. (2001), "Driven to Spend: Longer Work Hours as a by Product of Market Forces, in Working Time," in Golden, L. and Figart, D. *International Trends, Theory and Policy Perspectives*, London: Routledge.

Gershuny, J. (2005), "Busyness as the Badge of Honor for the New Superordinate Working Class." *Social Research*, 72(2) Summer: 287–314.

Godet, M. (2006), "L'erreur collective des 35 Heures," *Le Monde*, February 7.

Goff, J. le (2001), *Droit du Travail et Societe*, Rennes: PUR: 1013.

Golden, L. (2001), "Flexible Work Schedules: What Are Workers Trading Off To Get Them?," *Monthly Labor Review*, 124: 50–67.

Hamermesh, D. and Slemrod, J. (2005), "The Economics of Workaholism: We Should Not Have Worked on This Paper," NBER Working Paper W11566.

Hirsh, F. (1976), *Social Limits To Growth*, London: Routledge and Kegan Paul.

Jalas, Mikko (2002), "A Time Use Perspective on the Materials Intensity of Consumption," *Ecological Economics*, 41: 109–123.

—— (2005), "The Everyday Life Context of Increasing Energy Demands," *Journal of Industrial Ecology*, 9(1–2): 129–145.

Jefferys, S. (2007), "Valuing Work: What Sarkozy Can Learn from Thatcher," communication for the 11th Biennial French Sociology of Work Conference, London, 20–22 June 2007.

Kodz, J., Davis, S., Lain, D., Strebler, M., Rick, J., Bates, P., Cummings, J., Meager, N. (2003), "Working Long Hours: A Review of the Evidence," *Employment Relations Research Series*, 1 and 2(16).

Landers, R.M., Rebitzer, J.B. and Taylor, L.J. (1996), "Rat Race Redux: Adverse Selection in the Determination of Work Hours in Law Firms," *American Economic Review*, 86(3): 329–348.

Lenzen, M. and Murray, S. (2001), "A Modified Ecological Footprint Method and its Application to Australia," *Ecological Economics*, 37: 229–255.

Lojkine, Jean and Malétras, Jean-Luc (2002), *La guerre du temps*, Paris: Harmatan: 239.

Maurin, E. (2004), *Le ghetto français: Enquete sur le separatisme social*, Le Seuil: La Republique des Idees: 96.

Marx, K. (1867), *Das Kapital*, French edition (1963) Paris: Editions Gallimard.

Messenger, J. (2004), *Working Time and Workers Preferences in Industrialized Countries*, London: Routledge.

Osberg, L. (2003), "Nobody to Play With? The Implications of Leisure Co-ordination," Working Papers of the Institute for Social and Economic Research, Paper 2005–19, University of Essex.

Pannenberg, M. (2005), "Long-term Effects of Unpaid Overtime: Evidence for West Germany," *Scottish Journal of Political Economy*, 52(2) May: 177–193.

Pocock, B. (2001), *The Effect of Long Hours on Family and Community Life*, report for the Queensland Department of Industrial Relations, August 2001.

Postel, N., Rousseau, S., and Sobel, R. (2006), "La Responsabilite Sociale et Environnementale des Entreprises: une reconfiguration potentielle du rapport salarial fordiste?," *Economie Appliquee*, LIX(2006/4): 77–104.

Prouteau, L. and Wolff, F.C. (2002), "La participation associative au regard des temps sociaux," E*conomie et Statistique*, 352–353: 57–80.

——— (2005), "Participation associative des salaries et temps de travail," *Travail et Emploi*, 101: 59–70.

Putnam, R. (2000), *Bowling Alone: The Collapse and Revival of American Community*, New York: Simon & Schuster.

Ropke, I. (1999), "The Dynamics of Willingness to Consume," *Ecological Economics,* 28(3) March: 399–420.

Rochefort, R. (1997), *Le Consommateur entrepreneur*, Paris: éditions Odile Jacob: 302.

Rose, N. (1989), *Governing the Soul: The Shaping of the Private Self*, London: Routledge.

Salin, P. (1995), "Restaurer la liberté du temps de travail," *Le Monde*, December 21, 1995.

Schief, S. (2005), "Les travailleurs hautement qualifies travaillent-ils partout plus longtemps?," *Revue de l'IRES*, 49.

Shields, M. (1999), "Les Longues heures de travail et la santé," *Rapports sur la santé*, 11(2) autumn.

Schor, J. (2005), "Sustainable Consumption and Worktime Reduction," *Journal of Industrial Ecology*, 9(1–2): 37–50.

Simpson, R. (1998), "Presenteeism, Power and Organizational Change: Long Hours as a Career Barrier and the Impact on the Working Lives of Women Managers," *British Journal of Management*, 9(1) September: 37.

Spurgeon, A. (2003), *Working Time: Its Impact on Safety and Health,* Geneva: International Labour Organisation.

Thompson, E.P. (1967), "Time, Work-discipline and Industrial Capitalism," *Past and Present*, 38(1): 59–97.

Walzer, M. (2004), *Spheres of Justice: A Defense of Pluralism and Equality*, New York: Basic Books: 345.

Wiedmann, T., Minx, J., Barett, J. and Wackernagel, M. (2006), "Allocating Ecological Footprints to Final Consumption Categories with Input Output Analysis," *Ecological Economics*, 56: 28–48.

6 Age differences in the consequences of overwork

*Beth A. Rubin and Charles J. Brody**

Time and energy are finite; the demands of the 24/7 global economy seem not to be. As the old social contract structuring employment relations shifts, so too have the ways in which individuals work. Most notably, work in the 24/7 global economy is characterized by long hours and reconfigured work days in which work time is deepened, accelerated, expanded and otherwise transformed from the previous ideal of a five day work week characterized by regular 9–5 work days. Transformed work-time has led to a reproblemetization of time and work and reconsideration of its costs and benefits. To that end, social scientists across disciplines have sought to understand, unpack and explore these phenomena (see, for instance the new research volume, *Research in the Sociology of Work: Workplace Temporalities*, Rubin 2007).

One persistent outcome of these changes is the feeling of being overworked as symptomatic of the quality of work in the new economy.[1] This chapter focuses on two major issues – the negative effects of feeling overworked and possible age differences in those negative effects. We focus on the negative effects of being overworked in the United States because overwork seems to be a ubiquitous characteristic of the contemporary US economy. Though there is evidence that the reshaping of workplace temporalities and subsequent problems of overwork are a global phenomenon (Poster 2007), we focus here on the US experience. The *Families and Work Institute* report, "Feeling Overworked in America," (Galinsky *et al.* 2004) indicates that roughly one-third of US workers are chronically overworked. Given the centrality of work to people's lives and to the life of a society, understanding and explaining the characteristics and consequences of how people work reveals much about the social world more broadly.

We are, however, interested in more than just the negative consequences of overwork. The research here tests hypotheses drawn from two competing explanations for the ways in which age might moderate the negative impacts of feeling overworked on employees' feelings of stress and anger in the workplace. While normative contract theory suggests that the shifting social contract renders the costs of overwork higher for older workers (Rubin 1996; Cappelli *et al.* 1997; Rubin and Brody 2005), life course theory (Moen 1992; Moen *et al.* 1995; Scheiman 2003) implies that costs are greater for younger workers. Normative contract theory assumes that social relations are driven by norms of reciprocity.

The underlying, shared understandings that govern the employment relationship are such that employees expect that in exchange for good work and committed effort, they will receive relative security, opportunity and other job related rewards. Life course theory examines employment issues in the context of multi-level, structured phenomena in which individual experience is understood in terms of age-graded trajectories (Elder 1994: 5). These perspectives, as we show below, make different predictions about the relationships between age and over-work in the context of contemporary economic transformation. Thus, our analyses consider plausible explanations drawn from these two perspectives about whether the next generation of employees differs systematically from their older counterparts in the negative consequences of overwork. Understanding how current work-times affect individuals' well-being illuminates how macro-level changes impinge on micro-level, individual, experience.

Following this introduction, the chapter proceeds in five parts. In the first, we provide an overview of the literature and research that points to overwork as a new norm for work life. In the second section of the chapter, we focus on the negative effects of overwork drawing on literatures and research in a number of disciplines. The third section of the chapter addresses the relationship between age and overwork in the new economy. Our arguments consider the under-examined possible ways in which the negative effects of overwork may differ by age. We develop hypotheses drawn from the two perspectives, normative contract theory and life course theory. In the fourth section of the chapter we present the empirical research, addressing first data, measures, analysis and results. The final section of the chapter presents our discussion, conclusions and suggestions for further research.

1 Overwork in the 24/7 economy

Global competition and technological change have transformed economies and the organizations that operate them in order to operate more flexibly and rapidly (Rubin 1995; 1996; 2007; Vallas 1999; Cappelli 1997). These changes have led to the transformation of work times and a de facto "assault" on the normative five days a week 9–5 work-day. Likewise, changes have transformed work-time itself. In the efforts to respond to the increasingly competitive environments, employers have relied on a wide range of strategies to transform large, slow and lumbering bureaucracies into nimble, flexible fast-paced organizations.

They've gutted unions, thus removing barriers to labor usage; they restructured employment relations to draw on part-time and contingent work rendering employment insecure, unstable, and uncertain. Likewise, employers have introduced technologies that create constant accessibility, thereby blurring the home–work boundary. Most germane to this chapter are the efforts to remove the constraints of normative time use and constructions. That is, the social construction of the "normal" working schedule has identified the eight-hour workday and five-day work week as a norm in the United States; that normative time structure has become for employers an additional rigidity to overcome. Thus, through the use of non-standard employment contracts, new technologies and other forms of workplace reorganization, employers have sought to run their business freed from temporal and spatial constraints.

These factors combine in a number of ways all of which contribute to the experience of overwork as the new norm and to the overwork cultures that perpetuate it (Wharton and Blair-Loy 2001). One major organizational change that generates this overtime culture is organizational "de-layering" (Cappelli *et al.* 1997). As companies compress their hierarchies, outsource positions and push remaining tasks down the flattened hierarchy, they provide greater responsibility and often more work to a smaller workforce that is comprised disproportionately of managerial, professional and administrative (typical white-collar) employees. While benefiting some employees, there is considerable evidence that these changes contribute to overwork and overpacing for many others. For instance, employed mothers, particularly those with young children, professionals and managers, and employees engaged in technologically complex work tend to experience considerable overwork and over pacing (Maume and Purcell 2007; Jacobs and Gerson 2004; Green and Tsitgianis 2005). Furthermore, these processes contribute to greater job insecurity (Maume and Bellas 2001) as persistent organizational change, downsizing and outsourcing render jobs insecure and working in them more stressful (Sweet *et al.* 2007; Jacobs and Gerson 2001; 2004).

Another social change that contributes to overwork is the intensification of work activities and employment instability that create new pressures on dual-earner families that have become the norm in most developed countries. Researchers consistently show that dual-earner families often characterize their work as "overwork" in that their actual hours are greater than their preferred hours (Kalleberg 2007; Reynolds and Aletraris 2007). Dual-earner families outsource many of the activities that were once household activities. By so doing, it creates market demand for new businesses and extended hours for existing businesses to allow families to engage in a variety of services or use services outside of the standard working day that in turn require business to provide services outside of typical hours (Jacobs and Gerson 2004; Presser 2003).[2]

The *Families and Work Institute* conducted two studies, one in 2001 and a follow up in 2004 that focused explicitly on "feeling overworked" (Galinsky *et al.* 2001; 2004). In both instances, the *Families and Work Institute* used Harris Interactive, a major polling firm, to conduct a survey of a representative sample of the United States population of adults over 18 years old who work for pay. The researchers at the *Families and Work Institute* developed the questionnaires based on extant literature, their own focus groups and consultation with experts (Galinsky *et al.* 2001; 2004). The first survey revealed considerable overwork. Well over one-quarter of adults sampled felt overworked, overwhelmed and that they lacked sufficient time to step back and consider their work process in the three months prior to the survey. In fact, when they took into account respondents who felt overworked or overwhelmed at all in the previous three months before the survey, well over one-half of respondents were thus affected. They conducted a subsequent study in 2004 that asked the same as well as additional questions. The findings presented the same descriptive image of an overworked and overwhelmed working population that continued to have insufficient time to step back from their work to sufficiently process it.

The most recent *Feeling Overworked* study in 2004 indicated that roughly one-third of all US employees report being chronically overworked. Galinsky and her colleagues created an index of overwork that averaged the answers to three questions: did respondents feel overworked at least sometimes in the last month? did they feel overwhelmed by how much work they had to do in the last month? and did they have time to step back and process or reflect on the work they were doing at least sometimes in the last month? The scale ranged from 1 (never) to 5 (very often). They concluded that "employees with average scores above *sometimes* (3) can be viewed as being chronically overworked" (Galinsky *et al.* 2004: 14, emphasis original). This finding is roughly comparable to what the previous (2001) study revealed. Moreover, the extent of overwork is much greater when the researchers asked if employees felt overworked at least some-times in the previous month (Galinsky *et al.* 2004). They also found that the technological accessibility to work contributed to feeling overworked. The feeling overworked study found that women were more overworked then men (see also, Sayer 2007) and that members of the baby boom generation (ages 40–59) felt more overworked then other employees. Parents felt more over-worked than did non-parents. Finally, the researchers identified those workers with managerial positions and high incomes as experiencing more overwork than others. In both studies, roughly three-quarters of those surveyed self-identified as managerial, professional or administrative, a finding that is largely consistent with the ways in which organizations have restructured. Overwork would not be of so much interest if it was prevalent and benign, but it is not. Overwork is one of the very predictable *causes* of negative work experiences – a topic to which we now turn.

2 The negative effects of feeling overworked

The negative effects of feeling overworked have long been of interest to scholars across disciplines and over time. Workers' responses to feeling overworked are implicated in social movements, policy change, and transformed employment practices. Employees who feel overworked create costs to the firm via low morale and slow productivity (Weakliem and Frenkel 2006), turnover, burnout and absenteeism (Schor 1991; Perlow 1997; Presser 2003). Likewise there are social costs as overworked employees bring the negative outcomes home to their families (negative work–family spillover), and are less likely to participate in civil life through decreased time for participation in voluntary associations (Voy-danoff 2007). Feelings of overwork may contribute to the growing sense of risk in society, as harried workers rush through work on sensitive technological developments in fields such as nanotechnology, biotechnology and nuclear energy (Fitzgerald and Rubin 2007).

Finally, and the focus of this chapter, is that the costs of overwork are considerable for individuals. While the United States has not witnessed overwork as a systematic cause of suicide as in Japan (Kalleberg 2007), overworked employees are characterized by greater stress (Sparks, *et al.* 1997), depression, anger toward their employers, ill health and more (Galinsky *et al.* 2001; 2004). There is, for example, a huge body of literature on work stress that details the ways in which interrelated levels of social structure shape individuals' experiences and result in stress and other related outcomes (Kohn and Schooler 1973; Pearlin 1989: 242; Scheiman *et al.* 2003; Barley *et al.* 2005).

In addition, as employees respond to these pressures, they generate high health care costs for individuals, employers and society (Kalleberg 2007). Besides higher health care costs, data suggest that the overwork culture (Wharton and Blair-Loy 2001) and excessive workplace demands serve as a disincentive for workers to seek workplace advancement. To the extent that is a widespread trend, it points to future problems filling the most demanding, and likely important, occupational positions. That conclusion also implies that exploring how these factors affect different generations is important. That is, if future generations of employees, a demographically shrinking group, reject demanding jobs, there will be a labor supply crisis (something to which pundits refer often).[3] There are, then, few benefits for the individual, firm or society of individuals feeling overworked. We turn now to a direct consideration of how age and feelings of overwork may interact to either increase or decrease the effects of overwork on employees' anger about the amount of work and their stress.

3 Age and overwork

In this section of the chapter we discuss how age and overwork may be related by drawing on the two theoretical perspectives introduced earlier, normative contract theory and the life course perspective. Studies of workplace change have focused considerable attention on the effects of overwork on dual-earner families but little attention on how these negative effects are moderated by the employees' age. This absence is unfortunate because research in other areas suggests different vulnerability among workers of different age groups. Research on displacement, for example, has pointed to the disproportionate impact of current economic and organizational changes on older workers (Smith and Rubin 1997; Rubin and Smith 2001; Quadagno *et al.* 2001; Brown *et al.* 2006).

Researchers argue that in the new fast-paced economy, employers seek employees who will be flexible and will not seek long-term (read inflexible) employment (Kalleberg 2001; 2003; Rubin and Brody 2005). As companies restructure and rely on outsourcing, information technology and other workplace innovations, they are, by some accounts, less interested in retaining and retraining "experienced" workers and, therefore, privilege a younger workforce (Smith 2001; Ferres *et al.* 2003).

While research on workforce restructuring has provided inconclusive evidence on which age group is most vulnerable to restructuring (Bridges 2001) there are obvious reasons to argue that younger workers are attractive to employers for a variety of reasons; chief among them is that they are less expensive than their older counterparts. Their skills also may be more contemporaneous. Also creating the greater vulnerability of older workers is the decline of internal labor markets and unions, both structures that privileged seniority. Furthermore, employers may favor younger workers because their expectations of employment relations more closely conform to their own.

Demographic trends also point us to consideration of age differences in the negative effects of overwork. Demographic changes indicate an aging population and smaller replacement workforce. That demographic reality, in conjunction with evidence that those who experience overwork are less likely to seek employment advancement, points to possible critical labor shortages in the future.

Thus, there are both empirical and theoretical reasons to focus on age differences in the negative effects of overwork. Empirically, people in different age groups differ in their involvement with labor force activity (Bridges 2001: 327). Research on how individuals experience job security demonstrates age differences that hinge on perceptions of the economy and employability (Bridges 2001).

Normative contract theory and age

Analysts have argued that younger workers' normative expectations of loyalty and long-term employment are qualitatively different from older workers who have developed careers under the old social contract (Rubin 1995; 1996; Cappelli *et al.* 1997). Older employees entered the workforce during an era in which they could expect that if they worked hard, were reliable, productive and increased their human capital, they could progress up career ladders embedded in internal labor markets.[4] That implicit social contract has been more or less broken or rewritten in the last couple of decades. Thus, workers who entered the labor market more recently have a different set of expectations about the trade-offs and rewards associated with employment. Younger workers, it is argued, are more interested in jobs that provide experience, knowledge and work–family balance and have a "free-agent" approach to employment (Barley and Kunda 2004).

Certainly the popular press and anecdotal accounts of generational differences (Boomers, Generation X, Generation Y) repeatedly depict differences in attitudes toward employment, job insecurity and work–family balance. Recent studies by the *Families and Work Institute* substantiate those accounts and demonstrate that baby boomers (those born prior to 1964) feel more overworked. Our previous research asked if feelings of overwork, job insecurity, and technological accessibility affected employees' organizational commitment. Most germane to the research here is our findings that lack of control over work hours, greater accessibility than employees thought necessary decreased the commitment of older workers more than that of younger (Rubin and Brody 2005). In a subsequent paper (Brody and Rubin 2005), we investigated these relationships with a fuller dataset. First, the younger cohort had significantly lower levels of organizational commitment net of job tenure. We also found that the frequency with which supervisors required overtime without notice negatively affected the commitment of only the older cohort. The cohorts also differed in how doing work-related emails from home affected commitment; it negatively affected the commitment of the older workers but not that of the younger ones. So while there were certain dimensions on which the cohorts did not differ, there *were* differences that might similarly impact the relationship between overwork and its consequences. In our previous work, we were really focusing on the negative impact for *employers* (since we view depressed organizational commitment as a cost to employers). In the research presented here, we test hypotheses about how cohort and age effects moderate the effects of overwork on employees' stress and anger in the workplace.

Our prior research that predicted differences in commitment by age focused on Boomers versus Generation X; these broad categories, while appropriate for testing hypotheses linking experience with the employment contracts to commitment, do not capture the varying ways in which individuals are connected to the labor market. That is, though this aggregation of employees into cohorts may capture shared values, normative expectations and preferences associated with employment, these same values expectations and preferences may vary considerably with age. For these reasons, we turn to the arguments from life course theorists and consider how these might explain the age–overwork relationship.

Life course theory

While the media and much of the literature on these topics (including the authors of the feeling overworked reports) focus on a variety of attitudinal and value differences between baby boomers (those born prior to or in 1964) and Generation Xers (those born after 1964) insights from life course scholars suggest a different way of thinking about how age would moderate the negative impacts of overwork. Life course analysts point out that differences in labor force attachment are more broadly tied to differences in the life course but might be similar across different cohorts (Moen *et al.* 1995).

A life course perspective examines issues from within the context of individuals' lives and views those lives as embedded in other social relationships, particularly family relations. Life course analysts focus on "linked lives" and individuals' agency with respect to those linked lives (Elder 1994). A huge body of literature bears out the utility of the life course perspective for understanding a variety of work and non-work related phenomena.[5]

Certainly recent studies on work time preferences link these preferences to life stage (Jacobs and Gerson 2004) and find that the gap between preferred and actual work hours is greatest for men aged 36–55. For women that gap is fairly constant across age groups. For many employees, at least those in non-marginal sectors of the labor force, these are years when they have families, maybe homes and established careers.

Research on job values demonstrates that job values over the life course change considerably (Johnson 2001). Young workers move into the labor market with unrealistically high expectations. Over time, they develop more realistic work values as they gain experience (Johnson 2001). While they may move into jobs with very high expectations about certain aspects of the job, there is also evidence that they begin work with far more anxiety about other aspects of work since organizational restructuring has broken career ladders and eroded benefits (Quadagno *et al.* 2001; Osterman 1996).

Likewise, from this perspective, older workers develop not only experience and expertise (greater human capital) but also wider networks of support that sustain them through employment related difficulties. Those same older workers, though likely to have difficulty obtaining re-employment if displaced (Rubin and Smith 2001; Smith and Rubin 1997), are also more likely to have access to retirement benefits and other cushions associated with employment instability. Scheiman (2003) for example, finds that older people report less anger than younger people and work roles are often implicated in anger.

One of the most well-researched of these difficulties is work stress. A long history of research on work-stress links work hours to well-being. Over 40 years of that research has indicated that long hours at work are major stressors and that age differences are important to these explanations of work-stress (Knudsen 2006). Thus, there are a number of reasons to examine directly whether and how employee age moderates the negative effects of overwork.

The current study

The previous discussion points to two distinct hypotheses for the ways in which the negative effects of overwork should be moderated by employees' age. From the social contract perspective, older workers who have been socialized and worked under the old employment contract should experience the negative effects of overwork more strongly than their younger counterparts. Prior research has also shown that the last 25 years or so are characterized by a shift in the employment contract in which the reciprocity between employers and employees no longer results in an exchange of stable employment for productive labor (Rubin 1995; 1996; Barley and Kunda 2004). Thus, the normative expectations associated with work should differ and the feelings of betrayal, anger and stress should be greater for older workers. This reaction is, essentially, a cohort difference.

The life course perspective would predict the opposite. Older worker with more experience should be able to better weather the vicissitudes of economic turbulence and workplace pressures. These workers are better established, have more knowledge and resources both inside and outside of work on which to rely. Younger workers, on the other hand, are attempting to establish careers, build families and generate economic security. In addition, organizational restructuring and the decline of internal labor markets and the elimination of employment benefits suggest that younger workers' objective experience may cause overwork to create more anger and stress. Likewise, their expectations are quite high, so the anger and stress associated with overwork should be greater for younger employees. The life course explanation attributes differences between older and younger workers to the particular life/family state that characterizes a particular age group.

4 Research design

In the following section we discuss the data we use for this study, the measures, our analysis and the results. In the last section of the chapter we turn to our discussion of these findings.

Data

The data for this study are the unpublished dataset from *The Families and Work Institute* that we discussed earlier. As previously described, they used Harris Interactive to conduct a telephone survey of 1,003 US adults aged 18 or older who were employed (not by self) at the time of the survey. The sample is a nationally representative sample appropriately weighted to represent the demographic distribution of the population (Galinsky *et al.* 2004: 51).

Measures

Dependent variables: We use two indicators of the negative effects of overwork from the *Feeling Overworked in America* study, "stress" and feelings of "anger." To measure "stress" we use the index created by the *Families and Work Institute* that is a composite of four items that asked respondents to indicate how often they:

- felt that you were unable to control the important things in your life ...
- felt that difficulties were piling up so high that you could not overcome them
- felt nervous and stressed
- had trouble sleeping to the point that if affected performance on and off the job.

(Cronbach's Alpha = 0.74).

The second dependent variable, "anger," is measured by asking respondents when "thinking about your [main] job, ... in the last month" how often they had "felt angry" that they "were expected to do so much at work."

Respondents could reply with a five point scale that ranged from "very often" to "never."

Independent variables: there are two independent variables in our analyses, "feeling overworked" and "age." Feeling overworked was measured using an index of three items from respondents' answer to the question:

Thinking about your [main] job,... how often have you experienced the following in the last month?

- felt overwhelmed by how much you had to do at work
- felt overworked
- felt that you didn't have time to step back and process or reflect on the work you're doing?"

As before, respondents could reply to each item using a five point scale that ranged from "very often" to "never" (Cronbach's Alpha = 0.82).

We measure age as age in years. We also create age groups to capture individuals' different likely relationship to the labor force. A true life course analysis would be longitudinal to capture not only the embeddedness of life stages but also the timing of different activities. Given the cross-sectional data, we cannot capture this dynamic component of life course thinking. Instead, we create five different age groups that represent likely stages in individuals' connection to the labor market (Bridges 2001). Specifically, we break down age to create the following: 18–24-year-olds are the youngest labor force entrants. These employees may first be trying to enter into jobs and least likely to have established households and careers. The next age group is 25–39-year-olds; employees in the early stages of establishing households and careers. Our third age group is comprised of employees who are 40–54. Bridges (2001: 327) identifies "age 40 as a critical point" since that is when employees are protected under the Age Discrimination in Employment Act." That coverage is an institutionalized life course demarcation. Bridges also identifies 55–64 as a distinct group that is in "transition to retirement," another demarcation that has clear life course attributes. Our final group, the excluded category in the analyses below, are those 65 and over.[6]

Controls: We have controlled for a number of employee characteristics that are correlated with the dependent variables and that are standard predictors in the work–family literature (where much of the overwork research occurs). Thus we include: sex (1 = male, 0 = female); education, a measure of whether or not the individual is a manager;[7] an indicator of the presence of children at home (1 = at least one child at home); marital status (1 = married or living with a significant other); years worked with current employer (tenure); organizational instability (a composite of three variables: Has the organization eliminated or downsized last year?; Has the organization had difficulty hiring last year?; Has the organization merged/acquired/been acquired last year?); family income; and average hours worked, paid or unpaid, at main job.

Analysis

In the analyses that follow we are particularly interested in possible moderating effects of age on the negative effects of overwork. To capture those effects, in addition to including a linear measure of age, we introduce product terms between age-group and overwork in order to test competing hypotheses about the way different age groups moderate the impact of overwork on anger, in Table 6.1 and stress in Table 6.2. We use Ordinary Least Squares (OLS) regression analysis to estimate the models.

Results

Overwork significantly increases feelings of anger about the amount of work employees want to do net of their tenure with the organization, family income, their position, organizational instability, hours worked, sex, education level, education, marital status, and children at home. Contrary to expectations derived from both theories, *age was not related to feelings of anger about the amount of work*. Consistent with other literature, employees with higher incomes were less angry about the work load. Interestingly, tenure with the organization did increase anger felt at the amount of work, a finding that suggests social contract reasoning.

In the next model, we include four product terms between each age group and overwork. As a reminder to the reader, social contract arguments would predict that older workers would be the angriest since their expectations of the benefits of seniority would be compromised. From the life course perspective, the expectation is that those at the earlier stages of the life course, whose social supports are weaker and whose expectations are still high, would be the angriest. All of

Table 6.1 Moderating effects of age on the relationship between anger and overwork

	Model 1		Model 2	
	b	*S.E.*	*b.*	*S.E.*
Independent variables				
Overwork	0.633***	0.030	0.361***	0.095
Age	−0.001	0.003	0.002	0.005
Age 18–24* overwork	–	–	0.328**	0.118
Age 25–39* overwork	–	–	0.239**	0.101
Age 40–54* overwork	–	–	0.266**	0.084
Age 55–64* overwork	–	–	0.292**	0.083
Controls				
Tenure	0.007	0.004	0.006	0.004
Organizational instability	−0.037	0.063	−0.024	0.063
Hours worked	0.003	0.003	0.003	0.003
Sex (M = 1)	−0.049	0.181	−0.034	0.065
Education	−0.028	0.025	−0.013	0.025
Marital status	0.102	0.077	0.096	0.077
Family income	−0.049**	0.019	−0.048*	0.019
Children <18	−0.003	0.066	0.012	0.067
R^2	0.353		0.365	
Significant F change?			0.002	

Notes
*$p < 0.05$; **$p < 0.01$; ***$p < 0.001$.

the product terms are positive and significant. The findings indicate that the effect of age increases employee anger relative to the oldest employees (those over age 64). This finding is slightly consistent with life course arguments since all of the age groups are angrier than the very oldest workers who, as literature suggests, may have adapted their expectations and developed strong support systems. They also may be nearing retirement so the costs of overwork are, in many ways, less onerous.

Table 6.2 presents the results of the models predicting the moderating effect of age on stress. Again, as with anger, overwork significantly increases the stress of all employees net of controls. Also consistent with the effects on anger, age is not significantly related to employee stress. In the second model, we introduce the product terms. Here, none of the age-group/overwork interactions is significant. The coefficient associated with the 18–24 age group and overwork is larger than that associated with the other age-group/overwork interactions and approaches significance. Thus, in the third model, we estimate the model with this product term alone. The results indicate that employees in the 18–24 age group are significantly more stressed by overwork than their older counterparts, a finding that is again consistent with the life course, not the social contract, hypotheses.

Table 6.2 Moderating effects of age on the relationship between stress and overwork

	Stress		Stress		Stress	
	b	S.E.	b.	S.E.	b	S.E.
Independent variables						
Overwork	0.486***	0.024	0.328***	0.077	0.377***	0.025
Age	−0.003	0.002	−0.002	0.004	−0.001	0.003
Age 18–24* overwork	–	–	0.121	0.095	0.084*	0.037
Age 25–39* overwork	–	–	0.032	0.082		
Age 40–54* overwork	–	–	0.057	0.071		
Age 55–64* overwork	–	–	0.052	0.067		
Controls						
Tenure	−0.002	0.003	−0.003	0.003	−0.002	0.003
Organizational instability	0.003	0.051	0.020	0.062	0.016	0.051
Hours worked	0.001	0.002	0.002	0.002	0.002	0.002
Sex (M = 1)	−0.025	0.053	−0.024	0.053	−0.029	0.052
Education	−0.002	0.020	0.006	0.020	0.002	0.020
Marital status	0.056	0.062	0.047	0.062	0.047	0.062
Family income	−0.059***	0.015	−0.053***	0.016	−0.052***	0.016
Children <18	0.030	0.053	0.041	0.054	0.047	0.062
R^2	0.244		0.250		0.248	
Significant F change?			0.135		0.024	

Notes
*$p < 0.05$; **$p < 0.01$; ***$p < 0.001$.

5 Conclusions

The negative consequences of overwork are considerable and consistent. Anger and stress, both of which have implications for society and individuals, are predictable responses to overwork, a now "normal" part of the contemporary economy. While studies and journalistic accounts have focused attention on the negative consequences for older employees, our research suggests that bigger harms lay elsewhere.

We tested hypotheses drawn from two different theoretical arguments. The social contract/normative expectations theory made specific predictions that older generations would feel greater anger about overwork and stress due to overwork than would younger generations. *We found no support for this hypothesis.* Alternatively, life course theory makes age-related predictions about the negative effects of overwork on employees' stress and anger on the job. The estimated results provide some supporting evidence for these arguments. From the life course perspective, the negative effects of overwork should be greater for younger workers. *We did find minimal support for this hypothesis.*

Clearly the lack of strong age effects suggests that there is additional research to do. One possible explanation for the lack of robust results is that the hypotheses are not mutually exclusive; that is, both social contract and life course dynamics could be driving the relationships between overwork and its negative effects. Supporting this idea are the effects of tenure on employee anger. Though only suggestive, the positive impact of tenure on employee anger is actually consistent, as we mentioned previously, with the logic of normative contract theory. Arguably, those employees who are with the company the longest are those who have survived waves of displacement and now find themselves doing more, under more demanding working conditions, thus increasing their anger at work. To the extent that both social contract and life course effects are operating though, they would cancel each other out. Unfortunately, with cross-sectional data, we are unable to disentangle these effects.

A fuller dataset that would allow us to consider more job characteristics would undoubtedly provide further explanatory detail. Likewise, there is some evidence (Galinsky *et al.* 2004) that some people return from vacation well rested whereas others return feeling greater work-stress. Future analyses might explore these differences to determine if the patterns are consistent with the predictions of life course or our social contract explanations. Also important for future research is consideration of the extent to which the relative autonomy of the job explains the relationships (or lack thereof) among age, overwork and their negative outcomes. Ultimately, answering these questions would also benefit from analyses over time, something we would like to pursue if data allow it.

Our final claim is that there is considerable evidence that overwork is problematic to all age groups and leads to a number of negative health and other outcomes, the costs of which are inevitably passed on to the firm, families and society at large. Increasingly, the literature on work–life and balance demonstrates that these are out of sync, that employees (regardless of sex, age, marital status and other characteristic) experience overwork, a situation that creates a lose–lose situation.

Echoing that thought is research on work–family negative spillover (Mennino *et al.* 2005, among others) that points to the preponderance of such negative effects of overwork on the family. Angry and stressed employees, regardless of age, bring those negative feelings into their home, to their communities and to their other relationships. There is little evidence that anyone, not even employers, receives any benefit from angry, stressed employees and considerable evidence to the contrary. In converse, there is considerable descriptive evidence that overwork leads to more mistakes, lower commitment and other business-costly outcomes.

It is particularly consequential that younger employees are the most stressed and angriest from overwork. Both anecdotal and scholarly evidence point to younger employees' reluctance to make the same life trade-offs as their older counterparts. If, indeed, the negative effects of overwork, are most difficult for those in the earlier stages of their careers, and these employees are launching those careers in more unstable, and insecure environments, the rational choice of younger employees may well be to eschew demanding careers and embrace the entrepreneurial, each-person-for her or himself mindset encouraged by current employment relations. That may not, however, be the type of work attitude most likely to assist businesses struggling for survival in the increasingly competitive global economy. If employers are to attract and motivate young talent, rethinking the way in which work time is organized is crucial.

Some businesses have recognized the importance of making these changes. Knowing the importance of innovation and creativity in a knowledge economy, there are companies that seek to create genuinely balanced, family-friendly and humane work settings. These are the companies that protect their employees' time through real vacations, freedom from technological chains, flexible scheduling and generous family leave; they're also likely to show up on various "100 best places to work" lists. These are the companies that have made the shift to what Gewirtz and Fried identify as "life-friendly" work policies (Gewirtz and Fried 2007).

A final thought, that extends beyond the workplace but that has implications for the workplace, concerns the nature of social relations in the contemporary world. Younger workers have grown up in a world that is both highly unstable *and* highly networked. We expect, though, that younger workers' networks are different from those of their older counterparts. These post-modern networks are ephemeral and technologically created simulacra of relationships. They create loose friendships, based on thin-trust and technologically mediated attachments. They may have 1,000 *best friends* in their "MySpace" page, but those friends are not likely to be the kinds who can provide the economic and social resources that older workers are able to draw from their networks. Ironically, these young employees may be particularly unprepared for the challenges of the twenty-first-century workplace in which persistent work intensification and instability punish any who do not have strong buffers and deep resources. Addressing these issues is important not only for employers and employees but for social life more broadly.

Notes

* An earlier version of this chapter was presented at the twelfth World Congress of Social Economics, Amsterdam June 7–9, 2007. We thank Ellen Galinsky at the *Families and Work Institute*, New York for making these data available to us and Julie McLaughlin, UNC-Charlotte and John B. Davis, University of Amsterdam and Marquette University for comments on an earlier draft. We retain responsibility for any errors.
1 Analysts of time-use in the new economy have an ongoing debate about whether family obligations have created a time squeeze leading to employees working more hours than they used to (Schor 1991) or whether long hours at work actually represent employees' preferences for the conviviality of work in comparison to the chaos at home (Hochschild 1997). Also challenging the "time squeeze" argument are those who point to greater use of employment hours for leisure activity (Robinson and Godbey 1997). Despite this academic debate, there is considerable evidence that employees *feel* they work longer hours.
2 Though not a focus in this chapter, technologically induced accessibility also contributes to overwork.
3 Thomas Friedman's *World is Flat* raises some of these concerns in terms of the United States' inability to successfully compete in a global economy.
4 Admittedly, career ladders and internal labor markets have not been options for all employees, but they were characteristics of "good jobs" and it is from good jobs that generalized expectations about "career" come from.
5 See research by Glen Elder (1994), Phyllis Moen (2003; 1995) their students and colleagues.
6 In this sample, there were 33 individuals in this group. The oldest employee was 79.
7 One of the biggest limitations of the data is the relative lack of information about the work or organization.

References

Barley, Stephen R. and Gideon Kunda (2004), *Gurus, Hired Guns, and Warm Bodies: Itinerant Experts in the Knowledge Economy*, Princeton: Princeton University.
Barling, Julian, E., Kevin Kelloway and Michael R. Frone (eds.) (2005), *Handbook of Work Stress*, Thousand Oaks: Sage.
Bridges, William P. (2001), "Age and the Labor Market," in Ivar Berg and Arne L. Kalleberg (eds.) *Sourcebook of Labor Markets: Evolving Structures and Processes*, New York: Kluwer Academic, 319–352.
Brown, C., J. Haltiwanger, J. Lane (2006), *Economic Turbulence: is a Volatile Economy Good for America?*, Chicago: Chicago University.
Cappelli, Peter, Laurie Bassi, Harry Katz, David Knoke, Paul Osterman, Michael Useem (1997), *Change at Work*, New York: Oxford University Press.
Crouter, Ann C., Matthew F. Bumpus, Melissa R. Head and Susan M. McHale (2001), "Implications of Overwork and Overload for the Quality of Men's Family Relationships," *Journal of Marriage and Family*, 63: 404–416.
Elder, Glen (1994), "Time, Human Agency and Social Change: Perspectives on the Life-Course," *Social Psychology Quarterly*, 57: 4–15.

Ferres, Natalie, Anthony Travaglione and Ian Firns (2003), "Attitudinal Differences between Generation-X and Older Employees," *International Journal of Organisational Behaviour*, 6: 320–333.

Fitzgerald, Scott and Beth A. Rubin (2007), "Constructing Risk: Media Coverage of Nanotechnology," presented to the Department of Sociology, UNC-Charlotte.

Galinsky, E., S.S. Kim and J.T. Bond (2001), "Feeling Overworked: When Work Becomes Too Much," *Families and Work Institute*, New York.

Galinsky, E., J.T. Bond, S.S. Kim, L. Backon, E. Brownfiled, K. Sakai (2004), "Overwork in America: When the Way we Work becomes Too Much: Executive Summary," *Families and Work Institute*, New York.

Gareis, Karen C. and Rosalind Chait Barnett (2002), "Under what Conditions do Long Hours Affect Psychological Distress?," *Work and Occupations*, 29: 483–497.

Green, F. and N. Tsitegianis (2005), "An Investigation of National Trends in Job Satisfaction in Britain and Germany," *British Journal of Industrial Relations*, 43: 401–429.

Gewirtz, Mindy L. and Mindy Fried (2007), "Organizational Strategies for Network Weaving Work–Life Integration into 24/7 Cultures," in Beth A. Rubin (ed.) *Research in the Sociology of Work: Workplace Temporalities*, Bingley, UK: Emerald Group Publishing, 466–497.

Hochschild, Arlie (1997), *The Time-Bind*, New York: Metropolitan Books.

Jacobs, Jerry and Kathleen Gerson (2001), "Overworked Individuals or Overworked Families? Explaining Trends in Work, Leisure and Family Time," *Work and Occupations*, 28: 40–63.

—— (2004), *The Time Divide: Work, Family, and Gender Inequality*, Cambridge, MA: Harvard University Press.

Johnson, Monica F. (2001), "Change in Job Values during the Transition to Adulthood," *Work and Occupations*, 28: 315–345.

Kalleberg, Arne (2007), *The Mismatched Worker*, New York: W.W. Norton.

Kohn, Melvin and Carmi Schooler (1973), "Occupational Experience and Psychological Functioning: An Assessment of Reciprocal Effects," *American Sociological Review*, 38: 97–118.

Knudsen, Hannah K. (2006), "Dominant Themes and New Directions in Work Stress Research," *Work and Occupations*, 33: 224–226.

Maume, David and M.L. Bellas (2001), "The Overworked American or the Time Bind?," *American Behavioral Scientist*, 44: 1137–1156.

Maume, David and David Purcell (2007), "The 'Over-paced' American: Recent Trends in the Intensification of Work," in Beth A. Rubin (ed.) *Research in the Sociology of Work: Workplace Temporalities*, Bingley, UK: Emerald Group Publishing: 251–283.

Mennino, Sue Falter, Beth A. Rubin and April Brayfield (2005), "Home-to-job and Job-to-home Spillover: The Impact of Demanding Jobs, Company Policies and Workplace Cultures," *Sociological Quarterly*, 46: 107–135.

Moen, P. (1992), "Successful Aging: A Life Course Perspective on Women's Roles and Health," *American Journal of Sociology*, 97: 1612–1638.

—— (2003), *It's about Time: Couples and Careers*, Ithaca: Cornell University.

Moen, P., Glen Elder and K. Luscher (1995), *Examining Lives in Context*, Washington, DC: American Psychological Association.

Moen, P., Julie Robinson and Donna Dempster-McClain (1995), "Caregiving and Women's Well-Being: A Life Course Approach," *Journal of Health and Social Behavior*, 36: 259–273.

Osterman, Paul (1996), *Broken Ladders: Managerial Careers in the New Economy*, New York: Oxford University Press.

Pearlin, Leonard I. (1989), "The Sociological Study of Stress," *Journal of Health and Social Behavior*, 30: 241–256.

Perlow, Leslie (1997), *Finding Time: How Corporations, Individuals and Families can Benefit from New Work Practices*, Ithaca, NY: Cornell University

Poster, Winifred (2007), "Saying 'Good Morning' in the Night: The Reversal of Work Time in Global ICT Service Work," in Beth A. Rubin (ed.) *Research in the Sociology of Work: Workplace Temporalities*, Bingley, UK: Emerald Group Publishing, 55–112.

Presser, Harriet B. (2003), *Working in a 24/7 Economy*, New York: Russell Sage Foundation.

Quadagno, Jill, David MacPherson, Jennifer Reid Keene and Lori Parham (2001), "Downsizing and the Life-course Consequences of Job Loss: The Effect of Age and Gender on Employment on Employment and Income Security," in Marshall, Victor W., Walter R. Heinz, Helga Krüger and Anil Verma (eds.) *Restructuring Work and the Life Course*, Toronto: Toronto University, 303–318.

Reynolds, Jeremy and Lydia Aletraris (2007), "For Love or Money? Extrinsic Rewards, Intrinsic Rewards, Work–Life Issues, and Hour Mismatches," in Beth A. Rubin (ed.) *Workplace Temporalities Research in the Sociology of Work Volume 17*, Bingley, UK: Emerald: 285–311

Robinson, J. and G. Godbey (1997), *Time for Life*, University Park, PA: Penn State Press.

Rubin, Beth A. (1995), "Flexible Accumulation, the Decline of Contract and Social Transformation," *Research in Social Stratification and Mobility*, 14: 297-323.

—— (1996) *Shifts in the Social Contract: Understanding Change in American Society*, California: Pine Forge Press.

—— (ed.) (2007), *Research in the Sociology of Work: Workplace Temporalities*, Bingley, UK: Emerald Group Publishing.

Rubin, Beth A. and Brian T. Smith (2001), "Re-employment in the Restructured Economy: Surviving Change, Displacement and the Gales Of Creative Destruction," in Daniel B. Cornfield, Holly McCammon and Karen Campbell (eds.) *Working in Restructured Workplaces*, California: Sage: 323–342

Rubin, Beth A. and Charles J. Brody (2005), "Contradictions of Commitment in the New Economy: Insecurity, Time and Technology," Social Science Research 34: 843–861.

Sayer, Liana C. (2007), "Gender Differences in the Relationship between Long Employee Hours and Multitasking." in Beth A. Rubin (ed.) *Workplace Temporalities: Research in the Sociology of Work Volume 17*, Bingley, UK: Emerald Group Publishing: 403–436

Schieman, Scott (2003), "Socioeconomic Status and the Frequency of Anger across the Life Course," *Sociological Perspectives*, 46: 207–222.

Schieman, Scott, Debra B. McBrier and Karen Van Gundy (2003), "Home-to-work Conflict, Work Qualities, and Emotional Distress," *Sociological Forum*, 18: 137–164.

Schor, J. (1991), *The Overworked American*, New York: Basic Books.

Smith, Gregory P. (2001), "Baby Boomer versus Generation X: Managing the New Workforce," *Citizen-On Line, Business*, May 9.

Smith, Brian T. and Beth A. Rubin (1997), "From Displacement to Reemployment: Job Acquisition in the Flexible Economy," *Social Science Research*, 26(3): 292–308.

Sparks, K., C. Cooper, Y. Fried and A. Shirom (1997), "The Effects of Hours of Work on Health: A Meta-Analytic Review," *Journal of Occupational Health Psychology*, 1999(4): 307–317.

Sweet, Stephen, Phyllis Moen and Peter Meiskins (2007), "Dual Earners in Double Jeopardy: Preparing For Job Loss in the New Risk Economy," in Beth A. Rubin (ed.) *Research in the Sociology of Work: Workplace Temporalities*, Bingley, UK: Emerald Group Publishing, 437–461.

Vallas, Steven (1999), "Rethinking Post-Fordism: The Meaning of Workplace Flexibility," *Sociological Theory*, 17: 68–101.

Voydanoff, Patricia (2007) *Work, Family and Community*, New Jersey: Lawrence Erlbaum Associates.

Weakliem, David and Stephen J. Frenkel (2006), "Morale and Workplace Performance," *Work and Occupations*, 33: 335–361.

Wharton, Amy and Mary Blair-Loy (2002), "The 'Over-time Culture' in a Global Corporation," *Work and Occupations*, 29: 32–63.

7 The implications of happiness research for work time reform

Robert M. LaJeunesse

A renewed interest in happiness

Mainstream economists have recently discovered what heterodox economists have long known – that the study of psychology is useful in understanding human behavior and the success of socioeconomic policy. Many orthodox economists now accept that happiness exists, can be objectively measured, has important individual and social consequences and can be externally altered (Easterlin 1974; Kahneman 1999; Blanchflower and Oswald 2004; Layard 2005). The new research on well-being suggests that economics must now go beyond the nineteenth century psychological approach that characterizes neoclassical analysis, toward a more "Veblenian" or Humanistic approach to human psychology (Cordes 2005). The utilitarian (Benthamite) psychology that has dominated mainstream economic thought for the last century tries to explain and predict human behavior as the outcome of self interested action, which is manifest, ideally, in voluntary exchange. Yet, among other failures, this hedonistic psychology is largely incapable of explaining why economic growth has not improved well-being in the developed world; it sheds little light on the abundance paradox experienced in many rich countries today.

The inability of economic growth to improve life satisfaction in the developed world is becoming increasing apparent. Given the social, psychological and environmental fallout of the last 50 years of economic growth, it is unclear whether "material abundance" in advanced nations is a reflection of social progress. Such questioning echoes the doubts of early socialist thinkers (such as Owen, Mill, Marx, and Keynes) that access to more goods will improve the human condition. Revealing the seamy side of growth, recent well-being research seriously questions whether the preponderant emphasis placed on production over the last 50 years has allowed individuals to "live wisely and agreeably well" (Keynes 1972).

The paradox of abundance

Although we have been conditioned to associate economic growth with progress, recent environmental, social, and psychological research suggests that economic growth does not enhance well-being invariably. Material "abundance" is not always analogous with social "progress." Indeed, happiness research indicates that some advanced countries, mostly in central Europe, have achieved social advancement and greater well-being with slower economic growth. If the industrial democracies of the world have achieved material abundance, the time-honored lodestar of economic growth will need to be abandoned for an alternative method of increasing socio-economic participation and life satisfaction.

Although it may be slightly premature to claim that industrial society has reached a state of widespread abundance, recent trends suggest that there is little hyperbole in such a description. The advanced economies of the world now possess the resources and ability to provide the whole of their populations with basic life necessities – food, shelter, healthcare, and education. General health and longevity are often taken as objective measures of social progress. Yet, it is unclear how closely improvements in these welfare proxies are related to economic growth. Although it is true that citizens of wealthy countries have become healthier over the last century – as evidenced by longer life-spans and lower rates of heart and lung disease – the technological advancements that rendered them possible may have still been available at lower levels of economic growth. Technological development is cumulative in nature and has been accelerating for some time now in both market and non-market societies. Indeed, it is possible that technological development could have been equally, or more, robust in the presence of slower or selective economic growth. Institutionalist economists, such as Clarence Ayres (1944), contend that mainstream economic thought falsely identified the growth of the market economy as a precondition of industrial technological development, when it was likely the reverse. The consolidation of private enterprise within a market system was but one way of structuring the large-scale capital investments required by the technological discoveries of the Industrial Age. Throughout history other non-capitalistic social systems have organized large-scale investment projects: witness the mobilization to explore space by the former Soviet Union and China. The connection between economic growth and general health is further complicated by the fact that market-based economic growth has introduced its own health risks: air and water pollution, food impurities, sleep deprivation, obesity, and mental disorders. In fact, a recent struggle for many governments has been finding ways to retard the excessive consumption of food and housing. Increasingly, the epidemics of obesity and urban sprawl have been recognized as creating large external costs to society in terms of the health, environmental and social problems they create.

The prospect of abundance is quite obvious in recent nutritional trends. In developed countries today a youngster is more likely to die of health complications related to obesity than to protein deficiency. The pandemic of obesity has spread across the globe. According the World Health Organization (2006), there were 1.6 billion people in the world that could be categorized as overweight in 2006. This figure is nearly double the 820 million people in the world that suffered from undernourishment in the same year (United Nations 2006). In a global context, there is clearly an abundance of food available, but its distribution and regulation leaves much to be desired.

Recent developments in housing are similarly suggestive of abundance, but could hardly be classified as sustainable. The size of a typical new home in the United States is now over 2,250 square feet (208 m²), double the average area of a house built 50 years ago. The expansion of home size is even more staggering when one considers that the average size of families has fallen; the median household size in the United States has fallen from 4.0 to 2.6 in the last 25 years. Housing trends are similar in Australia where the size of new homes now averages 2,484 square feet (230 m²), while household size has also fallen precipitously. In Germany, housing space per person has expanded from 162 square feet (15 m²) in 1950 to 400 square feet (37 m²) in 1990. New homes are commonly equipped with central air conditioning and an array of appliances and conveniences that are rarely used to their potential, such as commercial grade stoves and refrigerators, extra dining rooms, and swimming pools. Certainly, construction trends in the advanced economies of the world indicate that adequate housing can be made available for the overwhelming majority of the population, but only if government regulation is implemented to ensure access and curb excesses that create expensive social and environmental externalities.[1]

Although far from universal, education is now more accessible than ever. In the United States the average adult has completed 12.3 years of education, the highest in the world (Easterbrook 2004). College degrees are held by one-quarter of American adults; two-thirds of high school graduates enroll in some college, while less than 10 percent drop out of high school. While improvements are sorely needed in terms of degree completion and racial access to higher education, the United States is nearing the milestone of becoming the first society in which the majority of adults are college graduates. In addition to the expansion of formal education, new information technology has broadened the frontiers of knowledge. Information, of varying veracity, is now more readily available than ever before.

Given the political will, many wealthy nations now possess the ability to feed, shelter and educate unprecedented numbers of the population. Yet, a free-market does not possess a mechanism to foster a "shared" abundance. By its very nature, a market distributes goods or services by rationing them on the ability to pay. Private markets have proven to be problematic in the distribution of basic necessities. Thus, government action will be required to ensure that individuals have access to the mere necessities of life that the industrial process is capable of furnishing when it is not usurped by pecuniary interests (Veblen 1919).

If there is no technical basis for a scarcity of life's basic necessities, what role does greater economic growth play in improving well-being? Herein lays the paradox presented by a growing field of psychological research that concludes that growing material affluence has resulted in virtually zero improvement in societal well-being in wealthy nations. While economic growth indicators have tripled in the developed world over the last 50 years, well-being indices have remained flat, mental illness has more than tripled, and unbridled individualistic behavior is unraveling our social fabric (Myers 1992; Putnam 2001; Layard 2005).

The role of happiness

Economists like Kahneman (1999) and Layard (2005) make a convincing case that happiness can be objectively measured and socially influenced. The supposition is a departure from the assumptions and policy implications of mainstream economics. Conventional thinking in economics has held that individual wants are innately derived, or fixed, and that the pursuit of those wants in perfectly competitive markets will promote the greatest happiness for all. Government's role was to promote market flexibility and the pursuit of self-interested behavior. In concert, these forces would spontaneously yield the greatest possible happiness. With the ascendancy of the free market and the disembedding of the economy from society, gross national happiness became synonymous with gross national product. Individual choice, descendent from the theories of Social Darwinism and Adam Smith's invisible hand and promoted by "highly artificial stimulants," assumed a pro-growth bias that still dominates the thinking and pronouncements of leaders in Western governments (Polanyi 1953).

In decades past, when many basic needs were unmet, economic indicators were a decent first approximation of how well a nation was performing. Yet, as wealthy nations have increasingly solved the economic problem of providing basic human needs to the whole of the population, growth indicators have proven to be largely ineffective at measuring societal well-being. Rather than deriving greater happiness from more income, the evidence suggests that those living in developed nations would benefit more from increased security – at work, in the family and in the community – and stronger personal relationships. The policy implication is that politicians will have to assume a more nuanced approach to improving the human condition than simply increasing material throughput. Indeed, the accurate monitoring and effective promotion of well-being should be of utmost concern to Western governments as the pursuit of happiness ranks with life and liberty as an "inalienable human right."

Are wealthy countries happier?

Easterlin (1974; 1995) was one of the first economists to suggest that economic growth may not enhance well-being. Easterlin (1974: 118) concluded that "in the one time series studied, that for the United States since 1946, higher income was not systematically accompanied by greater happiness." His research further suggested that subjective measures of individual well-being are generally the same across poor and rich countries. Easterlin's findings lent credence to the psychologist's suggestions that happiness is relative; that we should think of people as getting utility from a comparison of themselves with other members of their reference group.

The lack of a "happiness payoff" from economic growth has since been corroborated by a growing body of economic and psychological research. Many researchers have found that large increases in national income, often a doubling or tripling of real income, have yielded no improvement to a variety of national well-being measures (Diener and Biswas-Diener 2002; Easterlin 1995; Oswald 1997; Diener and Oishi 2000; Blanchflower and Oswald 2004). In their review of the literature on income and happiness, Diener and Seligman (2004: 2) state that "it is clear that rising income has yielded little additional benefit to well-being in prosperous nations." Logically, the well-being effects of income growth are larger in poor nations then in wealthy nations. But as basic human needs for food, shelter, clothing and health care are satisfied, the return to happiness from greater income diminishes and eventually disappears. In 2002, Frey and Stutzer (2002) placed this per capita annual income level at around $10,000. When the correlates of national wealth, such as health, quality of government, and human rights, are controlled for, the effect of national income on well-being is nonexistent. Helliwell (2003: 355) concludes that the happiest people "are not those who live in the richest countries, but those who live where social and political institutions are effective, where mutual trust is high, and corruption is low."

The putative correlation between income and happiness also breaks down at the regional or neighborhood level. Hagerty (2000) found that when personal income was statistically controlled, individuals living in higher-income areas of the United States recorded lower happiness scores than those living in lower-income neighborhoods. Similarly, Putnam (2001) suggested that higher state-wide income was associated with lower well-being once individual income was statistically controlled. Thus, at both regional and national levels, economic growth seems to have exhausted its ability to produce more happiness in developed nations. As Diener and Seligman (2004: 10) write, "income, a good surrogate historically when basic needs were unmet, is now a weak surrogate for well-being in wealthy nations."

In the remarkable case of Japan, even a six-fold increase in per capita income from 1958 to 1991 failed to produce any increase in reported well-being (Diener and Oishi 2000). Since World War II, the Japanese economy experienced one of the most spectacular growth spurts in history, yet average happiness rating did not budge. The case of Japan illustrates that there are cultural variations in the manner in which income is connected to well-being. People in many developed nations, for instance, are socialized to work for pay and to feel as if they are contributing to society if gainfully employed. Yet, a different culture might put more emphasis on non-market activities, such as nurturance or gift-giving. These cultural variations help explain why individuals living in poorer countries and communities sometimes report high well-being. Although they may not produce high levels of material throughput, they can still be engaged in activities that are respected in their culture.

Cultural influences are also consistent with findings that the unemployed in wealthier neighborhoods and countries are significantly less happy, particularly when they are surrounded by a culture of high income and employment. Clark (2001) found that unemployment is associated more strongly with lower well-being in regions that have low unemployment than where it is high. Unemployed people on average are dissatisfied even if they had a relatively high income and a presumably larger accumulation of wealth – perhaps because they are no longer performing a task that is respected by their culture. The elderly offer an interesting contrast. Retired people are not expected to work in most cultures, and consequently retirement does not typically harm their well-being the way unemployment otherwise would (Diener and Biswas-Diener 2001).

The idolatry of work often suggests that non-employment is a social calamity on par with unemployment. The thinking is summarized in the aphorism that "the only thing worse than being exploited is *not* being exploited." This view holds that paid employment affords the worker structure for the day, social contact, and a source of respect, engagement, challenge and meaning. Yet new research on happiness suggests that those who choose not to partake in the labor force are not so lacking after all. Layard (2005: 138) writes,

> The data totally refute this [as a source of misery] ... Moves between work and being "out of the labour force" involve much smaller changes in happiness than moves between work and unemployment ... and retirement is not bad for happiness either.

The implication of these findings is that the social virtues that paid work may provide in the existing social structure can be provided by other cultural or organizational means. Indeed the aged and the wealthy have established multiple social arrangements that provide social contact, respect, challenges, engagement, and meaning in ways that may be more sustainable for the community and environment than remunerative employment.

Are wealthier individuals happier?

Research on the relationship between well-being and *individual* income suggests that the link is slightly stronger, but largely ephemeral. Moreover, individual income is largely irrelevant when formulating national policy. It is impossible for legislation to make everyone wealthier than everyone else. Yet, even if the government did attempt to produce more "winners," it is unclear that the net effect on well-being would be positive. The correlation between greater personal wealth and well-being is insignificant, of questionable causation, and short-lived.[2]

At the micro level, studies of the association between individual income and well-being show mixed results. Consistent with James Duesenberry's (1949) hypothesis that individuals care mostly about relative income, Blanchflower and Oswald (2004: 1375) find that "relative income has some explanatory power in a happiness equation even when absolute income is held constant." Yet, in US longitudinal studies, Diener *et al.* (1993) report the confounding findings that those with declining income reported an increase in their happiness, and the group whose income increased reported diminished well-being. In a study of job satisfaction, Clark and Oswald (1996) found that satisfaction with one's work depended on the pay relative to other similarly-qualified workers, rather than on absolute pay. Most telling in this regard is the finding by Alesina *et al.* (2004)

that greater income inequality is associated with lower well-being in Europe and the United States, even after controlling for income. The effect is statistically stronger in Europe than the United States. Explaining the growth of redistributive policies in the United States and Europe over the last century, Alesina *et al.* (2004: 2010) point out that "even the net losers from distributive schemes [the wealthy] may favor them because they perceive poverty and inequality as social harms."

When it comes to windfall changes in personal wealth, the evidence is also mixed. An experimental study by Smith and Razzell (1975) found that gamblers who won large soccer betting pools in England were significantly more likely to report being happier than the comparison group. Researching the impacts of financial windfalls, Brickman *et al.* (1978) find that lottery winners are little happier, or even less happy, than they were before they won the big prize. More recently, Gardner and Oswald (2001; 2007) find that lottery winners and heirs receiving windfall inheritances reported higher well-being. Their 2007 study found that a small sample of Britons who experienced a moderate lottery windfall (between £1,000 and £120,000 in 1998) reported an improvement in their mental well-being two years later to the tune of a 1.4 point increase in the 36-point General Health Questionnaire.

It is important to note, however, that these positive effects largely occur at the individual level and are negated by the tendency for average incomes and desires to rise over time. Kapteyn *et al.* (1976) estimate that up to 80 percent of the benefit of increasing individual income disappears due to rising aspirations and descriptions of "adequate" consumption as income rises. Van Praag and Fritjers (1999) have studied how people's actual income affects their desired income. Across nine countries the authors find that a dollar rise in actual income causes a rise of between 35 and 65 cents in desired income.[3] Highly apposite to work time reform, Solnick and Hemenway (1998) have shown that although people are not rivalrous with their leisure time they tend to make self-defeating comparisons to others when choosing their preferred income. When asked to choose between two earning situations with constant price structures, the majority of Harvard students in the School of Public Health chose to make themselves materially worse off in order to improve their relative income (or social status). Their choices were between: (a) receiving $50,000 per year while others average $25,000; or (b) receiving $100,000 per year while others average $250,000. Yet, only 20 percent were concerned with relative position when it came to choosing between the following two vacation regimes: (a) receiving two weeks vacation while others average one week; (b) receiving four weeks vacation while others average eight weeks.

As first blush the happiness research at the individual level appears to be inconsistent with the findings that aggregate happiness is not improved by economic growth. Yet, if the bulk of the individual happiness improvement comes from making relative income comparisons rather than the act of consumption, then the two findings can logically coexist. Clark *et al.* (2008) explain the findings,

The broad consensus in the literature is that the paradox points to the importance of relative considerations in the utility function, where higher income brings both consumption and status benefits to an individual. Comparisons can either be to others to oneself in the past. Utility functions of this type can explain the positive slope found in much of the empirical literature [for individuals]. However, since status is a zero-sum game, only the consumption benefit of income remains at the aggregate level. Since the consumption benefit approaches zero as income rises, happiness profiles over time in developed countries are flat.

A misplaced emphasis on relative income sets individuals up for despair when they realize, often gradually, that consumption does not provide the happiness they imagined. David Myers (1992: 38) cogently summarizes the literature,

> The second helping never tastes as good as the first. The second fifty thousand dollars of income means much less than the first. Thus the correlation between income and happiness is modest, and in both the United States and Canada has now dropped to near zero.

Research by Ronald Inglehart (1990) indicates that income has a negligible impact on happiness in Europe as well.

As adaptive and emulative creatures, we tend to adapt our expectations about what will make us happy and continually compare ourselves to different groups of people. Yet, the race for social status is a zero-sum game as one person's relative success comes at the expense of another person's success. If two people excel commensurately, there is no change in relative social status and the competition continues. Contemporary market societies that place a premium on individualism and social status therefore devote prodigious effort to changing what cannot be changed in total. Layard (2005: 105) comments,

> The struggle for relative income is totally self-defeating at the level of the society as a whole. If my income rises relative to yours, your income falls relative to mine by exactly the same amount. The whole process produces no net social gain, but may involve a massive sacrifice of private life and time with family and friends. It should be discouraged.

If the need to invidiously distinguish yourself from your peers takes on a materialistic bent, it is likely to further diminish your happiness. Contemporary research on acquisitive behavior suggests that encouraging individuals to lead a highly materialist lifestyle will not enhance well-being. Materialistic individuals have been characterized as having lower self-esteem, greater narcissism, a greater tendency for social comparison, less empathy, less intrinsic motivation and highly-conflictual relationships (Kasser *et al.* 2004). People with intrinsic goals, i.e. they define their values by themselves, are typically happier than those with extrinsic goals, i.e. those motivated by some external reward such as financial success (Kasser and Ryan 1993). Nickerson *et al.* (2003) also found that materialism predicts lower well-being later in life. Lyubomirsky *et al.* (2003) conclude that happiness is linked to what one gives rather than what one gets. Materialism may result in lower well-being because materialistic individuals tend to downplay the importance of social relationships and seem to have a continually large gap between their incomes and material aspirations (Solberg *et al.* 2004).

Economic growth and other social ills

If the failure of economic growth to increase our well-being was simply a matter of societies reaching a maximum happiness threshold, there may be little cause for concern. Yet, many other measures of our social health have been deteriorating in the face of economic growth. Nowhere is the need to buffer the pernicious effects of the materialistic bent and the growth fetish more poignant than in the incidence of mental disorder and suicide. Diener and Seligman (2004: 16) write that "in stark contrast to the improvement in economic statistics over the past 50 years, there is strong evidence that the incidence of depression has increased enormously over the same time period." Controlling for population growth, ten times as many people in contemporary Western society suffer from unipolar depression – unremitting bad feelings without a specific cause – than did 50 years ago.

Although better diagnosis and lower stigmatism associated with depression explain some of the higher incidence, they scarcely account for a ten-fold increase across a generation or two. Evidence of the prodigious increase in depression among mature adults is provided by the Cross National Collaborative Group. In 1992, this study sampled nearly 40,000 adults from America, Puerto Rico, Germany, France, Italy, Lebanon, New Zealand, and Taiwan and revealed dramatic increases in risk for depression across the twentieth century, despite robust economic growth in most of the countries. Klerman *et al.* (1985) found that 65 percent of American women born in 1950 had one depressive episode before the age of 30, whereas only 5 percent of women born before 1910 had such an episode. In a study of the Old Order Amish living in Lancaster County, Pennsylvania, Egeland and Hostetter (1983) estimated that the Amish have about one-fifth to one-tenth the risk of unipolar depression than their neighboring Americans in modern communities. Despite repudiating the use of electricity, automobiles and modern necessities, the Amish experience little mental despair and are equally satisfied with their lives as the Forbes magazine's "richest Americans" (Diener and Seligman 2004). In the context of work time reform, it should be noted that the Amish devote very few, if any, hours to paid work in a hierarchical labor market.

Oswald (1997) notes the continued presence of suicide in modern society and a weak positive correlation between income per capita and suicide rates. Using data from the US General Social Survey from 1972 to 1998, Blanchflower and Oswald (2004: 1366) conclude that, despite rapid economic growth, Americans have "become more miserable over the last quarter century." Myers (1992: 43) comments, "no matter how we define depression, the finding persists: Today's younger adults have grown up with more affluence, more depression, and more marital and family misery." They are also more familiar with the consequences of depression – suicide, alcoholism, and substance abuse. A doubling of per pupil spending, smaller class and family sizes, declining household poverty, and increased parental education between 1960 and 1980 did little to reverse the social degradation of teenagers that was manifest in a doubling of the delinquency rate, a tripling of the suicide and homicide rates, and the quadrupling of unmarried births (Myers 1992). It would seem that household or governmental spending on adolescents is no replacement for parental supervision of teenagers. Indeed, antisocial behavior among adolescents may be the most immediate bellwether of the social costs associated with long hours and contingent work arrangements, but they are certainly not the only costs as these youngsters represent the future workforce.

The psychological literature suggests that economic growth as a national public policy has exhausted its ability to generate widespread well-being in the developed world. Once people attain threshold income levels, additional increases in wealth have a very small influence on happiness. Poverty and wealth equally fail to improve happiness. There may be some improvement to individual well-being from a single financial windfall, but for a neighborhood, region or nation as a whole, income growth beyond modest affluence is not a source of greater well-being. Eventually, developed nations intent on enhancing social well-being will have to abandon economic growth as a policy lodestar.

Implications for work time reform

There are a host of issues that emerge from the psychological research on happiness that are of particular relevance to work time reform. Perhaps the most important finding is the influence of relative income on well-being. In the context of work time, the psychological importance attached to relative income, under current social norms, may encourage workers to opt for greater income and the attendant longer hours when given the choice between labor and leisure. This is not to say that workers have absolute choice in the matter. Labor has been shown to be "lumpy" with employers offering workers long-hours regimes on a take-it-or-leave-it basis. Surveys of worker preferences that indicate a large disconnect between actual working hours and desired hours suggest that workers are not free to vary their work hours (Kahn and Lang 1991; Fagan 2004). When employers offer inflexible work time regimes, workers must resort to changing employers, continually exiting the labor market, or retiring early to achieve their preferred hours (Böheim and Taylor 2004).

The importance placed on relative income is germane to work time policy because it is consistent with both the neoclassical model of work time determination and Juliet Schor's (1995) "work-and-spend" theory. Although the working time outcomes of each theory may be similar, the assumptions and policy implications are quite different. Based on Veblen's (1934) theory that consumption desires are prone to emulation and invidious comparisons, the "work and spend" approach holds that workers have been encouraged, if not inveigled, to receive productivity dividends in the form of income and consumption instead of free time. As workers get locked into consumption habits, they adapt their stated preferences so that consumption is revealed as a preference over leisure. If workers have some prerogative to influence work hours regimes, a strong desire to emulate the consumption standards of wealthier individuals may influence the allocation of time between labor and leisure. Workers may be more prone to emulate the consumption of the rich rather than their leisure because consumption is a more visible, or conspicuous display of status. Veblen (1934: 71) writes,

> One's neighbours, mechanically speaking, often are socially not one's neighbours, or even acquaintances; and still their transient good opinion has a high degree of utility. The only practicable means of impressing one's pecuniary ability on these unsympathetic observers of one's everyday life is an unremitting demonstration of the ability to pay.

In a test of the "Veblen effect" on work hours, Bowles and Park (2005) show that long hours are positively correlated with inequality across OECD countries, but caution that the returns to skill and the greater rewards associated with "winning the race" are equally important as Veblen effects in explaining long hours.

Rather than the current distribution of work time reflecting the neoclassical outcome of sovereign workers "getting what they want," the work-and-spend model contends that workers come to "want what they get" from the productivity bargain with their employers (Schor 1995). Employers prefer that any productivity benefit that flows to the working class takes the form of higher consumption rather than leisure in order to perpetuate the status quo of consumerism, the market mentality, and labor market segmentation (Philip 2001). For Schor (1995), the adaptation of preferences explains why workers are less willing to part with current income in pursuit of more leisure, and more willing to part with future income. Indeed, Hart and Associates (2003) found that while only 15 percent of survey respondents would work fewer hours for less pay in the present the number increased to 42 percent that would definitely or probably do it in the future. This suggests a role for government intervention in improving the ability of workers to access future productivity gains in the form of work time reduction.

The impact of relative income and social inequality on happiness warrants particular attention by policy makers as work time reduction could be designed to transfer hours and income from the overworked to the under-worked. Studies have shown that people routinely forego an absolutely higher, but relatively lower, income for a lower absolute income that is above average (Solnick and Hemenway 1998). Similar experiments have confirmed that extra dollars make less difference to happiness for a rich person than for a poor person. Logically then, if money is transferred from a richer to a poorer person, the poor person gains more happiness than the rich person loses, feelings of injustice aside. Thus, the more equally a country's income is distributed the higher the average level of happiness – all else equal. This is extremely relevant to work time reform because, as Bosch and Lehndorff (2001) have shown, the reduction of average work hours in Europe has resulted in a more equitable distribution of paid work and earned income. If relative income is more important to well-being than absolute income, work time reform that compresses relative income will lead to a Pareto improvement in well-being. Although the over-employed would lose some income, they would be gaining proportionately more leisure (due to productivity gains) and the greater happiness associated with greater equality. When the enhanced well-being of the over-employed is added to the income gains of the under-employed, it is clear that a redistribution of work hours could improve happiness in the aggregate.

A corollary finding from the psychological research, which is likely to confound many economists, is the influence of non-financial variables on well-being. Dispelling the notion that income buys happiness, the evidence suggests that marital status, education, and labor force participation – independently of their influence on income – are more important to well-being than absolute income. In fact, Blanchflower and Oswald (2004: 1373) calculate that to "compensate" an individual's happiness for being widowed or divorced it would require an additional income of approximately $100,000 per year. Although such estimates should be wielded cautiously, it suggests the relative insignificance of money in the average respondent's happiness index. If money plays such a peripheral role in our happiness, then a less materialistic distribution of work hours could be welfare-enhancing.

Another finding relevant to work time reform is that well-being is "U-shaped" with respect to age, meaning that happiness (US) or life satisfaction (UK) usually reaches its doldrums at midlife (Blanchflower and Oswald 2004; Clark *et al.* 1996). In both the United Kingdom and the United States, well-being tends to hit a low around the age of 40 before rising again in later working life and rapidly in retirement. Doubtless, this comes as little surprise to working parents as the mid-life low corresponds to the peak-earning and harried-parenting years of both American and British workers. The fact that well-being reaches a nadir during the peak earning years suggests that recent labor market trends in the United States and the United Kingdom – the feminization of the labor force, the growth of single parenting, and the polarization of work hours – have not been managed in a favorable manner and that there is scope for work time reform to alleviate some of the burden.

A final research finding with implications for work time reform is that the strength of social relationships is one the best predictors of well-being. According to Eckersley (2004), happiness comes from being connected in a web of relationships and engaged in a variety of activities that give life meaning. In *A General Theory of Love*, Lewis *et al.* (2000) argue that the human desire for love and intimacy is a physical necessity that has evolved with humanity; that the brain evolved a chemical need for closeness as part of the stimuli that allow it to function properly. On the whole, married people are happier than singles, people from large families are happier than those from small families, and those that engage in multiple activities, where they interact with many other people, are happier than those who tend to stay at home (Lewis *et al.* 2000). Lane (2000) estimates that while 3 percent of Americans described themselves as "lonely" in 1957; the figure has grown to 13 percent today. Americans appear to be living longer and lonelier lives than ever before. These studies show what people in wealthy countries subconsciously know; that more money and more possessions do not increase individual well-being. The psychological research suggests that when unfettered capitalism is allowed to demand long hours, worker mobility and alienating work, social relationships will suffer and create feedback effects on health, labor productivity, and civility.[4] Work time reform offers the potential to serve as a brake on the liberalization of the labor market that has wrought deleterious effects on worker well-being.

In Australia, New Zealand, the United States, Japan and the United Kingdom from 15 to 28 percent of the workforce toils for 50 hours or more per week, while many others are relegated to short (part-time) hours.[5] Given the polarization of work hours extant in wealthy countries, there is cause for concern that workers lack either the time or resources to cultivate their social relationships and fulfill their social responsibilities. A new body of research is emerging that documents the social costs of this maldistribution of work hours. Unicef's *Child Poverty in Perspective: An Overview of Child Well-being in Rich Countries* (2007) provides some recent evidence that long hours and growth do not translate into improved social outcomes for children. Likewise, the Relationship Forum's *An Unexpected Tragedy: Evidence for the Connection between Working Hours and Family Breakdown in Australia* (2007) manifests the large social costs associated with a work fetish that is maintained at the expense of family time. Both reports suggest that long working hours are a major contributor to at-risk teen behavior. Yet, the social costs do not end with adolescents. The *Study of Early Child Care and Youth Development* (2007) financed by the US National Institute of Child Health and Human Development – tracking more than 1,300 children in various childcare arrangements – found that keeping a preschooler in a large day care centre for a year or more increased the likelihood that the child would become disruptive in class. The study used teacher ratings of each child to assess behaviors like interrupting class, teasing and bullying, and found that the effect persisted through the sixth grade.

Sociological research suggests that if long hours result in a dearth of parenting time the social costs will be immediately apparent in deviant youth and teenage behavior. Yet the social costs of long hours are much more severe and persistent when one considers that today's under-supervised children are tomorrow's leaders and workers. Therefore, labor market regulation designed to subordinate the economy to critical social needs could be viewed as vital industrial policy since it affects a nation's future social well-being, productivity, and international competitiveness.

If the growing dissatisfaction with the fruits of economic growth does not militate for an alternative social division of labor, structural changes emerging in market societies will continually press the issue. Most developed economies have matured from agrarian societies to industrialized nations and then to a service-oriented economy. In their post-industrial condition, many countries have struggled to redefine the relationship between work, income and socio-economic participation. Even more vexing, many observers anticipate a "post-service" economy in which a growing number of service-sector employees will become technologically unemployed, further blurring the delineations between work and socio-economic participation (Gross 1971). In such a context, a rethinking of the role of economic growth and paid work will be imperative.

Well-being research also casts suspicion on the long-standing emphasis that American, Canadian, British and Australian labor unions have placed on wage negotiation, to the general exclusion of work time. As evidenced by the success of European unions in negotiating for work time reduction, labor unions can be an effective vehicle for social change. If labor unions want to enhance the life satisfaction of their members, they should return to their older doctrines that labors' share of income would increase if working hours were shortened because this would make labor scarce and thus more expensive. Even if wages do not increase as a consequence of short hours, workers are still likely to be happier with stable incomes and more leisure time.[6]

A broad policy prescription

Applying a new desideratum of greater socioeconomic participation to the labor market militates for a much more active regulation of the distribution of work hours and tax structures that attenuate income inequalities and curtail the work and spend cycle. Layard (2005) equates the social costs arising from the quest for relative income advantage as a negative externality or a form of pollution. Bowles and Park (2005: 407–408) write that

> Veblen effects cascade downward through the income distribution, with the richest group inflicting subjective costs on the next group, whose emulation of the consumption of the rich then augments its own consumption level, thus passing additional subjective costs to the groups further down.

The economic elite are unlikely to know, or care, that they are polluting other people in this way, so society must alter the attractiveness of longer hours as a means of displaying an invidious distinction.

Taxation is widely used to modify anti-social behavior, but its application needs to be as targeted as possible to minimize unintended consequences. If we make taxes commensurate to the damage that an individual does to others when they earn more, then they will only work harder if there is a true benefit to society as a whole. Given the asymmetry of incentives involved with longer hours, a progressive tax system is the most appropriate policy. Although many have advocated a flat tax on consumption, such a tax is not designed to address the social costs of conspicuous consumption. Bowles and Park (2005: 410) contend that "the consumption of those who, like the well-to-do, are directly or indirectly reference models for many would ideally be taxed at a higher rate than the consumption of those who are models to none or to few."

Although a progressive consumption tax may curtail some of the conspicuous waste related to consumption, there may well remain a desire to invidiously distinguish oneself on the basis of earnings or net worth. In other words, taxing consumption only indirectly impacts the labor–leisure trade-off. The possibility of deferring consumption (saving) can still yield pressures toward long hours. Moreover, Hamermesh and Slemrod (2008) have recently shown that many individuals work long hours out of an addiction to work, which blinds the addict to the pernicious health effects of the activity in ways similar to traditional addictions. Since many workaholics have the ability to determine their own hours and influence the hours of their co-workers and spouses, they create negative spillovers by compelling others to work longer hours and realize lower utility levels than they would in the absence of an addiction (Hamermesh and Slemrod 2008). Dismissing a more targeted but less tractable tax on hours, Hamermesh and Slemrod (2008: 20) espouse a progressive income tax, "the optimal tax system not only features higher marginal tax rates than otherwise, but also marginal rates that rise with income more rapidly than otherwise."[7] A progress tax on income offers a more direct means of altering the labor/leisure calculus than a consumption tax and is consistent with the sin taxes applied to other types of addictions. Finally, only taxing consumption, irrespective of the progressiveness of the tax, is more regressive than an income tax, which can be designed to have similar effects on the consumption patterns of the wealthy. Layard (2005: 228) writes in favor of a progressive income tax, "taxation is a way of containing the rat race, and we should stop apologizing for its 'dreadful' disincentive effects. If tax-cutters think people should work still harder, they need to explain why."

Although progressive income taxes would have a general impact on the marginal attractiveness of working longer hours, a direct tax on overtime hours would have a more expedient effect without disrupting the many other types of activities related to income taxes (i.e. capital investments). Income taxes would not have to be as progressive if coupled with an overtime tax in the form of a double-time pay premium in which 50 percent went to the worker and 50 percent went to the government (to pay for the social costs associated with long hours). Taxing long hours would address the polarization of work hours in a more efficient manner than solely increasing the progressivity of taxes on multiple forms of income. In many countries, a "long-hours tax" would need to be combined with greater white-collar inclusion in overtime pay requirements or work hour limits to be effective in redistributing hours. Short of strengthening overtime inclusions, the success of Dutch legislation that grants workers the right to switch to part time work arrangements suggests that many professional workers, who are currently excluded from overtime regulations, will voluntarily choose shorter hours if given adequate legal protections. Thus new overtime penalties, thresholds, and inclusions could be strengthened by weekly work time limits (i.e. maximum allowable hours), protections for full-time workers seeking hours reductions, and government subsidies for goods that are complementary to the leisure activities.

If the appropriate policy mix is achieved, work time redistribution could successfully increase socioeconomic participation by generating more family time for some and more family income for others. Since it serves to increase socioeconomic participation, work time reform is consistent with Nussbaum's (2000) notion of greater human "functioning" and Amaryta Sen's espousal that public policy strive to enhance human capabilities. Sen (1985) defines capabilities as what people are able to do or to become – the opportunities they have to achieve various lifestyles and the ability to live a rewarding life. Since work time reform can be designed to enhance socioeconomic participation, it represents a precondition for human flourishing.

Conclusions

Large numbers of people in the developed world can now empathize with the plight of Midas. The psychological research suggests that a rapacious appetite for material goods has not translated into greater happiness. The finding that wealth accretion in the aggregate has done little to improve life satisfaction or happiness, suggests that the efficacy of growth-based public policy is quickly waning. Consequently, denizens of the developed world are re-evaluating the pinnacle of civilization as something more than material goods squirreled away in self-storage. Myriad measures of well-being have suggested that the robust economic throughput of the last half-century has not made our lives "richer" in terms of individual or social well-being. Whether the chosen index emphasizes environmental, familial, or social degradation, the conclusion is the same; the developed world has been sold a bill of goods labeled the "growth consensus."

It bears mention that many activities that enhance our well-being – parenting, sex, love, friendship, social interaction, – are also critical to the perpetuation of our species. Curiously, however, many of these activities are not part of economics proper. We do not rely on the "market" or "voluntary exchange" to ration activities such as sex, love, parenthood, friendship, and democracy, and in many instances the marketplace is antithetical to them. Simply pursuing economic growth as an objective policy target is therefore unlikely to promote greater well-being. Layard (2005: 235) comments that, "Through science, absolute material scarcity has been conquered in the West, and we need to think hard about what would now constitute progress." Indeed, socioeconomic policy will have to be more subjective, nuanced and value-based if it is to improve life satisfaction in the future.

The new research on happiness suggests that reformation of the labor market is the first step toward achieving the good economy. As Britain's New Political Economy Working Group (Compass 2006: 23) has pointed out,

The good economy is a caring economy. It provides living wages, secure pensions and affordable housing for all. It supports a progressive shortening of working hours, with productivity gains taken as time as well as income, as happened through much of the twentieth century but has stalled since the 1980s. It offers everyone the opportunity to enjoy the fulfillments of both work and caring, rather than having too much of one or the other. It supports the household, care and voluntary economies ... The good economy is environmentally sustainable ... The good economy outperforms the deregulated "feral" economy in traditional economic terms.

More importantly for the denizens of the developed world, the new research on happiness suggests that the "good economy" outperforms the free-market economy in humanistic terms as well. Thus, labor market reform that increases socioeconomic participation by reversing the polarization of work hours holds the prospect of improving both the performance of the economy and the well-being of society.

Notes

1 The social costs of urban sprawl and gated-communities are readily apparent in many blighted inner-cities and under-funded school districts across America.

2 The psychological research suggests that the *causation* between individual wealth and well-being is nebulous. Diener *et al.* (2002) found that cheerfulness in the first year of college was associated with higher income when respondents reached their 30s. In their review of the literature on the subject, Diener and Seligman (2004: 8) conclude that, "longitudinal findings indicate that some part of the association between income and happiness is likely due to happy people going on to earn more money than unhappy people."

3 Stutzer (2003) reports a rise in desired income of 40 cents with every additional dollar earned.

4 In terms of declining civility, another social indicator that has deteriorated despite decades of economic growth is crime. Conservative reformers hoped that a large economic pie would sow the seeds for a less violent society. Instead, recorded crime increased by 300 percent in most countries between 1950 and 1980 (Layard 2005). Although there have been substantial reductions in crime of late in the United States, Australia, Canada and Britain, the incidence of crime is still far above its 1950 level. Surely, many factors influence national crime statistics, but it is quite telling that this important measure of our social fabric deteriorated so sharply during one the most robust periods of economic growth on record in the capitalist world.

5 In 2005, 25 percent of Australia's ten million workers worked more than 45 hours per week. The Australian Bureau of Statistics (ABC 2007) classified some 544,600 as underemployed one year later.

6 Hayden (1999) provides many examples of workers, who were initially hesitant to trade income for leisure time, coming to cherish their "new lifestyle" after experimenting with short hours.

7 Hamermesh and Slemrod (2008) point out the class bias in the relatively little attention given to workaholism. Behavioral economists advocate sins taxes that regressively burden the poor on activities such as smoking, drinking, gambling and unhealthy eating, yet the addiction to long hours concentrated among highly educated, well-paid workers is largely ignored.

132 *R.M. LaJeunesse*

References

ABS (Australian Bureau of Statistics) (2008), Australian Labour Market Statistics, July 2008. Online, available at: http://www.abs.gov.au/AUSSTATS/abs@.nsf/DetailsPage/6105.0Jul%202008?OpenDocument accessed September 4, 2008.

Alesina, A., R. di Tella and R. MacCulloch (2004), "Inequality and Happiness: Are Europeans and Americans Different?," *Journal of Public Economics*, 88: 2009–2042.

Ayres, C.E. (1944), *The Theory of Economic Progress*, Chapel Hill: University of North Carolina Press.

Blanchflower, D.G. and Oswald, A.J. (2004), "Well-being Over Time in Britain and the USA," *Journal of Public Economics*, 88(7–8) July: 1359–1386.

Bosch, G. and Lehndorff, S. (2001), "Working-time Reduction and Employment: Experiences in Europe and Economic Policy Recommendations," *Cambridge Journal of Economics*, March 25(2): 209–243.

Bowles, S. and Park, Y. (2005), "Emulation, Inequality, and Work Hours: Was Thorstein Veblen Right?," *Economic Journal*, 115 November: F397–F412.

Brickman, P., Coates, D. and Janoff-Bulman, R. (1978), "Lottery Winners and Accident Victims: Is Happiness Relative?," *Journal of Personality and Social Psychology*, 36: 917–927.

Böheim, R. and Taylor, M.P. (2004), "Actual and Preferred Working Hours," *British Journal of Industrial Relations*, March (42): 1: 149–166.

Clark, A.E. (2001), "What Really Matters in a Job? Hedonic Measurement using Quit Data," *Labour Economics*, 8: 223–242.

Clark, A.E. and Oswald, A.J. (1996), "Satisfaction and Comparison Income," *Journal of Public Economics*, 61(3) September: 359–381.

Clark, A., Oswald, A. and Warr, P. (1996), "Is Job Satisfaction U-shaped in Age," *Journal of Occupational and Organizational Psychology*, spring (69): 57–81.

Clark, A.E., Frijters, P. and Shields, M.A. (2008), "Relative Income, Happiness and Utility: An Explanation of the Easterlin Paradox and Other Puzzles," *Journal of Economic Literature*, forthcoming.

Compass (2006), "Direction for the Democratic Left," *A New Political Economy: Compass Program for Renewal*, London: Lawrence and Wishart Limited.

Cordes, C. (2005), "Veblen's 'Instinct of Workmanship,' Its Cognitive Foundations and Some Implications for Economic Theory," *Journal of Economic Issues*, XXXIX(1) March: 1–20.

Diener, E. and Biswas-Diener, R. (2002), "Will Money Increase Subjective Well-being?," *Social Indicators Research*, 57: 119–169.

Diener, E. and Oishi, S. (2000), "Money and Happiness: Income and Subjective Well-being across Nations," in E. Diener and E.M. Suh (eds.) *Subjective Well-being across Cultures*, Cambridge, MA: MIT Press.

Diener, E. and Seligman, M. (2004), "Beyond Money: Toward an Economy of Well-being," *Psychological Science in the Public Interest*, 5(1): 1–31.

Diener, E., Sandvik, L. and Diener, M. (1993), "The Relationship between Income and Subjective Well-being: Relative or Absolute?," *Social Indicators Research*, 28: 195–223.

Diener, E., Nickerson, C., Lucas, R.E. and Sandvick, E. (2002), "Dispositional Affect and Job Outcomes," *Social Indicators Research*, 59: 229–259.

Duesenberry, J.S. (1949), *Income, Saving and the Theory of Consumer Behavior*, volume lxxxvii, Cambridge, MA: Harvard University Press.

Easterbrook, Gregg (2004), *The Progress Paradox*, New York: Random House.

Eckersley, R. (2004), *Well and Good: How We Feel and Why It Matters*, Melbourne, AU: Text Publishing.

Egeland, J. and Hostetter, A. (1983), "Amish Study: I. Affective Disorders among the Amish," *American Journal of Psychiatry*, 140: 56–61.

Esterlin, R. (1974), "Does Economic Growth Improve the Human Lot? Some Empirical Evidence," in P. David and M. Reder (eds.) *Nations and Households in Economic Growth: Essays in Honor of Moses Abramowitz*, New York: Academic Press: 89–125.

—— (1995), "Will Rising the Income of All Increase the Happiness of All?," *Journal of Economic Behavior and Organization*, 27(1): 35–48.

Fagan, C. (2004), in J.C. Messenger (ed.) *Working Time and Workers' Preferences in Industrialized Countries: Finding the Balance*, New York: Routledge.

Frey, B.S. and Stutzer, A. (2002) *Happiness and Economics: How The Economy and Institutions Affect Human Well-being*. Princeton, NJ: Princeton University Press.

Gardner, J. and Oswald, A.J. (2007), "Money and Mental Wellbeing: A Longitudinal Study of Medium-sized Lottery Wins," *Journal of Health Economics*, 26: 49–60.

—— (2001), "Does Money Buy Happiness? A Longitudinal Study Using Data on Windfalls," *Mimeo*, Warwick University.

Gross, B. (1971), "Planning in an Era of Social Revolution," *Public Administration Review*, May–June.

Hagerty, M.R. (2000), "Social Comparisons of Income in One's Community: Evidence from Nation Surveys of Income and Happiness," *Journal of Personality and Social Psychology*, 78: 746–771.

Hamermesh, D.S. and Slemrod, J.B. (2008), "The Economics of Workaholism: We Should Not Have Worked on This Paper," *B.E. Journal of Economic Analysis and Policy*, Contributions, Article 3 8(1). Online, available at: www.bepress.com/bejeap/vol. 8/iss1/art3.

Hart, Peter and Associates (2003), *Imagining the Future of Work*, New York: Alfred Sloan Foundation.

Hayden, A. (1999), *Sharing the Work, Sparing the Planet*, Toronto: Between the Lines.

Helliwell, J.F. (2003), "How's Life? Combining Individual and National Variables to Explain Subjective Well-being," *Economic Modeling*, 20: 331–360.

Inglehart, R. (1990), *Culture Shift in Advanced Industrial Society*, Princeton: Princeton University Press.

Kahneman, D. (1999), "Objective Happiness" in D. Kahneman, E. Diener and N. Schwarz. (eds.) *Well-being: The Foundations of Hedonic Psychology*, New York: Russell Sage Foundation: 3–25.

Kapteyn, A., Praag, B.M. and F.G. van Herwaarden (1976), "Individual Welfare Functions and Social Reference Spaces," *Economic Letters*, 1: 173–178.

Kasser, T. and Ryan, R.M. (1993), "A Dark Side of the American Dream: Correlates of Financial Success as a Central Life Aspiration," *Journal of Personality and Social Psychology*, 65: 410–422.

Kasser, T., Ryan, R.M., Couchman, C.E. and Sheldon, K.M. (2004), "Materialistic Values; Their Causes and Consequences," in T. Kasser and A.D. Kanner (eds.) *Psychology and Consumer Culture: The Struggle for a Good Life in a Materialistic World*, Washington, DC: American Psychological Association: 11–28.

Klerman, G.L., Lavori, P.W., Rice, J., Reich, T., Endicott, J., Andreason, N.C., Kellor, M.B. and Hirschfield, R. (1985), "Birth Cohort Trends in Rates of Major Depressive Disorder among Relatives with Affective Disorder," *Archives of General Psychiatry*, 42: 689–693.

Lane, R.E. (2000), *The Loss of Happiness in Market Democracies*, New Haven, CT: Yale University Press.

Layard, R. (2005), *Happiness: Lessons from a New Science*, New York: Penguin Press.

Lewis, T., Fari, A. and Richard, L. (2000), *A General Theory of Love*, New York: Random House.

Lyubomirsky, S., King, L. and Diener, E. (2003), "Happiness as a Strength: A Theory of the Benefits of Positive Affect," *Mimeo*, University of California, Riverside.

Myers, D. (1992), *The Pursuit of Happiness: Who is Happy – and Why*, New York: William Morrow and Company.

Nickerson, C., Schwarz, N., Diener, E. and Kahneman, D. (2003), "Zeroing in on the Dark Side of the American Dream: A closer Look at the Negative Consequences of the Goal for Financial Success," *Psychological Science*, 14: 531–536.

Nussbaum, M.C. (2000), *Women and Human Development: The Capabilities Approach*, Cambridge, UK: Cambridge University Press.

Oswald, A.J. (1997), "Happiness and Economic Performance," *Economic Journal*, 107: 1815–1831.

Philip, B. (2001), "Marxism, Neoclassicism and the Length of the Working Day," *Review of Political Economy*, 13(1): 27–39.

Polanyi, K. (1953; reprint 1994), *The Great Transformation*, Boston: Beacon Press.

Praag, B. van and Fritjers, P. (1999), "The Measurement of Welfare and Well-being: The Leyden Approach," in D. Kahneman, E. Diener and N. Schwarz (eds.) *Well-being: The Foundations of Hedonic Psychology*, New York: Russell Sage Foundation.

Putnam, R. (2001), *Bowling Alone: The Collapse and Revival of American Community*, New York: Simon & Schuster.

Relationships Forum (2007), *An Unexpected Tragedy: Evidence for the Connection between Working Hours and Family Breakdown in Australia*. Online, available at: www.relationshipsforum.org.au/assets/downloads/rfa_an_unexpected_tragedy_executive_summary.pdf.

Rowe, J. (1999), "The Growth Consensus Unravels," *Dollars and Sense* (224) July–August.

Schor, J. (1995), "Trading Income for Leisure Time, Is There Public Support for Escaping Work-and-Spend?," in V. Bhaskar and A. Glyn (eds.) *The North, the South and the Environment, Ecological Constraints and the Global Economy*, Tokyo: Earthscan Publications, United Nations University Press.

Sen, A.K. (1985), *Commodities and Capabilities*, Amsterdam: North-Holland.

Smith, S. and Razzell, P. (1975), *The Pools' Winners*, London: Calibon Books.

Solnick, S. and Hemenway, D. (1998), "Is More always Better? A Survey on Positional Concerns," *Journal of Economic Behavior and Organization*, 37: 373–383.

Solberg, E.C., Diener, E. and Robinson, M. (2004), "Why are Materialists Less Satisfied?," in T. Kasser and A.D. Kanner (eds.) *Psychology and Consumer Culture: The Struggle for a Good Life in a Materialistic World*, Washington, DC: American Psychological Association: 29–48.

Stutzer, A. (2003), "The Role of Income Aspirations in Individual Happiness," *Journal of Economic Behavior and Organization*, 54: 89–109.

Veblen, T.B. (1919; reprinted in 2002), *The Vested Interests*, New Brunswick, NJ: Transaction Publishers.

—— (1934), *The Theory of the Leisure Class*, New York: Modern Library.

Unicef (2007), *Child Poverty in Perspective: An Overview of Child Well-being in Rich Countries: Innocenti Report Card 7*, Florence: The United Nations Children Fund.

United Nations (2006), "World Hunger Increasing," *FAONewsroom* (Food and Agriculture Organization, Rome), October 30. Online, available at: www.fao.org/newsroom/ en/news/2006/1000433/index.html accessed March 26, 2008.

US National Institute of Child Health and Human Development (2007) *Study of Early Child Care and Youth Development*, US National Institute of Child Health and Human Development. Online, available at: https://secc.rti.org/summary.cfm accessed May 25, 2009.

World Health Organization (2006), "Obesity and Overweight," *Fact sheet no. 311*, September. Online, available at: www.who.int/mediacentre/factsheets/fs311/en/print.html accessed March 26, 2008.

8 Social time in international work environments

Esther Ruiz Ben

Introduction

Information technologies (IT) are bound up with time and space issues and embedded in social and cultural dimensions of life. In the context of international IT, organizations using and producing IT, information technologies play a double role in shaping social life and organizing work in enterprises while serving as a model for structuring time and social relations in other social contexts. In multinational IT enterprises when several teams are involved in the production of software in different national contexts, information technologies play a crucial role for coordination and synchronization of activities expecting an acceleration of working processes. However communication using email or instant messaging does not substitute and often does not even sustain personal contact (Sharpe 2001). Emails for example, are often written in schematic and context related language needing additional explanations to clarify misunderstandings and thus represent sometimes a factor for working processes when the use of information technologies is not integrated in day-to-day working habits. Thus, expectations for overcoming time and space constraints in global IT offshoring processes using IT often fail because of cultural divergences in time structures and habits at the workplace. Social contexts have their own rules about time and also about places and space, so that even using the same information technology tool, the nature of relations between the context of use and the process of using such technologies can much vary and bring many different social implications. In order to overcome intercultural conflicts multinational IT organizations develop and use several methods under the label of quality management methodology (i.e. ITIL, Six Sigma, BS 7799, Balance Score Card) focusing on completion of deliverables on time (Carmel and Beulen 2004: 142) and contributing to the rationalization of international work. Such methods function as common sharing rules and serve as a legitimate basis for action in international environments, and as a basis for distant action taking place on the Internet. However, local cultures do not lose their importance.

Employees working in international teams are not only integrated into the flows of work and global temporalities, but also into local social and cultural life. Working in different national locations also means involvement in particular *time regimes* of scheduling qualifications, continuous education, and entrance into labor market and occupational as well as professional prospectives, and also institutionalized work–life balance programs influencing career opportunities of men and women (Ruiz Ben 2007). Such bundling of time norms institutionally supported in particular countries shape day-to-day situations as well as biographical trajectories. Information technologies create a new social space connecting local places and time norms, thus challenging contingent time and space concepts. Information technologies alter the intrinsic relationship between time and space allowing communication between persons in unlimited distanced locations shrinking distance in time to a minimum. Face to face properties of communication get lost (facial or body gestures with different meanings in different cultural settings) whereas written and oral language, particularly English, predominates. However, as Giddens (1984: 60ff.) points out, routine forms of behavior must be worked out by those sustaining them. This means particularly for the situations of no co-presence of collaborating teams in dispersed geographical locations that day-to-day routines and social relations between distant groups must be created through mediated communication and through sporadic encounters, coordinated and synchronized. Consequently, enterprises and also employees are increasingly confronted with multiple and divergent temporalities (Castells 1996: 472). The question at this point is how are such multiple temporalities synchronized and coordinated? In this chapter I attempt to build a theoretical model to explain this on the basis of Lewis and Weigert's (1981) typology of social time and some concepts of Orlikowski's (1992) structurational model of technology to approach an understanding of the interrelation between social time and the use and design of information technologies in international working environments.

The chapter is organized in three sections. First, I briefly explain some theoretical perspectives concerning the transformation of time in relation to work and information technologies in order to explain the different levels of social time in the workplace. Second, I explain Lewis and Weigert's (1981) typology of social time to provide a theoretical basis for the analysis of temporalities in international IT workplaces. Third, I discuss how this theoretical basis for understanding time experiences might be improved in international working settings.

Understanding social time in digital workplaces

Time constitutes a fundamental category of human existence crucially shaping social experiences. In the social sciences many authors have paid attention to this category (Durkheim 1915; Elias 1988; Hassard 1996; Luckmann 1968; Maurer 1992; Nassehi 1993; Nowotny 1993; Urry 1991; Zerubavel 1981). Particularly since the expansion of the Internet during the last decade of the twentieth century, scholars have paid more attention to the time related implications of information technologies regarding innovation, forms of work control, expertise timing, and the transformation of work–life time experiences.

Castells (1996) and Urry (2000) have shown how information technologies change the experiences of time and the relation to space and places. Through increasing the speed of data delivery information technologies constitute a medium in the dynamic of disembedding and reembedding of social relationships. Giddens refers to this phenomenon as time–space distantiation, Harvey emphasizes time–space compression in this regard, whereas Robertson focuses on the dialectic between the global and the local (glocalization). Castells suggests that information technologies take us into an era of timeless time, in which the different time levels get mixed and in which time is no longer cyclic, but arbitrary, not recursive, but incursive (Castells 1996: 464). This new concept of temporality is "the emerging, dominant form of social time in the network society, as the space of flows does not negate the existence of places" (Castells 1996: 465). More concretely considering how working time is institutionalized in industrial countries, Castells points out that the regulation of labor markets differ institutionally between and within countries. High level professional and unskilled service workers are the two main groups in which longer working hours are concentrated (1996: 472). Thus, Castells suggests that the *network society* is characterized through an unequal distribution of time between working categories and also through a general diversification of working time. This means that working time is often distributed in non-fixed terms. Information technologies have allowed an acceleration of production through the instant transmission of information between different places and also the development of the network model of firm organization through the distant and just in time distribution of information between several organizations. Moreover, the central way of organizing work is increasingly focused in project work (Kalkowski and Mickler 2002), giving more and more self-responsibilities for the work outputs to employees and a higher degree of autonomy and self-regulation. Regarding working time, Voss-Dahm (2005: 136) points out that self-organization of work like trust-based working hours can mean a "self-organized extension of working time." In Pongratz and Voß's (2003) *Arbeitskraftunternehmer* – "entreployee" model or entrepreneur of his/her own labor power, one of their three characterizing dimensions is directly related with the self-organization of work–life time or what they call *self-rationalization*. This refers to the self-determination of day-to-day activities and of long term plans willingly accepting the primacy of the company as a basic part of life. The other two dimensions of the *entreployee* are self-control or the independent planning and control of work by their own self-commercialization, meaning the production and commercialization of self-competencies in the labor market and in the enterprise. However, as *entreployees* represent an ideal type of worker occupied in knowledge based occupations, they are difficult to find accomplishing the three characteristics identified by the Pongratz and Voß (2003). Thus, though control over work is increasingly being delegated to employees frequently working in projects, particularly in international projects, new forms of work control are needed to coordinate work processes and synchronize disparate working times. Project management and quality assessment gain a crucial role in this situation. Indeed, Project managers are confronted with both the synchronization of plural individual and team temporalities for which they need information technologies. At the same time, such coordination tasks become more and more complex and are increasingly professional-ized, allowing an extension of the task scope beyond the boundaries of the enterprise and of geographical location.

The rapid development of information technologies has in addition increased productivity and facilitated monitoring and control of employees working in distant locations (DiMaggio 2001: 22). Labor becomes controllable and compa-rable across countries through programmed work flows on the Internet. Such a programming of work based upon previous processes of standardization allows the conversion of different forms of work into codes that are able to flow on the Internet. Aneesh (2006) explains how programming codes function as a basis for connection among persons working in disperse environments through data banks or computer screens, and how programming and coding are symptomatic for a new kind of power: *algocracy*.[1] Programming codes represent a key structure for organizing virtual work and are intrinsic to "the emerging transnational labor regime, which is ordered and integrated through different relations of power and governance" (Aneesh 2006: 5). Aneesh (2006) asserts that spatial, temporal and algocratic integration serve to organize work globally.

Such integration has been dramatically accelerated in recent decades and has developed hand in hand with the formation of global networks with flat-tened work hierarchies monitored through heterogeneous governance tools and oriented to the market with increasingly shorter innovation cycles. Due to rapid technological changes trust-based relational contracting oriented toward outcomes while involving risk-sharing as well as benefit-sharing among the parties and recognition of collaborators' expertise is favored over integration among firms, as Gibbons (2001: 198) points out. Such trust-based relational contracting needs time to establish a trust relation among the parties and involves risks related to the outcomes that are often external to the contractors. Thus, it is very difficult to foresee how these relations will develop among dif-ferent nationally based firms embedded in differing institutional backgrounds (for example in the case of the New Eastern European Member States) and transformation rhythms. In addition, temporal disparities constitute zones of uncertainty (Crozier and Friedberg 1977) that global IT consulting enterprises attempt to define and dominate. Governance is practiced through multiply located quality standards, routines meaningful in interaction and resources, particularly time resources. Expertise related risks, those regarding cultural, language and communication differences among disperse teams, knowledge control and transfer issues, management of different time zones or human capital aspects emerge in everyday practices in international work environ-ments. To recover such a loss and to mitigate such risks, companies use various mechanisms such as global tools like ITIL and quality management systems on the basis of global recognized standards such as ISO. Systematiza-tion of processes and making knowledge explicit through mechanisms such as documentation are needed to implement such tools in day to day practices. Thus, expertise, as the ability to act knowledgeably in a determined context (Oshri *et al.* 2007: 54; Gasson 2005: 2) on the basis of contextual practice and knowledge, experience and qualification can be made explicit through formalized practices such as documentation.

For documenting individuals use concepts that they share in the group and combine with genres as shared conventions practices. At the organizational level such conventions crystallize into quality standards that serve as rationale for the practice and legitimize particular forms of work. Moreover, global management tools serve to coordinate disperse expertise in distributed work environments. Both quality standards and global management tools capture organization practices and conventions and serve as socialization basis for newcomers in the organization, so that continuous training on such tools are very important to support knowledge transfer. At the same time, depending on the grade of employees' engagement on the development of both quality standards and global management tools, professional autonomy and discretion will be considered as supported or threatened by employees (Ruiz Ben 2008). For employees in international workplace environments firm loyalty disappears more and more since professional itineraries are increasingly determined through projects prerogatives and learned competences in the long run.

Summarizing, social time at the workplace links different levels of social relations: those regarding global enterprises relations, national and regional institutional settings embedding group relations and individual day-to-day activities and trajectories. Information technologies function as a synchronization medium between different time and social levels in international environments. In the next section I attempt to build an analytical model for the analysis of international workplace temporalities on the basis of Lewis and Weigert's (1981) model and integrating some concepts of Orlikowski's (1992) structurational model of technology.

Social time in international working settings: the role of information technologies

Lewis and Weigert (1981) propose a typology in which they distinguish several levels of social time. Cyclic time takes place at the social-cultural and organizational levels including daily, weekly and yearly cycles or repetitions influencing social interaction. Interaction time refers to the embeddedness of social acts within larger social acts; this means those happening at the macro level of society. And self time is the time that the individual experiences. Lewis and Weigert (1981) argue that these three levels of social time are embedded, stratified, and synchronized. First, embeddedness, refers to the links of different structures of time within one another, with "microstructures" of time constrained by "macrostructures" of time. Embeddedness integrates varying social times while involving temporal stratification and synchronization. In the words of Lewis and Weigert:

> Embeddedness recognizes that human life and the social actions which constitutes it are a complex overlap of actions and meanings at various stages of

enactment... Temporal embeddedness works as a mechanism making the experience of self-continuity, a permanent identity across differing situations, plausible. Temporal embeddedness is a plausibility structure for the experience of the unity and continuity of an increasingly complex modern self.

(Lewis and Weigert 1981: 450)

Second, stratification of time systems is considered a reflection and outcome of different relations of power. The three levels of social time are stratified with cyclic time as precedent over interaction and further over personal time.

Lewis and Weigert (1981: 451) point out that stratification of time is a mechanism that makes the experience of self-control and social-control plausible a single reality. Thus, for example, individuals apparently act freely when they schedule and synchronize their work–life timetables following given deadlines in projects or institutional schedules of expected biographies, this means, those biographical trajectories that best fit to, for example, given career traces in particular contexts.

Regarding synchronization, Lewis and Weigert (1981: 451) explain that "[synchronization] is a derivative of temporal embeddedness and stratification and works as a mechanism for making the rationality of human action and planning plausible." Synchronization is linked to the ordering of actions and expectations regarding future goals, which are involved in rationality and which Lewis and Weigert (1981: 451) understand as a "public reality by which a number of individuals make the same sense of the future."

At this point I suggest that a same sense of the future is framed in different national settings in which biographical time phases are institutionalized. Such institutionalized time limits at the national level I call National Time Regimes. National Time Regimes refer to definitions of time limits for qualifications, continuous learning, entrance into the labor market and to working time regulations in a particular national setting, but also to established time limits for caring provisions. In situating National Time Regimes in the model of Lewis and Weigert (1981), I suggest that they function as legitimate basis for time stratification and influence the three time dimensions of the model. National Time Regimes are linked to the gendered patterns of expertise and professionalism definition, since they differently structure time orientations of men and women in ICT organizations and networks, and serve as different orientation for both men and women.[2]

Table 8.1 Typology

Time dimension	Social level	Features
Cyclic Time	Socio-cultural and organizational	Embeddedness
Interaction	Interaction	Synchronization
Self-Time	Individual	Stratification

Source: Dimensions of time in Lewis and Weigert (1981).

National Time Regimes are also closely related to commercial pressures to reduce "time to market" and involve disparate forms of regulating time norms and resources at various levels of the ICT production. National Time Regimes thus represent crucial structuring principles in Giddens' (1984: 6) sense. In international working settings, organizations must integrate timing of projects, of network relations in different nations and also of allocations of employees. Information technologies serve as a medium for integrating different National Time Regimes and institutionalized time norms and resources at the organization level. Using Lewis and Weigert's (1981) model, information technologies are crucial for synchronization of social time while at the same time they function as an embeddedness basis. As Orlikowski (1992: 411) points out, technologies are the product of human action and mediate workers' activities. They also influences institutional properties of an organization, while at the same time institutional properties influence humans in their interaction with technologies: "when acting on technology [whether designing, appropriating, modifying, or even resisting it], human agents are influenced by the institutional properties of their settings. They draw on existing stocks of knowledge, resources and norms to perform their work." Thus, whereas information technologies are used for synchronizing social time, they influence time structures of signification in different cultural locations and with it they transform the embeddedness of varying social times.

Given the *interpretive flexibility* of technology explained by Orlikowski (1991: 408) as the degree to which users of technology are engaged in its constitution, institutional properties affect workers in their interaction with information technologies. This means that the distribution and signification of time in the organization and in different cultural settings will affect how workers use information technologies. Thus, different concepts and meanings of time in different organization locations and those inscribed in information technologies as means for synchronizing distant organization locations influence each other and contribute to global embeddedness of different time dimensions (cyclic time, interaction time and self time). Documenting and storing project information with information technologies creates a history of the organizations as a common identity that creates expectations in the organization and represents a part of the cyclic time of the organizations. Information technologies makes such history available for workers in international working environments, so that their self time and interaction time are also integrated in such history records.

However, although information technologies enable synchronization of timings in distant working settings and the creation of common history records within organizations, National Time Regimes still influence biographical trajectories. Bryce and Singh (2001) assert for instance that from an evolutionary perspective of the analysis of organizational forms institutional disparities among nations make cross-nation convergences difficult. Thus, such national institutional disparities should be also taken into account in examining social time in international working environments.

Improving the understanding of social time in international work environments

In this section I have attempted to build a theoretical basis for the analysis of social time in international IT working environments. I suggest distinguishing between cyclic time of nations and organizations, interaction time in groups and self time of individuals following the model of Lewis and Weigert (1981). Information technologies serve as a basis for synchronizing different such social time levels and contribute to their embeddedness in international environments.

Regarding cyclic time, although information technologies allows for a global acceleration of working processes, for productivity growth and new forms of governance and domination (Aneesh 2006) through the flow of work in the Internet, many institutions related to the timing of work, employment, education, caring and professional trajectories still remain tied to national state contexts. Qualification paths still differ very much among nations and even among regional settings. In addition, the work habits, including forms of timing work experienced during education phases for example at the university, differ very much among countries. Also the links between temporalities at work and "private" places are very differently structured and experienced among national contexts (Rubery and Grimshaw 2003).

Thus, for organizations operating internationally and pressured by the acceleration of innovation cycles such heterogeneity of national related timings constitutes an obstacle to overcome in global competition arenas. In this situation, to adjust multiple environments to institutional infrastructures of law, international consulting and educational programs aided by information technologies have emerged challenging National Time Regimes. In organizations information technologies support the share of a common recorded history of projects and individual experiences that create expectations for future projects, working outputs, as well as work timings from employees in different locations. This common history enables comparison between different timings and outputs, and contributes to rationalization of international work. In addition, information technologies influence time structures of signification in different cultural locations, and with it they transform the embeddedness of varying social times.

At the interaction level, due to the increasing use of contingent employees, particularly in low wage countries because of the substitution of fixed jobs in organizations through projects and the cost-saving imperatives, plural and divergent temporalities often come into conflict retarding work flows and creating unexpected costs (Ruiz Ben *et al.* 2008). New governance tools such as Six Sigma and quality management systems integrated in IT organization infrastructures serve as a normative share basis which employees make meaningful in their day-to-day interactions with project members.

At the self time level, following Lewis and Weigert's (1981) model, employees working at a distance are confronted with disparities between time regimes operating at local and national levels and the timing demands of multinational firms. Timing demands of multinational firms refers to the increasing responsibility of employees for timing work–life activities in the short run (projects deadlines) and in the long run (professional itineraries through projects). Information technologies allow a transgression of workplace borders, blurring work–life boundaries, enabling a prevalence of work time above other life time contexts. This corresponds to Adams' (1995) views on the subordination of all other aspects of life to work, the producing and structuring of out-of-work time. Moreover, the individual level of the employees "flexibility and self-responsibility credo" corresponds to the *self-control and self-rationalization* dimensions of what Pongratz and Voß (2003; 2004) describe as the "entreployer" (*Arbeitskraftunternehmer*), who is entrepreneur of her/his own labor power. Employees must be responsible for their own planning of work, which means that they themselves have to control their work timing, but also for the "stratification" and "synchronization" of time spheres in the Lewis and Weigart (1981) sense: they themselves determine the organization of their daily plans and their long-term plans, willingly accepting the prevalence of work time prerogatives. Summing up, I suggest that information technologies permit the synchronization of "distant times" in different national settings and contribute to the embeddedness of different levels of social time. Following Orlikowski's (1992) model, I argue that institutional properties also affect information technologies, so that different time concepts as resources and also as institutional properties in different contexts influence how information technologies are used, appropriated and developed.

Notes

1 The term "algocracy" has recently been introduced by Aneesh (2007) in his book *Virtual Migration* to refer to the governance of dispersed code and capital in "virtual" work through the "rule of algorithm." Aneesh focuses on the programming code used in transnational projects to define such a "rule of code," which organizes transnational labor through an optimal algorithm of code and capital, space and time (2007: 5). Algocracy is thus not only "a new kind of power," but also a distinguishing marker of the current era of globalization.
2 It is important to emphasize here also the interrelation of gender with other social categories such as age or qualification.

References

Adam, B. (1990), *Time and Social Theory*, Cambridge: Polity Press.
—— (2003), "Reflexive Modernization Temporalized," *Theory, Culture and Society*, 20(2): 59–80.
Aneesh, A. (2006), *Virtual Migration: The Programming of Globalization*, Durham and London: Duke University Press.
Barley, S.R. (1986), "Technology as an Occasion for Structuring: Evidence from Observations on CT Scanners and the Social Order of Radiology Departments," *Administrative Science Quarterly*, 31: 78–108.
Bergmann, W. (1983), "Das problem der Zeit in der Soziologie. Ein Literaturüberblick zum Stand der 'zeitsoziologischen' Theorie und Forschung," *Kölner Zeitschrift für Soziologie und Sozialpsychologie*, 35: 462–504.
Bryce, D.J. and Singh, J.V. (2001), "The Future of the Firm from an Evolutionary Per-

spective," in P. DiMaggio (ed.) *The Twenty-first-century Firm: Changing Economic Organization in International Perspective*, Princeton, NJ: Princeton University Press: 161–186.

Carmel, E. and Beulen, E. (2005), "Managing the Offshore Transition," in E. Carmel (ed.) *Offshore Information Technology: Sourcing and Outsourcing to a Global Workforce*, Cambridge, UK: Cambridge University Press: 130–148.

Castells, M. (1996), The Rise of the Network Society, Oxford: Blackwell.

Cook, S.D.N. and J.S. Brown (1999), "Bridging Epistemologies: The Generative Dance Between Organizational Knowledge and Organizational Knowing," *Organization Science*, 10: 381–400.

Crozier, M. and E. Friedberg (1977), L'acteur et le systéme, Paris: Ed. du Seuil.

DiMaggio, P. (ed.) (2001), The Twenty-first-century Firm: Changing Economic Organization in International Perspective, Princeton, NJ: Princeton University Press.

Durkheim, E. (1915), *The Elementary Forms of the Religious Life: A Study in Religious Sociology,* New York: Macmillan.

Elias, N. (1988), *Über die Zeit.* Frankfurt: Suhrkamp.

Gasson, S. (2005), "The Dynamics of Sensemaking, Knowledge and Expertise in Collaborative Boundaryspanning Design," *Journal of Computer-Mediated Communication*, 10(4): 1–23.

Gibbons, R. (2001), "Trust in Social Structures: Hobbes Meets Repeated Games," in Karen S. Cook (ed.) *Trust in Society*, New York: Russell Sage.

Giddens, A. (1984), *The Constitution of Society*, Berkeley: University of California Press.

—— (1987), "Time and Social Organisation," in A. Giddens, *Social Theory and Modern Sociology*, Cambridge: Polity Press: 140–166.

—— (1995), *Die Konsequenzen der Moderne*, Frankfurt a.M.: Suhrkamp.

Gottschall, K. and Voß, G.G. (eds.) (2003), *Entgrenzung von Arbeit und Leben: Zum Wandel der Beziehung von Erwerbstätigkeit und Privatsphäre im Alltag*, Rainer Hampp, München/Mehring, S. 307–331.

Harvey, D. (1989), *The Condition of Postmodernity*, Oxford: Blackwell.

Hassard, J. (1996), "Images of Time in Work and Organization," in S.R. Clegg, C. Hardy and W.R. Nord (eds.), *Handbook of Organization Studies*, London: Sage: 581–598.

Kalkowski P. and Mickler O. (2002), "Zwischen Emergenz und Formalisierung: zur Projektifizierung von Organisation und Arbeit in der Informationswirtschaft," *SOFI Mitteilungen*, 30. Online, available at: http://webdoc.sub.gwdg.de/edoc/le/sofi/sofi0230.html, accessed January 10, 2003.

Lam, A. (1997), "Embedded Firms, Embedded Knowledge: Problems of Collaboration and Knowledge Transfer in Global Cooperative Ventures," *Organization Studies*, 18(6): 973–996.

Lewis, J.D. and Weigert, A. (1981), "The Structures and Meaning of Social Time," *Social Forces*, 60(2): 432–462.

Luckmann, T. (1968), "Zeit und Identität: Innere, soziale und historische Zeit," in F. Fürstenberg and I. Mörth (eds.) *Zeit als Strukturelement von Lebenswelt und Gesellschaft.*

McCall, L. (2001), *Complex Inequality: Gender, Class and Race in the New Economy*, New York: Routledge.

Maurer, A. (1992), *Alles eine Frage der Zeit? Die Zweckrationalisierung von Arbeitszeit und Lebenszeit*, Berlin: Sigma.

Nassehi, A. (1993), *Die Zeit der Gesellschaft: Auf dem Weg zu einer soziologischen Theorie der Zeit*, Opladen: Westdeutscher Verlag.

Newell, S., Bresnen, M., Edelman, L., Scarbrough, H. and Swan, J. (2006), "Sharing Knowledge across Projects: Limits to ICT-led Project Review Practices," *Management Learning*, 37: 167–185.

Nowotny, H. (1993), *Eigenzeit: Entstehung und Strukturierung eines Zeitgefühls*, Frankfurt: Suhrkamp.

Orlikowski, W.J. (1992), "The duality of Technology: Rethinking the Concept of Technology in Organizations," *Organization Science*, 3(3): 398–427.

Oshri, I., J. Kotlarsky and L. Willcocks (2007), "Managing Dispersed Expertise in IT Offshore Outsourcing: Lessons from Tata Consultancy Services," *MIS Quarterly Executive*, 6(2): 53–65.

Pekruhl, U. (2001), *Partizipatives Management. Konzepte und Kulturen*, München: Mering.

Pongratz, H.J. and G.G. Voß (2003), *Arbeitskraftunternehmer: Erwerbsorientierungen in entgrentzten Arbeitsformen*, Berlin: Sigma.

Robertson, R. (1995), "Glocalization: Time–Space and Homogeneity–Heterogeneity," in M. Featherstone, S. Lash and R. Robertson (Eds.) *Global Modernities*, London: Sage: 25–44.

Rubery, J. and D. Grinsham (2003), *The Organization of Employment*, London: Palgrave.

Ruiz Ben, E. (2005), *Professionalisierung der Informatik: Chance für die Beteiligung von Frauen?*, Wiesbaden: DUV.

—— (2007), "Defining Expertise in the Practice of Software Development while doing Gender," *Gender, Work and Organisation* (Special Issue Gender and Technology), 14(4): 305–311.

—— (2007), "Quality Standardization Patterns in ICT Offshore Projects," in M. Raisingiani (ed.) *Handbook of Research on Global Information Technology*, London: IGI Global: 312–328.

—— (2008), "Quality Standardization Patterns in ICT Offshore Projects," in Mahesh S. Raisinghani (ed.) *Handbook of Research on Global Information Technology Management in the Digital Economy*, Texas: Texas Woman's University.

Ruiz Ben, E. and M. Wieandt (2006), "Growing East: Nearshoring und die neuen ICT-Arbeitsmärkte in Europa," *FIfF-Ko. 23. Jg./3.* S: 36–42.

Ruiz Ben, E., Wieandt, M. and Maletzky, M. (2007), "Offshoring in the ICT Sector in Europe: Trends and Scenario Analysis," in Mahesh S. Raisinghani (ed.) *Handbook of Research on Global Information Technology Management in the Digital Economy*, London: IGI Global: 328–356.

Sharpe, R. (2001), "Globalization: The next tactic in the Fifty-year Struggle of Labor and Capital in Software Production," in Rick Baldoz, Charles Koeber and Philip Kraft (eds.) *The critical Study of Work: Labor, Technology and Global Production*, Philadelphia: Temple University Press.

Urry, J. (2000), *Sociology Beyond Societies*, London: Palgrave.

Voss-Dahm, D. (2005), "Verdrängen Minijobs 'normale' Beschäftigung? Warum die Neuregelung der geringfügigen Beschäftigung erfolgreich und zugleich problematisch ist: das Beispiel des Einzelhandels," *Institut Arbeit und Technik: Jahrbuch 2005*. Gelsenkirchen: 232–246.

Zerubavel, E. (1981), *Hidden Rhythms: Schedules and Calendars in Social Life*, Berkeley: University of California Press.

Part III

Gender, poverty transmission and ageing

9 The rise of the adult worker model

Balancing work and family life in Europe

Janneke Plantenga

1 Introduction

Throughout Europe, employment rates are steadily increasing, to a large extent because of the changing labor market behavior of women. As a result of the strong increase in female employment, the gender gap in employment rates has narrowed to 14.2 percentage points in 2007, compared to a gap of almost 18 percent in 2000. This development, in which especially the labor market behavior of women has changed rather dramatically, has been referred to by Jane Lewis as the rise of "the adult worker model" (Lewis 2001). The male breadwinner model, with the gendered division of paid and unpaid work, no longer describes the behavior of a significant proportion of families. Rather, the adult worker model, in which it is assumed that both men and women are active at the labor market, serves as a normative framework, inspiring both the labor market behavior of individual men and women as well as the policy measures at national and international level.

The concept of the adult worker model is especially strong at the level of the European Union, both for social and economic reasons. Within the European Employment Strategy, growing labor force participation is favored as a means to promote gender equality and social inclusion, as well as to increase economic competitiveness and to broaden the tax base of the European welfare states. It is exactly for these reasons that the Lisbon council of 2000 has set targets for the overall employment rate of 70 percent and a female employment rate of 60 percent by 2010. Raising the female participation rate is even more acute given the ageing of Europe's population. The potential for growth, and the sustainability of pensions and benefits, necessitate a higher employment rate for both older workers and women. Men and women have to become "citizen workers."

In terms of gender equality, these developments and the changing policy discourse might be rated rather positively. After all we have long argued in favor of women's economic and financial independence. Paid work generates access to wages, social security, power, independence and a sense of significance. At the same time, the economic imperative to increase female labor employment has resulted in a rather instrumental vision of gender equality. Gender equality is translated into higher female participation rates which are required for the health of the economies of EU member states and the EU social model. Critical in this line of thinking is that the gendered division of paid and unpaid work is not taken into account; women still perform most of the unpaid care work, as a result of which their position at the labor market is fundamentally different from men. In the ideal adult worker model, the individual is no longer bothered by care responsibilities. Care is being sourced out, reorganized and commodified, for example by increasing formal childcare facilities and facilities for the old and disabled. In real life, though, the opportunities for an outsourcing strategy may be limited, by services not being available or too expensive. As a result the integration of women into the labor market may not further gender equality because women are forced into part-time, flexible or marginal jobs.

In addition, there are real limits to the pursuit of a full adult worker model based on the commodification of care. Care, as Lewis and Giullari (2005) emphasize, is more than just a task. It involves emotional labor and relationship. It is both active and passive, emotional and relational, involving physical and non-physical presence. By implication, the organizational and personal dimension of care work in the family is difficult to substitute. This means that an affordable, accessible and high quality service infrastructure is not enough. It is also necessary to be able to provide time to care. From a social policy point of view, this requires investments in leave facilities and/or in rights to reduce working time for parents. At the same time, it has to be noted that leave facilities may lower the participation rate and/or may deepen the gender inequality because women will take up most of the leave. This raises the question of the optimal design of the care infrastructure, taking into account the importance of both paid and unpaid work.

In this chapter, I will firstly analyze the rise of the adult working model in the EU member states. An important conclusion, perhaps not surprisingly, is that the European Union still exhibits a highly diverse picture and that although the male breadwinner model has eroded, the social reality is still far from a "family comprised of self-sufficient autonomous individuals." Second, I will illustrate the changing care infrastructure in the different EU member states, focusing especially on childcare services and leave facilities. It appears that several countries are in a process of making their care infrastructure more compatible with the demand of the adult worker model, while at the same time being confronted with the different logic of care policy. Finally, I will try to assess the current state of affairs and try to answer the question as to which policy domains need to be elaborated upon in order to further a gender equal adult worker model.

2 Employment rates

Figure 9.1 gives an overview of the total employment rate of all the EU member states and the three EEA countries (Iceland, Liechtenstein and Norway) in 2007. The difference between the highest and lowest ranking country is almost 30 percentage points, with Iceland having a total employment rate of 85.1 percent and

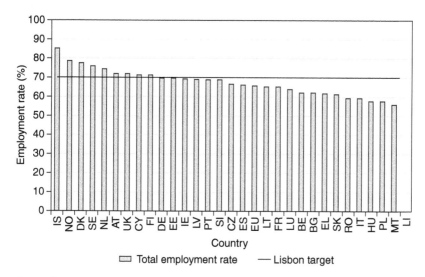

Figure 9.1 Total employment rate 2007 (source: Indicators for monitoring the Employment Guidelines 2008 Compendium (14/03/2008); for Iceland and Norway:
Eurostat Employment Statistics 2006).

Note
EU = EU27.

Malta an employment rate of 55.7 percent (data for Liechtenstein missing). From
the graph it also appears that among the EU member states Denmark, the Netherlands, Sweden, Austria, the United Kingdom, Cyprus and Finland have already
met the Lisbon target for total employment, with Germany, Estonia and Ireland
close behind. At the lower end of the ranking are Hungary, Poland and Malta.

Figure 9.2 gives the employment rate for women, indicating on the one hand
the decline of the breadwinner model in quite a few European member states
while on the other hand illustrating the rather diverse position of women in the
European labor markets. Again, the highest-ranking country is Iceland, with a
female employment rate of almost 81 percent, whereas in Malta the female
employment rate is just below 37 percent (data for Liechtenstein missing).
Figure 9.2 also indicates that 15 EU member states (and Iceland and Norway)
have already met or exceeded the Lisbon target of 60 percent female employment. At the other end of the ranking it appears that Greece, Italy and Malta are
still far from the Lisbon target, as female employment rates are under 50
percent.

The difference between total and female employment rates indicate that
throughout Europe there is still a large gap between the employment rates of
men and women, with women falling significantly behind. Figure 9.3 ranks all
the countries in this respect. The highest employment gender gaps are found in
the Southern part of Europe: Malta, Greece, Italy, Spain and Cyprus. Ireland and
Luxembourg also score rather unfavorably in this respect. Relatively small

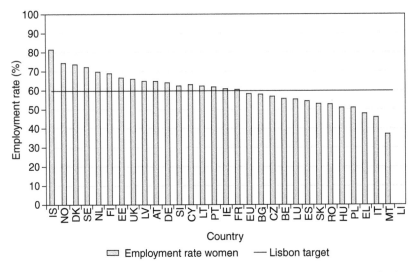

Figure 9.2 Employment rate of women 2007 (source: Indicators for monitoring the
        Employment Guidelines 2008 Compendium (14/03/2008); for Iceland and
        Norway: Eurostat Employment Statistics 2006).

Note
EU = EU27.

gender gaps (less than 10 percentage points) are found in the Scandinavian countries and the Baltic States. When interpreting these data, it has to be noted that
the Lisbon targets – and related to this the employment data – are based on a
headcount. Differences in working hours are not taken into account. As women
work part-time more often than men, the employment gender gap, as presented
in Figure 9.3, is in fact underestimated. When measured in full-time equivalents,
the gender gap calculated for all the member states of the European Union
(EU27) increases to 20.6 percentage points compared to 14.2 percentage points
when measured in headcount. The Dutch gender gap particularly increases from
12.6 percentage points when calculated in headcounts to 29.1 percentage points
when calculated in full-time equivalents.

An important reason for employment differences between men and women is
the different impact of parenthood. Whereas men with children tend to work
more than men without children, the opposite is true for women: women without
children have higher employment rates than women with children. The different
impact is illustrated in Figure 9.4, which compares the difference in employment
rates of men and women without the presence of any children and with the presence of a child aged 0–6 within the age group 20–49. Remarkably, the impact of
parenthood on men is rather similar in the member states and hovers around −10
percentage points (data for Sweden, Iceland, Liechtenstein and Norway missing).
For women, however, the impact differs considerably. The highest figures are
found in the Czech Republic, with women without a young child having a

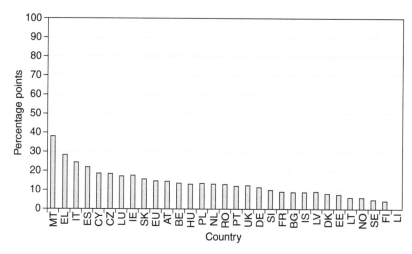

Figure 9.3 Employment gender gap 2007 (source: Indicators for monitoring the Employment Guidelines 2008 Compendium (14/03/2008); for Iceland and Norway: Eurostat Employment Statistics 2006).

Note
EU = EU27.

participation rate which exceeds 40.5 percentage points the participation rate of women with a young child, in Hungary (a difference of 33.6 percentage points) and in Slovakia (a difference of 32.8 percentage points). In Romania and Belgium, on the other hand, the difference is rather small (2.1 and 0.9 percentage points respectively). Portugal and Slovenia are the only countries where women are more likely to be employed after having children. The employment impact of parenthood on women is −3.9 percentage points in Portugal and −5.5 percentage points in Slovenia. Figure 9.4 also points out that the typical gendered division of labor of the male breadwinner model, in which men have the primary responsibility to earn and women to care, is still valid in most European member states. The Czech Republic, Hungary and Slovakia are the three countries where women are most affected by parenthood, but practically all countries still follow to some extent this general pattern.

Summarizing this part, it seems fair to state that there is still a large gap between the assumptions of the adult worker family and the rather diverse labor and care patterns in the social reality of the EU member states; men and women are not equal worker citizens yet. At the level of the European Union this (familiar) conclusion is translated into a continuous appeal to member states to promote female employment. Several documents underline the importance of further measures in this respect, emphasizing the importance of assisting in care responsibilities either by investing in services or by facilitating the combination of work and care. For example the Joint Employment Report 06/07 (the annual report published at the level of the European Union to

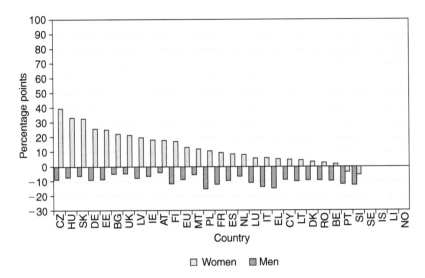

Figure 9.4 Employment impact of parenthood on men and women 2006 (source: Indicators for monitoring the Employment Guidelines 2008 Compendium (14/03/2008).

Note
EU = EU27.

monitor the European Employment Strategy) assesses the current state of affairs as follows:

> The employment rate for women has increased in almost all Member States. However, the potential contribution of women to raising the aggregate employment rate is still not fully exploited. Further policies to promote child and elderly care, and the reconciliation of work and family life would continue to improve the labor market position of women.
>
> (JER 2007: 10)

This brings us to the issue of the care infrastructure and the nature and scope of reconciliation policies. First we deal with childcare services; the section following will focus on leave facilities.

3 Childcare services

Personal services are extremely important in the lives of working parents. This applies in particular to childcare services, as care responsibilities constitute a major obstacle to (full) employment. The importance of affordable and accessible quality childcare provision has long been recognized by the European Council and the European Union. In March 1992, the Council of the EU passed a recommendation on childcare to the effect that member states "should take and/or progressively encourage initiatives to enable women and men to reconcile their occupational, family and upbringing responsibilities arising for the care of children" (Directive 92/241/EEC). At the 2002 Barcelona summit ten years later, the aims were formulated more explicitly and targets were set with regard to childcare. Confirming the goal of full employment, the European Council agreed that member states should remove disincentives to female labor force participation and strive, taking into account the demand for childcare facilities and in line with national patterns of provisions, to provide childcare by 2010 for at least 90 percent of children between three years old and the mandatory school age and for at least 33 percent of children under three years old.

Figure 9.5 summarizes the use of childcare services for children in the youngest age category, on the basis of the EU-SILC statistics for the year 2006.[1] These figures indicate children cared for in formal arrangements, as a proportion of all children of the same age group. Formal arrangements in this respect refer to education at pre-school or equivalent, childcare at center-based services outside school-hours, a collective crèche or another day-care centre including family day-care organized/controlled by a public or private structure. On the basis of this indicator, it appears that seven member states (Denmark, Netherlands, Sweden, Belgium, Spain, Portugal and United Kingdom) and Iceland and Norway have already met the Barcelona target with France and Luxembourg close behind.[2] At the lower end of the ranking we see Slovakia, Lithuania, Austria, the Czech Republic and Poland with a score of 5 percent or less (figures for Bulgaria, Romania and Liechtenstein are missing). A more detailed analysis would reveal that the countries are also highly diverse with regard to the number of hours that formal arrangements are used. In countries like Denmark, Iceland, Portugal, Slovenia, Finland, Latvia, Greece, Hungary, Slovakia, Lithuania and

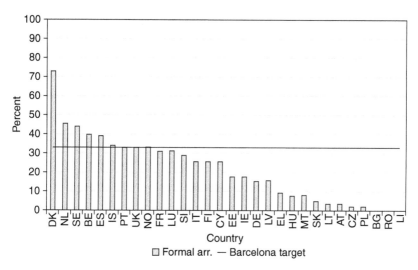

Figure 9.5 Use of formal childcare arrangements, 0–2 year olds (source: EU-SILC 2006 (provisional); data for DE and NO: EU-SILC 2005)

Poland, most formal childcare services are used for 30 hours or more per week. In other countries (the Netherlands, United Kingdom, Germany, Hungary, Austria and Czech Republic), part-time arrangements are much more common. In the United Kingdom, for example, employed mothers typically work part-time, which corresponds to a high part-time use of childcare services (Plantenga and Remery 2008).

Figure 9.6 provides data on the use of formal childcare services for the age category three years old to the mandatory school age. The Barcelona target states that the actual coverage rate should be at least 90 percent. The SILC-data indicate that nine EU member states meet the Barcelona target or score rather high: Belgium, Denmark, France, Ireland, Sweden, Spain, Italy, the Netherlands and the United Kingdom. Other countries score at least 50 percent; the exception being Poland with a score of only 28 percent. Compared to the scores for Figure 9.5 it seems that the use of formal care arrangements increases with the increasing age of children. Of course this is, to a large extent, due to the inclusion of pre-school arrangements under the heading of formal arrangements and the high coverage rate of pre-school arrangements for children in the age category three years old to the mandatory school age. It has to be taken into account, though, that in most countries pre-school is only part-time, as a result of which working parents still need additional childcare facilities which may be much less available.

Recent developments

Information on the use of childcare facilities is helpful for assessing the relative importance of this particular reconciliation policy; it does not, however, answer

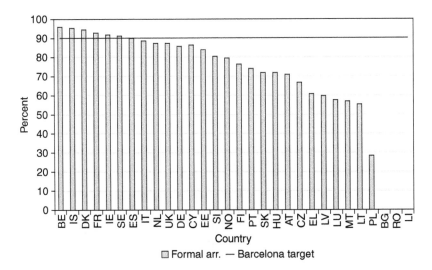

Figure 9.6 Use of formal childcare arrangements, three years – the mandatory school age (source: EU-SILC 2006 (Provisional); data for DE and NO: EU-SILC 2005).

the question whether demand is fully met. The actual demand for childcare is influenced by the participation rate of parents (mothers), levels of unemployment, the length of parental leave, the opening hours of school and the availability of alternatives such as grandparents and/or other (informal) arrangements. In Finland, for example, the coverage rate of formal arrangements for the youngest age category is, according to Figure 9.5, 26 percent, which is well below the Barcelona target of 33 percent. Yet childcare facilities are not in short supply. In fact, since 1990 Finnish children under three years old are guaranteed a municipal childcare place, irrespective of the labor market status of the parents. In 1996 this right was expanded to cover all children under school age. This entitlement complements the home care allowance system, which enables the parent to stay at home to care for his/her child with full job-security until the child is three years old. Partly due to the popularity of the home care alternative, the supply of public day-care services has met the demand since the turn of the 1990s (Plantenga and Remery 2005: 35)

If we combine the information of Figure 9.5 and Figure 9.6 with information on the national care and school system we should acknowledge that childcare is framed as a social right in Finland, Denmark and Sweden. Also in a few other countries, notably Norway, Belgium, France and Slovenia, policies seem to be targeted at full coverage. Slovenia for example, has a rather high coverage rate of childcare services. Unlike many other countries in Eastern and central Europe that underwent economic and political transition at the end of the last century, the availability of public care services did not diminish after the transition. Most women choose to stay at home for one year (taking up the whole length of their maternity/parental leave) and then to return to full time work. Yet another example is France. For some time the childcare system has offered almost total coverage for children aged 2–3 for working parents as well as quite long openings hours that are almost compatible with full time employment.

In a number of other countries, childcare services are still in short supply, yet there is a movement toward a fuller coverage of childcare services. This concerns in particular the United Kingdom, the Netherlands, and Germany. In the Netherlands, for example, childcare services have increased especially since the mid 1990s. In 2005 the financial structure has become demand driven which, in principle, should be compatible with a full coverage (Plantenga and Remery 2008). The level of provision is also increasing in Luxembourg, Portugal, Italy, Spain, Austria and Greece although at a somewhat more moderate pace and/or from a relatively low starting point. In Italy, for example, the scarcity of formal childcare for young children is particularly due to cultural factors that still persist in the country, as well as to the structure of the Italian care regime, which relies more on financial transfers than on the supply of services in kind (Ferrara 1996; Bettio *et al.* 2006). However, a new, more positive attitude toward formal childcare for young children is spreading, translating into an increasing supply of day-care centers, albeit at a slow pace.

In other countries, though, the developments are still extremely limited – perhaps hardly existing. Barriers to investing in childcare services seem to be financial as well as ideological. Perhaps one of the most complicated challenges refers to the fact that the policy objectives on participation, fertility and social integration are not always easily compatible. Child development concerns, for example, or the ambition to increase the fertility rate may either translate into a policy targeted at increasing childcare services, or into a policy favoring extended leave facilities and/or increasing the provision of childcare allowances. Especially in continental Europe leave facilities and financial support have been favored over childcare services. Long parental leave facilities, however, or a favorable financial incentive structure may not promote labor supply and may result in large differences in male and female working time patterns. This brings us to the provision of leave facilities.

4 Leave facilities

Besides childcare, leave facilities are an important element of reconciliation policy. Especially when children are young, time related provisions such as leave entitlements, career breaks and the reductions of working time are extremely important for combining work and private life.

At the level of the European Union, national policy in the field of leave arrangements has been underpinned since June 1996 by a directive of the European Council which obliges member states to introduce legislation on parental leave that will enable parents to care full-time for their child over a period of three months. In principle this refers to an individual, non-transferable entitlement. This directive ensures that a certain minimum standard is guaranteed within the member states. Over and above this, however, there is a broad range of national regulations. The duration of parental leave, for example, differs substantially, ranging from three months in some countries to the period until the child's third birthday in others. Also the level of payment varies widely, with some countries providing unpaid leave and others compensating leave takers more or less for their loss of earnings. In addition to differences in length and level of payment, parental leave can be organized along family or individual lines. If the former is used as the basis, parents are in a position to decide who will make use of the parental leave allocated to the family. If both parents have an individual, non-transferable entitlement to parental leave, they can both claim a period of leave. If one parent does not take advantage of this entitlement the right expires. Especially in the ten new member states, the parental leave is often framed as a family right (see for a detailed overview of leave entitlements Plantenga and Remery 2005; Fagan and Hebson 2006).

The differentiated nature of leave facilities makes a neat comparison of the 27 member states rather complicated as the impact and importance of the leave facilities in the national context cannot be assessed by simply ranking the countries by the length of the consecutive weeks of leave. Country differences may be overestimated, as formal regulations say little about the actual impact. This calls for information on the take up rate; that is the actual use of leave facilities. Ideally, information on take up rates should be combined with information on the length of leave, in order to make a proper comparison between countries and/ or between men and women (Bruning and Plantenga 1999). Unfortunately, detailed figures in this respect are not available; only the Nordic countries provide regular consistent statistical accounts of the use of leave (Rostgaard 2005; Deven and Moss 2005).

We do know, however, that the use of parental leave depends in particular on whether the leave is unpaid or paid and, if paid, at what level (Deven and Moss 2005). It is therefore possible to compute a kind of "effective leave indicator" by weighting the duration of the leave by the level of payment. Such an indicator is provided by the EU within the context of the European Employment Strategy. This index gives the number of months of maternity/paternity and parental leave with benefits replacing at least two-thirds of salary. So, only leave that is relatively well paid is taken into account. The outcomes of this exercise are presented in Figure 9.7. On the basis of this indicator, Sweden has the highest score – providing parents with 16 months of well paid leave. Other scores seem to converge around 10–12 months and four months. The United Kingdom has the absolute minimum with 1.5 months, as a result of the fact that only the first six weeks of maternity leave are paid by 90 percent of the former income.

Recent developments

Although leave facilities are an important means of reconciling work and family, the outcomes in terms of labor force participation may be rather uneven or even negative, especially if the leave is long. In addition, the gender effects may be rather negative as leave is mostly taken up by women. Given the emphasis on

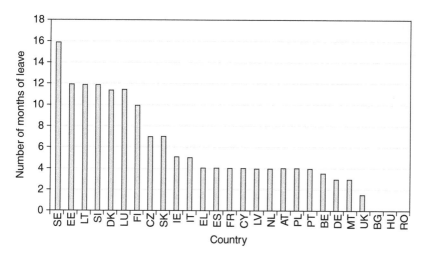

Figure 9.7 Month of (paid) maternity, paternity and parental leave, 2005 (source: EU compendium update 143/05/2008).

Note
Salary replacement for SK 55%.

increasing the employment rate, especially with regard to women, several countries have changed the actual design of the schemes, taking into account the need to increase the activity rate and/or trying to reach a more equal sharing between men and women.

The negative employment impact of long leave systems may be overcome by shortening the statutory right. An important recent example in this respect is provided by Germany. After a long and controversial political debate a new parental allowance act came into force in January 2007. Parents still have the right to parental leave for a maximum of three years, but the parental allowance during leave has changed. The parental allowance now is 67 percent of the previous gross earnings (with a minimum and maximum) for the parent on leave and is paid for 12 months; if the other partner takes the leave as well, two additional months are conceded. It is assumed that due to the new regulation especially mothers will return earlier to gainful employment (Leitner *et al.* 2008).

Another remedy to counter the negative employment effects is to create more opportunities for leave takers to participate at the labor market; examples of this strategy are provided by Czech Republic, Hungary and Slovakia. In the Czech Republic, for example, since 2004 parents on parental leave have been allowed to engage in paid employment without any limitations on the amount of earnings, while at the same time receiving parental allowance. From February 2006 it is also possible for a parent that is receiving parental allowance to use public childcare services for up to four hours a day for a child older than three years. This may be helpful for mothers trying to return to the labor market, as in the fourth year of parental leave they lose the right to return to their original employment (Plantenga and Remery 2008).

Yet another way to overcome the negative effects of long parental leave schemes is to foster equal sharing between men and women – although such a strategy may be rather neutral in terms of participation effects. Equal sharing proves to be rather difficult, however; in practically all countries there are major differences in the take up between women and men. Even in countries in which the take up of leave among fathers is relatively favorable, the duration of the leave taken by men is most of the time shorter, as a result of which the labor market (and care) impact of the take up is less pronounced. One of the most positive examples comes from Sweden. Here the proportion of all parental allowance days used by fathers increased from 7 percent in 1990 to 19 percent in 2004 (Björnberg and Dahlgren 2008: 52).

Summarizing this section: leave facilities are important to reconciling work and private life. Yet, the employment effects must not be overestimated. Especially lengthy periods of leave may reduce (female) participation and damage future career paths and earnings. In quite a number of European welfare states, these effects have inspired a redesign of parental leave systems making it more compatible with paid work and/or trying to facilitate equal sharing.

5 Toward a gender equal adult worker model?

So far we have covered changing employment rates and the developments in the different national care systems – focusing especially on the care system with regard to young children. The overview indicated a large gap between the implicit assumptions of the adult worker model and the actual reality of most European member states. Only a few countries, with the Nordic countries as the most well-known examples, have developed a system of leave and childcare arrangements that seem to be based on the assumption that fathers and mothers will be fully engaged in the labor market. At the same time the overview illustrated that quite a number of countries are trying to redesign the care infrastructure, making it more compatible with the demands of the adult worker model: the number of childcare places is increasing and/or the leave system is being reorganized in order to limit the negative labor market effects.

The problems in this respect are rather large, however. In fact, one of the basic problems of the adult working model seems to be that care policy can only to a certain extent be redesigned as "employment led." Whereas fiscal policy and social security policy becomes more and more targeted toward increasing the employment rate, care policies are motivated by different issues, like the fertility rate, family values or child well-being. Although policies in these areas may not by definition contradict labor market considerations, it seems likely that some tradeoffs exist between facilitating care and stimulating labor supply. This raises the question of the optimal design of the care infrastructure: how to reconcile the interest of the family, the market and the state in a way that is both efficient and just from a social, demographic and economic perspective.

The optimal design of the care infrastructure becomes even more complex if the issue of parental choice is added. Parents may differ in their preferences with regard to work and family outcomes and most public policies tend to enhance parental choice. Several countries (for example France, Finland, and Norway) have set up alternative trajectories: after a period of leave parents have the choice between childcare provisions or a home care allowance which may be conditional on not using childcare facilities and may typically last for several years. Although this model ranks high from the perspective of parental choice, one of the drawbacks is that differences between families and/or men and women in working and caring patterns increase, because especially mothers with low labor market chances will opt for the home care allowance. Indeed, there may not be much choice in a context in which the labor market is strongly segregated by sex and where parental obligations have remained gendered.

Yet, despite all the difficulties, there appears to be a certain consensus on the importance of available and affordable childcare services within the context of a gender equal adult worker model. Care services seem to escape the trade-offs between facilitating care and stimulating labor supply as there is strong evidence that the availability of good quality childcare services has a positive impact on the female participation rates, while at the same time increasing fertility rates, by making a child less costly in terms of income and career opportunities. In fact, the increasing participation rate has been a decisive factor in formulating the Barcelona childcare targets as part of the European Employment Strategy. In addition, good-quality childcare services may serve a child-development purpose, providing the child with a rich, safe and stimulating environment. As such childcare services may offer an important contribution to child development and socio-economic integration. These arguments do not imply, however, that the childcare issue is beyond debate. Rather, the debate seems to be shifting toward the maximum number of hours per day, the age at which a child should start making use of childcare services and the price to be paid by parents. Even in countries where childcare (for older children) is accepted and used on a large scale, as in the Nordic countries, every now and then "good motherhood" and the well-being of children in childcare are topics of public discussion (Plantenga and Remery 2008). The outcome of these debates will to a large extent structure the work and care patterns of young families.

The optimal design of leave within the context of a gender equal adult worker model is also a matter of debate. From a narrow labor market perspective, the optimal length of leave seems to be around 4–6 months (Jaumotte 2003; OECD 2007). A longer leave period weakens career opportunities and makes the goal of gender equity harder to attain. Yet in terms of child development or in terms of overall fertility it may be important to extend this period, indicating a trade-off between stimulating employment and facilitating care. There is more unanimity with regard to the payment level: higher payment levels have a positive impact on the take up rate. There is also abundant evidence that the take up by men increases if parental leave is well paid and organized as an individual entitlement. In addition, it is extremely important to provide a continuum of support to families. The period of leave, therefore, should be attuned to the provision of childcare services (OECD 2007).

As an overall conclusion it seems fair to state that redesigning the care infrastructure will remain an important policy priority in the near future. Despite all the effort and improvements, high quality and affordable childcare facilities are still in short supply in quite a number of European member states. In addition, leave facilities are still not geared toward a situation in which both men and women fully engage in the labor market. The concept of the adult worker model therefore not only necessitates a restructuring of employment policy but also a restructuring of the care infrastructure, keeping in mind the policy goals with regard to participation, gender equity, fertility and social integration.

Notes

1 EU-SILC refers to the European Statistics on Income and Living conditions, which is supposed to become the new reference source for statistics on income and living conditions and common indicators for social inclusion.
2 For a correct interpretation of scores of Figure 9.5, it is important to note that national boundaries between formal and other arrangements may not completely comply with the EU-SILC data. For France, for example, child minders who are paid directly by parents (*assistantes maternelles*) are not included. However, in France, the great major-

ity of child minders must be registered and are therefore considered as a form of formal care in the national statistics. This is, in fact, the main form of childcare of very young children (Plantenga and Remery 2008).

References

Bettio, F., A. Simonazzi and P. Villa (2006), "Change in Care Regimes and Female Migration: The 'Care Drain' in the Mediterranean," *Journal of European Social Policy*, 16(3): 271–285.

Björnberg, U. and L. Dahlgren (2008), "Family Policy: The Case of Sweden," in I. Ostner and C. Schmitt (eds.) *Family Policies in the Context of Family Change: The Nordic Countries in Comparative Perspective*, Wiesbaden: VS – Verlag.

Bruning, G. and J. Plantenga (1999), "Parental Leave and Equal Opportunities: Experiences in Eight European Countries," *Journal of European Social Policy*, 9(3): 195–209.

Deven, F. and P. Moss (eds.) (2005), *Leave Policies and Research: A Review and Country Notes*, CBGS Working Papers 2005/3, Brussels: CBGS.

Fagan, C. and Hebson, G. (2006), *Making Work Pay Debates from a Gender Perspective: A Comparative Review of Some Recent Policy Reforms in Thirty European Countries*, Luxembourg: Office for Official Publications of the European Communities.

Ferrera, M. (1996), "The Southern Model of Welfare in Social Europe," *Journal of European Social Policy*, 6(1): 17–39.

Jaumotte, F. (2003), *Female Labour Force Participation: Past Trends and Main Determinants in OECD Countries*, Paris: OECD.

JER (2007), *Joint Employment Report 2006/2007*, Brussels: Council of the European Union.

Leitner, S., I. Ostner, C. Schmitt (2008), "Family Policies in Germany," in I. Ostner and C. Schmitt (eds.) *Family Policies in the Context of Family Change: The Nordic Countries in Comparative Perspective*, Wiesbaden: VS – Verlag.

Lewis, J. (2001), "The Decline of the Male Breadwinner Model: Implications for Work and Care," *Social Politics*, 152–169.

Lewis, J. and Giullari, S. (2005), "The Adult Worker Model Family, Gender Equality and Care: The Search for New Policy Principles and the Possibilities and Problems of a Capabilities Approach," *Economy and Society*, 34(1): 76–104.

OECD (2007), *Babies and Bosses. Reconciling Work and Family Life: A Synthesis of Findings for OECD Countries*, Paris: OECD.

Plantenga, J. and C. Remery (2005), *Reconciliation of Work and Private Life: A Comparative Review of Thirty European Countries*, Luxembourg: Office for Official Publications of the European Communities.

—— (2008), *The Provision of Childcare Services: A Comparative Review Of Thirty European Countries*, Luxembourg: Office for Official Publications of the European Communities (forthcoming).

Rostgaard, T. (2005), "Diversity and Parental Leave," in F. Deven and P. Moss (eds.) *Leave Policies and Research: A Cross-national Review*, CBGS Working Papers 2005/3, Brussels: CBGS: 29–39.

10 Redistribution, intergenerational inequality and poverty transmission

Germany and the United States compared

Veronika V. Eberharter[*]

1 Introduction

The reduction of income inequality and poverty counts among the general objectives of social policy in industrialized countries. Public transfers and redistributive taxes traditionally are framed as redistribution schemes and targeted to reducing income inequality and poverty, and improving the living standard of the population. Countries differ concerning macroeconomic indicators, institutional labor market settings, family role patterns, and the degree of social mobility, as well as to the extent the countries protect the citizens from income inequality and poverty. The instruments and transfer packages for achieving higher income equality and anti-poverty effects tell a great deal about the working of the underlying welfare regime.

According to the way the state influences the system of social stratification and affects the social citizenship rights the conservative-corporatist and the liberal welfare regimes are the most contrasting (Esping-Andersen 1990). Germany among other European countries is a representative of a conservative-corporatist welfare system, whereas the welfare regime in the United States is characterized as liberal. The German welfare system was developed on the basis of mutual aid associations, which are subsequently the basis for social protection. The structure of social services and social benefits are closely related to the people's position in the labor market. Social insurance, which covers the system costs of health, some social care and much income maintenance, is managed by a system of independent funds. The liberal welfare regime in the United States promotes the market, rather than the state in guaranteeing the welfare needs of the citizens and stresses the sense of individualism, laissez-faire, and a punitive view of poverty. The state reacts only in case of social failures and limits the help only to special groups. The transfers are modest and the rules for entitlement are very strict. The labor market policies offer less protection for workers and thus induce a more flexible labor market.

Cross-section empirical evidence show lower poverty rates in countries with high-level or carefully targeted public transfers (Canada, Northern Europe) or heavily insured countries (Sweden, Belgium, and Germany). In these countries disposable income inequality is less than market income inequality, suggesting that the tax and benefit system reduces overall inequality. In the United States, the social-insurance and direct (payroll and income) tax system is weak, and the social-assistance system makes only a small contribution to poverty reduction (Smeeding *et al.* 2001).

The analysis of the intergenerational effects of public transfers on individual behavior and economic outcomes is mostly based on US data and yields ambiguous results. On the one hand, the results point out that parental welfare use leads to an attenuation of labor market opportunities, reduces welfare participation costs, and encourages the welfare use of the children thus perpetuating intergenerational poverty cycles. Public transfers prevent persons from developing their resources or to take advantage of existing opportunities, and thus human capital such as education and work experience is not valued, and there is little motivation to pursue full-time employment (Gottschalk 1992; An *et al.* 1993; Bane and Ellwood 1994; Mayer 1997; Corak and Heisz 1999; Vartanian 1999; Pepper 2000; Vartanian and MacNamara 2000; Page 2004; Vartanian and MacNamara 2004; Corak 2006). On the other hand, public transfers and redistributive taxes are designed to narrow the intergenerational income gap, and result in an overall improvement of the living standard of the poor, so that the incomes of the children converge to the mean more quickly (Ellwood and Summers 1986; Corak 2006).

This chapter aims at producing a better understanding of the impact of different redistribution policy regimes on income inequality, poverty intensity, income mobility, and poverty persistence in an intergenerational context. Based on nationally representative data from the German Socio-Economic Panel (GSOEP) and the Panel Study of Income Dynamics (PSID) in the United States, the chapter compares the implications of redistribution policy measures on intergenerational income inequality and poverty, the extent and the determinants of income mobility and intergenerational poverty in Germany and the United States, two countries that differ concerning welfare policy regimes, labor market settings and family role models. The chapter deals with the following questions:

- To what extent do the social policy regimes in Germany and the United States change relative income positions within and between generations?
- What is the impact of the public transfers on overall income inequality and poverty?
- To what extent do redistribution policy and individual characteristics contribute to intergenerational income mobility?
- To what extent does redistribution policy reduce or perpetuate intergenerational poverty and what are the determinants of cross-generational poverty?

According to the cross-sectional results of the implications of redistribution policy measures we hypothesize that in Germany – known as a country with a strong redistribution policy and a high social safety net standard – public transfers and redistributive taxes reduce income inequality and poverty intensity to a higher extent than in the United States with its more liberal social policy concept. As a more liberal society we expect higher intergenerational income mobility and a stronger influence of family background variables on intergenerational income mobility in the United States than in Germany. On grounds of weaker social welfare safety nets we also expect stronger intergenerational poverty persistence in the United States than in Germany.

We analyze the equivalent family income before (pre-government) and after (post-government) taxes and subsidies of parent–child pairs in different time windows to address to non-linearities in the intergenerational income mobility setting (cf. Hyson 2003; Hertz 2004). The analysis of the intergenerational inequality and poverty intensity is based on commonly used inequality measures and poverty indexes presented in Foster *et al.* (1984). In the analysis of the intergenerational income mobility we employ linear and non-linear regression approaches on the permanent income variables of different cohorts in different time windows.

The chapter proceeds as follows: Section 2 describes the database; Section 3 characterizes the inequality and poverty measures, as well as specifies econometric approaches used; Section 4 presents the empirical results; and Section 5 concludes with a discussion of the implications of these findings and the directions for further research.

2 Database and sample organization

The empirical analysis is based on data from the German Socio-Economic Panel (GSOEP) and the US Panel Study of Income Dynamics (PSID), which were made available by the Cross-National-Equivalent-File (CNEF) project at the College of Human Ecology at Cornell University, Ithaca, NY. The PSID started in 1980 and contains a nationally representative unbalanced panel of about 40,000 individuals in the United States. From 1997 on, the PSID data are available bi-yearly. The GSOEP started in 1984 and contains a representative sample of about 29,000 German individuals that includes households in the former East Germany since 1990. Both the surveys track the socioeconomic variables of a given household, and each household member is asked detailed questions about age, gender, marital status, educational level, labor market participation, working hours, employment status, occupational position, income situation, as well as household size and composition.[1] The income variables are measured on an annual basis and refer to the prior calendar year. For the accompanying analysis we use the income variables referring to the wave of the interview (e.g. to the 1984 wave), but questioned in the following wave (e.g. in the 1985 wave).

We analyze the economic and social situation of children living in the parental household and as adults in their own households. The data do not provide a sufficiently long time horizon to observe the parents and the children at identical life cycle situations, but cover a sufficiently long period to allow us to observe the socioeconomic characteristics of the parental household and to link this data with the children's socioeconomic characteristics when becoming members of other family units. Thus, the data can be used to draw inferences about the effects of being exposed to redistribution policy measures in the parental household on the income situation of young adults. The data do not allow us to identify parent–child relations exactly. The accompanying analysis considers adults whose marital status is "married," or "living with partner" and who are living in households with persons with the marital status "child" as parent–child pairs.

The sample includes persons aged ten to 18 years, co-resident with their parents in 1980 (United States) or 1984 (Germany). We do not consider children older than 18 years to avoid the overrepresentation of children staying at home until a late age (Kolodinsky and Shirey 2000). The children are at least 24 years old when we analyze their income situation in the years 1999–2005 (Germany) or 1994–2003 (United States). This selection process leads to a sample of 1,430 individuals in Germany and of 2,569 individuals in the United States. Due to sample selection design we observe West German persons only.

We follow the standard conventions and assume that income is shared within families and thus household income is arguably a better measure of the economic and social status than individual income variables. To analyze the impact of redistribution on economic outcomes the study is based on equivalent pre- and post-government household income. The pre-government household income, that is the income before taxes and subsidies, includes labor earnings (wages, salaries, non-wage compensation, income from on the job training, self-employed income and bonuses), and the cash income from private sources (property, pensions, alimony and child support) of all household members. Post-government household income equals the pre-government household income plus household public transfers (social benefits: dwellings, child or family allowances, unemployment compensation, assistance, and other welfare benefits), plus household security pensions (age, disability, widowhood), deducting household total family taxes (mandatory social security contributions, income taxes, or mandatory employee contributions). To take into account family structure we adopt the OECD-equivalence scale to arrive at the equivalent pre-government household income and equivalent post-government household income. The household income variables are deflated with the national CPI (2001 = 100) to reflect constant prices. To exclude the impact of transitory shocks and cross-section measurement errors we use 4-year averages of the equivalent household income variables. The equivalent household incomes 1984–1987 (Germany) or 1980–1983 (USA) capture the income situation of the persons living in the parental household. The economic and social situation of these persons living in their own households is observed in the periods 1999–2002, 2000–2003, 2001–2004, and 2002–2005 (Germany), or 1996–1999, 1997–2001, and 1999–2003 (United States).

3 Methodology

Intergenerational income inequality and poverty measures

Change in the overall level of inequality and poverty between market income and disposable income is an important dimension of the well-being of the population in a country and reflects the functioning of the redistribution policy. To evaluate the extent of income inequality we employ the coefficient of variation, the Gini coefficient, and the Generalized Entropy inequality measure $GE(2)$.

The coefficient of variation

$$CV(y) = \frac{1}{\bar{y}}\left[\frac{1}{n}\sum_{i=1}^{n}(y_i - \bar{y})^2\right]^{1/2} = \frac{\sigma_y}{\bar{y}} \tag{1}$$

captures the relation of the standard deviation of the income variable and its arithmetic mean. The higher the value of the coefficient of variation, the higher the degree of inequality.

The Gini coefficient measures v-times the surface between the Lorenz curve, which maps the cumulative income share on the vertical axis against the distribution of the population on the horizontal axis, and the line of equal distribution. The easiest mathematical expression of the Gini coefficient is based on the covariance between the income of an individual (y_i) and the rank (F) the individual occupies in the income distribution. The rank takes a value between 0 for the poorest and 1 for the richest. Denoting $\bar{y}$ as the mean income, the Gini coefficient is then defined as

$$Gini(v) = \frac{v\,\mathrm{cov}(y, F^{v-1})}{\bar{y}} \tag{2}$$

The parameter v is used to emphasize various parts of the income distribution, and the higher the weight, the more emphasis is placed on the bottom part of the income distribution. The parameter $v = 2$ characterizes the standard Gini coefficient

$$Gini = \frac{2\,\mathrm{cov}(Y, F)}{\bar{y}} \tag{3}$$

which ranges from 0 (perfect equality) to 1 (total inequality).

The inequality measures of the Generalized Entropy class

$$GE(\alpha) = \frac{1}{\alpha^2 - \alpha}\left[\frac{1}{n}\sum_{i=1}^{n}\left(\frac{y_i}{\bar{y}}\right)^\alpha - 1\right]$$

with

$$GE(0) = \frac{1}{n}\sum_{i=1}^{n}\log\frac{\bar{y}}{y_i}, \quad GE(1) = \frac{1}{n}\sum_{i=1}^{n}\frac{y_i}{\bar{y}}\log\frac{y_i}{\bar{y}}, \quad \text{and } GE(2) = \frac{1}{2n\bar{y}^2}\sum_{i=1}^{n}(y_i - \bar{y})^2 \tag{4}$$

are sensitive to changes at the lower end of the income distribution for α close to 0, equally sensitive to changes across the distribution for α equal to 1 (Theil index), and sensitive to changes at the upper end of the distribution for higher values of α. The analysis here employs the $GE(2)$ inequality measure which is half the squared coefficient of variation

$$GE(2) = \frac{1}{2}CV(y)^2 = \frac{1}{2}\left[\frac{1}{\bar{y}}\left[\frac{1}{n}\sum_{i=1}^{n}(y_i - \bar{y})^2\right]^{1/2}\right]^2, \tag{5}$$

with n as the number of individuals, y_i as the income of individual i, and $\bar{y}$ as the mean income.

To describe poverty intensity and the extent of inequality below the poverty line we employ distance measures used in poverty analysis (Foster *et al.* 1984). To identify the poor we employ the poverty threshold of half the median income variable (z). The headcount ratio (FGT(0)) indicates the amount of poor persons in the total population. The average normalized poverty gap (FGT(1)) expresses the relative average distance of the income of individual i (y_i) to the poverty line (z)

$$pg = \frac{z - |\frac{1}{n}\sum_{i=1}^{n} z - y_i|}{z} = \frac{z - d}{z}, \text{ with } d = |\frac{1}{n}\sum_{i=1}^{n} z - y_i|. \tag{6}$$

Contribution of income sources to total inequality

We decompose the $GE(2)$ inequality measure to evaluate the contribution of the labor market income and public transfers to total pre-government income inequality. The total inequality, I, sums to S_k absolute contributions of the (k) income sources $I = \sum_k S_k$, which can be written as

$$S_k = s_k GE(2) = \rho_k \chi_k \sqrt{GE(2)GE(2)_k} \tag{7}$$

The $s_k = S_k/I$ indicates the proportional contribution of the income component k to total inequality, ρ_k is the correlation between source k and total income, $\chi_k = \frac{y_k}{y}$ is the share of source k in total income, and $GE(2)$ and $GE(2)_k$ are one-half the squared coefficient of variation of total income and the kth income source respectively. A large value of S_k implies that income source k is an important source of income inequality. If $S_k > 0$, the kth income source provides a disequalizing effect, and if $S_k < 0$ the income source k provides an equalizing effect.

Intergenerational income elasticity

The most common approach to measure how economic (dis)advantages are transmitted across generations is to estimate the intergenerational income elasticity applying ordinary least squares (OLS) to the regression of a logarithmic measure of the children's income variable (y_c) on a logarithmic measure of the income variable in the parental household (y_p)

$$y_c = \beta_0 + \beta_1 y_p + \varepsilon_c \tag{8}$$

The constant term β_0 represents the change in the economic status common to the children's generation, and the slope coefficient, β_1 is the elasticity of the children's income variable with respect to the parents' income situation. The larger β_1 the more likely an individual as an adult will inhabit the same income position as her parents, which implies a greater persistence of the intergenerational economic status. The closer β_1 is to zero the higher is the intergenerational income mobility. The random error component ε_c is usually assumed to be distributed $N(0, \sigma^2)$.

The extension of equation (8)

$$y_c = \beta_0 + \beta_1 y_p + \delta_c X_c + \varepsilon_c \tag{9}$$

includes a set of control variables (X_c) to account for the individual characteristics of the children which partly express the indirect effects of the parental income on the children's income. To the extent that these variables lower the coefficient β_1, these other effects "account for" the raw intergenerational income elasticity, β_1, from equation (8). The (X_c) controls are observed in 1999 (2002) for the German sample, and 1994 (1997) for the US sample. We include the educational years as an indicator of human capital. In the case of missing values the educational attainment is set equal to the amount reported in the next year, for it is possible to increase educational attainment but impossible to decrease it. The higher the income of the parents the higher their investment in the education of the children, which in turn causes a higher income of the children. The labor market engagement is considered with the annual working hours of the persons. Finally, the gender dummy (1 male, 0 female) controls for gender differences in the effects of redistribution policies on intergenerational income elasticity.

Intergenerational income transitions

The intergenerational income elasticity measures average income mobility but does not throw important light on the probabilities of economic success conditional upon the economic background of the parents. The movement from one income position to another and the factors that influence it are the key issues from a welfare point of view (Heckman 1981). The transition matrix allows us to analyze the intergenerational persistence of income positions at different points of the income distribution. We use the log equivalent income variables of the parents' and the children's households and split them into five equal segments to create transition matrices. The entries sum to 1 along the rows. Each element m_{ki} of a transition matrix indicates the probability (in percent) that a person belongs to the k-th quintile of the income distribution given that she belongs to the i-th quintile of the income distribution of the parental household. The more independent the income variable in both the households, the greater the likelihood that the elements of this transition matrix are close to 0.2, representing an equal distribution across all quintiles. The more the elements of the transition matrix differ from 0.2 the greater is the intergenerational similarity. The comparison between the transition probabilities according to the pre-government household income and the post-government household income allows us to evaluate the impact of redistribution policy on the intergenerational mobility or persistence of economic status.

Determinants of intergenerational poverty persistence

To evaluate the extent to which sex, educational attainment, and labor market engagement determine the probability of intergenerational poverty persistence we employ a binomial logit model. Intergenerational poverty persistence exists if a person is positioned in the first or in the second income quintiles given that her parents are positioned in the first or second income quintiles. The dependent variable (*pov*) indicate the intergenerational poverty transition of the equivalent household income variables and takes the value 1 if the person experienced intergenerational poverty persistence, and takes the value zero if a person experienced an intergenerational transition out of poverty.

The probability of intergenerational poverty persistence is estimated to be

$$Prob(pov = 1) = \frac{e^z}{1 + e^z}, \text{ or equivalently } Prob(pov = 1) = \frac{1}{1 + e^{-z}}. \tag{10}$$

The Z characterizes the linear combination $Z = B_0 + B_1X_1 + \ldots + B_nX_n$, the $X_i = 1, \ldots, n$ are the independent variables and the $B_i = 1, \ldots, n$ are the regression coefficients. In general, if the probability is greater than 0.5, we predict cross-generational poverty, and if the probability is less than 0.5, we predict an inter-generational transition out of poverty.

The interpretation of the regression coefficients B_i is based on the relation between both these probabilities, the so called "odds"

$$\frac{Prob(pov = 1)}{Prob(pov = 0)} = e^{B_0 + B_1X_1 + \ldots + B_nX_n} = e^{B_0}e^{B_1X_1} \ldots e^{B_nX_n}. \tag{11}$$

The $\exp(B_i)$ are the factors by which the "odds" change when the i-th independent variable increases by one unit, e.g. this value expresses the relative risk of intergenerational poverty persistence with a one-unit change in the i-th independent variable. For the underlying analysis the X_i include a gender dummy, the years of education to control for human capital, and the employment hours to capture the labor market engagement of a person.

4 Empirical results

In both the countries, the Gini coefficient and the Generalized Entropy inequality measure ($GE(2)$) indicate that the tax and benefit systems reduce the equivalent pre-government income inequality. The $GE(2)$ income inequality measure, which is more sensitive to changes at the higher end of the distribution, reveals a significantly higher inequality of the equivalent pre-government household income in the United States than in Germany. In Germany, the redistribution

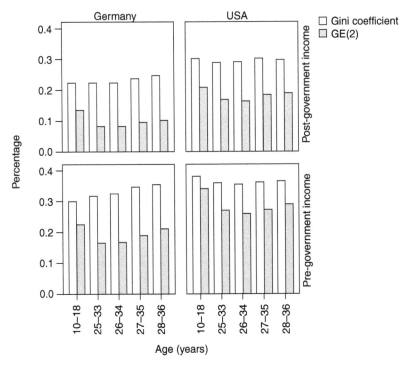

Figure 10.1 Income inequality in Germany and the USA (source: PSID-GSOEP 1981–
2006, author's own calculations).

policy halves income inequality, whereas in the United States redistribution
reduces income inequality by about one-third. The Gini coefficient, which is
more sensitive to changes at the bottom part of the income distribution, suggests
that the tax and benefit system reduces income inequality to only a low extent in
both the countries (Figure 10.1).

For both the countries, the decomposition of the Generalized Entropy
(*GE*(2)) inequality measure corroborates the results of Fields (2004) that labor
income is the most important source of income inequality in industrialized
countries. In Germany, the labor income of persons living in parental households adds 84 percent to total pre-government income inequality. With increasing age labor income contributes up to more than 90 percent to the total
pre-government income inequality. Public transfers equalize total equivalent
pre-government income inequality by between 1 percent and 4 percent. In the
United States, the contribution of labor income to total pre-government household income equality is lower than in Germany due to the structural differences
in the income composition. Labor income shares between 64 percent and more
than 80 percent of the total equivalent pre-government income inequality. In
contrast to the German case, the equalizing effect of public transfers decreases
in the life course (Figure 10.2).

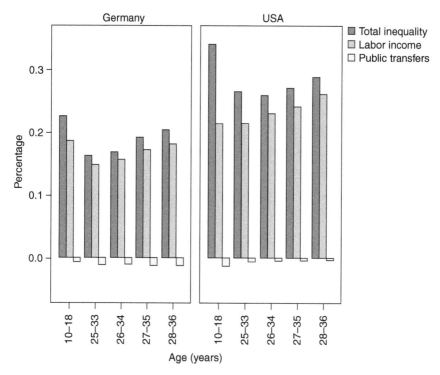

Figure 10.2 Contribution of income source to total income inequality (source: PSID-GSOEP 1981–2006, own calculations).

As Jäntti and Danziger (1994) and Smeeding (2005) among others found, labor income disparities are important determinants of poverty intensity. For the German sample, pre-government income poverty intensity in the parental household amounts to about 10 percent, and then increases up to 23 percent for persons aged between 28–36 years. The before-redistribution poverty gap widens with increasing age indicating a growing dispersion in the lower tail of the income distribution. In the United States, both the poverty rate and the poverty gap do not differ significantly by age groups. In Germany, redistribution halves the poverty rate and reduces the poverty gap to under 5 percent in the different age groups. In the United States, redistribution policy reduces the poverty intensity by about 6–8 percent points (Figure 10.3).

The regression results indicate higher intergenerational pre-government income persistence in the United States than in Germany. In Germany, redistribution policy increases the intergenerational income elasticity and thus lowers the intergenerational income mobility of persons aged 28–36 years from 0.160 to 0.407. In the United States, redistribution policy leads to a further increase of the intergenerational income elasticity up to 0.492 for persons aged 25–33 years and to 0.489 for persons aged 28–36 years. Including a set of control variables, the regression results reveal country differences concerning the contribution of

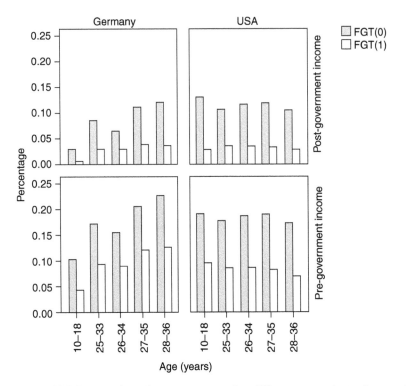

Figure 10.3 Poverty intensity, poverty gap for different age cohorts (source: PSID-
GSOEP 1981–2006, own calculations).

family background characteristics to intergenerational income mobility. In the
United States, gender, educational attainment, and labor market engagement significantly lower the intergenerational post-government income elasticity by more
than 10 percent. In Germany, the labor market presence significantly contributes
to the post-government income elasticity, but the influence of gender and education is not significant. Possible explanations may be that the public transfer
system and the various welfare-state programs in Germany (Federal Childcare
Payment, Parental Leave Act (Bundeserziehungsgeldgesetz, BErzGG 2001))
"overrule" the influence of family background characteristics on intergenerational income mobility. Another explanation could be that labor market segrega-
tion and discrimination partly diminishes the importance of gender and
educational attainment (Table 10.1).

Intergenerational income mobility differs over the income distribution and for
different age cohorts, therefore the intergenerational elasticity at most summarizes the overall degree of intergenerational mobility, and should not be used as
a target for redistribution policy measures. The intergenerational transition
matrices based on the log equivalent household income variables reveal a notice-
able persistence of the relative income positions at the very tails of the income

Table 10.1 Intergenerational income mobility, Germany 2000–2005, USA 1999–2005

Equation	Estimated coefficients	Germany				USA			
		Pre-gvt-income 1999	Pre-gvt-income 2002	Post-gvt-income 1999	Post-gvt-income 2002	Pre-gvt-income 1994	Pre-gvt-income 1997	Post-gvt-income 1994	Post-gvt-income 1997
(8)	Constant	8.05***	7.91***	7.00***	5.55***	5.06***	5.54***	4.82**	4.97***
	pre-gvt income, parents Germany1984;USA 1980	0.14*	0.16*			0.476***	0.444***		
	post-gvt income, parents Germany1984; USA 1980			0.237**	0.409***			0.492***	0.489***
	R^2adj	0.0159	0.0154	0.0277	0.0997	0.229	0.242	0.244	0.238
	RMSE	0.886	0.984	0.495	0.417	0.814	0.735	0.480	0.471
	LL	–391	–379	–216	–147	–1265	–916	–725	–401
(9)	Constant			6.73***	5.47***			4.63***	4.89***
	post-gvt income, parents Germany1984; USA1980			0.274***	0.377***			0.385***	0.361***
	GENDER 1male 0female			–0.1	0.0833			0.114***	0.114**
	EDUCATION Germany: 1999; 2002 USA: 1994; 1997			0.018*	0.00735			0.0759***	0.0711***
	EMPLOYMENT Germany: 1999; 2002 USA: 1994; 1997			0.232**	0.251**			0.177***	0.324***
	R^2adj			0.0546	0.165			0.351	0.379
	RMSE			0.488	0.402			0.445	0.425
	LL			–211	–136			–642	–338

Source: GSOEP-PSID 1981–2006, own calculations.

Notes
* $p < 0.05$; ** $p < 0.01$; *** $p < 0.001$.

distribution in both the countries. Most of the transition probabilities significantly differ from 0.2, indicating that the income positions of the children are far from being perfectly predicted by the relative income position of the parental household. The probability that a child ends up in a transfer quintile different from the one occupied in the parental household tends to be monotonically decreasing.

Tables 10.2a–10.2d show the intergenerational transition probabilities for the pre-government income situation and the post-government income situation (bold). The transition probabilities do not suggest that redistribution policy is an effective instrument to reduce intergenerational poverty situations in both the countries. In the United States redistribution policy enforces the intergenerational persistence of income positions at the very top and the very bottom of the income distribution to a higher extent than in Germany. In Germany, redistribution policy measures attenuate the intergenerational income persistence at the very bottom of the income distribution. However, the degree of immobility in the tails of the income distributions might be exaggerated, for upward mobility is not possible for those born at the top, and downward mobility is not possible for those born at the bottom. The higher probability for the stayers at the very top and very bottom of the income distribution in part represents the non-linearity in the mobility process (Atkinson *et al.* 1983).

Table 10.3 shows the estimated regression coefficients B_i and their significance level. In both the countries, gender, educational attainment and labor market experience significantly determine the probability of intergenerational poverty persistence before redistribution: each additional year of education and each additional working hour significantly reduce the risk to experience intergenerational poverty persistence. Female persons have a lower risk to inherit poverty from their parents. In the United States, gender, educational attainment and labor market presence determine intergenerational poverty persistence after redistribution. In Germany, the influence of the working hours is not significant. A possible explanation may be that redistribution policy works according to the principle of "equal shares for all."

5 Conclusions

The analysis here contributes to the understanding of intergenerational effects of redistribution policy on income inequality, poverty intensity, income mobility, and poverty persistence. We have analyzed the question whether redistribution policy succeeds in attenuating income inequality and poverty, income mobility and poverty persistence for Germany and the United States, two countries differing in social policy regimes, labor market institutions, and family role models. The results point out that

*   redistribution policy reduces income inequality, and poverty intensity to a greater extent in Germany than in the United States, which corroborates the higher level of benefits and public services in conservative-corporatist welfare regimes;

Table 10.2a Intergenerational income transition Germany 1984/1999

Germany Deciles parents' income pre-gvt 1984 post-gvt 1984	Deciles children's income pre-government income 1999 post-government income 1999				
	1	2	3	4	5
1	0.3065	0.2419	0.1935	0.1774	0.0806
	0.3279	**0.2623**	**0.2459**	**0.1148**	**0.0492**
2	0.2063	0.1905	0.2381	0.1905	0.1746
	0.1818	**0.2576**	**0.1818**	**0.1818**	**0.1970**
3	0.2063	0.2063	0.2540	0.1587	0.1746
	0.2206	**0.2059**	**0.1618**	**0.2353**	**0.1765**
4	0.1296	0.1852	0.1296	0.2407	0.3148
	0.1321	**0.1887**	**0.1697**	**0.2642**	**0.2453**
5	0.1000	0.1333	0.2167	0.2333	0.3167
	0.1250	**0.0893**	**0.1607**	**0.2500**	**0.3750**
Total	0.1921	0.1921	0.2086	0.1987	0.2086
	0.2007	**0.2039**	**0.1842**	**0.2072**	**0.2039**

Chi2(16)=26.0035* **Chi2(16)=35.5212*****

Source: PSID-GSOEP 1981–2006, own calculations.

Notes
* $p<0.05$; ** $p<0.01$; *** $p<0.00$.

Table 10.2b Intergenerational income transition Germany 1984/2002

Germany Deciles parents' income pre-gvt 1984 post-gvt 1984	Deciles children's income pre-government income 2002 post-government income 2002				
	1	2	3	4	5
1	0.2931	0.3103	0.1724	0.1034	0.1207
	0.3750	**0.2857**	**0.1429**	**0.1071**	**0.0893**
2	0.2449	0.2245	0.2653	0.1633	0.1020
	0.2069	**0.2069**	**0.3448**	**0.1207**	**0.1207**
3	0.1324	0.2353	0.2206	0.2206	0.1912
	0.1967	**0.1967**	**0.2295**	**0.1967**	**0.1803**
4	0.1224	0.1224	0.1633	0.2245	0.3673
	0.1154	**0.1154**	**0.1346**	**0.3269**	**0.3077**
5	0.1702	0.0638	0.1489	0.3404	0.2766
	0.1304	**0.0217**	**0.2174**	**0.2609**	**0.3696**
Total	0.1919	0.1993	0.1956	0.2066	0.2066
	0.2088	**0.1722**	**0.2161**	**0.1978**	**0.2051**

Chi2(16)=38.3936*** **Chi2(16)=54.2697*****

Source: PSID-GSOEP 1981–2006, own calculations.

Notes
* $p<0.05$; ** $p<0.01$; *** $p<0.00$.

Table 10.2c Intergenerational income transition USA 1980/1994

USA Deciles parents' income pre-gvt 1980 **post-gvt 1980**	Deciles children's income Pre-government income 1994 **Post-government income 1994**				
	1	*2*	*3*	*4*	*5*
1	0.5584	0.2532	0.0974	0.0584	0.0325
	0.5472	**0.2453**	**0.1069**	**0.0629**	**0.0377**
2	0.3350	0.2792	0.1980	0.1320	0.0558
	0.3450	**0.2650**	**0.1950**	**0.1150**	**0.0800**
3	0.1636	0.2409	0.3045	0.1864	0.1045
	0.1644	**0.2785**	**0.3014**	**0.1826**	**0.0731**
4	0.1324	0.2146	0.2009	0.2740	0.1781
	0.1345	**0.1928**	**0.2197**	**0.2735**	**0.1794**
5	0.0470	0.1107	0.1779	0.2685	0.3960
	0.0493	**0.1086**	**0.1645**	**0.2796**	**0.3980**
Total	0.2123	0.2086	0.2004	0.1985	0.1801
	0.2145	**0.2072**	**0.2000**	**0.1982**	**0.1801**
	Chi2(16)=343.0760***		**Chi2(16)=352.1448***		

Source: PSID-GSOEP 1981–2006, own calculations.

Notes
* $p < 0.05$; ** $p < 0.01$; *** $p < 0.00$.

Table 10.2d Intergenerational income transition USA 1980/1997

USA Deciles parents' income pre-gvt 1980 **post-gvt 1980**	Deciles children's income Pre-government income 1997 **Post-government income 1997**				
	1	*2*	*3*	*4*	*5*
1	0.5407	0.2222	0.1333	0.0889	0.0148
	0.4569	**0.2845**	**0.1293**	**0.0948**	**0.0345**
2	0.3452	0.2500	0.1905	0.1667	0.0476
	0.3699	**0.2192**	**0.1712**	**0.1712**	**0.0685**
3	0.1650	0.2650	0.3200	0.1850	0.0650
	0.1783	**0.2420**	**0.2803**	**0.2229**	**0.0764**
4	0.1692	0.1891	0.2040	0.2239	0.2139
	0.1301	**0.2192**	**0.2534**	**0.2260**	**0.1712**
5	0.0300	0.1423	0.1948	0.2322	0.4007
	0.0337	**0.1180**	**0.1742**	**0.2360**	**0.4382**
Total	0.2122	0.2070	0.2132	0.1895	0.1782
	0.2153	**0.2100**	**0.2046**	**0.1965**	**0.1736**
	Chi2(16)=292.4887*		**Chi2(16)=214.5830***		

Source: PSID-GSOEP 1981–2006, own calculations.

Notes
* $p < 0.05$; ** $p < 0.01$; *** $p < 0.00$.

Table 10.3 Determinants of intergenerational poverty transmission

	Germany		United States	
	Pre-gvt-income parents 1984 children 1999	*Post-gvt income parents 1984 children 1999*	*Pre-gvt-income parents 1980 children 1994*	*Post-gvt income parents 1980 children 1994*
Gender				
1male, 0female	−1.1844***	−1.2228***	−0.6275**	−0.9442***
Education	−0.1890***	−0.1409***	−0.1737***	−0.2031***
Employment	−0.0004*	−0.0004**	−0.0004**	−0.0001
N	609	609	1785	1785
LR chi2	627.09	557.65	1831.95	1888.07
Prob > chi2	0.0000	0.0000	0.0000	0.0000
Pseudo R2	0.7428	0.6605	0.7403	0.7630
LL	−108.579	−143.304	−321.293	−293.231

Source: GSOEP-PSID 1981–2006, own calculations.

Notes
* $p<0.05$; ** $p<0.01$; *** $p<0.00$.

- labor income contributes the largest part of total pre-government household income inequality in both the countries;
- intergenerational income persistence is stronger in the United States than in Germany. In Germany, the redistribution policy measures contribute to a higher social mobility between generations, whereas the more liberal and market oriented welfare regime in the United States entails a stronger intergenerational income persistence;
- gender, educational attainment, and labor market engagement significantly determine the intergenerational post-government income elasticity as well as the intergenerational poverty persistence in the United States. These results corroborate the higher influence of individual characteristics on the social position and the social mobility of a person in market oriented countries;
- regardless of the different welfare regimes, redistribution policy enforces intergenerational income persistence in the tails of the income distribution in both the countries.

These results call for broader thinking on the mechanisms and causes of income inequality and poverty, the structural features of the labor markets and their institutions, and how families, labor markets and social policy interact in determining the degree of intergenerational income mobility and poverty persistence. Social policy should not adopt the general view that redistribution policy is able to break the intergenerational transmission of income inequality and poverty. In fact, redistribution policy is forced to encourage active labor market engagement across generations.

Notes

* Acknowledgments: The author wishes to thank John B. Davis and the members of the review committee for clarifying the exposition, and the participants of the twelfth World Congress of Social Economics in Amsterdam, June 7–9, 2007, for helpful comments and discussions. The shortcomings and errors remain the author's as usual.
1 For a detailed description of the databases see Burkhauser *et al.* 2001.

References

An, C., R. Haveman and B. Wolfe (1993), "Teen Out-of-wedlock Births and Welfare Receipt: The Role of Childhood Events and Economic Circumstances," *Review of Economics and Statistics*, 72: 195–208.

Atkinson, A.B., Maynard, A.K. and Trinder C.G. (1983), *Parents and Children: Incomes in Two Generations*, London: Heinemann Educational Books.

Bane, M.J. and Ellwood, D. (1994), *Welfare Realities: From Rhetoric to Reform*, Cambridge, MA: Harvard University Press.

Burkhauser, R.V., Butrica, B.A., Daly, M.C. and Lillard, D.R. (2001), "The Cross-National Equivalent File: A Product of Cross-national Research," in I. Becker, N. Ott and G. Rolf (eds.) *Soziale Sicherung in einer dynamischen Gesellschaft*, Frankfurt: Campus.

Corak, M. (2006), "Cross-country Comparison of Generational Earnings Mobility," in J. Creedy and G. Kalb (eds.) *Research on Economic Inequality, Volume 13: Dynamics of Inequality and Poverty*, Amsterdam: Elsevier.

Corak, M. and A. Heisz (1999), "The Intergenerational Earnings and Income Mobility of Canadian Men: Evidence from Longitudinal Income Tax Data," *Journal of Human Resources*, 34: 504–533.

Ellwood, D. and L. Summers (1986), "Is Welfare Really a Problem?," *Public Interest*, 83: 57–78.

Esping-Andersen, Gosta (1990), *The Three Worlds of Welfare Capitalism*, Cambridge, UK: Polity Press.

Fields, Gary (2004), "Dualism in the Labor Market: A Perspective on the Lewis Model after Half a Century," *Manchester School*, 72: 724–735.

Foster, J.E., Greer, J. and E. Thorbecke (1984), "A Class of Decomposable Poverty Measures," *Econometrica*, 52: 761–766.

Gottschalk, P. (1992), "The Intergenerational Transmission of Welfare Participation: Facts and Possible Causes," *Journal of Policy Analysis and Management*: 254–272.

Heckman, J.J. (1981), "Statistical Models for Discrete Panel Data," in C.F. Manski, D. McFadden (eds.) *Structural Analysis of Discrete Data with Econometric Applications*, Cambridge: MIT Press.

Hertz, T. (2004), "Rags, Riches and Race: The Intergenerational Economic Mobility of Black and White Families in the United States," in S. Bowles, H. Gintis and M. Osborne (eds.) *Unequal Chances: Family Background and Economic Success*, Princeton, NJ: Princeton University Press.

Hyson, R. (2003), *Differences in Intergenerational Mobility across the Earnings Distribution*, US Bureau of Labor Statistics, WP 364.

Jäntti, M. and Danziger, S. (1994), "Child Poverty in Sweden and the United States: The Effect of Social Transfers and Parental Labor Force Participation," *Industrial and Labor Relations Review*, 48: 48–64.

Kolodinsky, J. and Shirey, L. (2000), "The Impact of Living with an Elder Parent on Adult Daughter's Labor Supply and Hours Of Work," *Journal of Family and Economic Issues*, 21: 149–174.

Mayer, S.E. (1997), *What Money Can't Buy: Family Income and Children's Life Chances*, Cambridge, MA: Harvard University Press.

Page, M.E. (2004), "New Evidence on the Intergenerational Correlation in Welfare Participation," in M. Corak (ed.) *Generational Income Mobility in North America and Europe*, Cambridge, UK: Cambridge University Press.

Pepper, J.V. (2000), "The Intergenerational Transmission of Welfare Receipt: A Nonparametric Bounds Analysis," *Review of Economics and Statistics*, 82: 472–488.

Smeeding, T. (2005), "Public Policy, Economic Inequality, and Poverty: The United States in Comparative Perspective," *Social Science Quarterly*, 86: 955–983.

Smeeding, T., Rainwater, L. and Burtless, G. (2001), "United States Poverty in a Cross-national Context," in Danziger, S.H. and Haveman, R.H. (eds.) *Understanding Poverty*, New York and Cambridge, MA: Russel Sage Foundation and Harvard University Press.

Vartanian, T.P. (1999), "Childhood Conditions and Adult Welfare Use: Examining Neighborhood Factors," *Journal of Marriage and the Family*, 61: 225–237.

Vartanian, T.P and MacNamara, J.M. (2000), "Work and Economic Outcomes after Welfare," *Journal of Sociology and Social Welfare*, 27: 41–78.

—— (2004), "The Welfare Myth: Disentangling the Long-term Effects of Poverty and Welfare Receipt for Young Single Mothers," *Journal of Sociology and Social Welfare*, 31: 105–140.

11 Pension reform and household financial position

GianDemetrio Marangoni, Chiara Marcomini and Stefano Solari[*]

1 Introduction: old-age insurance and financialization

Developed countries' pension systems have been the subject of a large number of economic studies which have analyzed a plurality of issues such as: long-term viability relative to the ageing of the population, distortions of production factor costs, incentives to investment, labor market flexibility, and the definition and allocation of national savings. However, only a minority of these economic studies assumes a view oriented toward understanding all direct and indirect consequences of the changed institutional environment produced for households. In fact, the welfare and the financial dimensions often enjoy strict inter-dependencies, which are worth being studied from one perspective. Indeed, the actual context in which households take their savings and providence decisions are neither separable nor regulated by "complementary" institutions. Moreover, economists seldom consider the relationship between pension reforms and the actual social values of citizens. The management and reform of pension programs are always considered as "objective" economic problems leaving little space for the study of contexts in which household savings-providence decisions are in harmony with social values. Throughout the 1990s and the 2000s we have experimented with an extensive series of reforms in this sector in most developed countries. The European case is particularly interesting due to the extent of its generous public PAYG[1] systems. Besides the reasonable aim of assuring the viability of pension schemes in the context of ageing societies, the set of reforms enacted in many Western countries was also geared toward improving the performance of financial markets. Such changes have produced a major modification in the way households save and invest, in what they can consider as sure and reliable and in what remains uncertain and therefore to be insured.

The focus here is the linkage between the changing form of pension systems and the adaptation of household financial positions at an aggregated level and in international comparison. In fact, the impact of such reforms is already displayed in the portfolios of households and in the redistribution of wealth which is induced by the changing patterns of saving. We adopt an applied approach by considering a few specific linkages as proposed by four families of studies and by reviewing some data on the structure of financial systems and on the role of

financial intermediaries devoted to social security. Four main families of theoretical notions and perspectives are connected in this chapter:

1   First, a distinction is usually made in financial systems between *market-
    based* and *bank-based* capitalism due to the relative importance of different
    sources for firm financing. This distinction has a long history and became
    popular when it was included in the Allen and Glade textbook (1990).[2] A
    further distinction is made between economic systems where *managerial
    capitalism* prevails (competitive or coordinated) and those where *family
    capitalism* exists (Amable 2003; 2004).
2   Second, beyond the standard dichotomy between PAYG and funded pension
    systems, and that between the "defined contribution" and "defined benefit"
    principle of benefit calculation (valid in both systems).[3] The distinction
    between the Bismarckian (corporative) welfare systems and the universalist
    (Beveridgian) systems is also relevant (Esping-Andersen 1990).
3   Third, a basic notion is that of *complementarities* between pension systems
    and financial institutions. Where PAYG systems are adopted, the financial
    system is underdeveloped due to the immediate redistribution of savings
    without any capitalization. Where pension systems are based on pension
    funds and capitalization of savings, the financial system is much more
    developed (Tyrrell and Schmidt 2001). In corporatist countries the leading
    financial role of banks goes hand in hand with the repartition schemes of
    pension systems. This also determines the confidence of investors in finan-
    cial markets as a solution for providence problems – which is much higher
    in countries such as the United States and Great Britain.
4   Fourth, connected to the previous two points, the notion of *financialization*
    of the economy concerns the relative importance of finance in the "gover-
    nance" of the economy. Looking at institutional arrangements, *financializa-
    tion* is a process in which financial values "become leading institutional and
    organisational design criteria" (Froud *et al.* 2000: 104).[4] It finds an institu-
    tional foundation in "shareholder value" principles in the governance of
    firms (Aglietta and Reberioux 2005). Financialization implies a "financial
    globalization" that reduces the autonomy of government policies and
    national regulations (Tiemstra 2007). It results in "inflated" credit and debt
    positions and therefore it may indirectly be measured as the rising diver-
    gence between the value of assets and liabilities of the main (private non-
    financial) institutional sectors relative to GDP. Financialization apparently
    increased everywhere in the 1990s, but the inflating effect of the bull market
    probably overestimated the effective changes and hid the real structural
    changes in the financial structure of the economy. The causes of this phe-
    nomenon are varied, but the introduction of pension funds based on capital-
    ization of savings may have significantly contributed to it.

Starting from these basic views of financial and welfare systems interdependencies we will develop a number of socio-economic theoretical issues. Moreover,

we will try to evaluate the changes in the financial structure that directly concern households which can be attributed to recent pension reforms in developed countries. As a consequence, we will first explore the theoretical connections and the complexity of this institutional interdependency; second, we will present evidence on the reforms enacted in some developed countries; then we will evaluate the real extent of reforms and the initial results and effects driven by these structural interdependencies, trying to separate those produced by other determinants; last, we offer some insights into the tenability of a shareholder society.

2 Pension system reforms: some basic socio-economic theoretical issues

Since the beginning of the 1990s, an intense effort has been made by many economists and international institutions to convince governments to implement pension reforms oriented to reducing the extent of public repartition schemes in favor of programs based on funded schemes. Actually, scholars like Gordon Clark (2003c) have conceived pension reforms as part of a set of structural reforms aimed at radically changing the structure of property and society as a whole.

In our present economic systems social security is a crucial institution for both intra- and inter-generational distribution of wealth. It is strictly intertwined with both the state and financial systems: it may assume a form that drives savings away from financial institutions or a form which may integrate and magnify their development. Consequently, the institutional arrangement of social security does not only affect the configuration of welfare entitlements, but it also affects the amount of financial assets and the property of productive capital. Also, these changes as well as labor market institutions affect the governance of firms. Therefore, complex complementarities of institutions exist between social security, state, finance, company governance, labor markets and (back to) welfare in general.

Consequently, the main reasons put forward for the widening of funded pension schemes are that, on the one hand, capitalization may reduce the risks that PAYG systems face with the ageing of society,[5] and on the other hand, pension funds may have positive effects on the supply side of the economy in two main ways: (*a*) they allow governments to reduce social contributions and thus increase the competitiveness of firms; (*b*) they contribute to developing financial markets and the mass of financial capital which, with the diffusion of shareholder value, would help to develop a best corporate governance (reducing insider control).[6]

Changes induced by the transition to capitalization are normally said to increase savings and supply them to producers through the investment activity of financial intermediaries, which operate through instruments alternative to commercial bank lending (Clowes 2001). As a consequence, we would expect to see an expansion in disintermediated financing patterns (stock exchange and issues of debt securities) and a reduction (at least relative) in the importance of bank lending for corporate finance. On the other side of the economy, households would accumulate financial wealth and become, directly or indirectly, the main proprietors of the production means. From this point of view we would expect to see an increase in the net financial wealth of households.

The changes involved, however, are more pervasive and interconnected than portrayed in this picture. Reforms substantively modify a complex set of interdependent risks, entitlements and duties characterized by their different nature and interconnection with the many socio-economic institutions. They also affect the very nature and logic of state intervention in the economy. On the other hand, the whole system configuration tends to be resilient because of sunk costs, institutionalized behavior, social structures and the long times required to modify the nature of capital assets. Christine André (2003), who has performed a structural analysis of European welfare systems, found that, up to 2003, the basic nature and the main differences between pension systems remained almost the same (reforms notwithstanding).

From the point of view of the *social insurance function*, reforms tend to induce a major shift in the legal status, logic and functioning of the instruments adopted. The first point is that social entitlements of repartition schemes granted by the state are replaced by (limited) individual property rights. This induces a shift in the kind of risks faced by the investment programs: the political risk typical of PAYG pensions (change in entitlements) is replaced by a risk due to economic instability and conflicts of interest. The logic of reciprocity politically defined is substituted by an individual and monetary logic of financial rent (Montaigne 2006). The pooling of (general economic) risk in a wide basin constituted by the whole political-economic system is replaced by a narrower pooling of (financial) risks in a trust. All this induces a distancing of state politics from social security institutions. The state, from its role as regulator, provider of services and shock absorber, becomes a simple regulator and controller of markets. We may add that in countries enjoying a corporatist welfare state, a "social capital" based on the culture of association and mutual aid, slowly built up over the last two centuries, is squandered with the transition to market-based and individualized forms of providence.

From the point of view of the *citizens' financial position*, the change from a public repartition scheme to a private capitalization program tends to modify the composition and nature of their assets. A major reason put forward for the introduction of pension funds (or life insurance) is that the accumulation of capital constitutes a pool of financial wealth which is safer and more solid compared to a system based on balancing flows of taxes and benefits.[7] The collective investment made in repartition-based pension systems is considered as a sunk investment where each generation owns pension entitlements and social contribution duties. Consequently, from the individual point of view, social contributions (or taxes oriented) to finance pensioners' benefits may be seen as a capitalization of an individual entitlement. Valdés-Prieto (2005) has analyzed this "securitization of taxes" implicit in PAYG schemes. From this point of view, it could be said that the reforms transform implicit non-monetary capital into financial capital which is securable and tradable, social entitlements into property rights, claims on the polity into claims on financial returns and social duties into economic choices. Therefore, there is a qualitative change in assets (and liabilities) of the citizen and an increase in real assets,[8] though people with lower income and, in general, those used to publicly managed repartition-based pensions may appear less confident in pension funds. All in all, there is something which is not convincing in listening to economists – a discipline born under the star of liberalism and therefore oriented to fight against rent positions – who promise a life based on financial rent for everybody.

From the point of view of the *general governance of the production system*, Gordon Clark (2003a; 2003c) has presented "pension fund capitalism" as a "fifth stage of capitalism" illustrating the many implications of this institutional change for the whole socio-economic system. Reforms would socialize capital ownership and transform the most quoted companies into public companies and shareholder-value oriented governance would socialize profits. Clark (2003c) consequently asks: why should we enforce stakeholder rights and corporate democracy (as in German codetermination) if we can all be shareholders? This is not a new idea. Liberal-conservatives like Röpke (1958) believed that only diffused wealth could make capitalism work well. Also Catholic economists like Vito (1949) imagined diffused shareholding as a solution to the social question. However, Engelen (2003) and many other economists worry that such a major change cannot succeed. They are concerned that the ensuing financialization would lead to instability and a shift of entrepreneurial risk toward social insurance.

In fact, not all of the (fragile) chains in the mechanism envisaged by Clark appear to work well. Investment in trusts (insurance or pension funds) does not represent a full property right in production assets (as imagined by Röpke). It represents a limited property right, typical of trusts – as clearly explained by Montaigne (2006) – which does not entail any of the positive effects of direct control over production means. As a consequence, all the benefits of the pension fund system depend on the absence of private benefits from control of firms by trustees and the absence of conflicts of interest inside finance. This is far from having been achieved as the role played by pension funds in mergers and acquisitions (M & A)[9] or as the many cases of "interested mis-management" sanctioned by regulatory authorities have shown in the recent past. As a consequence, institutional investors tend to constitute a concentration of economic power instead of socializing it.

From the point of view of the *stability of the economy*, two basic views still prevail with regard to these themes. Orthodox economists, including some new-Keynesians, tend to see in the financial development resulting from said reforms a step that reduces market imperfections and contributes to enforcing a competitive order, which is better able to drive efficiency. The instability of finance, from this point of view, is due to underdeveloped markets (Rajan and Zingales 2002). Contrary to this, Keynesians and institutionalists tend to relate instability to uncertainty and to the speculative nature of finance. As a consequence, the more financialized the economy, the more unstable it is (Toporowski 2000). Even if the Rajan and Zingales (2002) argument that financial markets are unstable because they are not sufficiently extended were correct, it would be difficult to understand why financial markets should be stabilized using the resources of pensioners, some of the most vulnerable citizens in our economic system.

In the following paragraphs we firstly single out the patterns and magnitude of pension reforms in the main developed countries (with a special reference to Europe where welfare systems are considered particularly unbalanced). We then try to read some signs of change in the main data available on the changes in financial structure.

3 The main pension reforms

The kinds of reforms which are relevant to this study are those oriented toward increasing the extent of funded schemes. They can be divided in two categories:

1 Reforms which reduce benefits of first pillar repartition schemes,[10] providing an indirect incentive to subscribe to a supplementary scheme – these are particularly relevant in extended repartition systems like those of the Scandinavian and continental European economies;
2 Reforms that directly provide an incentive to subscribe to a supplementary pension scheme. These can be weak (e.g. tax benefits) or strong (e.g. coercion); they can involve a partial opting out from PAYG programs or involve supplementary saving. They can also be more or less attractive in terms of prospective returns and risk in the sense that schemes based on "defined benefit" are more attractive and transparent compared to those based on "defined contribution." However, policies oriented to develop "defined contribution" programs at the expense of "defined benefit" are more developed in countries where pension funds are already well diffused (United States, United Kingdom and the Netherlands).

Pension reforms aimed at making funded schemes compulsory were introduced in Denmark, Finland, the Netherlands and Switzerland in the 1980s; in 2000 they were also introduced in Sweden. The United Kingdom also radically modified pensions in the 1980s and provided incentives for autonomous pension funds (PFs). In the 1990s they were also introduced in Belgium, Austria and Germany, and now have a medium coverage. They have been implemented but have achieved a low coverage in the remaining countries.

Continental countries (corporative "Bismarckian" welfare states)

In the Netherlands pension funds were developed many years ago due to the low level of basic pensions. Supplementary pensions are a non-compulsory complement of the basic pension and most pension funds are organized by sectors or by firms (in particular in medium and large firms). Some 91 percent of laborers participate in pension funds and 50 percent of pensioners receive benefits due to them (Observatoire des retraites 2004/4). This system has not seen major changes in the arrangement of pensions other than incentives to delay retirement (Van Riel *et al. 2003*).

In Germany, following the corporatist logic, the pension system is fragmented according to sectors and different tiers. Mandatory pensions include almost all categories of laborers (except some self-employed) while the second tier supplementary occupational scheme is provided for civil servants, white and blue-collar workers and miners (about 50 percent of employees are covered by a supplementary pension). Firms supply most of the second tier by accumulating book reserves or by collective agreements in the public sector (one-third of workers in commerce and two-thirds of those in industry are covered by occupational plans) (Schmäl 2003).

A recent reform has been implemented, where the principle of reinforcing pension funds on a voluntary basis has a major role. The aim is to keep the public contribution rate at a stabilized level. The envisaged development of pension funds takes specific forms different from the traditional book reserves. The 2001 reform was aimed at promoting the development of supplementary pension schemes whilst slightly reducing the target replacement ratio in the social security scheme. The 2004 old-age pension Insurance Sustainability Act introduced a sustainability factor in the pension indexation formula.

In Belgium, one-third of employees are covered by occupational schemes. The state has decided to enlarge tax incentives for the second tier schemes and individual plans, but the effects are still moderate (31 percent of coverage). Reforms in 2003 were oriented toward introducing collective agreements to develop professional schemes such as in Scandinavian corporatist regimes. The generosity of France's compulsory schemes has left relatively few possibilities for development of other supplementary pensions. Life insurance has taken on this business. A special form of long-term savings, *épargne salariale*, which contributes to stabilizing the financing of companies, is promoted by the state. Reforms have been oriented toward making the compulsory PAYG scheme viable and offering tax benefits to individual or company pension savings. In Austria, the severance indemnity has been transformed into company pensions. Recent measures have increased pension fund incentives, but the latter are not developed (11 percent coverage). Reforms have increased the retirement age and have linked benefits to contributions paid in the entire career.

Scandinavian countries

In Scandinavian countries social partners play an important role in occupational schemes (similarly to the Netherlands). They conclude collective agreements on occupational pension provision at the level of sectors, and membership in these schemes is mandatory. As a result, coverage rates of such schemes are particularly high.

Supplementary private pensions are more important in Denmark (80 percent coverage) than in Sweden because first tier pensions are less generous. In

Denmark, in fact, the repartition scheme is fairly limited and flat. In the nineties the Danish trade unions promoted some development of occupational regimes.

The major Swedish pension reforms, from 1994–1998, introduced the notional defined contribution system (as in Italy) and promoted the institutionalization of compulsory pension funds. These funds are now integrated into the pension system (2.5 percent of sums paid for pensions are assigned to public or private funds, on individual accounts) (Palme 2003).

In Finland, the organization of supplementary schemes is mandatory and financed by both principles of PAYG and funding. They are often managed by private organizations under public supervision. The main change is that the benefit calculation of these schemes shifts toward defined contribution. In 2001 and 2005 a major reform was implemented which modified the calculation of benefits in the first pillar and introduced a defined contribution mechanism.

Mediterranean countries

Italy has implemented frequent pension reforms since 1992. They have introduced "notional defined contribution" principles in repartition schemes and created incentives to divert some existing deferred savings previously in book reserves of firms' balance sheets in favor of pension funds (7.5 percent of gross salaries per year). However, the reluctance of laborers to participate in pension funds is still high.

Spain authorized pension funds in 1987. From 2002 to 2005 reforms were implemented to make the PAYG more flexible. Recently, the development of occupational schemes, particularly in small and medium-sized companies, has been specially promoted.

In Portugal, private pensions have increased since 1987, due to the low level of basic pensions. Tax incentives to promote the development of supplementary pension schemes have been recently introduced.

In Greece, a legislative framework has recently been established for funded schemes and incentives have been established to expand this system. At the same time the relatively generous public pensions have been reformed and benefits reduced.

United Kingdom, the United States and Japan

Pension funds were implemented several years ago in the United Kingdom and, therefore, their relative share in percent of GDP is high. Pension schemes are voluntary for the employee, but employers above a certain size (five or more employees) have to make pension products available if they are currently not offering an appropriate occupational pension scheme (the "stakeholder pensions"). In a first period, in 1978, public schemes with pensions linked to wages were made compulsory (SERPS), but eventually it was possible to "contract out." Large tax incentives were implemented in 1988 and in the 1990s to help private pension funds. A general trend has been to put an end to defined benefit plans and to replace them by defined contribution plans. In the United Kingdom, the "state second pension" provides a compulsory earnings-related additional pension, which is particularly beneficial to people on low incomes or people with interrupted careers. Opting out of this system is possible, but only into a private or occupational scheme that has fulfilled certain criteria and which provides at least the benefits of the foregone state scheme (Emmerson 2003).

The United States has not experimented with major pension reforms in the last 20 years, except for a recent increase in retirement age. Japan, on the other hand, has increased the contribution rate to public pensions and linked benefits to the ageing of the population (the first country so far to enact such automatic measure).

Instruments for promoting private pension provisions are diverse and include collective bargaining, tax incentives or direct financial support in the form of subsidies (as introduced by the latest German and Czech Republic pension reforms) and rules that make membership in such schemes mandatory (or quasi-mandatory). Some countries plan to partly compensate people for the decline in statutory replacement rates by the development of privately managed pension provisions (in particular Germany, Italy, Denmark and to a lesser extent Belgium). On the other hand, an incentive relevant (in theory) for subscribing to a pension fund is provided by the general retrenchment of first pillar pensions. In many countries minimum pensions have been raised, but occupational schemes have in general, undergone a cut in the way pensions are calculated. With these reforms Bismarckian welfare systems tend to become more akin to Beveridgian systems, but they remain more difficult to modify. The attempts of the European Union to harmonize pension systems have not yet achieved significant results.

In the next sections we analyze to what extent reforms have produced the expected changes and modified the financial structure of European countries.

4 The contribution of life insurance and pension funds to capital increase

The data elaborated by the OECD on financial intermediaries and pension funds are of reasonably good quality. However, the extreme diversity between the institutional frameworks of the various countries affects the availability and significance of data and the distinction between life insurance and pension funds is not always clear, due to the specific country's rules. As a consequence, the following statistics allow us to propose some empirically based reflections but no "sharp" quantitative measurements and evaluations.

The net acquisition of financial wealth by institutional investors of this sector (both pension funds and life insurance) represents a share of the total flow of net financial assets, which is variable in time and between countries (Table 11.2a). Surprisingly, this share is not growing in the majority of the countries considered. If we consider pension funds only, the shares become negligible in most countries. Only in Japan and the Netherlands does this kind of investment absorb a large and increasing share of the flow of net financial assets. In the United

Table 11.1 Pension reforms

	General first pillar pensions			Pension funds			
	Benefit definition	Replac. rate first pillar, 2005	Reforms	Introduction	Coverage	Incentives	
Netherlands	DC	30.0 =	1996 Reform of survivors benefits 2006 Reduction of early retirement incentives	1997 Mandatory	High (P2)	P(3)	
Belgium	DB ↓	39.0 ↓	1997 *Reduction of benefits* 2003 New scheme of *"sectoral pensions"* to extend second pillar, besides existing complementary pension commitments *Reduction of benefits* (standard retirement age (W) increase to 65 in 2009); contribution period to early retirement increased	Voluntary	Medium (P2)	P(2) P(3)	
Austria	DB ↓	64.0 ↑↓	1993 *Introduction of new benefits* (partial retirement, credit pension related to family status) 1996–7 *Reduction in benefits* (pension formula; ↓ replacement rate) 2003–4 *Reduction in benefits* (2003 abolish early retirement scheme; longer contribution period; greater pension fund incentives)	Voluntary	Medium (P2)	P(2)	
Germany	DB ↓	43.0 ↓	1997 Pension reform law: replacement rate reduced (in 30 years) 2001–2004 promoted development of supplementary pension schemes (funded DC	Voluntary	Medium	P(2)	

continued

Table 11.1 continued

	General first pillar pensions			Pension funds		
	Benefit definition	Replac. rate first pillar, 2005	Reforms	Introduction	Coverage	Incentives
			scheme) on a voluntary basis. *"Riester pension"*, 2002, reduction in statutory pension scheme to be compensated by private savings; promoted by bonuses (independent of wages) or by tax-deductible contributions. *Reduction in benefits* (increase in statutory retirement age)			P(3) (lower)
France	DB ↓	66.0 ↓	2003 Reform, incentives to work longer; *reduction in benefits* (longer period for full pension; contribut. rate increased 0.2% from 2006)	Voluntary	Low	P(3) Low (insurance)
Denmark	DC	45.1 ↑	2003 DB to DC	1964/1985 mandatory	High (P2)	P(3)
Sweden	NDC	53.0 ↓	1998 DB to NDC 2000 reduction in benefits	1986 Voluntary, 2001 mandatory	High (P2) Medium (P3)	P(3)
Finland	DB	57.0 =	2001 early retirement discouraged in private sector 2005 Reformed "earnings-related pensions" (P1); DB to DC and reduction of benefits*	1986/1985 Quasi mandatory	Low (P2)	P(3)
Luxembourg	DB	91.0 =	1996 Restrictive measures for public sector pensions. Progressive retirement. 2002 New legislation on individual old-age savings introduced, favouring development through tax incentives	Voluntary	Low	P(3)
Switzerland	DB ↓	58.2 ↓	2003 Equalization of male–female conditions	1982 Quasi mandatory occupational	High	

Japan	DB	34.4	1994 Increase of retirement age 2004 Rise of contribution rate and link to life expectancy risk	Before 1990, voluntary	Medium P(2)	P(2)
Italy	DB to NDC	79.0 ↓	1992 Amato reform: introduction of occupational private schemes (with tax advantages); gradual increase in retirement age (60w; 65m); minimum contribution requirement for old age benefits (from 10 to 20 years); extension of reference period for pensionable earnings (5 to 10 years; whole career for new entrants); increase in contribution requirement for early retirement (36 years); increase in contribution rates (*reduction in benefits*) 1993 New legislative framework on supplementary pensions 1995 Dini reform – DB to NDC – old earnings-related formula to new contribution-related formula by 2013; 1997 Stringent contributory/age requirements for seniority pensions; increase in contributions (for self-employment; artisans etc.); increase in minimum pensions; new framework on occupational (supplementary) pensions, *significant tax incentives for transformation of TFR (severance indemnity) into funded schemes* 1998 New compulsory pension contribution for all self-employed income earners 2000 Tax incentives for returns of pension funds (11% instead of 12.5%) 2004 (Pension system regime: earnings-related, mixed, contribution-defined), early pensions will be tightened	1992–1997 Voluntary. 2006 Quasi mandatory	Low P(3)	

continued

Table 11.1 continued

	General first pillar pensions			Pension funds		
	Benefit definition	Replac. rate first pillar, 2005	Reforms	Introduction	Coverage	Incentives
Spain	DB	91.0↓	1987 Authorized creation of pension funds 1991 Universalization of minimum pension system 1994 Pensions indexed to expected inflation for subsequent year 1997 *New incentives for development of supplementary pension schemes reduction in benefits; change of calculation of benefits: best 15 years; greater proportionality to contribution career in initial amount of pensions* 1997 Reduction of early retirement incentives 1999 Incentives to continue working 2000 Creation of a fund for the transition to a mixed PAYG-funded system 2002–2005 (reduction in benefits) Incentives to continue working. Early retirement is discouraged. 2002 reform of legal framework for private pensions (taxes)	1987 Voluntary	Medium	P(2) P(3)

continued

Country						P(2)
Portugal	DB	75.0 ↑↓	1993 Pension reform 1997 National guaranteed minimum income scheme 1997 Reduction of minimum contribution base 1998 Great Plan Option enlargement of financing sources; *developing supplementary pension schemes* 1999 Flexible retirement system 2001/2002 principles for supplementary occupational pension plans, *pension calculation rules*: lifetime earnings; supplementary pension rights: principle of portability 2005 public sector pensions aligned; increase in contribution period (reduction in benefits)	voluntary	Low	P(2)
Greece	DB	105.0 ↓↑	1992 Pension reform: (reduction in benefits) limits to supplementary pensions and to lump sum received at retirement by wage earners; reduction of replacement rates; increase in both employers' and employees' contributions three pension funds for the self-employed merged into one, another 65 smaller funds either wound down or amalgamated 2001 mandatory individual accounts for funded tier, allowing for switch of part of statutory social security pension into private pension funds since 2002, over half the labour force has joined funded schemes second pillar pensions have been established quite recently, in 2002 limits to pension entitlements; contributions are raised (reduction in benefits)	2002 Voluntary	Low to medium	

Table 11.1 continued

	General first pillar pensions			Pension funds		
	Benefit definition	Replac. rate first pillar, 2005	Reforms	Introduction	Coverage	Incentives
Ireland	DB	31.0 ↑	1998/99 basic pension increased by around 6.5%–7% 1999 first steps to encouraging personal responsibility for pensions 1999 National Pension Reserve fund: pre-funding in part the future Exchequer cost of social welfare and public service pensions, statutory obligation on the Government to pay a sum equivalent to 1% of GNP into the fund 2000 Tax incentives introduced for pension provision of self-employed, employers and proprietary directors 2003 Personal Retirement Savings Accounts: promote supplementary pension coverage. Cost-neutral early retirement scheme with actuarially reduced benefits introduced.	Voluntary	Medium	P(3)
United Kingdom	DB	17.0 ↑	1988 Personal pension: private second pension to people without access to an occupational scheme or who change jobs frequently (today 14% in UK)	Voluntary, also P(1)	Medium P(2)	P(2) opting out

	1995 Pension reform: 1. strengthen safeguards on occupational pension funds; 2. introduction of a new Occupational Pensions Regulatory Authority				Medium P(2)
	1999 Stakeholder Pension introduction of a scheme to encourage people to take out private pensions (personal pension, moderate incomes without access to a company pension scheme); equitable pension rights				
	2002 introduction of State Second Pension (replaces State Earning Related Pension (SERP), introduced in 1978) – higher benefits				
	2003 Introduction of Pension Credit (increases income-related benefits to over 60); basic State Pension increased			Before 1990, voluntary; plurality of schemes	
United States	DB	41,2	(1983) Recent increase in retirement rate		

Notes
P(1): first pillar; P(2): second pillar; P(3): third pillar.
DB: defined benefit; DC: defined contribution; NDC notional defined contribution.

Table 11.2a Net acquisition of PFs and life insurance as percentage of flow of net financial assets

	Pension funds and life insurance			Pension funds only		
	1995	2000	2004	1995	2000	2004
Belgium	19.7	44.1	74.3	2.4	1.7	4.5
Germany	38.4	54.4	36.0			
France	58.1	92.2	58.2			
Austria*	31.9	24.5	24.5	3.2	3.3	5.4
Netherlands	61.4	53.3	53.7	33.2	30.4	42.6
Portugal	31.1	17.1	28.7	17.6	5.3	5.5
Greece	2.6	2.0	2.4	0.0	0.1	0.9
Spain	19.9	29.0	14.5	2.0	10.2	8.4
Italy	15.6	32.2	39.1			
Finland	23.2	120.4	21.2	0.0	0.0	9.1
Sweden	66.7	92.0	46.9	32.2	48.3	26.0
Denmark	54.1	58.4	39.2			
United Kingdom	50.3	46.7	35.4	19.4	19.0	21.9
United States	44.4	245.0	37.3	34.5	193.8	32.6
Japan	47.7	62.2	83.1	19.1	61.8	83.1

Notes
* 1996.
Data not available when empty.

Table 11.2b Net acquisition of PFs and life insurance as percentage of GDP

	Pension funds and life insurance			Pension funds only		
	1995	2000	2004	1995	2000	2004
Belgium	1.89	3.62	5.51	0.23	0.14	0.33
Germany	2.75	3.14	2.13			
France	4.57	4.72	4.07			
Austria*	1.88	1.68	1.77	0.19	0.22	0.39
Netherlands	6.76	6.25	6.30	3.65	3.56	5.00
Portugal	3.57	2.60	2.86	2.02	0.81	0.55
Greece	0.40	0.19	0.29	0.00	0.01	0.11
Spain	1.86	2.62	1.44	0.19	0.92	0.84
Italy	1.90	3.07	3.56			
Finland	1.02	2.74	1.14	0.00	0.00	0.49
Sweden	2.95	5.23	4.21	1.43	2.74	2.34
Denmark	2.72	3.74	3.42			
United Kingdom	4.22	2.75	3.45	1.62	1.12	2.13
United States	2.80	2.46	2.26	2.18	1.94	1.98
Japan	5.19	1.55	2.07	2.08	1.54	2.07

Notes
* 1996.
Data not available when empty.
OECD Financial statistics, Net equity of households (S14_S15:) in life insurance and pension funds reserves (F61AS); National currency, current prices. GDP: OECD Annual National Accounts, Gross Domestic Product, Annual, in millions of Current Prices (National Currrency).

Kingdom and the United States – which are often considered the homelands of pension funds – it reaches respectively one-third and one-fifth of the total accumulation of financial wealth. The real extent of these flows can be calculated relative to GDP (Table 11.2b). In this case we can see that the Netherlands and Sweden invest a high ratio of GDP in this form of saving, in particular pension funds. Belgium and France display a sizeable flow into life insurance but not into pension funds. With the exception of Portugal, the importance of pension funds as attractors of household savings is increasing, but not in very strong proportion. Where reforms have been implemented to consolidate a second pension pillar, such figures rise to appreciable numbers, but the figures are not likely to cause radical changes in the financial structure.

5 Do pension funds contribute to develop the shareholder society?

The most significant change occurs in the ownership of shares. Unfortunately, despite the common statistical standard, national accounts are not totally comparable and do not always single out pension funds. Individuals tend to lose importance as owners of companies (except in Italy), and the same happens to non-financial companies (except in France).

The item that grows in every country is "rest of the world." This is a sign of globalization of capital and, unfortunately, is not divided into institutional sectors. We can nonetheless presume that institutional investors play a major role in the increase in this item. When specifically analyzed, pension funds show a steady increase (except in Denmark) but little importance. In the United Kingdom their importance decreases. This can be attributed to the fall in share prices and to the internationalization of investments. Financial intermediaries, in general, increase their importance as owners of shares, but with remarkable differences between countries. Consequently, in national accounts, pension funds do not emerge as major players in the management of productive wealth. There are certainly institutions (with other financial intermediaries) contributing to the internationalization of capital ownership and to the loss of the national dimension of the economies. Households tend to disappear as direct owners of productive activities. In conclusion, there is no shareholder society emerging from the past experience of pension reforms; the property of companies is more globalized and increasingly in the hands of other companies and not of households.

6 What difference for household assets?

As regards aggregated household financial wealth and in particular the impact of pension funds (and life insurance) on the accumulation and structural transformation of financial wealth, Ertürk *et al.* (2005) have observed how, in the last 15 years, household portfolios have preferred riskier assets. This is due to many causes. First, when people increase their wealth, they do not leave it in liquid forms (and this changes the composition of wealth). Second, low interest rates,

Table 11.3 Share ownership as percentage of total in value

France	1990	1995	2000	2003	Italy	1990	1995	2000	2003
Pension funds and insurance	4.8	6.4	7.2	7.9	Pension funds and insurance	2.1	4.2	3.5	3.2
Banks and fin. interm.	9.3	10.9	15.0	18.2	Banks and fin. interm.	1.7	4.6	7.1	8.4
Mutual funds	2.8	2.2	2.5	2.2	Mutual funds	5.5	0.9	5.3	3.7
Individuals (*)	36.9	30.4	21.5	20.7	Individuals (*)	43.0	45.3	37.0	39.6
Companies	27.7	31.2	32.0	30.4	Companies	33.5	24.9	29.9	27.1
Rest of the world	11.9	12.9	17.9	16.3	Rest of the world	6.5	9.6	11.8	12.4
Other (gvt)	6.7	6.0	3.8	4.2	Other (gvt)	7.7	10.5	5.5	5.7
Total	100	100	100	100	Total	100	100	100	100

Germany	1993	1995	2000	2005	Denmark	1990	1998	2001	2005
Financial institutes	6.0	6.2	14.4	13.7	Financial institutes		16.2	13.7	18.3
Banks and fin. interm.	12.8	12.9	11.5	10.7	Banks and fin. interm.		4.4	3.5	4.0
Insurance	6.6	6.3	8.2	12.4	Pension funds and insurance		23.1	20.1	16.5
Individuals	19.9	18.2	16.1	12.5	Individuals		14.5	12.7	13.9
Companies	42.8	44.0	35.0	27.8	Companies		17.8	23.4	22.1
Rest of the world	10.0	8.2	12.5	20.1	Rest of the world		16.2	21.3	19.4
Other (gvt)	2.0	4.2	2.3	2.8	Other (gvt)		7.9	5.4	5.7
Total	100	100	100	100	Total		100	100	100

United Kingdom	1990	1994	2000	2004	Sweden	1990	1995	2000	2005
Individuals, no profit	22.2	21.6	11.4	9.4	Non-fin. corporations	25.3	11.8	7.1	10.6
Insurance	20.4	21.9	17.8	13.7	Banks and fin. interm.	1.1	0.7	2.4	2.6
Pension funds	31.7	27.8	9.8	6.9	Mutual funds	8.5	9.1	8.5	11.5
Investm. trusts etc.	7.7	8.8	2.9	4.1	Investment comp.	10.5	6.7	6.4	5.4
Banks	0.7	0.4	1.4	2.7	Insurance companies	14.6	13.3	9.8	8.4
Other fin. institutions	0.7	1.3	4.1	10.2	General government	8.9	7.9	9.3	7.5
Priv. non fin. Institut.	2.8	1.1	1.5	0.6	Households	23.6	20.8	15.7	17.0
Public sector	2	0.8	0.0	0.1	Foreign owners	7.7	29.6	39.0	35.6
Rest of the world	11.8	16.3	22.7	27.7					
Not on crest	0	0	28.4	24.6					
Total	100	100	100	100	Total	100	100	100	100

Source: Data from national accounts. Germany: financial accounts for Germany 1991–2005 Deutsche Bundesbank; France: Banque de France, comptes nationaux financiers annuels; Italy: Banca d'Italia, relazione annuale. Sweden: Statistics Sweden, financial accounts, balance sheets; Denmark: Danmark Nationalbank, kvartalsvise finansielle konti for Danmark; United Kingdom: National Statistical Office, statbase, share ownership.

Notes
Incomparabilities due to national accounts.

on the one hand, and the bull market at the end of the 1990s, on the other, have induced savers to shift toward riskier forms of investment compared to deposits and government bonds. Pension reforms can be certainly included in the causes of these changes. They can be related to both the increase in financial wealth and to the difference in the degree of institutionalization of saving.

In countries that have introduced pension funds, household financial wealth is clearly higher (Table 11.3). This is in accordance with the fact that the provision of social security in such countries is based on the service of accumulated financial wealth while in pension systems it is based on direct repartition of savings no accumulation is needed.

Gross financial wealth as well as financial debt grows everywhere, although with different intensity. However, when institutionalized saving becomes compulsory (or at least when significant incentives are introduced), this appears to crowd out spontaneous saving. When we exclude pension assets and life insurance reserves (presuming that countries where PFs are low enjoy reasonably extended public PAYG systems) we discover very different data. In fact, the net financial wealth of the Netherlands, Denmark and the United Kingdom is rapidly decreasing while Italy and Belgium emerge as the richest countries.[11] This is mainly the effect of the rising debt of families for both durables and real estate purchases. It is difficult to say whether this is a sign of the development of financial markets or simply, from a macroeconomic point of view, a symptom that these countries are consuming their capital.

Table 11.4a Different measures of household financial wealth, %GDP

	Gross financial wealth			Net financial wealth			(Fin. debt)
	1995	2000	2004	1995	2000	2004	2004
Belgium	246.6	292.5	248.8	206.9	249.6	205.6	43.2
Germany	145.6	175.9	184.1	83.4	102.8	113.1	71.0
France	139.6	174.9	171.8	97.9	127.4	120.1	51.7
Austria	120.8	131.5	139.9	78.9	85.1	89.3	50.6
Netherlands	241.3	297.8	267.7	179.1	216.0	162.6	105.1
Portugal	181.0	187.7	201.3	140.2	113.7	110.5	90.8
Greece	127.2	175.3	135.0	117.0	152.5	91.6	43.4
Spain	141.7	166.1	162.0	99.7	112.1	92.9	69.1
Italy	171.9	230.8	226.2	151.3	203.0	192.9	33.3
Finland	58.0	110.2	112.2	20.7	77.6	67.5	44.7
Sweden	119.6	161.7	165.7	72.6	109.7	102.6	63.1
Denmark	156.8	185.2	205.3	65.0	83.5	88.0	117.3
United Kingdom	272.0	327.0	268.0	198.1	250.0	168.3	99.7
United States	292.6	339.5	312.5	223.7	264.2	220.4	92.1
Japan	266.5	287.9	298.8	179.9	201.2	217.9	80.9
Switzerland*		370.9	348.6		256.9	226.3	122.3

Sources: OECD Financial statistics, GDP from general statistics.

Note
* 2003.

Table 11.4b Not financial wealth GDP net of pension funds, percentage GDP

NFWGDP net of PFs	Net financial wealth minus life insurance and pension funds			Life insurance and pension funds			Variation
	1995	2000	2004	1995	2000	2004	2004–95
Belgium	187.5	215.2	159.5	19.4	34.4	46.1	26.8
Germany	48.1	56.8	61.5	35.3	46.0	51.7	16.4
France	68.8	79.8	65.6	29.2	47.6	54.5	25.4
Austria	64.2	63.3	64.2	14.7	21.8	25.1	10.4
Netherlands	56.3	62.5	12.2	122.9	153.5	150.4	27.5
Portugal	123.7	87.2	79.1	16.5	26.5	31.5	14.9
Greece	115.2	149.2	88.5	1.8	3.3	3.1	1.3
Spain	87.0	91.1	70.6	12.6	21.0	22.3	9.7
Italy	136.3	179.4	159.9	15.0	23.7	33.0	18.0
Finland	15.3	61.0	47.4	5.5	16.6	20.2	14.7
Sweden	41.6	58.6	50.8	31.1	51.0	51.9	20.8
Denmark	–2.7	–1.7	–7.4	67.7	85.2	95.4	27.8
United Kingdom	63.6	82.3	32.0	134.5	167.7	136.3	1.7
United States	138.5	163.7	124.2	85.3	100.6	96.2	10.9
Japan	112.5	125.8	140.8	67.4	75.4	77.1	9.7
Switzerland*		117.0	85.8		140.0	140.5	–

Notes
OCDE data (*)2003.
OECD Financial statistics, GDP from general statistics.

As a consequence, an unexpected positive relationship emerges between the debt of households and the wealth accumulated in pension funds and life insurance (Figure 11.1). It may be read according to many perspectives. It could mean that institutional investors contribute to developing a more sophisticated financial system where people can best discount their consumption preferences in the present. It could – instead – mean that this form of compulsory saving crowds out other forms of saving. This may also be related to the asset restructuring effect we discussed previously: an immaterial capital (redistribution entitlements) is transformed into a financial capital (pension funds).

Social security investment is fairly differentiated. Continental countries such as France, Belgium and Germany prefer life insurance (where there is some powerful insider). In Table 11.4a and Table 11.4b OECD data are reported, which also include mutual funds that can be used as spontaneous social security investment (third pillar) and is also useful for comparison. In the Netherlands, Denmark and Japan both life insurance and pension funds are well developed. In Germany, pension funds include company schemes such as *Direktzusagen* and other forms of employee benefits. Also, in the United Kingdom and United States, a large part of funds include company schemes which are funded in many different ways, though often not through a pooled fund.

However, we can highlight how in the countries where pension funds are well developed such institutions mainly take the form of "defined benefit" or "hybrid"

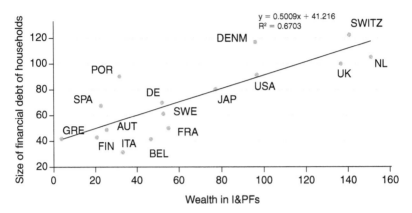

Figure 11.1 Household debts.

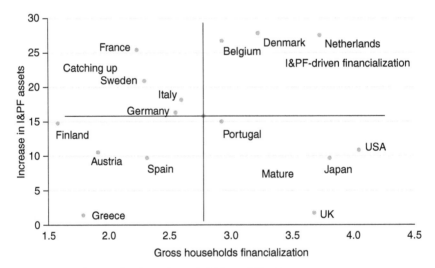

Figure 11.2 The contribution to household financialization.

schemes. In the other countries, reforms have been implemented to increase second and third pillars, but they have introduced "defined contribution" schemes. This induces little trust in employees because defined contribution shifts all risk to savers. This may explain the poor success – so far – of pension funds despite all incentives assured by governments.

Finally, to summarize the changes concerning households, we can relate the increase in assets of life insurance and pension funds (I and PF, in percentage to GDP) to the gross household financialization (value of financial assets plus liabilities as a percentage of GDP) (Figure 11.2). In this way, we can distinguish four categories of countries. In the Netherlands, Denmark and Belgium, I and PF

Table 11.5 Detail of household assets, 2000–2004 percentage GDP

	Belgium		Germany		France		Austria	
	2000	2004	2000	2003	2000	2005	2000	2004
Investment fund shares	44.6	39.5	19.8	21.5	18.4	16.6	14.6	14.4
Life insurance reserves	18.7	30.2	28.0	30.9	44.5	54.5	17.3	20.0
Pension funds	15.7	16.0	18.0	20.0	3.1	4.2	4.5	5.0
Autonomous PFs	4.4	3.9	8.6	9.4	3.1	4.2	4.5	5.0
Defined benefit	9.8	11.8			1.7	1.8		
Hybrid	0.0	0.0						
Defined contribution	0.1	0.1			1.3	2.4	4.5	5.0
Non-financial assets			222.3	220.6	209.6	345.4		
Dwellings	149.1	153.4			125.2	146.2		

	Netherlands		Spain		Italy		Finland	
	2001	2004	2000	2005	2000	2004	2000	2004
Investment fund shares	11.8	8.6	24.0	22.4	38.6	24.7	3.9	6.3
Life insurance reserves	40.2	45.0	11.3	12.1	13.9	22.4	7.8	9.9
Pension funds	102.5	105.4	9.7	10.6	2.0	2.2	8.8	10.3
Autonomous PFs	102.0	105.4	6.1	8.1	1.4	1.9	2.7	3.0
Defined benefit	102.0	104.6	0.1	0.1	0.1	0.1	5.7	9.3
Hybrid	0.0	0.0	1.6	2.0				
Defined contribution	0.5	0.8	4.3	4.9	1.9	2.1	0.4	0.9
Non-financial assets	117.0	123.2						
	102.9	109.5			139.9*	161°		

Table 11.5 continued

	Denmark		United States		Japan		Switzerland	
	2000	2004	2000	2004	2000	2004	2000	2003
Investment fund shares	10.8	14.5	39.1	39.4	6.8	7.7	33.6	31.4
Life insurance reserves	43.7	49.1	8.4	9.1	51.3	49.9	23.6	23.5
Pension funds	38.5	42.3	93.8	88.4	28.4	30.1	116.4	117.0
Autonomous PFs	38.5	42.3	78.2	70.8			92.1	91.6
Defined benefit			51.6	46.4				
Hybrid	38.5	42.3	26.6	24.5			92.1	91.6
Defined contribution								
Non-financial assets			130.8	162.8	250.1	217.9		
Dwellings	82.0							

Source: OECD data.

Notes
* Bank of Italy, 2002.

contribute to further increasing financialization, but this is also due to the developing financial debt in the former two. Then we have "catching up" countries such as Sweden, Italy, France and Germany where financialization is low due to a low debt. "Mature countries" are the United States and United Kingdom where I and PF do not greatly increase their assets.

7 Conclusion

The general aim of reforms oriented toward increasing the extent of funded "defined contribution" programs was also to enjoy positive synergies with financial markets. Such reforms have been implemented with different intensities, and starting from very differentiated systems. Direct and indirect incentives have been supplied to create and address massive flows of savings in this direction. However, the capitalization of funds is not proceeding at high speed and it finds some resistance in the lack of confidence that the employees of (most) corporatist countries have in financial markets. This lack of confidence may be due to the conflict of interest existing in bank based financial systems of corporatist economies. As a consequence, pension funds rapidly develop only in some countries where financial markets are already well developed and where people are used to these instruments. Consequently, the strategy to substitute many forms of relatively low risk pension programs (from public PAYG to "defined benefit" funds) with riskier programs (defined contribution pension funds) appears to be having little success.

On the other hand, there is no trade-off between social security systems: the cases of Switzerland and the Netherlands demonstrate that pension funds can overlay PAYG systems. These countries, rather than nations like the United Kingdom and the United States where pension funds are not highly capitalized, represent the benchmark for the development of funds of corporatist countries which have reformed their systems. Little, however, can still be said about the changing form of the social insurance function performed by these systems.

Citizens' financial positions are changing also as a consequence of these reforms. However, the expansion of their assets is not, in the main, due to PFs. The unexpected fact, which requires an explanation, is that high levels of financial wealth accumulated in pension funds tend to trade off with net financial wealth. This could be due to the fact that pension funds develop best in well-developed financial systems, but these are also the countries where household debt rises considerably decreasing the real net financial assets of households. In any case, no sign of a rising shareholder society appears on the horizon. On the contrary, the property of production means is leaving the hands of households.

Notes

* We acknowledge funding from EC, FP6, contract CIT2-CT-2004–506077, ESEMK project.
1 PAYG, "pay as you go" denotes pension systems based on the repartition financing system where social contributions finance pension expenditure and which therefore are exposed to the problem of "ageing" of population causing an unbalance between contributors and receivers.
2 A related (more abstract) distinction is that between *intermediated* and *disintermediated* systems. In the 1990s the relevance of these distinctions was questioned or defended by a number of authors.
3 The "defined contribution" in PAYG systems is called "notional defined contribution" (NDC).
4 See also Boyer (2000), Engelen (2002), Froud *et al.* (2000; 2006).
5 This point is controversial, however. Funded schemes would be too late relative to the evolution of the age structure of the society to provide a positive effect when the maximum unbalance between in and out-flows of PAYG systems occurs.
6 Supporters of funded schemes provide a large list of benefits (Lindbeck and Persson 2003), mainly assuming that institutional intermediaries and the increase in financial assets will make financial markets more like a perfect market. Such studies (e.g. Feldstein 1996) fail to explain how and why such factors may heal the present imperfections of financial markets, which are qualitative and not due to insufficient quantities of financial assets.
7 However, the accumulation of financial capital may not be such safe ground on which to base pension benefits. In fact, some scholars have started questioning the dangers

of financial instability due to the effect (via sale of financial assets by pension funds) of the retirement of baby boomers (Poterba 2001; Brooks 2002).

8 The problem of transition makes this transformation even clearer, as the Chilean experience shows: the opting out of employees from PAYG to funded programs left the former pension payment unbalanced, which then had to be financed by public debt. The latter rose by a value comparable to the growth of the private financial assets of pension funds. In the end, from the macroscopic point of view, the Chilean economy found itself with more financial capital, but also with a larger public debt, which was bought by pension funds (Minns 2000).

9 A well-known case is the role of pension funds in the acquisition of Mannesmann by Vodafone in Germany.

10 "First pillar," as understood by the European Union pension framework, is the basic scheme of basic pensions granted to all laborers and based on a repartition financial mechanism.

11 This however does not take into account the public debt, which is high in these countries.

References

Aglietta, M. and A. Reberioux (2005), *Corporate Governance Adrift: a Critique of Shareholder Value*, Cheltenham: Edward Elgar.

Allen, F. and D. Gale (2000), *Comparative Financial Systems*, Cambridge, MA: MIT Press.

André, C. (2003a), "Ten European Systems of Social Protection: An Ambiguous Convergence," in D. Pieters (ed.) *European Social Security and Global Politics*, Netherlands: Kluwer Law International: 3–44.

—— (2003b), "Ongoing Changes of Pensions in the European Union," communication at the Conférence du European Thematic Network EPOC on Privatisation of Public Pension Systems – Forces, Experiences, Prospects, Vienne, June 19–21: 68. Online, available at: www.epoc.uni-bremen.de/home.htm.

Amable, B. (2003), *The Diversity of Modern Capitalism*, Oxford: Oxford University Press.

Aoki, Masahiko (2001), *Toward a Comparative Institutional Analysis*, Cambridge, MA: MIT Press.

Boyer, R. (2000), "Is a Finance-led Growth Regime a Viable Alternative to Fordism? A Preliminary Analysis," *Economy and Society*, 29: 111–145.

Brooks, R. (2002), "Asset-market Effect of the Baby Boom and Social Security Reform," *American Economic Review*, 92(2): 402–406.

Clark, G.L. (2003a), "Pension Security in the Global Economy: Markets and National Institutions in the 21st Century," *Environment and Planning A*, 35: 1339–1356.

—— (2003b), "Comment on Ewald Engelen: The European Model is Unsustainable," *Environment and Planning A*, 35: 1373–1376.

—— (2003c), *European Pensions and Global Finance*, Oxford: Oxford University Press.

—— (2005), "Pension Fund Corporate Engagement: The Fifth Stage of Capitalism," *Industrial Relations*, 59(1): 142–171.

Clark, G.L. and N. Whiteside (eds.) (2003), *Pension Security in the 21st Century*, Oxford: Oxford University Press.

Clowes, M.J. (2001), *The Money Flood: How Pension Funds Revolutionized Investing*, New York: John Wiley.

Diamond, P.A. and P.R. Orszag (2005), "Saving Social Security," *Journal of Economic Perspectives*, 19(2): 11–32.

Disney, R. (2004), "Are Contributions to Public Pension Programmes a Tax on Employment?," *Economic Policy*, July: 267–311.

Engelen, E. (2002) "Corporate Governance, Property and Democracy: A Conceptual Critique of Shareholder Ideology," *Economy and Society*, 31: 391–413.

—— (2003a), "The Logic of Funding European Pension Restructuring and the Dangers of Financialization," *Environment and Planning A*, 35: 1357–1372.

—— (2003b), "Comment on Gordon Clark: The False Necessities of State Retreat," *Environment and Planning A*, 35: 1377–1380.

—— (2006), "Resocializing Capital: Putting Pension Savings in the Service of 'Financial Pluralism'," *Politics and Society*, 34(2): 187–218.

Ertürk, I. and S. Solari (2007), "Banks as Continuous Reinvention," *New Political Economy*, 12(3): 369–388.

Ertürk, I., Froud, J., S. Johal, S. Solari and K. Williams (2005), "The Reinvention of Prudence: Household Savings, Financialization and Forms of Capitalism," CRESC Working Paper 11.

Esping-Andersen, G. (1990), *The Three Worlds of Welfare Capitalism*, Cambridge, UK: Polity Press.

—— (1999), *Social Foundations of Post-industrial Economies*, Oxford: Oxford University Press.

European Commission (2005), Financial Integration Monitor, annex to the background document. Online, available at: http://ec.europa.eu/internal_market/finances/fim/index_en.htm.

Feldstein, M. (1997), "Transition to a Fully Funded Pension System: Five Economic Issues," NBER Working Paper 6149.

Ferrera, M. and M. Rhodes (2000), "Building a Sustainable Welfare State – Reconciling Social Justice and Growth in the Advanced Economies," *West European Politics*, 23(2): 1–10 and 257–282.

Froud, J., C. Haslam, S. Johal and K. Williams (2000), "Shareholder Value and Financialization: Consultancy Promises and Management Moves," *Economy and Society*, 29: 80–110.

Froud, J., S. Johal, A. Leaver and K. Williams (2006), *Financialization and Strategy: Narrative and Numbers*, London: Routledge.

Galbraith, J.K. (1975), *Money*, Boston: Houghton Mifflin.

Hackethal, A. and R.H. Schmidt (2004) "Financing Patterns: Measurement Concepts and Empirical Results" Working Paper J.W. Goethe Universität Frankfurt.

Lindbeck, A. and M. Persson (2003), "The Gains from Pension Reform," *Journal of Economic Literature*, XLI: 74–112.

Minns, R. (2001), *The Cold War in Welfare: Stock Markets versus Pensions*, London: Verso.

Montagne, S. (2006), *Les Fonds de Pension: Entre protection Sociale et Spéculation Financière*, Paris: Odile Jacob.

Munnell, A.H. (2003), "Restructuring Pensions for the Twenty-first Century: The United States' Social Security Debate," in G.L. Clark and N. Whiteside (eds.) *Pension Security in the 21st Century*, Oxford: Oxford University Press: 193–223.

Observatoire des retraites (various years) La Lettre. Online, available at: www.observatoire-retraites.org.

OECD (2005) *Ageing and Pension Reform, Implications for Financial Markets and Economic Policies*, Paris: OECD.

—— (2007), *Pensions at a Glance*, Paris: OECD.

Orszag, P.R. and Stiglitz J.E. (2001), "Rethinking Pension Reform: Ten Myths about Social Security Systems," in Holzman R. and Stiglitz J.E. (eds.) *New Ideas about Old Age Security: Toward Sustainable Pension Systems in the Twenty-first Century*, Washington, DC: World Bank.

Palme, J. (2003), "Pension Reform in Sweden and Changing Boundaries between Public and Private," in G.L. Clark and N. Whiteside (eds.) *Pension Security in the 21st Century*, Oxford: Oxford University Press: 144–166.

Poterba, J.M. (2001), "Demographic Structure and Assets Return," *Review of Economics and Statistics*, 83(4): 565–584.

Rajan, R.G. and L. Zingales (2002), "Banks and Markets: The Changing Character of European Finance," in V. Gaspar, P. Hartmann and O. Sleijpen (eds.) *The Transformation of the European Financial System*, Frankfurt: ECB: 123–167.

—— (2003), "The Great Reversals: The Politics of Financial Development in the 20th Century," *Journal of Financial Economics*, 69: 5–50.

Riel, B. van, A. Hemerijck and J. Visser (2003), "Is there a Dutch Way to Pension Reform?," in G.L. Clark and N. Whiteside (eds.) *Pension Security in the 21st Century*, Oxford: Oxford University Press, 64–92.

Röpke, W. (1958 [1998]), *Humane Economy: The Social Framework of the Free Market*, Wilmington, DE: ISI books.

Schmähl, W. (2003), "Private Pensions as Partial Substitute for Public Pensions in Germany," in G.L. Clark and N. Whiteside (eds.) *Pension Security in the 21st Century*, Oxford: Oxford University Press: 115–141.

Schmidt, R.H. and M. Tyrell (2003), "What Constitutes a Financial System in General and the German Financial System in Particular?," Working Paper J.W. Goethe Universität Frankfurt.

Schmidt, R.H., A. Hackethal and M. Tyrell (1999), "Disintermediation and the Role of Banks in Europe: An International Comparison," *Journal of Financial Intermediation*, 8: 36–67.

Solari, S. (2004), "The Impact of Welfare Systems Reforms: The Case of Italian TFR," *Rivista Italiana di Scienze Economiche e Commerciali (*RISEC), 51(3): 367–392.

Shiller, R.J. (2000), *Irrational Exuberance*, New York: Broadway Books.

Sinn, H.W. (2000), "Why a Funded Pension System is Useful and Why it is not Useful," NBER Working Paper 7592.

Stockhammer, E. (2004), "Financialization and the Slowdown of Accumulation," *Cambridge Journal of Economics*, 28(5): 719–741.

Tiemstra, J. (2007), "The Case against Financial Globalisation," paper presented at ASE conference, Amsterdam, June 7–9.

Toporowski, J. (2000), *The End of Finance*, London: Routledge.

Tyrell, M. and Schmidt R.H. (2001), "Pension Systems and Financial Systems in Europe: A Comparison from the Point of View of Complementarity," *IFOStudien* (4): 469–503.

Valdés-Prieto, S. (2005), "Securitisation of Taxes Implicit in PAYG Pensions," *Economic Policy*, April: 215–265.

Vito, F. (1949), *Economia e Personalismo*, Milan: Vita e Pensiero.

Part IV
Ethics and social economics

12 Market operation and distributive justice

An evaluation of the ACCRA confession

*Johan Graafland**

1 Introduction

In August 2004 the General Council of the World Alliance of Reformed Churches (WARC) committed itself to a declaration of faith about the world economy in Accra (Ghana). The declaration is a response to the growing world-wide economic injustice and environmental destruction.[1] The declaration refers to the huge differences between rich and poor. To illustrate: the annual income of the richest 1 percent is equal to that of the poorest 57 percent; 24,000 people die each day from poverty and malnutrition; the debt of poor countries continues to increase.

According to the WARC the main cause of these problems is the current economic globalization led by the United States, together with international finance and trade institutions (IMF, World Bank, WTO), who use political, economic and military alliances to protect and advance the interests of capital owners. According to the declaration, the economic system is based on the following beliefs:[2]

- Unrestrained competition, consumerism and the unlimited growth and accumulation of wealth is best for the whole world;
- The ownership of private property has no social obligation;
- Capital speculation, liberalization and deregulation of the market, privatization of public utilities and national resources, unrestricted access for foreign investments and imports, lower taxes and the unrestricted movement of capital will achieve wealth for all;
- Social obligations, protection of the poor and the weak, trade unions, and relationships between people are subordinate to the processes of economic growth and capital accumulation.

The character of the declaration is most visible where the WARC connects this analysis to biblical teaching. The declaration is very pronounced in its wording. It claims that the worldwide economic system causes accumulation of the wealth of the rich at the expense of the poor, and considers this as unfaithfulness to God. The declaration refers to Luke 16: 13, where Jesus teaches that we cannot serve both God and Mammon.

The strong condemnation of the free market system is particularly strongly stated in the third part of the declaration that alternately makes a statement of faith, followed by a rejection of an aspect of the free market economy. To illustrate, the declaration states in articles 18 and 19:

> We believe that God is sovereign over all creation. "The earth is the Lord's and the fullness thereof" (Ps. 24: 1). Therefore, we reject the current economic order imposed by global neoliberal capitalism and any other economic system, including absolute planned economies, which defy God's covenant by excluding the poor, the vulnerable and the whole of creation from the fullness of life.

And in articles 20 and 21:

> We believe that God has made a covenant with all of creation (Gen. 9: 8–12). God has brought into being an earth community based on the vision of justice and peace … Jesus shows that this is an inclusive covenant in which the poor and marginalized are preferential partners… Therefore we reject the culture of rampant consumerism and the competitive greed and selfishness of the neoliberal global market system, or any other system, which claims there is no alternative.

The WARC states that the integrity of Christian faith can be questioned if churches refuse to act against the current economic system of globalization. In this it seems to endorse Duchrow's claim that the global economy is a confessional issue for churches (Duchrow 1987). The declaration therefore ends with a commitment that churches should devote their time and energy to change, renew and restore the economy. This is considered to be a matter of a choice for life: "so that we and our descendants might live" (Deut. 30: 19).

The declaration of Accra appeals to a commonly shared feeling of uneasiness about the current worldwide economic order and the lack of a just income distribution. Still, many local churches feel that the declaration lacks a nuanced view on the causes of worldwide poverty and the role of globalization. As a result, it risks missing its purpose of convincing and activating church members. In this chapter, we review the declaration's main point that the free market economic system is unjust. More specifically, we investigate two claims on which the declaration rests: a theological statement that extreme poverty is unjust in the eyes of God; and an empirical statement that the free market system benefits the rich at the expense of the poor and causes extreme poverty. For that purpose, we first present various different criteria of distributive justice. Next, we investigate which of these modern concepts of distributive justice are supported by biblical texts. Although the Bible is not a handbook of ethics (Gorringe 1994), we will see that many texts support one of the various modern criteria of distributive justice. Next, we turn to empirical evidence that free markets increase worldwide inequality within countries and between countries. The last section summarizes the main conclusions.

2 Distributive justice: an overview of standards

In all cases where different people put forth conflicting claims of property rights which cannot be satisfied simultaneously, questions of distributive justice arise. The formal principle of distributive justice requires that equals should be treated equally and unequals should be treated unequally in proportion to the degree to which they are unequal. This is an evident principle, but the difficulty starts with the question: when are people equal and when are they unequal? Which criteria should be applied to compare different persons? There are several alternative answers to this question, ranging from socialist principles that stress equality in income to the libertarian principle that gives priority to individual freedom (Graafland 2007a; see Table 12.1).

The first norm is absolute egalitarianism. Absolute egalitarianism holds that all people are equal in all aspects. There are no relevant differences that justify unequal treatment. This implies an equal share in the benefits and burdens. An example of an economic application is a strict communist system in which each person obtains an equal income. Such a system requires that all incomes are taxed at a rate of 100 per cent and completely redistributed by a central authority.

An absolute communist system of income distribution may, however, be very harmful for the economy. If everyone receives the same income, the lazy person

Table 12.1 Ten alternative standards of distributive justice

Principle	Description
Absolute egalitarianism	Everybody an equal share
Difference principle	Inequalities allowed up to the point where the least advantaged get most in comparison to other distributions
Needs and ability principles	People get in accordance to needs, people should contribute in accordance to ability
Capability	People who need more to develop capabilities, get more
Utilitarianism	Equalize marginal utility of all individuals
Equal opportunity	Positions are open to all under conditions of fair equality of opportunity
Reward to effort	Distribution according to the efforts of individuals
Reward to productivity	Distribution according to the productivity of individuals
Reward to market price	Distribution according to the market mechanism
Freedom	Distribution by free transactions

will earn as much as the industrious person. Hence, there will be no economic incentive to work. A less extreme variant of egalitarianism, the difference principle of Rawls (1999), acknowledges that allowing some inequalities will benefit all people, including the least advantaged. The difference principle requires that the primary social goods of the least advantaged group be maximized. Primary social goods are goods that any rational person wants and include income and wealth (besides rights, liberties, opportunities and self respect). The difference principle may still require substantial redistribution, although less than 100 percent, because some inequality will render everyone better off, including the least advantaged.

The Rawlsian difference principle is, however, insensitive to special needs, such as of the disabled, the old, or the ill. These groups may be unable to produce anything worthwhile and at the same time need more income than healthy persons to obtain a similar level of well-being. This notion is captured by the third principle which states that benefits should be distributed according to people's needs and burdens should be distributed according to people's ability (Velasquez 1998).

A standard that is closely related to the needs principle is the capability approach of Sen (1984). His theory concentrates on the realization of certain powers or capabilities. The crippled individual's entitlement to more income arises in this view from the deprivation of his ability to move about unless he happens to have more income or more specialized goods (for example, vehicles for the disabled).[3] There are, according to Sen (1984), some specific differences between a needs approach and his own capability approach. First, in the needs approach needs are defined in terms of commodities. Particular goods and services are required to achieve certain results, even though it is acknowledged that different persons need different commodities to satisfy their needs. However, the relation between commodities and capabilities may be a many–one correspondence, with the same capabilities being achievable by more than one particular bundle of commodities. Second, the commodity requirement for specific capabilities may be dependent on the social context. A third difference is that "needs" is a more passive concept than capability. A final difference is that the needs approach tends to focus on basic needs, i.e. on a minimum quantity of particular goods. This may lead to a softening of opposition to inequality when the average level of welfare increases. Equality of capabilities is not prejudiced by the special concern with basic needs and can be used for judging justice at any level of development.

In utilitarianism, all that matters is maximization of the total amount of happiness or desire-fulfillment. Utilitarianism does not exclude a high degree of equality, because the utilitarian criterion of maximizing total utility prescribes that income should be redistributed until the marginal utility of all persons is equalized. As Singer (1972) argues, this implies a moral duty to give money if it is in one's power to prevent damages without thereby sacrificing anything of comparable value.

The sixth principle, the principle of equal opportunities, is also proposed by John Rawls (1999). This principle does not focus on outcomes but on opportunities. Although this principle is more liberal in nature than the preceding principles, it is still closely related to them, because the principle of equal opportunity requires that the influence of social contingencies and natural fortune should be mitigated. This may require, for example, affirmative action to rectify the effects of past discrimination.

The next three principles reflect capitalistic norms of fairness, which distribute benefits according to the value of the contribution that individuals make. This kind of principle is also called distribution according to moral desert. This principle states that each person should obtain that which he deserves. When a person has performed labor on some property, he or she has engaged in an activity that either displays some sort of human excellence (such as working hard) or confers a needed benefit on surrounding others (like making an object they want to buy) (Christman 1998). Thus, if a worker adds value to the lives of others in some permissible way and without being required to do so, that person deserves a fitting benefit. There are several ways of measuring this value. A first approach is to relate benefits to the individual work effort of a person. However, this approach encounters several problems such as measurement of work effort and a lack of compensatory justice if people work hard but not in a productive way. For this reason, it might be better to relate the value to the productivity of the person. This criterion of justice is consistent with Locke's property concept, that each person has a right to ownership over his own body, his own labor and the products of his labor. However, just as with work effort, it is often difficult to determine the exact productivity of workers, especially if their work is complementary to the work of others. The third approach, the market mechanism, determines one's contribution on the basis of the market price of the worker. In a perfect market each factor of production will be paid its marginal product. The total income reaped by an owner of production factors is the product of the price of the goods and labor he holds and the amount of his endowment of that factor.

The final and most liberal principle of justice is the entitlement theory of Nozick (1974).[4] Nozick does not accept any end-result principle. Justice only consists in an unhindered operation of the just procedures of justice in acquisition, transfer and rectification. Justice in acquisition concerns the appropriation of unowned things, which is subject to the proviso that there be enough and as good left in common for others. Justice in transfers requires that parties involved in a transfer voluntarily agree to the transfer. Justice in rectification requires that injustice resulting from a violation of the other two principles should be rectified. Nozick's theory slightly differs from the capitalistic principle of income in accordance to contribution. For example, Nozick also accepts voluntary transactions that do not allocate income according to merit, for example by inheritance or gifts, provided that these transactions are voluntary.

3 Which principles does the Bible support?

According to the WARC declaration, the root causes of massive threats to life are above all the product of an unjust economic system. The globalized free market system is opposing the covenant that God has made with all of creation. In article 20 of the declaration, the WARC states that the covenant is an inclusive covenant in which the poor and marginalized are preferential partners. It calls on us to put justice for the "least of these" (Mt 25: 40) at the centre of community life. Jesus did not only identify himself with the poor (Sider 1977), but proclaimed that he would do justice to the oppressed, give bread to the hungry; free the prisoner and restore the sight to the blind (Luke 4.18). In article 24 the WARC declares that God is a God of justice. God calls for just relationships with all creation. More specifically, God is in a special way the God of the destitute, the poor, the exploited, the wronged and the abused (Ps. 146: 7–9).

These statements indicate that the concept of justice that the WARC declaration assumes is egalitarian. The poor and marginalized are the focus of justice. They are preferential partners in the covenant of God. In Christian ethics, defining justice in terms of the so-called privilege of the poor (De Santa Ana 1977) is, however, not uncontested. There is some discussion regarding which standard of justice is endorsed by the Bible. In Christian ethics, two opposing views can be distinguished. On the one hand, libertarian Christians like Beisner and Novak defend the capitalistic or libertarian views on justice. According to Novak (1982: 345), God is not committed to equality of results. The Bible stresses ultimate competition; there are winners and losers. According to Beisner (1994), the biblical concept of justice can be summarized as rendering impartially to everyone his or her due in proper proportion. This would lend support to the last four standards of distributive justice described in Section 2. Other Christian ethicists defend the priority of the poor. The Bible favors a special treatment of the poor in justice and law and acknowledges their special needs. The poor are given priority, not because God loves them more, but because their wretchedness requires greater attention if the equal regard called forth by the equal merit of all persons is to be achieved (Mott 1994). In this section we will discuss both views and investigate whether the Bible supports the last view, which is also expressed by the Accra declaration.

3.1 Capitalistic justice

Let's start with the libertarian principle of procedural justice. The Bible indeed mentions many texts that express the right to private property, condemn stealing (Exod. 20:15; Lev. 19:11; Prov. 23:10; Eph. 4:28), require compliance to contracts (Jer. 22:13) and demand rectification if the principle of justice in transfers is violated (Exod. 22:4–7; Lev. 5:14–16, 6:1–5, 22:14; Num. 5:5–8; Prov. 6:30–31). Beisner (1994) argues that if justice defined along libertarian and capitalistic lines would really have been taken seriously in biblical times, the poor would not have been abused and in many cases they would not have become poor. In this view unjust oppression of the poor is in the Bible always linked to violation of their (negative) rights to freedom. The complaints of the Old Testament prophets should be read against the background of a hierarchical structure that developed during the reign of Solomon. During this time, the pressure of the royal court on the population increased (Van Leeuwen 1956; Soggin 1993). For example, 1 Kings 5:13 reports that 30,000 men were forced to labor for Solomon's building. In addition, 80,000 men were forced to work in quarries and another 70,000 were porters. The forced labor and the high taxes for the royal organization especially hit small peasants (Davies 1989). This situation continued during the period of kings following Solomon. Excavations have shown that during this time the royal court inhabited large palaces, whereas the common people had to live in slums (De Vaux 1989).

There are also many texts that support the capitalistic principle of moral desert. Trade should be honest. One should use true and honest weights and measures and not cheat the other trading partner (Deut. 25:13–16; Ezek. 45:10; Mic. 6:10; Amos 8:5; Prov. 20:10). So one should be rewarded in accordance to what one really brings to the market. Many texts in the Old Testament and New Testament support the idea that effort or productivity should be rewarded. Jesus applies this principle in the parable of the three servants (Matt. 25:29) and the parable of the gold coins (Luke 19:26). Also in the Kingdom of God, everybody shall be rewarded in accordance to his or her deeds (Matt. 6:3, 19:29; Luke 6:38, 18:29–30). The apostle Paul defends a similar standard (1 Cor. 3:8, 12–15; 1 Tim. 5:18; 2 Thess. 3:10).

3.2 Socialist justice

So, basically, the Bible supports at length the capitalistic principles of justice. But is that all? According to Calvin Beisner it is. Although Beisner acknowledges that God commands the rich to show mercy to the poor and that mercilessness is a sin (Deut. 15:7–11), relief to the poor is a matter of charitas, not of justice. The poor do not have an unqualified positive right to assistance by others, just because they are poor. There is no perfect duty for the rich to guarantee a subsistence level of welfare for the poor that can or should, if necessary, be enforced by the state.

This argument seems invalid for two reasons. First, violation of negative rights of freedom is not the only cause of poverty. An example is Naomi. Others did not harm her negative rights to freedom. Nevertheless, she was impoverished as a result of the early death of her husband and sons. Also periods of drought could impoverish small farmers. According to Frick (1989), the general climatic patterns in Palestine have not changed significantly since around 6000 BC. Palestine suffers from occurrences of a series of sub-normal years. Farmers often experience three consecutive dry years. Coincidentally, this explains the possibility of disastrous drought in the time of Elijah (I Kgs. 18:1). Whereas a farmer could weather a single dry year, a series of such years caused severe want.

A second argument against the libertarian view on biblical justice is that the Bible commands several institutions that protect the poor, independently from the causes of their poverty (Mott 1994). For example, the poor received food during the sabbatical year (Exod. 23:10) and from what was passed over in the first harvest (Deut. 24:19–22). The hungry were to be allowed immediate consumption of food in the grain fields (Deut. 23:24) and farmers were not to cut the corn at the edges of the fields, but leave them for the poor (Lev. 19:9–10). Other examples are the law of the tenth (Lev. 27:30; Num. 18:2 1; Deut. 12:6; Amos 4:4), the law to share with the poor food at the harvest festival (Deut. 16:11) and the prohibition on demanding interest from the poor (Exod. 22:25; Lev. 25:36; Deut. 23:19; Prov. 28:8). Thus, aid to the suffering is not merely a matter of personal duty to be merciful.

These rules fit with the needs principle of distributive justice. There is no qualification in any of these texts stating the poor people thus provided for are victims of procedural injustice. They merely are needy. The need principle is also behind prohibitions to delay the payment of a worker's wage (Deut. 24:14–15; Lev. 19:13) or the hoarding of grain during times of hunger (Prov. 11:26). There are many other texts that confirm the relevance of the need principle. An example is how God provided Israel with manna in the desert: "Every morning each gathered as much as he needed" (Exod. 16:15–18). Also Paul refers to this text in 2 Cor. 8:15.[5] However, it should also be noted that most provisions to sustain the poor required their own effort. The rule of leaving corn in the fields uncut for the poor helped them, but they could only get food by doing relatively unproductive work.

What about the other standards of distributive justice? Does the Bible support these principles as well? First, some texts can be used to defend the capability theory of Sen. The poor should not only receive aid to keep them alive, but also be provided with the means to develop their capacities and maintain their freedom. Only then would they be able to live a life of dignity. An example is Deuteronomy 15:13–14, which commands slaveholders to free the slaves in the sabbatical year and to provide them with sheep, corn and wine. This would enable the released slave to build up a new and independent life. With the deliverance from slavery the exploitation of the weak by the powerful is rejected. Like many social laws, this is motivated by Israel's own deliverance from the slavery in Egypt (Meeks 1989). Another example is the prohibition to demand a working tool as security for a loan, such as a millstone, because this would take away the family's means of preparing food to stay alive (Deut. 24:6). A third example is the law of the jubilee year (Lev. 25:8–22). In this year, all property that had been sold should be restored to the original owner or his descendants. The text justifies this prescription by the principle that God is the owner of the land (Klenicki 1997). The land was a gift of God imparted to all the people of Israel. No member of the community was to be denied the privilege of enjoying the benefits of the land and its produce (Graafland 2001). One can interpret this institution as an application of the capability principle of Sen, since land was a necessary resource for people to develop their capabilities and exercise real freedom. It did not only provide people with the capital that allows one to earn an income, but also offered the possibility to participate fully in the community. The loss of land did not only involve economic hardship, but also a loss of representation in the local assembly (Davies 1989).

The law of the Jubilee year can also be interpreted as an application of the principle of equal opportunities. Land was the main capital in Israel. The Jubilee year implies that once in 50 years the next generation should have the opportunity to start anew. They received the capital that they needed to be economically successful. But, of course, the assigned land was just a start. They had the responsibility to use the capital in the right way to build up a prosperous life.

There are no biblical texts that support utilitarianism or the difference principle. The Bible is largely unfamiliar with the modern concepts of (marginal) utility and efficiency. It does not propose some kind of maximization of total happiness or of the social primary goods of the least advantaged group. Nor does the Bible defend absolute egalitarianism, because it does not force everybody to have exactly the same. Nevertheless, it should be acknowledged that the egalitarian ideal is not completely unfamiliar. For example, after the occupation of Canaan, the Israelite tribes were each allotted their territorial areas. It is clear from Joshua 13–19 that the land was allocated on a broadly equitable basis, so that each clan and each individual household had a right to a share in the inheritance of God's people (Wright 1983). Also the eschatological ideal, as expressed, for example, in Micah 4:4 ("Everyone will live in peace among his own vineyards and fig trees") pictures a situation where everybody will be happy and will equally enjoy life. That does not allow very unequal positions.

4 Market operation and socialist justice

In this section we review some empirical research on the relationship between markets and socialist justice. Is it true that, as the Accra declaration claims, that the current economic system causes accumulation of the wealth of the rich at the expense of the poor? More specifically, is there empirical information that provides insight into whether the internationalization of the market system contributes to or harms distributive justice?

4.1 Indicators

We focus on a subset of socialist principles of distributive justice, namely the needs principle and egalitarianism. The number of people living below certain poverty lines and the human development index are used as approximations of the fulfillment of basic human needs. The degree of egalitarianism is approximated by indices of income (in)equality within countries, such as the Gini index, and between countries. For the other socialist standards of distributive justice empirical indicators are much harder to obtain.

Also the measurement of the degree of market operation is problematic. There is no literature that relates indicators of the degree of competitiveness (such as the relative profit measure; the price-cost margin; the labor income ratio and the Herfindahl index[6]) to poverty, human development or to income inequality. Often the index of economic freedom (or sub-indices which are used for its construction, such as the size of a country's trade relative to potential, see Table 12.2) is used as an indicator for free market operation.

Table 12.2 Aspects of economic freedom according to the Fraser Institute

International trade	Taxes on international trade (−)	*Monetary policy and inflation*	Volatility of inflation (−)
	Size of a country's trade relative to potential (+)		Monetary growth rate (−)
International capital flows	Restrictions on capital flows (−)	*Price controls and regulation and market entry*	Price controls (−)
			Controls on borrowing and lending rates (−) Freedom to compete in markets (+)
Black market	Differences between an official exchange rate and black market rate (−)		
Government intervention	Public consumption as a % of GDP (−)	*Banking*	Citizens' rights to hold bank accounts abroad (+)
	Subsidies and transfer payments as a % of GDP (−)		Citizens' rights to hold foreign currency accounts domestically (+)
	The role and presence of state-operated enterprises (−)		
Taxes	Top marginal tax rates (and income threshold at which it applies) (−) Conscription (−)	*Property rights*	Equality of citizens under law and access to judiciary (+)

Note
a The nature of the impact (positive or negative) of the variable on the index of economic freedom is mentioned in brackets.

This index captures what Thomas Friedman has termed the Golden Strait-jacket[7]: tight money, small government, low taxes, flexible labor legislation, deregulation, privatization and openness all around, and thus provides a conceptualization of the economic system that the WARC criticizes. Since a number of studies find a positive causal influence of economic freedom on GDP per capita (Easton and Walker 1997; Dawson 1998; De Haan and Sturm 2000; Sturm and De Haan 2001; Scully 2002), we also investigate the relationship between GDP per capita and the fulfillment of needs or income equality.

4.2 Market operation and basic needs

A first indication of the impact of international markets on the fulfillment of needs is absolute poverty. The globalization of the world economy during the last decade has been accompanied by a relative decline in poverty. From 1990 to 2004, the absolute number of people living below the poverty line of $1.08 per day declined from 1.25 billion to 980 million (UN 2007). Poverty particularly substantially declined in East Asia. An example is China: after the transformation to a market system in 1978, the number of people living in poverty (below $1 per day) declined from 634 million in 1981 to 212 million in 2001 (World Bank 2006). In Africa, the absolute number of poor people remained high, but as a percentage of population the statistics also show a modest decline, particularly after 1999.

The analysis of the impact of markets on poverty is hindered by the fact that pure market liberalization seldom takes place. China grew because it allowed more private initiative, but flouted many other rules of the free market (Rodrik 2002). In order to calculate the effects of trade liberalization on poverty, computable general equilibrium (CGE) models are often used (Ackerman 2005). CGE models, such as the Global Trade Analysis Project (GTAP) model and the LINKAGE model of the World Bank, project that full trade liberalization would generate a one-time, not continuing, rise of 0.44 percent of GDP in developing countries. Using "poverty elasticities" calculated by the World Bank,[8] full trade liberalization would lift an estimated 66 million people out of poverty (using the $2 per day poverty line). For the world as a whole, this would represent a 3.4 percent reduction in poverty. Under the lower $1 per day poverty line, full liberalization would reduce poverty by 32 million people. This outcome indicates that trade liberalization may contribute to a reduction in poverty, but only to a very limited degree. It should be noted, however, that these estimates are surrounded with a high degree of uncertainty.

Empirical studies broadly support the view that trade liberalization will be poverty alleviating in the long run and on average (Winters *et al.* 2004). Winters *et al.* distinguish several channels. First, trade liberalization will stimulate economic growth and economic growth tends to decrease absolute poverty. Trade liberalization also fosters productivity growth. Although the effect on poverty

Table 12.3 Poverty (less than $1.08 per day, as a percentage of population)

Region	1990	1999	2004
East Asia	33.0	17.8	9.9
Southeast Asia	20.8	8.9	6.8
Latin America and Caribbean	10.3	9.6	8.7
Western Asia	1.6	2.5	3.8
Southern Asia	41.1	33.4	29.5
Sub-Saharan Africa	46.8	45.9	41.1

Source: UN (2007).

reduction is uncertain, productivity growth is seen as a necessary part of any viable poverty reduction strategy for the long term. The empirical evidence for other channels through which trade liberalization may reduce poverty – through more economic stability, through price reduction of consumer goods, through the creation and destruction of markets, through the creation of employment or increase in wages, through more government revenue – is, however, not unambiguous and highly dependent on local institutions and complementing policies of the government. There is quite a lot of evidence that poorer households may be less able than richer ones to protect themselves against adverse effects from more trade liberalization or to take advantage of new opportunities created by openness. Therefore, there is an important role for additional policies to provide social protection and to enhance the ability of poorer household to benefit from new opportunities.

Another indicator of the fulfillment of basic needs is the Human Development Index (HDI). This index combines three dimensions of human welfare: life expectancy (as an indicator of a long and healthy life); the adult literacy rate combined with primary, secondary, and tertiary gross enrollment ratios (as an indicator of knowledge); and real GDP per capita (as an indicator of the standard of living). Biermans (2005) shows that the first two aspects (health and knowledge) are positively related to the third aspect of the HDI (standard of living). This is particularly true for poor countries. Diener and Diener (1995) provide similar findings for the so-called basic needs fulfillment index (including percent of population having safe drinking water, rate of infant mortality, mean life expectancy, percent of population with sanitary facilities and mean daily calorie supply per person). They showed that this index is significantly positively related to GDP per capita at low levels of income, but then levels off at higher levels of income.

This positive relationship does not prove, however, a causal influence of economic welfare on human development, because the causal link can run in both directions. Ranis and Stewart (2005) present empirical support for both directions of causality by using lag structures that reduce the simultaneity bias. They also argue that the influence of economic welfare on human development crucially depends on the degree of income equality. The propensity of households to spend their income on products that contribute most to the fulfillment of basic needs – food, potable water, education and health – increases if the incomes of the poor rise. One estimate suggests, for example, that if the distribution of income in Brazil was as equal as that in Malaysia, school enrollments among poor children would be 40 percent higher.

4.3 Market operation and income equality within countries

Income equality is not only important for the fulfillment of basic needs through economic growth, but is also an important condition for economic growth as such. There is now a growing consensus that countries with an initial egalitarian distribution of assets and income tend to grow faster than countries with initial high inequality (Van de Hoeven 2009). This means that reducing inequality strikes a double blow against poverty. On the one hand, a growth path characterized by greater equality at the margin directly benefits the poor in the short run. On the other hand, an initial high level of equality contributes to economic growth as well. The question that we discuss in this section and the next section is how a free market system affects equality.

Equality can be based on income, wealth, consumption or any other reasonable proxy for well-being (such as job opportunities and social security). Most of the empirical research focuses on equality of annual income, because data for other types of equality are less available. In this section we first consider income equality within countries.

According to the so-called Kuznets curve, income inequality will initially rise with GDP per capita but then fall, as countries get richer. The history of the poor and rich countries seems to confirm this relationship (Glaeser 2005). Cornia (2004) argues that the last two decades have witnessed a rise in within-country inequality in developing countries. Also the World Bank (2006) refers to various researches that show that trade liberalization has a positive influence on wage inequality. This is confirmed by a recent overview article of Goldberg and Pavcnik (2007). They show that the exposure of developing countries to international markets as measured by the degree of trade protection, the share of imports and/or exports in GDP, the magnitude of foreign direct investment and exchange rate fluctuations has increased inequality in the short and medium run, although the precise effect depends on country and time specific factors. They research seven representative developing countries that have substantially reduced import tariff levels and non-tariff barriers to trade during the 1980s and 1990s. All these countries have experienced an increase in wage dispersion between high and low skilled labor, coinciding with the trade reforms.[9] Goldberg and Pavcnik offer several explanations. First, the recent rise of China and other low-income developing countries (India, Indonesia, Pakistan, etc.) may have shifted the comparative advantage in middle-income countries from low skill to intermediate or high skill intensity and therefore increased the demand and wage for skilled labor at the expense of unskilled labor. Some of the middle-income countries started to outsource their production to the upcoming low-income developing countries and this also raised the skill premium in the developing countries. Second, globalization has fostered international capital inflows into the developing countries. Since the utilization of capital normally requires the use of a higher share of skilled labor, the demand for skilled workers has increased as well. A similar mechanism is skill-biased technological change. This technological change may have taken the form of increased imports of machines, office equipment and other capital goods that are complementary to skilled labor. Liberalization may also have raised the demand for skilled labor, because it advantages companies that are operating more efficiently or closer to the technological frontier. Trade shifts resources from nonexporters to exporters and there is ample empirical evidence that exporters tend to be more productive than nonexporters. Trade openness may also have induced an additional upgrading of these firms, which are partly passed on to skilled workers in the form of higher wages. Finally, some research indicates that trade liberalization has increased the prices of consumption goods (such as food and beverages) that have a large relative share in the consumption bundle of the poor, and decreased the prices of goods that are consumed in greater proportion by the rich. The latter effect seems, however, to be relatively small compared to the effects on the wage dispersion between unskilled and skilled labor.

For the longer run, the effects are uncertain. Some studies indicated that market operation decreases income inequality in the longer run. Scully (2002) estimates that the index of economic freedom has a small but significant negative impact on the Gini index. Also Berggren (1999) finds that sustained and gradual increases in economic freedom influence equality measures positively. According to Berggren (1999), trade liberalization and financial mobility are driving these results, perhaps because poor people are employed in industries that expand and flourish with freer trade.

Market operation does not guarantee, however, that the income distribution will become more equal (once a certain point of welfare has been reached). This is illustrated by the United States. Initially, the economic process in the United States was very much in line with the Kuznets curve. The share of national wealth earned by the top 1 percent rose from 15 percent in 1775 to 30 percent in 1855 and 45 percent in 1935. After 1935 inequality declined, but this process stopped at the end of the 1960s. A similar pattern has been observed for the Gini-index. After a substantial decline between the 1930s and the second half of the 1960s, it has substantially increased since 1975, partly as a result of economic factors (skill based technological change, increased trade and globalization,[10] the decline of unions) and partly as a result of political factors (less progressive taxation, lower minimum wages and unemployment benefits). Table 12.4 confirms that European countries with a large government share show more income equality than the United States. Obviously, the institutions in the United States are less egalitarian and probably do not meet the difference principle of Rawls.

The negative relationship between market operation and the Gini index for the rich countries is also confirmed if we compare the index of economic freedom of the Fraser Institute with the Gini coefficient for the countries reported in Table 12.4. This index of economic freedom is negatively related to government intervention (measured by public consumption spending as a share of GDP, subsidies and transfer payments as a share of GDP and the presence of state-operated enterprises) and the level of top marginal tax rates. This explains why, *ceteris paribus*, this index is higher for the United States than for European countries. Estimation results of Scully (2002) for a larger sample of 80 advanced countries confirm that income inequality depends negatively on the share of government expenditures in GDP (both government consumption and transfers and subsidies).

Whether market operation contributes to income equality also heavily depends on the type of institutions governing the capital, output and labor

Table 12.4 Income distribution, government share and economic freedom

	% government. expenditure in GDP[a]	Gini index [b]	Index of economic freedom[c]
Denmark	56.3	24.7	7.7
Sweden	57.3	24.9	7.3
Finland	50.7	26.9	7.6
Norway	46.4	25.8	7.3
Scandinavia	52.7	25.6	7.5
Belgium	49.3	25.0	7.4
Germany	46.8	28.3	7.5
Netherlands	48.6	32.6	7.7
France	53.4	32.7	6.9
Mid. Europe	49.5	29.7	7.4
Ireland	34.2	35.9	7.9
U.K.	43.9	36.0	8.1
U.S.	36.5	40.8	8.2

Sources:
a GGDC database (2005). Online, available at: www.ggdc.net/dseries/totecon.html.
b United Nations Development Program (2004).
c Index of economic freedom. Online, available at: http://en.wikipedia.org/wiki/Index_of_Eonomiic_Freedom.

markets (World Bank 2006). In many developing countries, access to the financial market is highly unequal. A small number of wealthy families exert extensive control over the financial sector. Fast liberalization and privatization allow powerful insiders to gain control over state banks (Stiglitz 2002). The poor often have to pay much higher interest rates. Prahalad (2006) mentions the example of Dhavarie (a district of Mumbai) in India, where the interest rate for the poor equals 600–1,000 percent, compared to 12–18 percent for the rich in Bombay. Also labor market institutions can lead to significant equity gains. Examples are: the right to be represented by unions, minimum wage legislation and labor security regulations. Important product market institutions are: antitrust legislation, good infrastructure and low transportation costs, and supply of information (for example by Internet connections in rural areas).

4.4 Market operation and equality between countries

According to Milanovic (2005), 70 percent of worldwide income inequality arises from income variation between countries and 30 percent from income inequality within countries. In order to determine the impact of international markets on equality, one should therefore not only look at income inequality measures for individual countries, but also consider the convergence between countries.

Table 12.5 indicates that the expansion of international markets has not contributed to more income equality between rich and poor countries. From 1820 to 2001 the ratio of per capita income between the richest and the poorest country

Table 12.5 Trends in worldwide income relations[a]

	Growth rate real income per capita[b]			Ratio of real income per capita compared to Western countries				
	Total 1820–2001	Annual 1973–1980	Annual 1980–2001	1820	1950	1973	1980	2001
Western countries	19.0	1.9	1.9					
East Europe	8.8	2.1	0.2	0.57	0.34	0.37	0.38	0.26
USSR	6.7	0.8	−1.6	0.57	0.45	0.45	0.42	0.20
Latin America	8.4	2.7	0.3	0.58	0.40	0.34	0.35	0.25
Asia	6.9	2.8	2.3	0.48	0.15	0.15	0.16	0.18
China	6.0	3.5	5.9	0.50	0.07	0.06	0.07	0.16
India	3.7	1.4	3.6	0.44	0.10	0.06	0.06	0.09
Japan	30.9	2.3	2.1	0.56	0.30	0.85	0.88	0.91
Africa	3.5	1.2	−0.1	0.35	0.14	0.11	0.10	0.07

Sources:
a UN (2006), World Economic and Social Survey, Table I.1.
b Gross National Product per capita in 1990 international Geary Khamis dollars.

has risen from 3:1 to 15:1. Also, during more recent periods, income inequality is growing. This contradicts the expectations of economists such as Lucas (2000) who argue that the spread of technology will diminish income inequality between countries in the long run. The major exceptions are Japan (during 1953–1973) and more recently India and China.

According to the UN (2006), the hypothesis that international markets will bring convergence of income levels across countries is only confirmed on a regional level. For example, in Europe the relatively poor countries like Greece, Spain, Portugal and Ireland could adapt to the economic welfare of other European countries, due to their geographical location and stronger trade relations with richer European countries, the transfer of technology and the financial support by the EU. Regional convergence also occurred in East and South Asian countries, whereas African and Latin American countries showed convergence in economic stagnation. In fact, 84 percent of worldwide income inequality is accounted for by income differences between regions and only 16 percent by income differences within regions (UN 2006).

This indicates that market forces alone will not be sufficient to bring about worldwide income equality. Calderón *et al.* (2005) show that financial and trade opening generally lead to higher economic growth, but this positive impact appears to be small for poor countries. Only as the country develops, does it become substantial. Another study by Dowrick and Colley (2004) shows that the positive impact of trade liberalization is also declining (see Table 12.6). During 1960–1979 trade openness promoted the convergence between poor and rich

Table 12.6 The contribution of trade openness to economic growth

	1960–1979		1980–1999	
	Poor countries	*Rich countries*	*Poor countries*	*Rich countries*
Trade share (% GDP)	41.0	60.0	63.0	71.0
Estimated total contribution of trade to growth in real GDP per capita, % points per year	1.1	0.6	–0.5	1.0

Source: Dowrick and Colley (2004), Table 3.

countries. But after 1980, the role of trade openness reversed. Specialization in the export of primary products by poor countries has been more harmful than beneficial to these countries.

According to the UN (2005) a country should have a certain amount of physical and human capital in order to compete on the worldwide market. Without basic infrastructure (roads, railways, harbors, energy facilities, telecommunication, safe drinking water, etc.), a good public governance and administration, education and a minimum of health services, local companies will not be able to compete on the world market.

5 Conclusions

This chapter investigates the claim of the Accra statement that the free market system causes accumulation of the wealth of the rich at the expense of the poor and that support of this system should be classified as unfaithfulness to God. This claim combines an empirical statement and a theological statement. The empirical statement is that the free market system with unrestricted competition, respect for private property, openness to world trade and international capital flows and privatization of state enterprises, benefits the rich at the expense of the poor and causes extreme poverty. The theological statement is that extreme poverty of the poor is unjust in the eyes of God.

In order to test the theological statement, we investigated the meaning of justice in the Bible. We find that the Bible supports several standards of distributive justice. On the one hand, we find that capitalistic standards of justice, such as respect of negative rights of freedom (property rights) and the principle of rendering to each his or her due (distribution according to moral desert), are amply supported by biblical texts. However, unlike the Christian libertarian view, justice is not limited to these capitalistic standards. There are several texts that also prescribe the positive duty to fulfill the basic needs of the poor, independent from the cause of their poverty, by various institutions. These texts provide support for socialist principles of distributive justice, such as the needs principle and the capability principle of Sen. This supports the view of the Accra declaration that extreme poverty is unjust according to Christian faith.

In order to test the empirical statement, we review some recent literature about the impact of free markets on poverty, human development and income distribution. The empirical evidence that free markets increase poverty is mixed. On the one hand, the empirical evidence so far broadly supports the view that trade liberalization will alleviate poverty in the long run. There are some obvious examples, such as China and India, that have witnessed a substantial decline in poverty after the economy was opened up to free market mechanisms. We also find empirical support that human development (measured by life expectancy and education) is strongly positively related to economic welfare for developing countries. Since empirical research has shown that free markets (approximated by the index of economic freedom) contribute to economic growth, we may conclude that markets are a necessary condition for human development and the fulfillment of basic needs. On the other hand, international markets are not a sufficient condition for justice. An important condition for a positive link between economic growth and human development is that the revenues of economic growth are equally distributed. This depends on the various types of institutions governing the capital, labor and product markets. Also the econometric evidence that economic freedom reduces income inequality is mixed. Econometric evidence shows unambiguously, however, that income inequality decreases with the intervention of the government. To illustrate, whereas in the Scandinavian countries the government share is relatively high, the Gini index is relatively low compared to, for example, the United States.

Since 70 percent of worldwide income inequality is accounted for by income inequality between countries and 30 percent by income inequality within countries, it is even more important to consider the impact of markets on income equality between countries. Except for Japan, India and China, there is no indication that the globalization of the economy has reduced income inequality between countries. Insofar as convergence takes place, it is mainly on a regional scale, welfare being spread among all the countries in rich regions and the lack of welfare being spread in poor regions. For the latter type of regions, trade openness has hardly contributed or even slightly harmed economic welfare. Thus, although we find no evidence that free international markets have been a major cause of poverty in the developing countries, we agree with the Accra declaration in the sense that the unrestricted free market system provides insufficient guarantees that the injustice of extreme poverty will be solved.

Notes

* The author thanks Irene van Staveren and Ian Smith and other participants of the International Conference of Social Economics in Amsterdam and the annual conference of ACE (Association of Christian Economists) in Cambridge for their comments on an earlier version of this chapter.

1 For the text of the declaration, see the World Alliance of Reformed Churches website. Online, available at: http://warc.jalb.de/warcajsp/side.jsp?news_id=1157&navi=45.
2 The Accra declaration calls the current economic system a neoliberal economic system. Since the meaning of this political concept is not unambiguous, I will not use this term but, instead, refer to a free market system in which the government's only task is to secure private property rights.
3 Sen (1984: 320) thinks that there are good reasons to assume that Rawls also – contrary to what Rawls states – is really after something like capabilities instead of primary social goods, because Rawls motivates the focus on primary goods by discussing what these goods enable people to do.
4 The capitalistic and libertarian standards of justice are also known as commutative justice. Commutative justice holds for free exchange of value for value in trade among individuals. Nevertheless, they can also be classified as standards of distributive justice, because these standards also have implications for the distribution of income outside the market. Distributive justice is a generalization of commutative justice.
5 Many other texts in the New Testament support the needs principle, such as Matthew 25:35 and Acts 4:34 ("There was no one in the group who was in need"). For a more extensive discussion of standards of distributive justice in the New Testament, see section 8.4 in Graafland (2007b).
6 For a definition of these indicators, see CPB (2007).
7 Cited in Rodrik (2002).
8 The poverty elasticity estimates the percent change in the number of people in poverty for each 1 percent growth in average income for each region in the world.
9 The experience of developing countries that globalized during the 1980s and 1990s (Mexico, Colombia, Argentina, Brazil, Chile, India and Hong Kong) contrasts with the experience of several Southeast Asian countries (South Korea, Taiwan, Singapore) that underwent trade reforms in the 1960s and 1970s and exhibited a decline in inequality as they opened their economies to foreign markets.
10 Kynge (2006) illustrates how outsourcing of industrial activities from the United States to China particularly hit middle class workers with the example of Rockford, Illinois, one of the industrial areas in decay. The example shows how globalization can induce polarization on the labor market. Also statistics of the US Census Bureau show that the number of employees in middle-income classes has declined compared to employees with an income lower than $25,000 or higher than $75,000.

References

Ackerman, F. (2005), "The Shrinking Gains from Trade: A Critical Assessment of Doha Round Projections," Global Development and Environment Institute, Tufts University, Working Paper 05–01.
Beisner, E.C. (1994), "Justice and Poverty: Two Views Contrasted," in H. Schlossberg, V. Samuel and R.J. Sider (eds.) *Christianity and Economics in the Post-Cold War Era. The Oxford Declaration and Beyond*, Grand Rapids: William B. Eerdmans Publishing Company: 57–80.
Berggren, N. (1999), "Economic Freedom and Equality: Friends or Foes?," *Public Choice*, 100: 203–223.
Biermans, M. (2005), "The Political Economy of Dignity: Monitoring the Advancement of Socio-economic Human Rights in a Globalized Economy," Discussion Paper 43, SEO Economisch Onderzoek, Amsterdam.
Calderón, C., N. Loayza and K. Schmidt-Hebbel (2005), "Does Openness Imply Greater Exposure?," World Bank Policy Research, Working Paper 3733, Washington, DC: World Bank.

Christman, J. (1998), "Property Rights," in *Encyclopedia of Applied Ethics*, 3, San Diego: Academic Press: 683–692.

Cornia, G.A. (2004), *Inequality, Growth and Poverty in an Era of Liberalization and Globalization*, Oxford: Oxford University Press.

CPB (2007), "Measuring Competition in the Netherlands," Research Memorandum 163, The Hague.

Davies, E.W. (1989), "Lands; its Rights and Privileges," in R.E. Clements (ed.) *The World of Ancient Israel: Sociological, Anthropological and Political Perspectives*, Cambridge, UK: Cambridge University Press: 349–370.

Dawson, J.W. (1998), "Institutions, Investment, and Growth: New Cross-country and Panel Data Evidence," *Economic Inquiry*, XXXVI: 603–619.

Diener, E. and C. Diener (1995), "The Wealth of Nations Revisited: Income and the Quality of Life," *Social Indicators Research*, 36: 565–591.

Dowrick, S. and J. Colley (2004), "Trade Openness and Growth: Who Benefits?," *Oxford Review of Economic Policy*, 20(1): 38–56.

Duchrow, U. (1987), *Global Economy, a Confessional Issue for the Churches?*, Geneva: World Council of Churches.

Easton, Steven T. and Michael A. Walker (1997), "Income, Growth, and Economic Freedom, *American Economic Review*, 87(2) May: 328–332.

Frick, F.S. (1989), "Ecology, Agriculture and Patterns of Settlement," in R.E. Clements (ed.) *The World of Ancient Israel: Sociological, Anthropological and Political Perspectives*, Cambridge, UK: Cambridge University Press: 67–94.

Glaeser, E.L. (2005), "Inequality," Harvard Institute of Economic Research, Discussion Paper 2078.

Goldberg, P.K. and N. Pavcnik (2007), "Distributional Effects of Globalization in Developing Countries," *Journal of Economic Literature*, XLV March: 39–82.

Gorringe, T.J. (1994), *Capital and the Kingdom: Theological Ethics and Economic Order*, London: Orbis Books and SPCK.

Graafland, J.J. (2001), "Social and Economic Aspects in the Old Testament," in H. Klok, T. van Schaik and S. Smulders (eds.) *Economologues: Liber amicorum voor Theo van de Klundert*, Tilburg: University of Tilburg: 147–158.

—— (2007a), *Economics, Ethics and the Market: Introduction and Applications*, London: Routledge.

—— (2007b), *Het oog van de naald. Over de markt, geluk en solidariteit*, Kampen: Ten Have.

Haan, J. de and J.E. Sturm (2000), On the relationship between economic freedom and economic growth, *European Journal of Political Economy*, 16, 215–241.

Hoeven, R. van de (2009), "Income Distribution," in J. Peil and I. Van Staveren (eds.) *Handbook of Economic Ethics*, forthcoming.

Klenicki, L. (1997), "Jewish Understandings of Sabbatical Year and Jubilee," in H. Ucko (red.), *The Jubilee Challenge. Utopia or Possibility? Jewish and Christian Insights*, Geneva: World Council of Churches: 41–52.

Kynge, J. (2006), *China Shakes the World: The Rise of a Hungry Nation*, Amsterdam and Tielt: Nieuw Amsterdam and Lannoo.

Leeuwen, C. van (1956), *Sociaal besef in Israël*, Baarn: Bosch and Keuning.

Lucas, R.E. Jr. (2000), "Some Macroeconomics for the 21st Century," *Journal of Economic Perspectives*, 14(1): 159–168.

Meeks, M.D. (1989), *God and the Economist: The Doctrine of God and Political Economy*, Minneapolis: Fortress Press.

Milanovic, B. (2005), *Worlds Apart: Measuring Interregional and Global Inequality*, Princeton, NJ: Princeton University Press.

Mott, S.C. (1994), "The Partiality of Biblical Justice: A Response to Calvin Beisner," in H. Schlossberg, V. Samuel and R.J. Sider (eds.) *Christianity and Economics in the Post-cold war Era: The Oxford Declaration and Beyond*, Grand Rapids: William B. Eerdmans Publishing Company: 81–99.

Novak, M. (1982), *The Spirit of Democratic Capitalism*, New York.: Simon & Schuster.

Nozick, R. (1974), *Anarchy, State and Utopia*, New York: Basic Books.

Prahalad, C.K. (2006), *The Fortune at the Bottom of the Pyramid: Eradicating Poverty through Profits*, Upper Saddle River: Wharton School Publishing.

Ranis, G. and F. Stewart (2005), "Dynamic Links between the Economy and Human Development," DESA Working Paper 8, United Nations. Online, available at: www.un.org/esa/desa/papers.

Rawls, J. (1999), *A Theory of Justice* (revised edition), Boston, MA: Harvard University Press.

Rodrik, D. (2002), "Feasible Globalizations," NBER Working Paper 9129.

Santa Ana, J. de (1977), *Good News to the Poor: the Challenge of the Poor in the History of the Church*, Geneva: World Council of Churches.

Scully, G.W. (2002), "Economic Freedom, Government Policy and the Trade-off between Equity and Economic Growth," *Public Choice*, 113: 77–96.

Sen, A.K. (1984), *Resources, Values and Development*, Oxford: Blackwell.

Sider, R. (1977), *Rich Christians in an Age of Hunger*, Leicester: Inter-Varsity Press.

Singer, P. (1972), "Famine, Affluence and Morality," *Philosophy and Public Affairs*, 3: 229–243.

Soggin, J.A. (1993), *An Introduction to the History of Israel and Judah*, Canterbury, UK: SCM Press Ltd.

Stiglitz, J. (2002), *Globalization and its Discontents*, New York: Norton & Company.

Sturm, J.E. and J. de Haan (2001), "How Robust is the Relationship between Economic Freedom and Economic Growth?," *Applied Economics*, 33: 839–844.

UN (2005), "Investing in Development: A Practical Plan to Achieve the Millennium Development Goals: Overview." Online, available at: www.unmilleniumproject.org.

—— (2006), *World Economic and Social Survey*. Online, available at: www.un.org/esa/policy/wess/index.html.

—— (2007), *The Millennium Development Goals Report 2007*, New York: United Nations.

Vaux, R. de (1989), *Hoe het oude Israel leefde*, deel I, vijfde druk, Den Haag: Boekencentrum.

Velasquez, M.G. (1998), *Business Ethics: Concepts and Cases*, fourth edition, Upper Saddle River, NJ: Prentice Hall.

Winters, L.A., N. McCulloch and A. McKay (2004), "Trade Policy and Poverty: The Evidence so Far," *Journal of Economic Literature*, XLII March: 72–115.

World Bank (2006), *World Development Report 2006*, Washington, DC: World Bank.

Wright, C.J.H. (1983), *Living as the People of God, the Relevance of Old Testament Ethics*, Leicester: Inter-Varsity Press.

13 The social economics of corporate social responsibility

Informational abundance and collective action

*Martha A. Starr**

1 Introduction

In the past 15 years, the idea of "corporate social responsibility" (CSR) has become an important part of contemporary business life. While varying definitions of CSR have been offered, the core principle is that businesses should make decisions based not on profitability alone, but also on the social and environmental consequences of their actions.[1] Ideally, businesses are supposed to behave "responsibly" toward all of their "stakeholders," where the latter include not only owners and shareholders, but also workers, customers, surrounding communities, and the environment.[2] The notion of "responsibility," while not necessarily corresponding closely to any well-defined ethical principle, implies conforming to certain expectations of how businesses should operate vis-à-vis their stakeholders, namely that they should produce safe and useful products; minimize the adverse environmental impacts of their operations; implement fair and equitable workplace practices; adopt labor standards for overseas operations; contribute positively to surrounding communities; and conduct their business in ways that respect human rights.[3] While CSR is a strictly voluntary matter, concern with it has become widespread in the corporate business sector. Many large corporations have CSR policies and issue annual reports on their progress in meeting CSR objectives; some even appoint "Chief Responsibility Officers" to spearhead their CSR work.

The concern with ethics in business life makes the CSR movement of strong inherent interest to social economists. Whereas mainstream economics has tended to draw a stark line between positive and normative analysis, insisting that economists confine their work to the positive domain, social economists have traditionally taken normative issues to be of central interest to economic analysis, since they permeate methods used by societies to organize production, consumption, investment, distribution, access to natural resources, household provisioning, and other dimensions of economic activity.[4] Thus, for example, whereas mainstream economists have recently started exploring economic behavior as governed in part by ethical considerations like fairness, social economists have long had a richer view of the person, wherein she acts according to both self-interested and other-oriented drives, and socio-cultural and institutional mechanisms are understood to regulate the dialectic between them (Lutz 1990; O'Boyle 1994; George 1998; Davis 2003). Moreover, social economists do not feel constrained to refrain from normative analysis, but rather delve seriously into questions of the moral, ethical, philosophical and ontological bases on which it can be done. With this far richer repertory of ideas about methods for studying ethical dimensions of economic life, social economics is a uniquely valuable lens through which to examine the "ethical turn" in contemporary business life.

This chapter aims to draw a link between corporate social responsibility and issues and methods of longstanding interest to social economists by reviewing relationships between CSR and broadly-held social values, identifying the sources of market pressures on firms to voluntarily bring their operations into better conformity with these values, and examining how these pressures work in practice through a case study. The argument of the chapter is that, in the present era of informational abundance – where new information and communication technologies, especially the Internet, make it is easy to craft and disseminate narratives about firms' violations of fairness norms – it has become considerably easier to get "mainstream" consumers and investors, whose behavior is not systematically shaped by ethical considerations, to participate in efforts to sanction such firms (e.g. by diverting their purchases to other firms, signing petitions or pledges, etc.). This possibility of mobilizing "moral sentiment" alters firms' incentives insofar as they may realize gains from behaving responsibly or penalties from behaving badly. This argument is illustrated through the case of the "No Dirty Gold" campaign, which has worked for several years to try to get transnational mining corporations to shift away from production methods that are environmentally destructive, unsafe for workers, and harmful for communities living around gold mines. The case study is valuable for identifying both the promise and the limitations of relying on CSR to improve the social responsibility of the profit system.

2 Explaining the "ethical" turn in contemporary business life

The idea that corporations should behave responsibly toward their stakeholders is of course strongly consistent with various normative perspectives on business life.[5] An important example concerns parallels between CSR and Catholic social thought, which are of interest for three reasons. First, like the discourse of CSR, Catholic social thought views unregulated business activity as a fundamentally good way to organize economic life, but shares its concern that pursuit of profit can lead people and businesses to engage in practices that are ethically problematic. Reflecting this common point of departure, Catholic investors have often been in the vanguard of CSR work (see below). Second, many of the tenets of Catholic social thought are broadly reflective of Judeo-Christian social values, which predominate in the advanced-industrial countries where CSR has become a facet of business life.[6] And third, Catholic social thought has special relevance for the field of social economics, given its origin in "Catholic economics."

The importance of treating all shareholders fairly is consistent with the Catholic social tradition of viewing businesses as embedded in networks of social relationships that are ideally governed by ethical principles. As stated in the Pontifical Council of Peace and Justice's *Social Agenda* (2000: 208),

> Man works ... to provide for the needs of his family, his community, his nation, and ultimately all humanity ... [H]e collaborates in the work of his fellow employees, and in the work of suppliers and in the customers' use of goods, in a progressively expanding chain of solidarity. [7]

Efforts to gain profits that do not expand the "work and wealth of society" in this way, but rather depend on "illicit exploitation, speculation, or the breaking of solidarity among working people," violate the fundamental social function of business: "Riches fulfill their function of service to man when they are destined to produce benefits for others and for society" (ibid.: 392). Thus, businesses that pursue profits at the expense of other stakeholders in fact invalidate their right to own and control productive resources, as this right is predicated on using them to serve the common good.

Many of the specific dimensions of corporate behavior taken to be integral parts of social responsibility also relate closely to ideas in Catholic social thought. For example, the tenet that companies should produce *safe and useful products* corresponds to the idea that businesses can and should contribute to the common good by creating new products that meet people's needs in better ways:

> A person who produces something other than for his own use generally does so in order that others may use it after they have paid a just price ... It is precisely the ability to foresee both the needs of others and the combinations of productive factors most adapted to satisfying those needs that constitutes [an] important source of wealth in modern society.
>
> (Ibid.: 240)

Moreover, the idea that companies should minimize adverse *environmental consequences* of their actions is consistent with respecting the principle that "God intended the earth, with everything contained in it, for the use of every human being and people" (ibid.: 202). Thus,

> As one called to till and look after the garden of the world..., man has a specific responsibility towards the environment in which he lives, towards the creation which God ... [intended] ... not only for the present but also for future generations.
>
> (Ibid.: 319)

By implication, "those responsible for business enterprises are responsible to society for the economic and ecological effects of their operations. They have an obligation to consider the good of persons and not only the increase of profits" (ibid.: 320). Finally, the idea that businesses should safeguard *human rights* is strongly consistent with the central importance given to human dignity in Catholic social thought: Because people have been entrusted with the defense and promotion of the dignity of the human person, "all men and women at every moment of history" should strive to uphold that dignity (ibid.: 45). Thus, "the rich and employers must remember that no laws, either human or divine, permit them for their own profit to oppress the needy and the wretched or to seek gain from another's want" (ibid.: 258).

Thus, to the extent that companies recognize and incorporate social responsibility into the ways in which they do business, CSR would seem to shift the business system toward a model that better reconciles the dynamism and innovation of profit orientation with respect for widely-held values. But at the same time, the "ethical turn" seems to contradict a parallel development in the United States in recent decades – wherein the importance of maximizing profits in corporate business activity has been substantially re-prioritized. Since the early 1980s, in response to the complaint that corporate managers tend to pursue objectives other than maximizing shareholder value (the canonical "principal-agent" problem of corporate finance), various tactics, including shareholder activism and leveraged buy-outs, have been used to pressure corporate executives to make maximum profit their overwhelming concern (Kaplan 1997; Fligstein 2001: chapter 7; Holmström and Kaplan 2001; 2003).[8] The restructuring of executive compensation to prioritize stock-price gains is also intended to align managers' incentives with those of stockholders.[9] This "ascendancy of shareholder value" would seem likely to pressure firms to operate in ways that are bad for stakeholders other than shareholders; see, for example, Froud *et al.* (2000) on "serial restructurings" in the United Kingdom and their consequences for workers.[10]

How then are we to reconcile increasing social responsibility with re-prioritization of maximizing profits? Certainly, pressures to maximize profits constrain the range of responsibility projects that firms can undertake; if a firm's CSR work is seen as appreciably eroding its profits, profit-oriented shareholders might try to persuade management to scale back its work, orchestrate moves to unseat the CEO, entertain an outside bid for the firm, etc. However, as the business literature on CSR establishes, there is not necessarily a contradiction between profits and social responsibility *if* companies can benefit financially from improving their treatment of stakeholders.[11] To delineate the avenues via which improving responsibility may increase profits, it is helpful to think of the determinants of the value of owning a share in a given company. The value of an ownership share in a given company i, P_i, will be a function of the expected present discounted value of the company's profit stream, $E[\pi_i]$, plus any premium or discount it receives in the capital market, λ_i, as a result of investors buying or selling shares in part on the basis of social responsibility:

$$P_i = f\,[E(\pi_i)] + \lambda_i \qquad\qquad [1]$$

In the case of a publicly-traded corporation, P_i is the company's stock price. The term λ_i primarily reflects the influence of "socially responsible investment" (SRI) – a segment of the capital market in which investors manage their assets with respect to both financial and social concerns.[12] In the past decade in the United States, socially responsible investors, which include both institutional investors like pension funds, foundations, endowments, and retail SRI mutual funds, have accounted for about 10 percent of the total value of financial assets under management (Social Investment Forum 2006). While the primary mechanism used in SRI is "screening" (wherein companies with strong social and environmental performance are "screened into" the portfolio, and those with poor performance are "screened out"), some socially responsible investors – including a number of Catholic pension funds and endowments, state-government pension funds like the California Public Employees' Retirement Funds (CalPERS), and retail mutual funds like those offered by Calvert and the Pax World Funds – also use more activist tactics like engaging in dialogue with companies about problematic areas of social performance, and filing shareholder resolutions to focus attention on possibilities for improvement.[13] If the stock of a given company is disfavored by SRI investors due to poor social performance – absolutely and/or relative to other companies – and if the influence of these investors in the market is non-negligible, then we would expect the company's stock to trade at some discount relative to what would be predicted from its expected profit stream. If on the other hand, SRI investors favor the company's stock because of its superior social performance, and again if their influence is non-negligible, we would expect its stock to trade at a premium. But of course, given the fact that SRI investors represent only a modest share of total financial assets, whether they have any potential to influence corporate behavior via this avenue is not clear a priori; we return to this issue below.[14]

At the same time, social performance also influences the expected profits component of P_i, $f\ [E(\pi_i)]$, in so far as it influences the company's expected revenue stream and/or its expected costs. Thus even investors motivated strictly by financial gain will favor improvements in social performance *if* they raise the company's revenues by more than they raise costs. One would expect programs that improve social responsibility to tend to raise costs; presumably, companies adopt methods of production that can be considered "irresponsible" (e.g. are highly polluting, or abusive of workers) because doing so is more profitable than other methods, so that abandoning them in favor of socially preferred methods would tend to push costs up. But this way of looking at the problem assumes that firms are perfectly informed about costs, benefits, and risks of alternative methods and calculatingly choose those which are profit-maximizing. If instead they are unaware of alternative production methods that have superior social properties and equivalent or lower costs, and these methods are brought to their attention through CSR discourse, then it is not necessarily inevitable that improving responsibility would be cost-increasing. Thus, for example, it is well-established that firms that make efforts to improve their environmental performance tend to see their stock prices go up, where at least some part of this increase reflects cost savings (Petzinger 1997). Similarly, others have argued that improvements in social performance lower risks of being sued (for example, for discrimination against women or minorities, causing environmental damage through oil or chemical spills, creating health problems within a community by failing to properly dispose of industrial wastes, etc.), or of being more tightly regulated by the government. In these cases, then, improvements in social performance are said to "pay for themselves."

On the revenue side, improvements in social responsibility may boost revenues if they increase demand for the company's products, or reduce slippage in demand due to public concern about poor social performance. For this to be the case, consumers would need to have some knowledge of how firms behave in terms of social responsibility, and to allocate their purchases across goods and/or across companies in ways that favor socially "good" companies and disfavor the "bad." Whether we can take consumption to be broadly influenced by ethical considerations is of course problematic. For one, distinguishing between "good" and "bad" companies is not necessarily easy for an average consumer, especially when companies that are "good" along some dimensions may be quite "bad" along others.[15] For another, the idea that consumers' spending allocations can be used to induce improvements in CSR would seem to embed the traditional collective action problem: if everyone steered their spending toward socially "good" companies and away from the bad, the broad-based increase in social responsibility that this might induce could raise social welfare; but individually people have incentive to free-ride on the efforts of others, allocating their own spending according to price/product-quality considerations only, so that the impetus to influence firms' behavior may be too weak to have much effect.

However, this way of looking at revenue-related pressures is based on two problematic assumptions: atomistic individuals whose behavior reflects fixed preferences, and aggregate outcomes derived by "aggregating up" from them. In terms of the first problem, as social economists have long believed and as experimental research is confirming, it is far more appropriate to think of people's behavior as reflecting mixtures of self-interested and other-oriented drives, where features of the social context can tilt behavior in one direction or another.[16] A notable finding in this respect concerns "fairness" – which generally means, in the experimental setting, splitting rewards with another person in a relatively even way (50/50, or 60/40), rather than keeping the lion's share for oneself (99/1). In various kinds of games, it has been found that some people go out of their way to negatively sanction unfair behavior and to positively sanction its opposite. Furthermore, they sanction whether the "unfairness" affects them or someone else, and whether they expect to have future dealings with the person or not, suggesting that they do it for intrinsic rather than strategic reasons. However, fairness-related sanctioning is not an everywhere-and-all-the-time phenomenon. Some people consistently engage in it; many others engage in it at some times but not others, or under some circumstances but not others; and the remainder behave like *homo economicus*, consistently acting out of self-interest.[17] Whether sanctioning makes "fair" behavior become predominant depends on the relative importance of the different types of people in the experiment, and on the consequences of getting sanctioned. If people who consistently sanction are common, and/or the costs of getting sanctioned are high, even those inclined to act according to self-interest will begin respecting fairness norms because of the incentives to do so. However, if too few people consistently sanction, and/or getting sanctioned is not very costly, self-interest may become the predominant way of dealing with others.

The fairness-sanctioning framework provides a valuable way for thinking about revenue-related pressures for corporate social responsibility. Companies identified as being notably deficient in social responsibility are often understood to be treating some stakeholders *unfairly* – in the sense of appropriating an unreasonably large share of the benefits of their economic interchange, without regard to the hardship, loss of dignity, or erosion of opportunities that their behavior causes for others. Issues pursued under CSR that have particularly strong resonance in this respect are those in which stakeholders are too poor or otherwise disadvantaged to accept or reject terms of economic transactions offered to them by the company, and where the company seems to be fully exploiting this fact – most notably, sweatshop labor and child labor. Producing goods under sweatshop conditions and/or using child workers is in clear violation of basic expectations of respect for human dignity; as the *Rerum Novarum* puts it, "It is shameful and inhuman ... to use men as things for gain and to put no more value on them than what they are worth in muscle and energy" (Leo XIII: 20). Reaction to use of sweatshop and child labor provokes especially strong and widespread reaction when the company pays workers so little yet sells the goods they produce for notably high prices – as attested by the international boycott against Nike's expensive athletic footwear after it emerged that labor conditions in its Asian factories were not infrequently abusive. While sweatshops and child labor are widely viewed as fundamentally unacceptable violations of fairness norms, other kinds of behaviors are also construed as being unfair although not necessarily with the same depth and breadth of resonance as these "obviously" wrong practices, such as those failing to take precautions against environmental disasters (e.g. the Exxon Valdez); unnecessary or cruel animal testing; and doing business with foreign governments that egregiously violate their citizen's human rights (South Africa under apartheid, or presently Sudan).[18]

Understanding how the perceived unfairness of these practices contributes to revenue pressures for improving CSR relates to the second problematic assumption of the standard narrative – of deriving aggregate outcomes by "aggregating up" from atomistic individuals. In this kind of framework, people are oblivious to what others are doing, so whether demand for a company's product is affected by variations in its social responsibility depends on whether there are enough individuals within the population who know about and react to these variations by adjusting their purchases of the company's products for it to make a difference for their bottom line. But again, the recent experimental literature suggests that the likelihood that people behave "pro-socially" – i.e. in ways that uphold fairness norms, even if doing so entails a personal cost – is greater when they know that other people will too. For example, Meier (2006) finds in a field experiment that people are more likely to make charitable contributions, and to contribute more generously, when told that others are contributing at generous rates. This is the opposite of the prediction of the traditional collective action model, in which people are more likely to free-ride in the provision of a public good when they think others are doing enough to ensure that it is provided.

For this issue to work in terms of revenue pressures for CSR, people who are not themselves "ethical" consumers or investors (that is, who do not systematically buy goods or make investments with ethical concerns in mind) need to learn about cases in which companies behave unfairly toward stakeholders and about efforts by others to do something about it. It is here that the onset of the present era of *informational abundance*, brought about by information and communications technologies (ICTs), makes a substantial difference in creating channels to bring irresponsible corporate behavior to the public eye. Relevant ICTs include the websites of corporations, non-governmental organizations (NGOs), news services, brokerages, and government agencies; forums attached to websites; freestanding forums like iVillage; email (including email alerts); blogs; digital images; user-posted video banks like YouTube; and electronic data repositories like LexisNexis.

These ICTs facilitate collecting and spreading information on corporate misbehavior and mobilizing efforts to change it in four ways. First, ICTs significantly lower the costs and improve the speed with which information on firms' activities can be collected, analyzed, and disseminated. Notably, the Internet makes it far easier to get a hold of corporations' press releases, annual reports, quarterly earnings statements, minutes of shareholder meeting, filings with the Securities and Exchange Commission, etc. Second, websites and email make it much easier to research and publicize alternative narratives on corporate behavior. For example, sweatshop working conditions or other poor corporate conduct abroad can now be readily brought to light by posting photos, interviews, and text that provide an immediate "feel" for the negative impact of the company's behavior on workers and/or communities. There are also sites like that of Coop America, an activist consumer group, that provide "thumbnail sketches" on the social responsibility of major companies, aiming to help ethically-concerned people steer their dollars toward "good" companies and away from "bad."[19] Third, hyper-linking of related websites greatly increases the odds that information collected and posted by one group will be noticed and read by people other than its immediate constituents.[20] Fourth, websites and related tools like electronic petitions and letter-writing campaigns make it faster and much less expensive to mobilize consumers, investors and activists to join sanctioning actions.[21]

The issue with this kind of informational abundance is that, especially in cases where the company's behavior will be widely viewed as unacceptable, ICTs make it relatively easy to take the issue out of the realm of consumers and investors who are regularly motivated by ethical concerns, and into the realm of the general public, possibly via the route of print and broadcast media. Here the issue is that many people who do not systematically use ethical criteria in consuming and/or investing can nonetheless decide to stop buying a company's products if they become aware that it has been treating stakeholders poorly, and feel there is a chance that a change in their purchasing behavior could make a difference. Evidence that this kind of effect can be appreciable is provided by Rock (2003), who studied how news about sweatshop labor conditions affected the stock prices of several major garment and shoe manufacturers; most of the effects he found were negative and significant, and some were very large.

Clearly, this ability to mobilize "moral sentiment" creates incentives for companies to try to minimize the chances that their behavior could be portrayed to the public as irresponsible. On one hand, it gives rise to the problem of corporations launching public-relations campaigns to *portray* themselves as engaged in broad and deep efforts to excel on social and environmental performance, when they may or may not be.[22] While such campaigns make it harder to distinguish between "good" and "bad" companies, they are also risky, in that highly deceitful self-representations are often readily spotted and publicized by NGOs, who may hold false narratives up as further proof of a company's poor ethics. On the other hand, the possibility of gaining or losing sales as a result of social performance can also lead companies to take a lot of initiative to change their position relative to competitors. Notable in this regard is that Reebok voluntarily implemented the kinds of serious anti-sweatshop measures that market-leader Nike was resisting in the 1990s, which enabled it make good inroads into Nike's dominant market share and gave its stock price a sizable boost (Rock 2003). Thus, as long as there is some potential sensitivity of revenues to differences in social performance, companies seeking to improve their competitive position within an industry or market may find improvements in social performance to be a valuable route, especially if the market leader is a laggard.

3 The case of the "No Dirty Gold" campaign

To understand the role of informational abundance in facilitating ethics-oriented collective actions, it is valuable to examine a case in which these dynamics have been at work. The "No Dirty Gold" (NDG) campaign was launched in 2004 by Oxfam USA and Earthworks, an NGO that focuses on curbing environmentally destructive mineral development. The objective of the campaign is to call attention to the poor labor and environmental practices of transnational mining companies, and put pressure on them to improve. Standard mining methods use cyanide to leach gold from ore, generating large amounts of toxic waste per unit of gold extracted; disposal of this waste, and related release of harmful chemicals like mercury into the environment, causes lasting environmental degradation and health problems for humans and animals in large areas around mines. Additionally, while mining is anyway a dangerous occupation, working conditions in gold mines in poor, remote areas are often notably deficient in safety and health precautions, resulting in high rates of injury, disability and mortality, and occupational illnesses.

To illustrate the context within which the NDG campaign operates, Figure 13.1 provides a schematic representation of stakeholder relations in the gold supply chain. The problematic social and environmental performance occurs in the "upstream" part of the web of stakeholder relations, with the behavior of transnational mining companies operating in Ghana, Indonesia, Peru, and other developing countries. While their traditional operating methods have been good for profits, these have come at the expense of the other upstream stakeholders – miners, the environment, and surrounding communities. Thus, the campaign aims to make the mining companies' treatment of these stakeholders transparent to the international community. Influencing the mining companies directly has proved relatively difficult, in part because the long-term character of mining operations means they can continue doing business as usual without much risk of losing contracts. Pressure from socially responsible investors alone has not had much effect, reflecting their small share of capital markets. Instead, the NDG campaign aims to incite collective action in the "downstream" part of the web of stakeholder relations – in particular by bringing mining companies' problematic practices to the attention of people who buy or may buy gold jewelry.

The peak period of the NDG campaign is around Valentine's Day, when it uses a variety of tactics – including full-page advertisements in newspapers, materials posted on their website, press releases, email and letter-writing drives, protests outside jewelers, etc. – to raise awareness of "dirty gold," and to differentiate between jewelers who have and have not adopted a code of conduct called the "Golden Rules," wherein they pledge to buy gold from suppliers whose social and environmental practices are respectful of and fair to all stakeholders. Its informational materials call attention to the contrast between the symbolism of gold – of eternal love and the beauty of nature – and the ugly

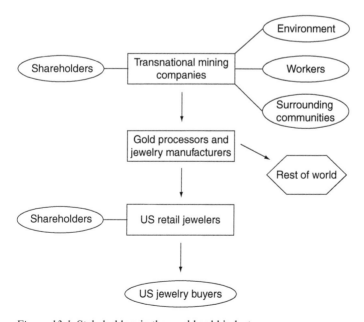

Figure 13.1 Stakeholders in the world gold industry.

reality of how it is extracted, underlining how wrong it would be to unthinkingly give gold jewelry to a loved one if its production was based on human suffering and indignity and environmental degradation. Thus, the website provides detailed information on a dozen communities around the world that are adversely affected by "dirty gold." Photos show, for example, a baby in Indonesia afflicted with skin problems resulting from dumping mine waste into a nearby bay, a rally in Peru demanding clean-up of a mercury spill, and an ancient sequoia-like tree threatened by plans to begin open-pit mining in Argentina.[23]

By differentiating between jewelers that are "leaders" and "laggards," the campaign aims to pressure the "laggards" to adopt the rules so as to avoid losing sales to the "leaders." As of mid-2007, 19 jewelers had adopted the Golden Rules, including some luxury jewelers (e.g. Tiffany, Cartier, Piaget); several major mall-based chains (e.g. Kay's, Zales); some major mass-market general-merchandise chains that do not specialize in gold but account for a sizable share of sales of gold jewelry (e.g. Wal-Mart, which adopted the code in 2007); companies that make class rings and other insignia merchandise; and some other specialty firms (internet jewelers, the Home Shopping Network). It should be noted, however, that the globally competitive and geographically dispersed nature of the "midstream" part of the gold supply chain makes it hard to ensure that adopting the Golden Rules translates tightly into ethically sourced gold: unlike the campaign against "blood diamonds," which was highly effective in good part because one company (De Beers) had strong control over much of the supply chain, it is more possible for "dirty" and "clean" gold to be mixed together after it moves from the mine to the companies that process gold and make it into jewelry before shipping it to end-user markets (see Marlin 2006).[24] It is notable also in this respect that the United States, while the second-largest importer of gold after India, buys only 15 percent of consumer gold sold on the world market (see Starr and Tran 2008). Again this complicates the process of putting pressure on mining companies.

To understand what factors influence jewelers to adopt ethical sourcing, we run some basic probit analyses of the probability of adopting the Golden Rules, using annual data on the 37 top gold retailers that have been named as "leaders" or "laggards" since the NDG campaign started. The explanatory variables include: whether the company is publicly-traded or private; a set of dummy variables indicating the market segment into which the company falls (luxury, mall-based, mass-market general-merchandise, insignia, or "other"); the year of the campaign; and whether or not a major player in the company's market segment had adopted the Golden Rules. The regression is estimated via a probit model because the dependent variable is discrete.

Results are presented in Table 13.1, in which estimated coefficients are shown as marginal effects (i.e. the difference in the probability of adopting the Golden Rules associated with the indicated firm characteristic). Publicly-traded companies were significantly and substantially more likely than privately-held companies to adopt the golden rules; *ceteris paribus*, the probability of adoption for publicly traded companies was 29.7 percentage points higher than that of private firms. This is strongly consistent with the idea that pressure from capital markets, either via profit-oriented shareholders concerned about depression of profits due to poor social performance and/or via socially responsible investors, is important in inducing firms to move promptly to address publicly circulating concerns about poor social performance. Different outlet types did not differ significantly in their probability of adoption, except in the case of mass-market general-mer-chandise retailers (like Wal-Mart, Sears, and Target): *ceteris paribus*, these were significantly less likely to adopt ethical sourcing rules than other types of stores, which makes sense because they probably viewed their reputations and profits as less likely to be damaged by adverse publicity about gold sourcing given that jewelry is only one of their many product lines. In contrast, some high-end jew-elers, like Tiffany's, were among the first outlets to adopt the Golden Rules, pre-sumably because they viewed their reputation for offering jewelry of unimpeachable quality as worthy of vigorous defense.[25]

The probit results also show the probability of adopting the rules to be con-siderably higher when a competitor within the firm's market segment has already adopted or is concurrently adopting the rules, although the estimated coefficient is significant at a 10 percent level only. This result is consistent with the idea that it is often competitive pressures that lead companies to undertake improve-ments in social performance. For example, in the insignia-jewelry market segment, where there are only a few major firms, student protests against them no doubt led firms to suspect that, if a competitor adopted the rules and they did not, they could lose contracts to that competitor; thus, perhaps not surprisingly, they all held out for awhile, but then all adopted the rules in 2007. Finally, the results suggest that the probability of adopting the rules ticked up in 2007, perhaps because of growing public awareness of the problem of "dirty gold," reflecting media coverage in such important outlets as the afternoon talk-show "Oprah" and the major bridal-industry magazine *Southern Bride*.[26]

Table 13.1 Retail jewelers: probability of adopting the "Golden Rules"

	Estimated marginal effect	*Standard error*
Publicly-traded company	0.2968*	(0.0925)
Luxury	−0.1727	(0.1627)
Mall-based	−0.2140	(0.1399)
Mass-market general merchandise	−0.3249*	(0.0659)
Class rings/insignia	−0.1825*	(0.0918)
Major competitor in market segment has adopted	0.3143+	(0.1708)
Dummy variable for 2006	0.0162	(0.1356)
Dummy variable for 2007	0.3942*	(0.1631)
Pseudo R2	0.36	

Notes
* = significant at 5% level, + = significant at 10% level.
Data cover 37 firms for 3 years; n = 111.

As argued, we might expect adoption of ethical-sourcing rules to boost a company's share price if it is expected to raise demand for the company's products and/or add a capital-market premium to its stock, but to lower the price if ethical sourcing is expected to raise jewelry costs; the net effect is therefore ambiguous. To investigate, we run regressions using daily stock price data from 1998–2007 for six major publicly-traded companies that have been named as leaders or laggards in the NDG campaign: Tiffany's, Zales, Finlay's, Signet, Wal-Mart, and Target. The dependent variable is the log change in the stock price. To gauge the effects of the NDG campaign, we include dummy variables for the period after the NDG campaign ramped up in earnest (February 2005 through the end of the period) and for the periods of the three Valentine's Day campaigns since then (the first two weeks of February in 2005–2007). Also included in the regressions are controls for other determinants of stock-price movements, including three lags of the dependent variable; the log change in the S&P 500 stock price index and its three lags; the log change in the world price of gold and its three lags; and a constant.[27] To allow for the possibility that stock-price volatilities are not constant over the period, the regressions are estimated as a Generalized Autoregressive Conditional Heteroskedasticity (GARCH) model with a generalized error distribution. Use of this model results in errors that are white noise.

Results for retail jewelers are shown in Table 13.2; italicized cells show estimated coefficients for Valentine's Day periods when the retailer had adopted the Golden Rules. There is only a bit of evidence that the NDG campaign had any effect on these companies' stock prices. The stock price of Finlay, which has not yet adopted the Golden Rules and is the eighth largest US jeweler, has consistently underperformed since the NDG campaign ramped up, relative to what would have been expected based on historical performance. The stock prices of two jewelers that adopted the rules – Tiffany and Zales – did significantly better than would have been expected during the 2007 Valentine's Day campaign, perhaps reflecting some shift in demand toward their products. But in general, most estimated effects of the NDG campaign are insignificant. For adopters of the Golden Rules, this is consistent with the idea that any increase in costs associated with ethical sourcing is offset by higher sales and/or a reduced capital-market discount; for non-adopters, it suggests that failure to adopt has not appreciably affected profit expectations or SRI-related capital-market discounts.

The important question is whether the campaign has created appreciable incentives for mining companies to clean up their acts. To address this question, we run similar regressions using data on three of the largest companies that concentrate on gold and are traded on US exchanges. To examine whether the campaign has dampened the ability of mining companies to transform higher gold prices into higher profits, we also add a variable that interacts with a dummy variable for the NDG campaign period with the world price of gold. As can be seen in Table 13.3, the results show an important difference between Newmont and Meridian – companies that have been singled out for criticism by the NDG campaign – and Rio Tinto, a UK-based mining company that was formerly the

Table 13.2 Retail jewelers: Estimated effects on stock prices of the NDG campaign

	Dummy variable for period since campaign ramped up (2005 on)	Dummy variable for Valentine's Day campaign in:			Joint significance of all campaign variables (p-val.)	R-squared
		2005	2006	2007		
	(1)	(2)	(3)	(4)	(5)	(6)
Tiffany	-0.0005	-0.0062	-0.0002	0.0051+	0.19	0.10
	(0.0007)	(0.0041)	(0.0034)	(0.0028)		
Zales	-0.0006	-0.0007	-0.0015	0.0075*	0.13	0.04
	(0.0007)	(0.0043)	(0.0038)	(0.0032)		
Signet	0.0005	0.0003	0.0018	-0.0009	0.91	0.03
	(0.0006)	0.(0035)	(0.0035)	(0.0027)		
Finlay	-0.0020*	-0.0027	-0.0055	-0.0004	0.02	0.02
	(.0008)	(0.0045)	(0.0034)	(.0035)		
Wal-mart	-0.0004	-0.0017	-0.0006	0.0003	0.75	0.32
	(.0005)	(0.0021)	(0.0024)	(0.0024)		
Target	-0.0007	-0.0055	0.0012	0.0024	0.27	0.30
	(0.0006)	(0.0035)	(0.0031)	(0.0026)		

Notes
The data are daily stock price changes, 1998–2007. In all regressions, the number of observations is 2,151. In each regression, the dependent variable is the log change in the company's stock price. In addition to the variables shown above, the right-hand side variables include three lags of the dependent variable; the log change in the S&P 500 stock price index and its three lags; the log change in the world price of gold and its three lags; and a constant. The regressions are estimated as Generalized Autoregressive Conditional Heteroskedasticity (GARCH) models with a generalized error distribution.
Standard errors are in parentheses.
* = significant at 5% level, + = significant at 10% level.
Shaded cells show estimated coefficients for Valentine's Day periods when the retailer had adopted the 'Golden Rules'.

Table 13.3 Major gold mining companies: effects on stock prices of the NDG campaign

	Dummy variable for period since campaign ramped up (2005 on)	Interaction of (1) with log change in gold price	Dummy variable for Valentine's Day campaign in:			Joint significance of Valentine's campaigns (p-val.)	R-squared
			2005	2006	2007		
	(1)	(2)	(3)	(4)	(5)		
Newmont	−0.0012 (0.0009)	−0.2353* (0.0823)	0.0010 (0.0047)	−0.0061 (0.0044)	0.0023 (0.0042)	0.51	0.05
Meridien	0.0004 (0.0014)	−0.2286* (0.1188)	−0.0092 (0.0082)	0.0044 (0.0071)	0.0016 (0.0079)	0.63	0.02
Rio Tinto	0.0010 (0.0009)	0.1308 (0.0845)	−0.0052 (0.0057)	−0.0030 (0.0047)	−0.0047 (0.0063)	0.63	0.01

Notes
The data are daily stock price changes, 1998–2007. In all regressions, the dependent variable is the log change in the company's stock price. In addition to the variables shown above, the right-hand side variables include three lags of the dependent variable; the log change in the S&P 500 stock price index and its three lags; the log change in the world price of gold and its three lags; and a constant. The regressions are estimated as Generalized Autoregressive Conditional Heteroskedasticity (GARCH) models with a generalized error distribution. Standard errors are in parentheses.
* = significant at 5% level, + = significant at 10% level.

"*bête noire*" of international mining but has made concerted efforts over the years to clean up its act, for example, by working with NGOs to develop plans to protect the biodiversity of an area before starting to mine (Bream 2006). For Newmont and Meridian, the effect of changes in the world price of gold on the stock price fell significantly after the NDG campaign started, but for Rio Tinto there has been no significant difference. This suggests that the NDG campaign, along with related bad press that Newmont and Meridian have attracted, has lowered mainstream investors' expectations of how profitably these companies can operate if they do not make efforts to improve their social and environmental performance. That social performance has became a concern among mainstream investors is reinforced by what happened at Newmont's 2007 shareholders' meeting: socially responsible investors filed a resolution asking the company to set up an independent committee to investigate the criticisms of how it operates abroad and make recommendations for change. The resolution passed by 92 percent, indicating that it was not just ethical investors who cared about this, but that shareholders generally had grown concerned that the company's failure to address social and environmental problems constituted a drag on profits.

4 Discussion and conclusions

The case of the NDG campaign illustrates the role of informational abundance in facilitating market-based pressure on companies to address shortcomings in social performance. As a mining industry spokesperson has observed, "News goes around the world quickly now and there is no place to hide" (quoted in Perlez and Johnson 2005: 1). The case also suggests that SRI's effectiveness lies not just in the capital-market premium or discount it creates, but equally if not more in its strategic partnerships with NGOs and other groups working to change a company's social performance. Thus, the fact that Newmont was screened out of many SRI funds due to its poor environmental and social performance may not have been a big concern to management, but a shareholder resolution is not something it can ignore.

At the same time, the findings of this chapter suggest important non-uniformities in the potential for fairness-related collective actions to lead to improvements in CSR. For one, the possibility of mobilizing "moral sentiment" against a company is likely to be much greater in consumer-goods industries than in industries selling their output to other businesses or government. Because the behavior of individuals reflects mixtures of self-interested and other-oriented drives, they can be expected to shop and act at least at times with social values in mind. But because the "shareholder ascendancy" puts large corporations under considerable pressure to prioritize profits (factoring in ethical criteria only insofar as they affect profitability), we would expect them to buy capital goods, intermediate inputs, and business services with their primary concern being first and foremost prices. Nonetheless, the rise of such practices as "green sourcing" – wherein companies deliberately try to buy goods and services produced "greenly" (e.g. paper made from post-consumer material or certified forest sources), and publicize that they are doing so – extends the pressures for improved social performance "upstream" to some degree.

For another, the possibility of mobilizing public sentiment against a company is greater on some issues than on others. As suggested above, issues that are broadly regarded as ethically wrong may provoke immediate and widespread reaction (as when they involve exploiting the lack of power of poor and marginalized people and eroding their dignity). But with issues that have some ambiguity to them, or that require more knowledge to understand what it is that is objectionable about the company's behavior, the market pressure on the company to improve its performance is often much weaker.

Thus, we conclude by pointing to three important unanswered questions about CSR on which social economists could fruitfully work. The first is the conceptual question of whether the CSR movement induces a shift in ethical norms in business life. Certainly firms' increasing attention to social responsibility has been promoted by possibilities of gaining over competitors by improving social performance, or avoiding risks of losing sales by appearing to be socially or environmentally "bad." But as Veblen outlined in his *Theory of Business Enterprise* (2005 [1904]), an important influence on how businesses do their business is "habitual ways of thinking" – i.e. the priorities and practices they think of as "normal" in the conduct of business life, which come to have a natural character to them. The idea that, to thrive, corporations in today's world need to be attentive to the ethics with which they treat their stakeholders is suggestive of a shift in business norms. However, more work needs to be done to determine, both conceptually and empirically, how to distinguish between a shift in business norms and a change in patterns of business behavior that does not involve an underlying change in habitual thinking. Understanding this question is important for determining whether CSR represents a shift in the business system that is likely to persist, or a more transitory discourse.

Second, even if it is possible to see CSR as having led to improvements in the social performance of corporations, there has been very little rigorous consideration of whether improvements undertaken voluntarily by profit-focused corporations go anywhere near far enough to make a difference on critical social and environmental issues – like reversing the process of climate change. Although it is of considerable interest that CSR has been able to re-infuse business life with concerns about social values, the fact that businesses can pick and choose which problems to address means that some classes of changes – those that would raise social welfare but at the expense of profits – will not be undertaken. Thus, social economists could valuably help develop conceptual frameworks for understanding when market pressures for social responsibility are likely to be insufficient for protecting the common good, and use them to identify empirically when government policies should (also) be used to compel businesses to adjust their practices.

And finally, there is the broader analytical question of why, in the past 15–20 years, the direct application of moral pressure on businesses – rather than government intervention – has come to be seen as the primary avenue for reducing contradictions between the profit motive and social values. Simple textbook economics holds that, when "market failures" result in market outcomes that are not welfare-maximizing, public policies must be used to shift them to the social optimum. The rise of CSR instead suggests the possibility of "government failure," wherein socio-political influences on government result in public policies that are not welfare-maximizing, so that market forces ironically become the avenue for moving market outcomes toward socially preferred points.[28] Thus, it is important to situate the rise of CSR in the context of broader reconfigurations of social, economic and political space – an analysis which social economists, because they do not extract economic processes from the societies and value systems in which they are embedded, but rather understand them in macro/social perspectives, are uniquely qualified to undertake.

Notes

* Many thanks to session participants at the twelfth World Congress of the Association for Social Economics, Amsterdam, June 2007, and to John B. Davis and Wilfred Dolfsma for valuable comments on earlier versions of this chapter.
1 A widely cited definition is that of the World Business Council for Sustainable Development (1999: 3), which defines CSR as "the continuing commitment by business to behave ethically and contribute to economic development while improving the quality of life of the workforce and their families as well as of the local community and society at large."
2 "Stakeholders" are broadly defined as those having legitimate claims to have voice in corporate decision-making processes. See Freeman (1984) for a seminal work, and Donaldson and Preston (1995) for valuable discussion.
3 See Vogel (2005) for an overview from an economic perspective.
4 See, e.g. Figart (2007) for discussion.
5 For broad review, see Graafland (2007).
6 Like the discourse of human rights, it is not clear that the general idea of CSR or its specific tenets make as much sense in value systems with other foundations. See, for example, Williams and Zinkin (2005) and Phoon-Lee (2006).
7 *The Social Agenda* is a collection of magisterial texts on Catholic social teaching (Pontifical Council for Justice and Peace 2000). Here we report the paragraph number in *The Social Agenda* in which the passage can be found. Original references are given in the Agenda itself.
8 See Lazonick and O'Sullivan (2000) on the rise of "shareholder value" as a dominant paradigm for corporate governance. On the extent to which American-style corporate governance is spreading internationally, see Lane (2003); Lee *et al.* (2003); and O'Sullivan (2003).
9 See Blair (1995) for a valuable overview. There is, however, much criticism of how performance-based executive compensation has worked in practice; see Bebchuk *et al.* (2002); Bebchuk and Fried (2004); and Boyer (2005).
10 Similarly, Bookman *et al.* (2007) find that CEOs of firms announcing lay-offs have significantly higher compensation than other CEOs, with the difference resulting from the stock-based component of their remuneration.
11 See Vogel (2005) for a review.
12 See Starr (2008) for further discussion.
13 See Tkac (2006) for empirical analysis of shareholder resolutions filed by socially responsible investors from 1992 to 2002. The lion's share was filed by investment funds of religious organizations.

14 One study by Angel and Rivoli (1997) suggests that a large share of investors would have to boycott a company's shares for their cost of capital to rise appreciably.
15 For example, Wal-Mart has worked hard to improve its environmental performance, but continues to pay its workers "everyday low wages."
16 See, for example, Fehr and Fischbacher (2002; 2004) and Fehr and Gächter (2000).
17 See Fehr and Fischbacher (2004) for discussion and data.
18 Starr (2008) provides data on "ethical preferences" among socially responsible investors.
19 See Coop America's website. Online, available at: www.coopamerica.org. As of June 23, 2007, the "Responsible Shopper" section of Coop America's website had profiles of 169 of the largest US consumer-goods companies (clothing, appliances, motor vehicles, groceries, restaurant chains, financial-services institutions, oil companies, consumer electronics, etc.).
20 In the case of Coop America, for example, its website has links to 67 other groups that work on its core issues (green energy, climate change, sweatshops, fair trade, and forestry and paper); 61 ongoing campaigns run by other organizations (in addition to eight of its own); a list of 95 SRI mutual funds (to which their websites are in turn linked); and hundreds of "green" businesses that it screens and lists in its National Green Pages.
21 Thus, for example, a petition urging Nike to agree to independent monitoring of its subcontractors was signed by 86,500 people (Human Rights Watch 1997).
22 For instance, in 2000 the oil giant formerly known as British Petroleum launched a $200 million advertising campaign aiming to reposition itself as a global energy company spearheading the drive to move "Beyond Petroleum" – while continuing to invest 25 times more on oil and gas than on wind and solar power (Frey 2002).
23 See No Dirty Gold campaign website. Online, available at: www.nodirtygold.org/community_voices.cfm (accessed July 7, 2007).
24 On the "Kimberley Process" to eliminate conflict diamonds from world supply, see Gold (2006).
25 See Tiffany (2006) for elaboration of its ethical and environmental stances. Note, however, that other high-end jewelers like Rolex have not followed suit.
26 That the NDG campaign has been successful in attracting public attention is also indicated by the fact that over 50,000 people have signed pledges not to buy gold jewelry from retailers who do not subscribe to the "Golden Rules" (Tepper 2006: 57).
27 Additional lags were of only spotty significance, and their inclusion did not qualitatively affect the results reported here.
28 This issue as it pertains to the United States was discussed compellingly by former Labor Secretary Robert Reich in his 2007 plenary address to the Association of Social Economics, in which he argued that the notion of "corporate personhood" gives corporations undue say in social outcomes by virtue of their legal rights to try to influence political processes.

References

Angel, James and Pietra Rivoli (1997), "Does Ethical Investing Impose a Cost Upon the Firm? A Theoretical Examination," *Journal of Investing*, 6(Winter): 57–61.
Bebchuk, Lucian and Jesse Fried (2004), *Pay without Performance: The Unfulfilled Promise of Executive Compensation*, Cambridge, MA: Harvard University Press.
—— and David Walker (2002), "Managerial Power and Rent Extraction in the Design of Executive Compensation," National Bureau of Economic Research, Working Paper No. 9068.
Blair, Margaret (1995), *Ownership and Control: Rethinking Corporate Governance for the Twenty-first Century*, Washington, DC: Brookings Institution Press.

Boyer, Robert (2005), "From Shareholder Value to CEO Power: The Paradox of the 1990s," *Competition and Change*, 9(1) March: 7–47.

Bream, Rebecca (2006), "Digging Deep: Mining Faces Up to the Cost of Presenting a Cleaner Image to the World," *Financial Times*, January 17: 17.

Brennan, Elizabeth (2000), "Gap Unfazed by Protests over Human Rights," *San Francisco Examiner*, January 14.

Brookman, Jeffrey T., Saeyoung Chang and Craig Rennie (2007), "CEO Cash and Stock-based Compensation Changes, Layoff Decisions, and Shareholder Value," *Financial Review*, 42(1) February: 99–119.

Davis, J. (2003), *The Theory of the Individual in Economics: Identity and Value*, London and New York: Routledge.

Donaldson, T. and L. Preston (1995), "The Stakeholder Theory of the Modern Corporation: Concepts, Evidence and Implications," *Academy of Management Review*, 20(1): 65–91.

Fehr, Ernst and Urs Fischbacher (2002), "Why Social Preferences Matter: The Impact of Non-selfish Motives on Competition, Cooperation and Incentives," *Economic Journal*, 112(478): c1–c33.

—— (2004), "Social Norms and Human Cooperation," *TRENDS in Cognitive Sciences*, 8(4) April: 185–190.

Fehr, Ernst and Gächter, S. (2000), "Cooperation and Punishment in Public Goods Experiments," *American Economic Review*, 90(4) September: 980–994.

Figart, Deborah (2007), "Social Responsibility for Living Standards: Presidential Address for the Association for Social Economics," *Review of Social Economy*, 65(4): 391–405.

Fligstein, Neil (2001), *The Architecture of Markets: An Economic Sociology of Twenty-first-Century Capitalist Societies*, Princeton, NJ and Oxford: Princeton University Press.

Freeman, R.E. (1984), *Strategic Management: A Stakeholder Approach*, Boston: Pitman.

Frey, Darcy (2002), "How Green Is BP?," *New York Times*, December 8: 99.

Froud, Julie, Karyn Williams, S. Johal and Colin Haslam (2000), "Restructuring for Shareholder Value and Its Implications for Labour," *Cambridge Journal of Economics*, 24(6) November: 771–797.

George, D. (1998), "Coping Rationally with Unpreferred Preferences," *Eastern Economic Journal*, 24(2): 181–194.

Gold, David. (2006), "The Attempt to Regulate Conflict Diamonds," *Economics of Peace and Security Journal*, 1(1): 49–52.

Graafland, Johan J. (2007), *Economics, Ethics and the Market: Introduction and Applications*, London: Routledge.

Holmström, Bengt and Steven Kaplan (2001), "Corporate Governance and Merger Activity in the US," *Journal of Economic Perspectives*, 15(2)(Spring): 121–144.

—— (2003), "The State of US Corporate Governance: What's Right and What's Wrong?," *Journal of Applied Corporate Finance*, 15(3)(Spring): 3–20.

Human Rights Watch (1997), *World Report, 1997*. Online, available at: www.hrw.org/reports/1997/WR97/index.htm, accessed June 24, 2007.

Kaplan, Steven (1994), "Top Executive Rewards and Firm Performance: A Comparison of Japan and the US," *Journal of Political Economy*, 102(3) June: 510–546.

—— (1997), "The Evolution of US Corporate Governance: We are All Henry Kravis Now," *Journal of Private Equity*, 1(2) (Fall): 7–14.

Lane, Christel (2003), "Changes in Corporate Governance of German Corporations: Convergence to the Anglo-American Model?," *Competition and Change*, 7(2–3) June–September: 79–100.

Lazonick, William and Mary O'Sullivan (2000), "Maximizing Shareholder Value: A New Ideology for Corporate Governance," *Economy and Society*, 29(1) February: 13–35.

Lee, Soo Hee, Jonathan Michie and Christine Oughton (2003), "Comparative Corporate Governance: Beyond 'Shareholder Value,'" *Journal of Interdisciplinary Economics*, 14(2): 81–111.

Leo XIII (1891), "On the Condition of Workers: Rerum Novarum: Encyclical of Pope Leo XIII," May 15, Publication 333-7, Washington, DC: United States Catholic Conference.

Lutz, M. (1990), "Social Economics in the Humanist Tradition," in Lutz, M. (ed.) *Social Economics: Retrospect and Prospect*, Boston, Dordrecht and London: Kluwer Academic.

Marlin, John Tepper (2006), "The 'No Dirty Gold' Campaign: What Economists can Learn from and Contribute to Corporate Campaigns," *Economics of Peace and Security Journal*, 1(2): 57–64.

Meier, Stephan (2006), *The Economics of Non-selfish Behavior*, Northampton, MA: Edward Edgar.

O'Boyle, E. (1994), "Homo Socio-economicus: Foundational to Social Economics and Social Economy," *Review of Social Economy*, 52(3): 286–313.

O'Sullivan, Mary (2003), "The Political Economy of Comparative Corporate Governance," *Review of International Political Economy*, 10(1) February: 23–72.

Perlez, Jane and Kirk Johnson (2005), "Behind Gold's Glitter: Torn Lands and Pointed Questions," *New York Times*, October 24: A1.

Petzinger, Thomas (1997), "Business Achieves Greatest Efficiencies When at Its Greenest." *Wall Street Journal*, July 11: B1.

Phoon-Lee, Christine (2006), "Corporate Social Responsibility and 'Putting People First' from a Chinese Cultural Perspective," *Journal of Corporate Citizenship* (22) (Summer): 23–25.

Pontifical Council for Justice and Peace (2000), *The Social Agenda: A Collection of Magisterial Texts*, Vatican City: Libreria Editrice Vaticana. Online, available at: www.the-socialagenda.org accessed June 24, 2007.

Rock, Michael (2003), "Public Disclosure of the Sweatshop Practices of American Multinational Garment/Shoe Makers/Retailers: Impacts on their Stock Prices," *Competition and Change*, 7(1) March: 23–38.

Social Investment Forum (2006), *2005 Report on Socially Responsible Investing Trends in the United States: 10-year review*, Washington, DC: Social Investment Forum. Online. available at: www.socialinvest.org/areas/research/trends/sri_trends_report_2005.pdf accessed February 20, 2007.

Starr, Martha (2008), "Socially Responsible Investing and Pro-social Change," *Journal of Economic Issues*, XLII(1) March: 51–74.

—— and Ky Tran (2008), "Determinants of the physical Demand for Gold: Evidence from Panel Data," *World Economy*, 31(3) March: 416–436.

Tiffany and Company (2006), "Sustainability: Our most Important Design." Online, available at: www.tiffanyandcofoundation.org/TiffanySustainabilityBrochure.pdf accessed June 18, 2007.

Tkac, Paula (2006), "One Proxy at a Time: Pursuing Social Change through Shareholder Proposals," *Federal Reserve Bank of Atlanta Economic Review*, 91(3) (3rd quarter): 1–20.

Veblen, Thorstein (2005 [1904]), *The Theory of Business Enterprise*, New York: Cosimo Classics.

Vogel, David (2005), *The Market for Virtue: The Potential and Limits of Corporate Social Responsibility*, Washington, DC: Brookings Institution Press.

Williams, Geoffrey Alan and John Zinkin (2005), "Doing Business with Islam: Can Corporate Social Responsibility be a Bridge between Civilisations?," Nottingham University Working Paper, October.

World Business Council for Sustainable Development (1999), "Corporate Social Responsibility: Meeting Changing Expectations." Online, available at: www.wbcsd.org/DocRoot/hbdf19Txhmk3kDxBQDWW/CSRmeeting.pdf accessed August 24, 2008.

World Gold Council (2007), "Gold Demand Trends, 1st Quarter 2007 (May)". Online, available at: www.gold.org/value/stats/statistics/gold_demand/index.html accessed 24 June 2007.

14 A proper choice

Jan de Jonge

1 Introduction

In this chapter the question is raised: how do we know whether the reasons for an action justify that action? Was there a good reason to act in that way: was it rational for the agent to do it and was it good that he did it? How can we decide on the goodness of actions? And how can we take account of it. I take the last two questions to be central to the problem of valuation.

A valuation is meant to establish the (natural) properties of the object or the state of affairs under consideration, to assess their (intrinsic) value and to qualify the object/event or state of affairs ("X is good/bad").

Valuations touch the frequent debated distinction between facts and values. The question is how evaluative conclusions can be drawn or be separated from descriptions of objects and/or states of affairs.

In the positivistic tradition evaluative conclusions can only be validated on the basis of natural facts. The basic tendency of science, therefore, has been to purge the world of meaning. As a consequence, any feature of reality that science cannot capture is downgraded as a (mental) projection. All meaning or value beyond what is required for natural facts to be articulated is conceived of as a reflection of our subjectivity.[1] Meaning is not to be found in nature, but rather projected unto objective reality. Value is a subjective variable that cannot be subjected to rational discourse. The obvious conclusion to be drawn is that valuations are merely subjective activities, lacking authority. Evaluative judgments do not make assertions that are either true or false, but rather express the speaker's own attitudes or feelings toward the matter under discussion. The standing of the judgment "X is good" is no more than the assertion, "I approve of X, do so as well."

Opposing this reasoning, Putnam has argued there is no decisive reason to regard scientific statements as purely factual, nor is there decisive reason to regard all normative statements as unfounded suggestions. All input to knowledge is to some extent shaped by our concepts. What makes a statement rationally acceptable is, in large part, its coherence and fit. A fact is something that is rational to believe (Putnam 1981: 54ff.). Putnam concluded that the fact/value distinction is not tenable, but he does not suggest that anything goes, because our justified perceptions of facts are constrained by the concepts of rationality and relevance.

Nagel denies that the objectivity of moral reasoning depends on its having an external reference. "There is no moral analogue of the external world – a universe of moral facts that impinge on us causally. Moral thought is not concerned with description and explanation of what happens, but with decisions, actions and their justification" (Nagel 1997: 101–102). Practical reasoning does not simply dictate particular actions, but rather governs the relations among actions, desires and beliefs.

Cognitivists criticize the noncognitivist creed that morality originates in the desires and emotions of the individual. Such an idea contradicts the ordinary understanding of ethics. How can we agree that it is rational to choose the better life, when it is just a matter of taste whether one lives a "good" or a "bad" life? An adequate theory of the nature of ethics must provide a plausible account of the way that reason supports moral judgments. Cognitivists resort to the term "necessity" to describe the authority of such norms. They assume that the authority of norms can be "seen" or "discovered" by human beings. Correctness in judgment is not determined by grounding them in facts of nature, but is just a matter of coming up with standards of shared practices. And these shared practices reflect that human beliefs, interests, dispositions, and so on, make up a "form of life." A form of life that consists in part in a certain shared set of values. "We live our lives in a setting of morally essential social institutions, conventions, and practices, on the one hand, and of prudentially essential personal commitments and involvements on the other" (Griffin 1996: 94). Both the goals of individual flourishing and our moral demands must be rendered compatible with our normative point of view and in our social nature (see also McDowell 1995).

This discussion finds its continuation in theories about motivation. In rational choice theory it is assumed that actions are only motivated by the preferences (in common language, the desires) of the agent. The expectations of an actor with regard to the outcome are based on his expectations (in common language, his beliefs). The expectations of an actor give expression to his knowledge of the situation (the restrictions, the opportunities) and, as mentioned, his expectations concerning the likely results of alternative actions. They are a product of knowledge, experience and information. Expectations guide the preferences of an actor, but only the preferences motivate an actor to act. As Hume once put it: "reason is the slave of passions." Reason is to be seen as an instrument for achieving ends that are not themselves given by reasons. The consequences are twofold: the goodness of ends cannot rationally be discussed and objective reasons play no role in motivating agents.

Therefore, there are three subjects for discussion: first, how to discuss the goodness of actions, second, how to take account of it, and third, if justifying reasons motivate agents. By way of introduction to the first issue, I shall discuss the question of how agents come to formulate their preferences. This concerns the question: "what is it that makes an action desirable?" I will formulate this as the question: "what attracts an agent, or why does he prefer this object or this state of affairs above an alternative?" The formulation of preferences is from this point of view not different from the task of valuing objects, actions or the state of affairs resulting from actions. Concerning the second issue, I will give special attention to Moore's criticism of the "naturalistic fallacy." I shall, furthermore, approach the relation between properties, of for instance objects, and their value as a relation between primary and secondary qualities: the supervenience relation. This culminates in the proposal, with regard to the question how to take account of the value of actions, that we should distinguish symbolic utility from substantive utility. Choices that aim at the realization of symbolic utility are intended to be what I call proper choices and therefore to be justified in retrospect. But we may not deduce from this that preferences for alternatives that do not articulate symbolic meaning are therefore unjustified. Whether decisions can be justified also depends on the alternatives that are available.

Thereafter, I will discuss the Humean theory of motivation and compare a motivated desire with a motivating reason. I shall propose replacing the Humean theory of motivation by a theory of motivation that admits that reasons can motivate.

2 The value of preferences

My point of departure is the way preferences are defined. Preferences can be seen as a relation between objects or commodities (a preference for apples above oranges); or as a relation between actions (a preference for eating an apple above eating an orange); or, as a relation between states of affairs (a preference for the state of affairs in which one eats an apple above the state of affairs in which one eats an orange). Although these different ways of picturing preferences result in the same choice, the different formulations are not irrelevant. The most important difference is that we can conceive of actions or states of affairs in a way that is not conceivable in connection with objects, namely as the making of meaning and/or fitting the world, which is realized in the action itself.

I shall discuss the following question: "are objects/states of affairs desired because they are valuable in one way or another, or is an object/state of affairs valuable just because it is desired?" Do preferential attitudes bestow value on the objects/states of affairs to which they are directed, or are these objects/states of affairs valuable for what they intrinsically are? Intuitively, it seems that the order of explanation must run from value to desire. But theoretically we can distinguish two answers to the question regarding what is valuable to an agent: is it (a) that our intrinsic desires and preferences are satisfied, or is it rather (b) that the states that are the objects of our desires/preferences are realized? (Rabinowicz and Österberg 1996: 2).

We have to consider two possibilities: is it the experienced enjoyment that follows from the fulfillment of an agent's rational and fully informed desires, or is it the state of the world that is realized that is valuable for the agent? Rabinowicz and Österberg give the following example: "when we wish that rainforests survive, is it then intrinsically valuable that we get what we wish or is it rather the survival of the rainforest?" Rabinowicz and Österberg could not solve this question. The implication of the first interpretation is that what has value is anything that contributes to the satisfaction of an agent's desires, whatever its content. It is good that people get what they want, because it is good for each person to get what he or she wants. According to the second interpretation the value of a preference satisfied is determined by the intrinsic value of the preferred state of affairs itself. The intrinsic value of state A supervenes on those internal features of A *for* which agents intrinsically value it.[2]

Quinn defends the second interpretation while formulating a similar problem as the one Rabinowicz and Österberg presented. His example is that someone wants to see famine ended in Africa. If she "attaches basic value to the end of famine, then it is the thought that doing such and such will help feed people that gives her the basic reason to do it – not the thought that it will bring her pleasure or save her pain" (Quinn 1993: 243). The pursuit is rationalized by the value of the object of the action.

The distinction between both interpretations does not make any real difference in practice. And, therefore, it does not lead to different normative conclusions in view of the fact that the two interpretations are equivalent in the following sense: given that a particular state of affairs is intrinsically preferred, the satisfaction of this preference takes place if, and only if, its objective is realized.[3]

However, value is defined very differently in the two approaches. We may, therefore, distinguish two theoretical grounds for attributing value: the constitutive argument and the supervenience argument. Either the fact that an object is desired or a state of affairs is preferred over alternatives determine its value (value is constituted by the desire) or, alternatively, the properties of the object or of the state of affairs determine its value.[4] This is the supervenience argument that grounds value in the natural properties of the preferred object/state of affairs.

Both the constitutive and the supervenience approach can be used to argue for the interdependence between an agent's desires and the characteristics of the state of affairs that results from an action, or from the properties of the object that is desired. This is aided by the fact that the desired thing will indeed have features or properties that make it desired, that enable it to arouse a desire etc. Mackie seems to have anticipated this, for he warned: "It is fairly easy to confuse the way in which a thing's desirability is indeed objective with its having in our sense objective value" (Mackie 1998: 98).

Cognitivists find it plausible to claim that, first, the features of the object exist independent of the provoked response, and second, that the response itself is a genuinely cognitive state of mind in some way directed to these features. They support the supervenience approach.

The problem is whether the intrinsic value of an object/state of affairs really is a non-relational property or that there exist interdependencies between the object's properties and the subject's psychological state toward the object.

Putnam opts for this possibility. *"Nothing at all* we say about any object describes the object as it is 'in itself' independently of its effect on us ..." (Putnam 1981: 61). The idea that value can simply be deduced from properties has to be rejected.[5] This statement does not deny that values or qualities can be objectively discussed; but it denies that it is possible to claim that there is one true result of a valuation process.

Wiggins even claims that we have to treat psychological states and their objects as equal and reciprocal partners. Consequently, it can be true both that we desire X because we think X is good, and that X is good because we desire it (Wiggins 1998: 158–159).[6] This claim goes much further than the idea that there are interdependencies. It undermines the idea of an interchange between intrinsic properties and the agent's perception of it and has, therefore, to be rejected.

3 Valuation and the naturalistic fallacy

The seminal statement with regard to the question how do we decide on the goodness of actions is Moore's assertion that many theorists have been victims of the naturalistic fallacy.

In the course of time there have been different readings of the content of this fallacy. Originally it was meant as a critique of Mill's argument that just as the only proof that an object is visible is that people see it, so the only evidence that anything is desirable is that people do actually desire it. Moore's objection to Mill was that he defines the word "good" as "desired," while it is clearly an open question whether what is desired is good. Desirable does not mean "able to be desired," as visible means "able to be seen." There may be desirable objects that are not desired. And since desirable includes the moral predicate "good" in its meaning, it is fallacious to define desirable by means of the empirical predicate "what people do actually desire" (cited in Crisp 1997: 73).

Moore was concerned with the equation of goodness, which he saw as a non-natural property, with a natural property.[7] He argued that being good cannot be identified with (or reduced to) any natural property, for "good" is a non-natural property, i.e. totally outside the physicalist ontology of the natural sciences. "Good" refers to a simple, indefinable, non-natural property. Everything that is good has this property. The apparent diversity of intrinsic values – such as, beauty, friendship or knowledge – is unified by the fact that they all share this good-constituting property. Therefore, the first definition of the naturalistic fallacy is that goodness is a non-natural property that cannot be equated with natural properties.

Moore has been attacked for relying on a mysterious and extravagant metaphysics. What could a non-natural property be, and how can one detect it? Since goodness is a non-natural property, it cannot be known by any of the senses. So it must be a matter of intuition (Mackie 1998: 94).[8]

Frankena was convinced that Moore's arguments against naturalism were inconclusive. He considered three interpretations of the "fallacy" (Frankena 1967: 51ff.):

1   it is the mistake of defining a non-natural property like goodness in terms of a natural one;
2   it is the mistake of defining a property in terms of another;
3   it is an attempt to define the indefinable.

Frankena argued that whichever version we take, Moore has failed to show that any mistake is involved. He has merely asserted things without proof.

The naturalist fallacy is only a fallacy because it involves a definitional fallacy. And a definitional fallacy is the process of confusing or identifying two properties. The fallacy is simply that two properties are treated as one and it is irrelevant that one of them is natural and the other non-natural (Frankena 1967: 57).

The objections of both Gauthier and Putnam are similar to the criticism expressed by Frankena. Gauthier agrees that a non-natural property such as good cannot be identified with some natural property. But a case of improper identification is not a case of unjustified correlation (Gauthier 1967: 315).

Putnam blamed Moore for conflating properties and concepts. From the non-synonymy of words nothing follows about the non-identity of properties. Temperature and mean molecular kinetic energy are two concepts that are not identical, but they correlate. The first is a practical concept, the second a theoretical one (Putnam 1981: 207ff). Gibbard formulated a similar objection (Gibbard 2002: 272–273).

The conclusion that can be reached from all this is that value corresponds to natural properties, goodness is the articulation of value and therefore goodness depends indirectly on these natural properties (Anderson 1993: 22–23).[9] This is a conclusion that we encountered before in connection with the supervenience approach.

If objects are equivalent in natural properties they must be equivalent in value. And if objects are equivalent in value, they must be equivalent in goodness. The supervenience approach is not the same as reductionism, but there is some similarity. If values are not reducible to facts, then at least they are dependent upon them.

Before introducing the second definition of the naturalistic fallacy, recall the subjectivist's or non-cognitivist's argument that meaning is not to be found in nature, but rather is projected onto reality. The language of evaluation is "emotive." It expresses a speaker's feelings and attitudes, as well as inducing similar feelings and attitudes in others. The making of any sincere evaluative judgment goes beyond description or assertion of fact. Hence, the apparently unquestionable distinction between "descriptive" and "evaluative" language. The second definition of the naturalistic fallacy therefore says that it is not possible to derive an evaluative conclusion from entirely non-evaluative premises. This definition is closely connected with the one that says that the naturalist tries to derive an "ought" from an "is." Both arguments are based on the strict distinction between values and facts, with the implication that values betray emotions that are not amenable to rational discussion.

Hare, for instance, explains that words like "good" and "should" are used evaluatively when they are used with commendatory force. He attacks ethical naturalism, defining a naturalist as someone who believes that he can deduce an ethical conclusion from descriptive premises. Geach agrees with Hare that "good" is an action-guiding word, for people should choose things that they consider to be good. But this does not mean that the word "good" must be used for commending, because it can have a straightforward descriptive sense. He distinguishes two sorts of adjectives: attributive adjectives (a good book) and predicative adjectives (this book is red). "Good" and "bad" are always attributive, not predicative adjectives (Geach 1967: 64).[10] Analytical philosophers wrongly claim that terms like "good" and "bad" are always being used in a commendatory way. That saying "this is a good book" means something like "I recommend that book." Geach rejected this view which denies that there may be a context in which good is primarily a descriptive term (remember also Putnam's remark that not all value judgments are meant to be recommending). He also denied that good is a non-natural attribute, "for nobody has ever given a coherent and understandable account of what it is for an attribute to be non-natural" (ibid.: 66). Hare responded that Geach's approach is only justified in the case of functional objects. In this case the term "good" is essentially an attributive adjective, which is applied in the form "X is a good A," where A stands for a specific class of objects (for instance a knife; and "X is a good A" means, this specific knife is a very good (sharp) knife). Thus we can use "good" as a descriptive term in the case that the term "good" qualifies as a functional (or instrumental) term, and when understanding the meaning of it requires knowledge of the use to which the object it denotes is typically put, or the end which that object serves (Hare 1967: 79). This corresponds to Thomson's use of first-order ways of being good, such as: good for use in, good at, good for, and so on (Thomson 1997). We can extend this, I suggest, to all cases in which we encounter instrumental values.

What Geach's argument tells us is that goodness can be directly deduced from the natural properties of objects or states of affairs when we know the ends or goals for which they are used, respectively, the states of affairs aimed at. This contradicts the common view among subjectivists that goodness can never be reduced to a natural property because it has emotive force. This argument is clearly wrong, as many descriptive predicates naturally acquire emotive force.

What, then, are the relations between the properties of states of affairs to be realized and the reasons that we have for behaving in a certain way. There seem to be two possibilities. The first is that when something has the right properties, it has the further property of being valuable, and that property gives us reason to behave in certain ways with regard to it. This is Moore's position. It is compatible with the supervenience approach to treat those properties as secondary qualities or properties. Secondary properties are powers that objects, states or actions have to produce effects in the consciousness of observers. "If an act is right (and if we ought to do it), then there is something about it that would evoke an attitude of approval in us, if only we could think clearly and objectively about it" (Rachels 1998: 16).[11] This view is a compromise between objective and subjective views of ethics.

It is objective in the sense that it identifies good and evil with something that is really there in the world outside us, but at the same time what is there has the power to produce feelings inside us. This view seems promising because it requires only ordinary objects, events and the like, and human beings who interact with them.

(Ibid.: 15)

The alternative, which Scanlon believes to be correct, is to hold that being good, or valuable, is not a property that itself provides a reason to respond in certain ways. Rather, to be good or valuable is to have other properties that constitute such reasons. It differs from the first alternative simply in holding that it is not goodness or value itself that provides reasons, but rather the natural properties that evoke these qualifications (Scanlon 1998: 97).[12]

The difference with the first interpretation seems superficial, and in a way it is. What Scanlon's view adds is that in order to understand the value of something it is not enough to know how valuable it is, but it is rather a matter of knowing how to value it – knowing what kinds of actions and attitudes are called for. This applies in particular to "moral" actions.

"Judgement rather than knowledge is what the practically wise person possesses" (Raz 2003: 48).

4 Symbolic utility

The question I want to address now is how we should take account of the goodness of actions. I propose that we focus on accounting for the value of the moral properties of actions. I shall present an approach that is suggested by Khalil, amongst others.

Khalil takes the view that is similar to the one we just have discussed, namely that moral properties supervene on the natural properties of actions. He describes moral properties in fact as symbolic qualities that supervene on the substantive qualities that can be derived from those characteristics of the states of affairs that result from the action. Symbolic utility is the expression of "goodness" that supervenes on the characteristics of an action, which underlie the substantive utility. Symbolic utility is a "by-product" of substantive utility.

Important in his approach is that every choice involves the sacrifice of foregone opportunities. Therefore, every choice involves costs. By stipulating that each action should be submitted to a cost–benefit analysis, Khalil wants to prevent actions from being judged without information about their comparative opportunity costs. He also wants to exclude irrational conduct (e.g. actions in which potential costs far exceed the expected benefits) from the domain of actions where symbolic utility is pursued.

Khalil's point of departure is that, theoretically, it is not fruitful to start with a moral/material dichotomy. As he put is: "there is no such thing as a moral action standing on its own, i.e. separate from the substantive input of interest ..." (Khalil 1997: 515). But neither is it fruitful to model the taste for, say, honesty as not different from other tastes. For this would entail that, as soon as the incentives for cheating increase, agents would substitute at the margin between honest and dishonest behavior. Khalil suggests we should treat the taste for moral sentiments as a by-product effect of the pursuit of an interest deemed preferred.[13]

Why should an agent aspire to act properly? Because he wants to preserve his integrity. "The moral by-product arises from executing what is determined to be the preferred interest. The connection between commitment and preferred interest is integrity" (Khalil 1997: 515). For an action to yield symbolic utility it is irrelevant who will be the recipient of the substantive utility. "It is granted that the agent can smoothly substitute between self-interest and other-interest" (Khalil 1997: 497). This is surprising for "moral choice" is habitually associated with other-regarding choice. But Khalil refuses to see a difference, in moral worth, between self-care and other-care. Building one's own house can be as worthwhile as volunteering one's labor to help the poor.

The next question that immediately announces itself is whether symbolic and substantive utility are interchangeable. Though Khalil denies that substantive and symbolic utility can be substituted along a smooth utility function, he does think they are comparable and, within certain limits, interchangeable. This allows for the possibility of a limited trade-off.

Summarizing: Khalil's approach to integrating moral sentiments and interests is characterized by three distinct features. His central idea is that, since there is no separate moral domain, moral qualities need a substantive stratum. The second feature is that symbolic utility is an intended by-product, and the agent wants to express commitment, appreciation and the like. In general, an act delivers symbolic utility when it is conducted properly. A third feature is that an agent does not want to act properly at every price. There is some (discontinuous) trade-off between symbolic and substantive utility.[14]

Thomson agrees with Khalil that being generous, kind or just can be very costly, and that there are cases in which paying these costs would be superogatory. Under normal conditions, morality may require us to incur costs, she argues, but it does so only when refusing to pay would be mean, cruel or unjust (Thomson 1997: 287). Her criterion for acting morally requires us to do a thing if, and only if, not doing it would be unjust, mean or cruel. In other words, we must prevent other subjects from being treated in an unjust, mean, or cruel way, even when we have to pay a (high) price. In these circumstances it is improper to apply a cost–benefit method, for a moral imperative applies.[15]

I will complicate matters further by introducing a distinction between prudent and moral action. This distinction is akin to Sen's well-known and useful distinction between actions driven by "sympathy" and actions driven by "commitment." My motive for this further distinction is that I want to retain the possibility of moral actions that are not instrumental to non-moral ends. Moreover, this distinction would resolve some of my objections against the trade-off between symbolic utility and substantive utility. Such a trade-off is permissible when moral behavior is instrumental to non-moral ends, i.e. in the domain of prudent acts.

Sandbu also introduces symbolic utility in his analysis of actions. Following Sen who showed how processes might enter preferences, he emphasizes the process character of actions. Agents may care about the way an action is executed. In such cases the agent is not indifferent to how an outcome is produced. We can say that the outcome is process-dependent or that the preference is process-nonseparable. The process is part of the preferred outcome; e.g. it is itself a valued end. These processes are neither independently nor instrumentally valued. They depend for their value on the causal connection with the outcome they aim for. In such preferences, processes have dependent non-instrumental value. "It is this dependent non-instrumental mode of valuation we need in order to account for process-nonseparability" (Sanbu 2007: 222). And he adds:

> By indicating or symbolizing something valuable – in other words, by representing it – an action is endowed with symbolic value over and above its instrumental or independent value.... These kinds of value are dependent – since they depend on the representative relation – but not instrumental – since their value is derived through ... symbolic relations, not a causal one.
>
> (Sandbu 2007: 225)[16]

By indicating or symbolizing something valuable an action is endowed with symbolic value over and above the value of its consequences. Rules and principles are particularly well suited to create representative relations.

5 Motivated desires and motivating reasons

In rational choice theory it is commonly assumed that an agent must want or desire to act properly before he or she will be inclined to do so, notwithstanding that there are good reasons to do it. Therefore, the question arises whether reasons that could justify an action could also motivate the agent. This question introduces a discussion about the Humean theory of motivation.

From a Humean point of view reason can tell us how to satisfy our desires, but it cannot tell us whether those desires are themselves "rational." There is no sense in which our desires or passions are rational or irrational. "All reasoning is concerned either with abstract relations of ideas or with relations of objects, especially causal relations.... Abstract relations of ideas are the subject of logic and mathematics; ... they yield no conclusions about action" (Korsgaard 1996: 331). Hume also argued that

> Reason is the faculty that judges of truth and falsehood, and it can judge our ideas to be true or false because they represent other things. But a passion is an original existence or modification of existence, not a copy of anything. It cannot be true or false, and therefore it cannot in itself be reasonable or unreasonable.
>
> (Korsgaard 1996: 218)

In the Humean approach, normative requirements only provide agents with reasons to act if they are appropriately related to the agent's antecedent desires. And since desires are non-rational states, there is no distinctively rational principle to enter into the explanation of motivation. Then, morality, for instance, cannot be a matter of knowledge, but is rather a matter of sentiment. The reason that moral considerations must be rooted in people's sentiments is precisely that nothing else can motivate them, leaving no room for justifying reasons as distinct reasons. Therefore, actions are justified by the reasons that motivate them. When facing conflicting desires, rational agents will do what they most want to do.

The idea that men are impelled by "desire" which can be assisted or impeded by reason but which is not itself rationally produced is quite unacceptable to a number of moral philosophers. The problem they have with the Humean theory of motivation is either that it does not "allow reason to have any critical impact on human behaviour at all" (Hampton 1998: 148). Or, that "it is irrational to have certain sorts of beliefs, but lacking the corresponding desires and motivations" (Wallace 1990: 382). They argue instead:

> We have reason to try to achieve some aim, when and because, it is relevantly worth achieving. Since these are reasons for being motivated, we would have these reasons even if, when we were aware of them, that awareness did not motivate us. But if we are rational, it will.
>
> (Parfit 1997: 130)

The non-Humean approach can be characterized as holding that people act for a reason, and that reasons are considerations in virtue of which actions are good in some respect and to some degree. One has a reason for action only if its performance is likely to produce, or to contribute to producing, good. In this conception of action the beliefs of an agent connect agency and value.

This approach allows that a gap may exist between what is good and what attracts the agent. And therefore the reason that justifies the action may not always motivate the agent. But when we deliberate about what we desire most, we deliberate about what it would be best for us to want.

> This feature is essential. It explains the sense in which desires are under control, rather than being states of minds visited upon us. A desire is reasonable when we have it because of a belief in the value of its object, and it would disappear were we to abandon that belief.... Our desires are, in this regard, like beliefs. We cannot want what we see no reason to want.
>
> (Raz 1999: 53)

There is a stronger point of view that claims that there are no rational desires that are not reason-based. The crucial distinction is between thinking of desires as being an essential part of a complete motivating state, or of thinking of them as identical with the state of being motivated. The state of being motivated needs an explanation and this must be given in terms of the nature of what is desired. A desire is an endorsement of a reason that is independent of it. If a desire is reason-based, then the desire does not itself add to those reasons. "Desires are held for reasons that they can transmit but to which they cannot add" (Dancy 2000: 39).[17]

In the opinion of Nagel,

> The assumption that a desire underlies every intentional act depends on confusion between two kinds of desires, motivated and unmotivated ones. Many desires are arrived at by decision and after deliberation.... Hunger is brought about by lack of food, not motivated by it. The desire to buy food is motivated by hunger. Motivational explanation is as much in order for that desire as for the action itself.
>
> (Nagel 1978: 155)

When one examines the logical reason why desires must always be among the necessary conditions of reasons for action, one sees that it may often be motivated by precisely what motivates the action. "And if it is motivated by that reason, it cannot be among the conditions for the presence of those reasons" (ibid.: 156).

Nagel's notion of a motivated desire then seems to meet the objection against the Humean theory that it gives no instrument for agents to critically reflect on their own behavior and at the same time to give in to the demand of Humean theory that agents ultimately have to have a desire to further an end. Be it that we have here a use of "desire" that indicates merely a motivational direction and nothing more.[18]

Pettit and Dancy, subsequently defend the idea that a motivating state can originate from cognitive considerations. Some of the desires that figure in motivating reasons are such that their presence is entailed by the presence of certain beliefs (desiderative beliefs). In such cases it would be natural to say, Pettit argues, that the desires are constituted by the beliefs. "We must regard the desire in that case as inheriting the cognitive or discursive status of the desiderative belief" (Pettit 1988: 531). A desiderative belief is just a motivated desire.

Dancy even argues that there are no desires (besides urges and inclinations) that are not reason-based. Dancy understands "desire" as a state of being motivated – as motivatedness – rather than as what motivates. "Starting from a state that is purely cognitive, it is conceivable that *motivation* should occur *without addition to or other change in* that psychological state of the agent to which the motivation (the motivatedness) is a response" (Dancy 2000: 92).[19]

The explanation of intentional action can always be achieved by laying out the considerations in the light of which the agent saw the action as desirable, sensible or required. The idea is that the "motivating reason" is the psychological state of the agent, the beliefs he is currently engaged in, and the normative reason is the content of those beliefs. Dancy understands motivating reasons in terms of justifying ones. The justification may turn out to be either true or false. It is not a theory about motivating reasons proper, as he admits.[20]

Nagel's insistence that the fact that the presence of a desire does not entail that it is a necessary condition for the presence of the reason fostered the fear among Humean theorists that the notion of a motivated desire might lead to the idea that (prudential) reasons are counterexamples to their thesis that all reasons for action depend on the agent's desires. And, this would be a refutation of the doctrine that deliberation always departs from existing desires, as Williams contended.

Smith responded, in defense of the Humean theory of motivation, that "the idea that there may be a state that motivates a desire, but which is not itself a desire, is simply implausible" (Smith 1987: 59). Instead of a motivated desire he argues in favor of a motivating reason.

Smith's approach is based on a strict distinction between beliefs and desires. Beliefs aim at truth, and beliefs should be changed to fit with the world. Desires aim at realization, and the world should be changed to fit our desires. From this distinction it follows that a cognitive propositional attitude (a belief) can give at most a partial specification of a reason for action. It needs in addition something non-cognitive, a state of the will or a volitional event (desire).

Essential in his version of the Humean theory is also a distinction between two concepts of desire. We may associate it with a feeling or an emotion. This is the phenomenological definition of a desire. It is modeled on the idea of sensations and it refers to psychological states. But in Smith's view desires differ from sensations in that they also have a propositional content. We should define desires as dispositions (ibid.: 47).

Now Smith has laid the foundations for the formulation of a motivating reason, i.e. there are cognitive states an agent can be in only if he is in some non-cognitive state. Then he states (ibid.: 55) that the Humean theory of motivation is entailed in the following premises:

1   having a motivating reason is, inter alia, having a goal;
2   having a goal is being in a state with which the world must fit;
3   being in a state with which the world must fit is desiring.

A motivating reason is thus the reverse of Nagel's motivated desire.

Smith, of course, is aware of the reservations about the non-cognitivism of Humean theory, namely that it leaves moral life too easy. It distorts the sense of authority that (normative) reasons have over us with regard to the desirability of the action. His reply is that, when we deliberate, we make judgments about the prima facie desirability of our options and, on this basis, reach a conclusion whether a particular option is desirable, all things considered. Someone who has a prudent (or moral) belief like, "it is right that I Ø" expresses a belief, a belief about the rightness of his Ø-ing. The point of view of the dispositional theory of value is that to be a value means that we are disposed, under ideal circumstances, to desire to desire (Smith 1989). The best way to see what a person prefers is to look at what he chooses when he is presented with a choice in imagination. This is the way to see whether a person values something. "The thoughtful person does not value what he desires but rather he values what he desires to desire" (Lewis 1989: 115).[21]

Does the dispositional theory of value appeal to a cognitive state? Reason plays a part in the process that Lewis describes: it is involved in bringing the agent into full imaginative acquaintance with the object. But once she has achieved this position, valuing is simply a sort of mental state directed toward the object that is valued. Whether or not she finds herself valuing the object has nothing to do with reason.

The criticism of Nagel's notion of a motivated desire has furnished us with an answer to the question whether the belief-desire account of action permits agents be moved, so to speak, "from both sides." That appeared not to be acceptable in the Humean tradition, as expounded by Smith.[22]

From this point of view a motivating reason is intelligible, a motivated desire is not. Wallace has termed this the "desire-out, desire-in" principle. "The process of thought which gives rise to a desire can always be traced back to a further desire, one that fixes the basic evaluative principle from which the rational explanation of motivation begins" (Wallace 1990: 370). The chain of explanation must eventually terminate in an unmotivated desire. Nagel's attempt to integrate justifying and motivating reasons is not acceptable in the eyes of those who represent the Humean tradition. I think we should not accept this conclusion.

6 Conclusion

Rational choice theory is about the efficient allocation of means over given ends. There is a silent agreement that ends should be taken for granted. Each person has the right to decide for him- or herself what he or she wants. Of course this is right, a discussion about a proper choice is not an invitation to meddle in the affairs of other people. My point of departure is that ends are being discussed in daily social practices (by individuals, firms, government agencies and the like) and that we should find a way to reflect this discussion in our theoretical framework. This would broaden the scope of rational choice theory that is too much focused on self-interested behavior. It would increase the relevance of rational choice theory and it would increase the social commitment of our students. I believe that this can be done within a modified framework of rational choice theory and this is what I have tried to explain in this chapter.

I started this chapter with the question what it means to say that there is good reason to act in a certain way. Is this just another way of saying that something is rational to do or does it mean something more, or something else, for instance to say that it is the proper way to do something? A second question was that if we could rationally discuss what is "good," if we had reasons to qualify a state of affairs as "good," reasons that would justify an action, would these reasons also be motivating agents?

How do we know whether an act is proper or good? The answer depends in the first place on the nature of our preferences for certain objects or states of affairs. Utilitarianism identifies the good with the object of a rational desire.

What is good is what an agent would desire if she were fully rational. This was the constitutive argument. The alternative view was the supervenience argument that grounds value in the natural properties of the preferred object/state of affairs. I concluded that there usually is some interdependence between the natural properties of an object and its desirability.

A second discussion concerns the nature of "good." Is it a natural or, as Moore argues, a non-natural property. Many scholars endorse the view that, leaving the functional or instrumental good aside, good is a non-natural property and defend the supervenience approach. Though values are not reducible to facts, they are dependent upon them. Extending this point of view to moral considerations, I have considered the approach of Khalil and of Sanbu, and adopted the concept of symbolic utility that expresses the rightness of an action. When an agent intends to act properly, she may obey certain norms or moral principles because she wants to express some symbolic meaning. The mere fact that she aspires to add symbolic meaning to her action does not necessarily explain the occurrence of that action, but it has some value or utility for that person and this utility is imputed back to the action, adding symbolic utility to its substantive utility. The fact that the action has been performed (the process) is included among the consequences of the action, and any value that the action may have is counted with the value of the outcome.

Symbolic meaning must be treated as a separate component of the utility an action can generate. The most important thing in valuing alternatives is to know what kind of actions and what kinds of attitudes are called for. The import of valuations for human beings is "to understand what matters to them, and so what is worth their aiming at" (Griffin 1996: 48).

Finally, I have discussed the question whether justifying reasons could also be motivating reasons. An affirmative answer to this question implies that we substitute the Humean theory of motivation for a non-Humean theory.

Notes

1 When I refer to natural facts I refer to facts about the world that the sciences study. This includes the human world as well as the natural world. The subjectivist view that is articulated here is partly the legacy of Hume who defended the view that all knowledge is derived from sensory perceptions against the rationalism of Descartes.
2 If X is an intrinsic good and X is a state of affairs, situation or fact, what is intrinsic to X is whatever is entailed or necessitated by X (Harman 2000: 141). This definition does not fit the satisfaction interpretation.
3 This suggests that defining desire as a disposition to realize itself could provide the solution to the theoretical impasse. A desire is a kind of proposition, a proposition to change the world in order to fit the desire (Smith 1987). This would make that the two interpretations coincide (see Section 4).
4 The object interpretation allows that something may be intrinsically valuable, even though nobody wants it (e.g. because it is hidden somewhere and nobody knows about its existence). Since the intrinsic nature of any object or state of the world is a non-relational property, it is not dependent on a state of mind such as interests or desires.
5 From Descartes we inherit the view of a strict dualism between an outer world that we

experience with our senses and an inner world, the world of our thoughts. What we find in this inner world can be described in isolation from the outer world. In fact a thought is a representation of our concepts that is depicted in the world outside. The opposing view reverses the sequence: a thought is a reflection of the state of affairs in the real world. Putnam opposes both views. There is, in his opinion, no gap between mind and world that must be bridged by representations. Our view of the world is the concerted action of our concepts and the real objects in the world. Perceptions are not passive acts, but active interferences of our thoughts to open up reality (Putnam 1981). Moreover, it is often difficult to separate the descriptive level from the evaluative. Pure descriptive terms turn out to be unavailable for a whole host of our key value terms like "courage," "gratitude," "honest," or "reliable' (see Taylor 1989: 54).

6 A specific person may think that she desires X because X is good. But from this we cannot conclude that it is good in general unless we know that the qualities of X can be objectively discussed, allowing for the possibility that the precise nature of that quality is under discussion. We have to stick to the distinction between objective properties and the awareness (and possibly distortion) of those properties. Wiggins thinks that anything that matters in life is arbitrary, contingent and unreasoned. It is something that cannot be criticized or adjusted with an eye to what is true or reasonable. Wiggins emphasizes that his position does not deny all objectivity to practical judgments. He only stipulates that practical questions often have more than one answer. This, of course, is true, but it does not require the belief that what is desired is therefore good.

7 But Mill did not claim that goodness is the same as what is desired. He only claimed that desire offers the only evidence for something's being good. Most of the objects of our desires we desire because we believe them to be valuable or desirable in some respect (Crisp 1997).

8 Out of this criticism came theories such as emotivism and expressivism. Since goodness does not refer to a natural property, it must be the expression of the commending of something.

9 Thomson's distinction between first-order and second-order ways of being good, whereby the second-order rests on the first-order can also be understood in this way (Thomson 1997).

10 Attributive adjectives must always be combined with a noun (as in "a good book" or "a good meal"). The meaning of predicative adjectives does not depend on any noun to which it is attached (see Rind and Tillinghast 2008).

11 Rachels suggests furthermore that the nature of secondary qualities provides a connection between recognizing something as right and being motivated to act. I agree on the condition that this relation is seen as a contingent one.

12 To be intelligible, values must have some link, even if indirect, with our beliefs. What demands respect, we must be able to see as respectable. What commands protection must be able to strike us as worth being protected.

13 The concept of a "by-product effect" should not be confused with Elster's (1983) description of by-products. Elster defines by-products as satisfactions that cannot be willed directly, such as enjoyment, sleep, good conversation, etc. To Elster, by-products emerge as the outcomes of situating oneself under proper conditions. The concept of a "by-product effect" should also not be confused with the idea of unintended consequences of an action. The idea of a "by-product effect" rather captures the shadow of an act that arises when such an act is meant to be a proper act.

14 In my opinion this is the only justification for a reference to a cost–benefit analysis when one intends to act properly. Since moral sentiments, as secondary qualities, are not quantifiable, symbolic utility can be quantified only indirectly by measuring the amount of substantial utility that the agent sacrifices in the next best option (the foregone opportunity). This equates the "moral worth" of an action with its "material

sacrifice." This view also underlines the importance of substantive utility. Excluding purely symbolic actions, most actions have, in the end, a substantive result.

15 Thomson's definition of a proper act resembles Scanlon's notion that an act is wrong if it will affect someone in a way that cannot be justified. See his formulation that acting proper requires that one has "the desire to be able to justify one's actions to others on grounds they could not reasonably reject" (Scanlon 1982: 116; 1998).

16 Symbolic utility cannot simply be incorporated in decision theory, for symbolic utility does not obey an expected utility formula (Nozick 1995). Process-nonseparable preferences can generate choices that violate WARP (Weak Axiom of Revealed Preference) (see Sandbu 2007: 214 for an example). Symbolic utility can be incorporated in a modified non-expected utility function.

17 I want to emphasize that what we are discussing are reasons that are meant to justify the actions they motivate. Of course, there are reasons that motivate actions but do not justify them.

18 In Nagel's terminology a motivated desire is a desire that follows from a reason. The desire would vanish should the reason disappear. The desire is just an animating force.

19 In my opinion the definition of "desire" as "motivatedness' is as close to Nagel's description of a motivated desire as it can be. Nevertheless, Dancy criticizes Nagel for not being a pure cognitivist Dancy 2000: 93–94). I must admit that the point escapes me.

20 The "motivating reason" in this context differs from the motivating reason that Smith introduced as a substitute for Nagel's motivated desire (see below).

21 It sounds as if Lewis is talking about a second-order desire, in which case he would be defending a motivated desire instead of a motivating reason.

22 In subsequent articles Smith seems to have made a surprising U-turn by defending cognitivism and declaring that the claim that a decision is justified is the expression of a belief rather than a desire. Thus, if we make a normative claim, we just express the belief that we would have certain desires if we had a set of desires that are maximally informed, coherent and justified. Beliefs can cause and rationalize desires without the aid of a further desire (Smith 2001). Nevertheless, I still consider his account of the Humean point of view as accurate.

References

Anderson, E. (1993), "*Value in Ethics and Economics,*" Cambridge, MA: Harvard University Press.

Broome, J. (1999), "Can a Humean be moderate?," in J. Broome, *Ethics out of Economics*, Cambridge: Cambridge University Press.

Crisp, R. (1997), *Mill on Utilitarianism*, London: Routledge.

Dancy, J. (2000), *Practical Reality*, Oxford: Oxford University Press.

Elster, J. (1983), "*Sour Grapes: Studies in the Subversion of Rationality,*" Cambridge, UK: Cambridge University Press.

Foot, P. (1978), "Morality as a System of Hypothetical Imperatives," in *Virtues and Vices and Other Essays in Moral Philosophy*, Oxford: Basil Blackwell.

Frankena, W.K. (1967 [1939]), "The Naturalistic Fallacy" in F. Foot (ed.) *Theories of Ethics*, Oxford: Oxford University Press.

Gauthier, D.P. (1967), "Moore's Naturalistic Fallacy," *American Philosophical Quarterly*, 4: 315–320.

Geach, P.T. (1967 [1956]), "Good and Evil," in F. Foot (ed.) *Theories of Ethics*, Oxford: Oxford University Press.

Gibbard, A. (2002), "Normative Explanations: Invoking Rationality to Explain Happenings," in Bermúdez, J.L. and A. Millar (eds.) *Reason and Nature: Essays in the Theory of Rationality*, Oxford: Clarendon Press.

Griffin, J. (1996), *"Value Judgements,"* Oxford: Clarendon Press.

Hampton, J.E. (1998), *The Authority of Reason*, Cambridge: Cambridge University Press.

Hare, R.M. (1967 [1957]), "Geach: Good and Evil," in F. Foot (ed.) *Theories of Ethics*, Oxford: Oxford University Press.

Hargreaves Heap, Shaun (2001), "Expressive Rationality: Is Self-Worth just Another Kind of Preference," in U. Mäki *The Economic World View*, Cambridge, UK: Cambridge University Press.

Harman, G. (2000), *"Explaining Value,"* Oxford: Clarendon Press.

Khalil, E.L. (1997), "Etzioni versus Becker: Do Moral Sentiments Differ From Ordinary Tastes?," *De Economist*, 145: 491–520.

Korsgaard, C.M. (1996), "Skepticism about Practical Reason," in C. Korsgaard, *Creating the Kingdom of Ends*, Cambridge: Cambridge University Press.

Lewis, D.K. (1989), "Dispositional Theories of Value," *Proceedings of the Aristotelian Society*, Suppl. LXIII: 113–137.

Mackie, J.L. (1998 [1977]), "The Subjectivity of Values," in J. Rachels *Ethical Theory*, Oxford: Oxford University Press.

McDowell, J. (1995), "Two Sorts of Naturalism" in R. Hursthouse, G. Lawrence and W. Quinn (eds.) *Virtues and Reasons: Philippa Foot and Moral Theory*, Oxford: Clarendon Press.

Nagel, T. (1978(1970)), "Desires, Prudential Motives, and the Present," in J. Raz (ed.) *Practical Resoning*, Oxford: Oxford University Press.

Nagel, T. (1997), *"The Last Word,"* New York: Oxford University Press.

Nozick, R. (1995), "Symbolic Utility," in R. Hursthouse, P. Pattanaik and K. Suzumura (eds.) *Choice, Welfare, and Development*, Oxford: Clarendon Press.

Parfit, D. (1997), "Reasons and Motivation," *Aristotelian Society*, LXXI: 99–130.

Pettit, P. (1988), "Humeans, Anti-Humeans and Motivation," *Mind*, XCVII: 530–533.

Putnam, H. (1981), *"Reason, Truth, and History,"* Cambridge, UK: Cambridge University Press.

Quinn, W. (1993), "Putting Rationality in its Place," in W. Quinn *Morality and Action*, Cambridge, UK: Cambridge University Press.

Rabinowicz, W. and J. Österberg (1996), "Value Based on Preferences: On Two Interpretations of Preference Utilitarianism," *Economics and Philosophy*, 12: 1–27.

Rachels, J. (1998), "Introduction," in J. Rachels (ed.) *Ethical Theory*, Oxford: Oxford University Press.

Raz, J. (1999), *"Engaging Reason: On the Theory of Value and Action,"* Oxford: Oxford University Press.

—— (2003), *"The Practice of Value,"* Oxford: Clarendon Press.

Rind, M. and L. Tillinghast (2008), "What Is an Attributive Adjective?," *Philosophy*, 83: 77–88.

Scanlon, T.M. (1982), "Contractualism and Utilitarianism," in A.K. Sen and B. Williams (eds.) *Utilitarianism and Beyond*, Cambridge, UK: Cambridge University Press.

—— (1998), *"What We Owe to Each Other,"* Cambridge, MA: The Belknap Press of Harvard University Press.

Sandbu, M. (2007), "Valuing Processes," *Economics and Philosophy*, 23: 205–235.

Smith, M. (1987), "The Humean Theory of Motivation," *Mind*, XCVI: 36–61.

Taylor, C. (1989), *"Sources of the Self,"* Cambridge, UK: Cambridge University Press.

Thomson, J.J. (1997), "The Right and the Good," *Journal of Philosophy*, XCIV: 273–298.

Velleman, J.D. (1992), "The Guise of the Good," *NOÛS*, 26 3–26.

Wallace, R.J. (1990), "How to Argue about Practical Reason," *Mind*, XCIX: 355–385.

Wiggins, D. (1998 [1976]), "Truth, Invention and the Meaning of Life," in J. Rachels (ed.) *Ethical Theory*, Oxford: Oxford University Press.

15 Toward an ethical economics of planning horizons and complementarity

Frederic B. Jennings, Jr.

1 Introduction

An economics of substitution and decreasing returns should yield to a new economics of complementarity and increasing returns (Jennings 2008a). The efficiency implications of any shift to cooperation, dismissing competition for its externalities and horizon effects, shall lead economics into an unfamiliar realm of challenging issues. Substitution has stymied the discipline, justifying neglect of interdependence and dynamic complexities still not well understood.

Substitution assumptions dodge the critical issue before it is raised. To impose static equilibria, treating increasing returns and complexity as not worthy issues for research, undermines the value of theory in its role as a guide to choice. Substitution assumptions say externalities shrink as they spread, relieving economists of much harder questions about cumulating effects (Myrdal 1978): if impacts grow once set into motion, then causal trajectories need to be traced on a path-dependent track. An economics of complementarity opens a larger challenge in a world that unfolds – in disequilibrium – along historical lines. This scenario has no balance, but is a process of falling – with some momentum – ahead in time, where wrong-headed theories steer choices awry irreversibly at significant cost.

The case for substitution rests on claims for decreasing returns, that marginal costs shall rise with new output as sales increase for a typical firm. But the justification for rising cost stands on nothing more than assertion, against sufficiently logical arguments that Pigou (1927: 197; 1928: 256) rejected the notion: "cases of increasing costs ... do not occur," and "supply price cannot ... increase with ... output." It was Hicks (1939: 83–85) who ushered economists into an Age of Denial – that grips us still – with "The Hicksian Getaway." Hicks asserted decreasing returns, called this "getaway ... well worth trying" though "we are taking a dangerous step," but dismissed the importance of falling cost which had driven the field for 20 years.[1] Samuelson (1947), Arrow and Debreu (1954) and others seized on the Hicksian frame, making it into a ruling orthodoxy in economics for 50 years.

Yet people like Kaldor (1972; 1975) rejected their claims, saying complementarity and increasing returns were the way of the world, that we must address them, understand how they work, and control the process when needed. Increasing returns and complementarity yield the world we inhabit, where there is no equilibrium but a trajectory open to chance circumstance and – maybe – intelligent choice. We have no escape from the problem, as we affect events whatever we do, for better or worse, every day. Ought we not try to apprehend truthfully how we might turn this unfolding mystery to our advantage, away from disaster? In a world of complementarity and increasing returns, there is no invisible hand transforming private gains into public goods (Smith 1776: 423). Instead, a framework of ethics and why they matter is urgently needed (Lux 1990; Foley 2006).

The rich culture of economics was stifled after The Hicksian Getaway into one neoclassical mold: the only acceptable economics became mathematical and determinate or econometrically honed to a fine technical tune. Thus has economics been narrowed almost beyond recall by excluding other "rival" analyses such as increasing returns, organization, institutional theory, human psychology, ethics, history and almost anything else in conflict with the ruling approach. The formalization of economics during the mid-to-late twentieth century had a very high cost due to rejection of diverse views. For sure, other outlooks survive – for the most part – though excluded from mainstream journals and often denied promotion. But things are changing in economics; perhaps it is soon to break free of The Hicksian Getaway – long after Hicks rejected it (Hicks 1977: v–vii; Jennings 2009a) – and move forward again.

A first step is to question the orthodox story on realistic constructs, since we cannot avoid decisions shaped by theory, useful or not. Then the case for increasing returns and complementarity is surveyed, to show why a new economics is needed. The concept of "planning horizons" is next developed to reinforce a claim for generalized complementarity in the economy and to explore what it means. Fourth, the chapter addresses the nature of trust and its impact on planning horizons, and the importance of ethics for the efficiency of an economy. The chapter will end with examples and applications where substitution assumptions have led us severely astray at a very high cost to social well-being. The overall aim of the chapter is to explore the need for a cultural change from competition to cooperation as the guiding organizational structure of economic society in an Information Age attuned to living ecologies.

2 The role of realistic constructions in the application of theory

The Age of Denial led by Hicks was smoothed by a Chicago School endorsement of unrealistic constructions,[2] based on a straw man definition of realism as *descriptive completeness* (Jennings 1968: 9–10). As all theory entails selective focus on (self-asserted) essentials, Friedman's (1953: 32–33) definition of realism makes it impossible to fulfill, letting him sidestep the actual challenge of framing essentiality and determining applicational relevance. Realism is central to any theory intended for use, since the value of economic constructions inheres in their reliability as a guide to choice. The impact of economic unrealism on the world has been disastrous, as further argued below.

Assumptions state the "ifs" surrounding our "then" conclusions in theory: *if* we are rational, blessed by perfect knowledge with no information constraints; *if* we are bound by resource scarcity; *if* we are motivated by self-concern untainted by altruism; and *if* our decisions are independently made and driven by market incentives; *then* free trade will likely yield gains to everyone in a transaction. But what about informational limits, spillovers (externalities) and ecological services in this analysis? Such are often treated as incidental, leaving us blind to their impact until duly explored. The selective focus of theory is at the same time a restrictive blindness, where theory is silent on what is ignored (treated as non-essential).

Trade-offs and substitution assumptions in neoclassical theory imply human interests stand in conflict: whatever you get is denied to me, as our bids show what we prefer (or maybe just how much money we have). Values in opposition, however, may not be the essence of economic relations out there in the world: do you rejoice in your neighbors' success or does it detract from yours? If you delight in others' good fortune, then your pleasures are complementary and not opposed. What if friends' suffering grabs us, subverting our peace until pain is relieved? Our real linkage of feelings and impact are more tightly entwined than we think. Constructions standing on grounds unfit to their realms of use leave us blind to the error, unless our unrealism is addressed and tested for its effects in contrast to some more realistic conception, which may not be as precise (Jennings 1968: 13–14).

For theory to be a reliable guide to action, assumptions should be realistic on all the essential facts. Any unrealism must be tested against some more realistic construct to establish the impact of its departures on the implied conclusions (Simon 1963: 230). Such assumes a prior existence of more realistic constructions on which a test of this kind can be based. The claim by Friedman (1953: 14) – "the more significant the theory, the more unrealistic the assumptions" – shuns the importance of testing for relevance through the impact on findings, since realism is defined unrealistically. It is the use of theory – and thus the efficiency of our decisions – that is subverted by unrealism. But "most practicing economists believe in [Friedman's] methodological tenets" (though are loath to admit it publicly), at least according to Boland (1984: 174). The Age of Denial legated by The Hicksian Getaway yet endures.

The focus of denial in economics is on increasing returns (Waldrop 1992: 18) and its implications for how economic agents are related. The question is whether human desire reflects a conflict or concert of value: whether social welfare outcomes are opposed or aligned. Economists have – since The Hicksian Getaway – opted for opposition and competition based on decreasing returns. And yet the Marshallian long-run supply curve falls, Pigou rejected decreasing returns and rising cost as inadmissible in the general case, and Kaldor endorsed increasing returns and tied it to widespread complementarities. So we will look at interdependence and its link to production technology.

3 The case for increasing returns and complementarity in economics

Kaldor (1972: 1240–1242) traced substitution and diminishing returns back to Adam Smith (1776), where:

> Economic theory went wrong ... in the ... fourth chapter of Vol. 1 of the Wealth of Nations ... [where] Smith ... gets bogged down in ... how values and prices ... are determined.... As a result, the existence of increasing returns and its consequences for the whole framework of economic theory have been completely neglected.

Marshall addressed the issue with a distinction of short from long run dynamics, where long-run supply curves decline with new output due to increasing returns (Shackle 1965: 27–42; Frisch 1950). Clapham (1922) opened the way to exploring and filling these "empty boxes" just two years before Marshall's death, after which Marshall's chair was taken by Pigou (1927; 1928) who endorsed increasing returns as a universal case. Subsequently Young (1928) wrote a paper on growth implications of falling cost, while his PhD student Chamberlin (1927; 1933) developed monopolistic competition in striking parallel to Robinson's (1933) work on imperfect competition. Shortly thereafter Keynes (1936) published his seminal *General Theory*: an acceptance of increasing returns seemed to energize economics.

It is hard to convey the audacity of The Hicksian Getaway in this context without reviewing the literature from the 1930s debates, a task beyond the scope of this chapter (cf. Jennings 2009a). Maybe it is sufficient to say that economists had accepted increasing returns as a general case, but never resolved the ensuing analysis into a post-Marshallian synthesis. Hicks (1939: 83–85) said they did not have to, indeed that under increasing returns "the basis on which economic laws can be constructed is ... shorn away" and dismissed that direction of thought as unimportant and probably fruitless. So economists were given permission to walk away from the question, into closed-system mechanical models encapsulated in doctrine. Hicks, Samuelson, Arrow and Friedman – along with many other economists – won Nobel Prizes for such work as it duly entranced the field. An example of the trend is found in Stigler's assertion of rising cost and substitution assumptions.[3] But there was a moment during the 1960s when time, learning and falling costs in production nearly emerged, but it was slapped down by specious arguments soon after it rose.

Alchian's (1959) paper on "Costs and Outputs" mapped time into dynamic cost, though his contribution was sidetracked by "The Hirshleifer Rescue." Hirshleifer (1962: 237–238) "rescu[ed] the orthodox cost function" with an assertion of rising cost, to claim a decisive verification that "the [neo]classical analysis is consistent and correct."[4] Oi (1967: 594) argued that this scheme merely echoed the Hicksian frame, preempting overt treatment of scale economies and knowledge in economics: "To attribute productivity gains to technical progress or learning is, I feel, to rob neoclassical theory of its just due." Alchian (1968: 319–320) ended this debate, declaring decreasing returns "a general and universally valid law." And so – in 40 short years – economics flipped from "inadmissible" (Pigou 1927; 1928) to "universal" (Alchian 1968) decreasing returns, based on nothing more than assertion.

Yet Alchian's (1968) statement did not go unchallenged; a paper by Kaldor (1975: 348) endorsed increasing returns and tied it to complementarity as our most general relation: "The principle of substitution … ignores the essential complementarity between … different types of activities … which is far more important for an understanding … of the economy than the substitution aspect." When Hicks (1977: v–vii) was given the Nobel Prize for his 1939 work, he had "mixed feelings" since he had come to view The Hicksian Getaway and its statics as "nonsense" based on an "indefensible trick" that devalued the role of time and history in economic analysis. But these concerns were ignored by mainstream economists; it was too late for revision: the Age of Denial endures.

Economics may now be emerging from its long isolation. Many reject the orthodox standards in the face of living ecologies and dynamic complexity (as well as the recent financial meltdown), despite that the Chicago School – as the most consistent defender of The Hicksian Getaway – penalizes graduate students for straying from decreasing returns as a "failure to absorb training" (Reder 1982: 19). This claim Leontief (1982: 105) flailed in a letter to *Science* opposed to senior economists' "tight control over the training, promotion and research activities of … younger faculty," comparing "the methods used to maintain intellectual discipline in this country's most influential economics departments … [to] those employed by the [US] Marines to maintain discipline on Parris Island."

The point is simply to show increasing returns as the way of our world and that generalized complementarity opens new doors in economics. The case for The Hicksian Getaway – and for The Hirshleifer Rescue – is based on assertion, not on substantive proof. Is it not time – as McCloskey (1994: 396) said – "for economics to grow up?" Planning horizons are introduced as a means to our maturation.

4 Planning horizons and their implications

Arrow (1969: 495) remarked that a theory of monopolistic competition "is forcibly needed in the presence of increasing returns, and is superfluous in its absence." Kaldor's (1972) paper ended with an appended "apology" to the late Chamberlin for rejecting his view on the divisibility of factors. Oi (1967: 594) argued dynamics and technical change were in the Hicksian frame, but under increasing returns a theory of time and knowledge is needed. Senge (1990: 79–80) identified three elements as the core of systems theory: negative feedback (substitution); positive feedback (complementarity) and time (planning horizons). Such are grounds for horizonal theories, spawned from monopolistic competitive frames and pricing analysis.

Planning horizons serve as an index of "bounded rationality' in an interdependent world where externalities are uncontained (Myrdal 1978). But if our effects grow as they spread then our rational limits of anticipation become an important constraint. Decisions are based on imagined projections, the range of which is the planning horizon. Knowledge brings a horizontal lengthening as will environmental stability, new energy and attention, motivation, self-confidence and other related phenomena. We cannot describe our planning horizons (H*) in cardinal terms; we only note their invisible immanence in every human choice. One might think of H* as a contingency-weighted average range of verified projection; Boulding (1966: 22–23) coined a unit – the "wit," like a "bit" of information – to measure the organization of knowledge. The planning horizon denotes an ordinal index of "wits'" in any decision, changes of which – "horizon effects" – show economic effects.

First we address the pricing implications of planning horizons. A longer H* will lower costs, markups and prices, and therefore raise output and growth, *ceteris paribus*:[5] so might horizons serve as an index of economic efficiency. Horizon effects support a complex systems theory of pricing and growth based on bounded rationality (Jennings 2008b).

Increasing returns and complementarity are joined in much the same manner as substitution and decreasing returns. As Arrow (1969: 495) observed, the former require a Chamberlinian theory. Yet how do we move from individual prices to group patterns? The usual way – an industry of firms with substitute products – supports economists' substitution assumptions, showing no role for complementarities save as a special case.

Taking a lead from Chamberlin's (1961) start with railroad pricing concerns, a transportation system model is more open to complex interdependencies. In transportation networks interrelations are of two kinds: substitution (parallel lines) and complementarity (end-to-end ties). But in a complex system, these connections are user-related: two associated routes – substitutes to one consumer – may be complements for another. Furthermore, these interdependencies are not decomposable; like wine, beer, cheese and pretzels, their relations are purpose-specific. When quenching a thirst we will choose to drink either beer or wine (as substitutes), but for throwing a party with friends all four products are purchased jointly (like complementary outputs). In transportation networks, these two forms of relation are intertwined.

Chamberlin's firms were unique individuals set in a systemic context, interacting complexly with their rivals under rising and falling cost. There was scant attention paid to joint or complementary ties. A composite mix of substitution and complementarity entails seemingly irresolvable trade-offs. Substitution will make competition efficient, though complementarity yields efficiency through cooperation. With both entangled, there is no optimal organizational form. Economics – so blinded by substitution – has seldom raised the question of complex interdependence nor has found any way to resolve it.

Horizonal theory does both. Think of a group of firms subsuming a mix of complex interdependencies and contrast the outcomes of *individual* and *joint* pricing: comparing them measures the "net interdependence" within that group with respect to any one member. If the individual profit maximizing price (P*) exceeds the joint profit maximizing price (P′) for a good, then *net complementarity* in the group prevails with respect to that member, whereas P* < P′ means *net substitution*. This is a way to incorporate complementarity into a grouping of firms, so allowing economists to transcend industry aggregation. Where rivals and complements are entwined, this scheme models such interdependence (Jennings 2006).

But how do horizons shape the mix of interdependencies here? Longer horizons shift this balance away from substitution and in favor of complementarity (Jennings 2008a), given another key assumption of "interhorizonal complementarity." Interhorizonal complementarity means that horizons adjust together across interpersonal space. Your horizon moves generally with and not against my own if we share a decision environment. If you become more predictable, I can plan better too. In sum, we all affect each other's horizons in every choice we make, mostly in complementary ways. We are role models for each other; most teaching and learning involves imitation; moods and emotional states shall radiate outward to others as well.

Interhorizonal complementarity is a new form of interdependence that changes the balance of substitution and complementarity in our relations. The longer our social horizons, then the more enlightened we are and the more commonality and less opposition that we find in our wants. Longer horizons shift the balance of human relations away from conflict toward a closer alignment of values and thus a reduction of conflict. Planning horizons serve as a social welfare standard in this sense and as a measure of organizational and ecological health (Jennings 2003; 2009b).

5 The ethical nature of planning horizons

The planning horizon – in its efficiency aspects – also offers an index of knowledge, organizational learning and time perspective in economics. Horizons reflect the internalization of otherwise external impacts, so will serve as a gauge of "conscience" in both an ethical and ecological sense. All human-caused ecological losses are horizonal: if consequence spreads outward forever, affecting all life on the planet, then our internalization of such "external" losses shall guard us against their occurrence. Caring is consequential; lack of conscience spawns social harm: ethics shall matter in the absence of substitution assumptions (Lux 1990; Foley 2006).

Learning also has an effect on the planning horizons in choice. Substitution has spawned a one-sided view of competitive virtue. Even Schumpeter (1942: 91) raised the question of sincerity here about economists' single-minded devotion to unrealistic competitive frames. Breaking away from The Hicksian Getaway also reveals substitution as special in a more general realm of complementary interdependence. Information and learning, for example, are complementary outputs: when people exchange information, no one loses and all of us gain both from the content and process of trade: "Teaching is in no sense an exchange, in which what the student gets the teacher loses" (Boulding 1962: 133–134).

In the presence of complementarity, cooperation is welfare-enhancing while competition is welfare-reducing. Learning is complementary in its effects: everyone gains from the process. Learning is shunted by competition, which shortens planning horizons, keeping us stupid, trivial, immature and fully ensnared in myopic concerns.

Economists have erected competition as an efficiency standard, though – while keeping horizons short – it threatens much we hold dear. We cannot measure horizon effects; substitution assumptions also force such phenomena out of frame. Theory, in its selective focus, is also restrictively blind to what is ignored as unimportant. We cannot see outside our own lens, save by adopting alternative views. Single-minded doctrines say nothing on what they omit: therefore rejecting complementarity yields an invisible loss. The way to assess opportunity cost is to look at the world through multiple lenses: each enlightens others' penumbrae so may avert some mistakes.

We have learned too well to compete; the ethical and ecological losses emerging from myopia, egocentrism and destructive violence stem from rivalrous systems. Substitution, decreasing returns and rigid dogma are the cause. A cultural shift to cooperation, needed to reverse such trends, shall lead economics into new realms. Successful cooperation is also a libertarian notion: cooperation through force is simply a contradiction in terms. The question of how to cooperate – to realize complementary gains – is less well addressed in economics than in organizational theory.[6] One key aspect of healthy institutional function is trust. The ethics and economics of trust deserve further regard.

Trust is a public good; trust is also "extremely efficient" (Arrow 1974: 22–23). There is scant demand for written contracts with those worthy of trust, and very few conflicts stay unresolved. Trust is also *horizonal*: its long-term value is often discounted against an immediate gain: the current financial crisis suggests the importance of ethics to economics. Short horizons sideswipe persistent devotion to truth; honesty yearns for expansive vision. If competition is keeping horizons short, it damages trust and efficiency: economists' substitution assumptions screen these effects from sight. More attention to complementarity is sorely needed.

Planning horizons serve as an ordinal index of ethical health in any economic society. Economists' substitution assumptions have led us severely astray if they contribute – through an exclusive focus on competitive virtue at the expense of failure resulting from perverse horizon effects – to ethical and ecological losses stemming from myopic concerns. Short horizons undermine trust, squander resources in conflict, and destroy options that we would desire were we able to see them. Some examples would help at this point, to show where this theory applies.

6 Examples and applications: ecology, education, information and social culture

The argument here is that competition – due to its fragmentation of effort and harmful impact on planning horizons – is spawning catastrophic effects in ecology, education, information and social culture. In each of these sectors, competition has had destructive effects on efficiency, functionality and diversity. Competition does not work in the presence of complementarity. Orthodox standards show why: competition is based on substitution, not complementarity. The counterproductive impact of competition among complementary outputs shows up in horizonal losses spawning a myopic culture. Perhaps the clearest example lies in the ecological impact of these horizon effects.

A Ecological impact

All human-caused ecological losses are horizonal, almost by definition. If what we do ripples outward forever, expanding in its effects – as is the case with complementarity – then our ranges of valid anticipation, namely our planning horizons, shape our results in their unfolding course. The Hicksian Getaway offered economists an illusion of fading effects, supporting partial analyses and neglect of externalities. Self-contained closed-system models emerge from these suppositions.

So with Hicks in 1939 economics shifted away from meaningful long-term problems into narrowly-focused short-term equilibria and determinate choice. Subjectivity is excluded from mainstream models in economics; "objectivity" opened a means to examine trade-offs and draw conclusions without the confounding effect of complexity or rational limits.[7] Substitution demands short-term models since fixed factors serve to raise the marginal costs of new output, allowing competitive frames to work as shown and described in our texts. Substitution warrants such models since impacts shrink as they spread due to negative feedback loops.

Substitution has held economists' study of long-term patterns at bay. The ecological impact of our depletion of nature's services is still ignored, despite its threat to well-being. The danger rises from competitive frames and their horizon effects. Competition extols the virtues of fragmentation and disaggregation of firms (and decisional agents) in the presence of substitution, while an ecology is an integral system of interlinked complementarities, all of whose components must be in balance for the whole process to work. You cannot attribute "the credit for a good cake to various inputs" (Nelson 1981: 1053–1055).

Competition does not function in complementary settings save at the cost of serious social losses. Indeed, the neglect of vital living ecologies as economic capital is an indictment of this approach: assets treated as "free" are wasted. One shudders to think of future generations' opinion of us, squandering goods in narcissistic consumption that we should have fostered for them, when they inherit a world deflowered by our rapacious savagery.

Ecological health should be our first priority as economists, since an economy is subservient to its vital life-support systems. Substitution assumptions say the interdependence of all living creatures simply can be ignored, without acknowledging this supposition. Theories stay silent on what they exclude, imposing invisible limits on our apprehension of fact. The ecological losses stemming from institutions standing on substitution are a direct effect of The Hicksian Getaway in economics. Only by weaning ourselves from mechanistic equilibrium models – and duly embracing complex systems – shall economics emerge from its Age of Denial and deal with the crises before us. Facing complementarity and increasing returns as the way of our world is only a small first step. But this advance shall not occur without an organizational shift to cooperation in education.

B The educational system

The impact of competition in education – as our primary means of social assimilation – is the association of fear with learning in an avoidance of error. Wrong answers give us a chance to unwind the incorrect derivations behind some misunderstanding. To penalize a mistake – instead of viewing it as a process of learning – creates an aversion to risky options. As Kohn (1986: 129–131) put it: "competition ... encourages rank conformity [and] ... dampens creativity ... [which is] a process of idiosyncratic thinking and risk-taking. Competition ... turns us into cautious, obedient people."

Comparable effects show up in the academic context as well in the way unorthodox theories are received and duly addressed. The orientation of outlooks in a competitive academic community is to examine new approaches for their relevance to one's ideas: support thereto will lead to endorsement with any challenge opposed. The patterns show an exclusive and defensive protection of views against those shedding new insight. The doctrinaire rigidity of neoclassical economics simply illustrates the point: our "rank conformity" is symptomatic of failure in learning environments where openness should be the norm (Georgescu-Roegen 1967: 104).

Reder's (1982: 19) report on Chicago training, criticized by Leontief (1982: 105), frames the basic conundrum. Teaching ideological dogma over intellectual inquiry – answers instead of questions – is indoctrination, not education. A flexibly open mind is axiomatic to honest science. The absence of such openness in academics should be seen as abnormal, even as pathological in a context devoted to learning (Jennings 2007). A key aspect of these shortcomings stems from the immaterial nature of information transactions.

C The information economy

The exchange of information is unlike that of physical goods, which are constrained by resource scarcity. Information – passed to others – is not lost to its source; rather the total value increases for all with access to it (Boulding 1962: 133–134). Trade-offs – so key to materialistic consumption – do not apply in this setting; instead, "what goes around, comes around" through a system of positive feedback. This situation is closely akin to one where rewards are aligned, not opposed, like beer and pretzels, wine and cheese, or end-to-end links in transport. In each case substitution assumptions state our relations wrongly, applied in a complementary setting.

Scarcity and worth are often correlated in economics: supply and demand are founded thereon, along with the explanation of price. Indeed, the whole equilibrium model and justification of partial analysis stand on this simple linkage: as Smith (1937 [1776]) might have said, the "rarer" things get, the "dearer" they become. But this is not the way our new Information Economy operates.

Here instead the relation of value and scarcity inverts, such that the more subscribers a product has, the greater its worth to each. As one observer remarked: "In the networked economy, the more plentiful things become, the more valuable they become.... Value is derived from plenitude, the concept of abundance" (Matthew 2001: 2). Elsner (2004: 1032–1033) expressed it in this way: "The 'new' economy, thus, has entered a stage of informational abundance which bears little resemblance to the mainstream economic assumption of scarcity," which calls for a greater emphasis on collaboration and coordination. We live in an Age of Information: knowledge is spread through instant contact, churning all we have learned. The inversion of the traditional linkage of value to scarcity is symptomatic of fundamental lacunae at the center of economics.

In these situations of information transmission and education, it is not substitution but complementarity that describes our relations. To impose a competitive frame upon transactions showing complementarities simply yields suboptimal outcomes and destructive behavior welfare-reducing in their results. Sundering complementary efforts shall limit their output and growth. If we all gain from any endeavor, rivalry is self-defeating in its opposition of aims. If instead we encourage each other by working in concert toward common needs, more will be done and learned. Competition in complementary settings is destined to fail; what we need is cooperation. Some of the symptoms of stress stemming from models unfit to their realms of application appear in the form of horizon effects with cultural implications.

D Our socioeconomic culture

The welfare-reducing impact of competition in complementary settings shows up in two related ways: in output declines and horizon effects. Interhorizonal complementarity means that private horizonal changes influence social planning horizons through role model and learning effects. In general – and surely for individuals – suppositions unfit to their realms of use shall limit our range of projection. Notions of competition based on substitution assumptions deployed in the presence of complementarity ought to reduce our planning horizons, so may yield a myopic culture as well.

Indeed, an economy – as it develops – shifts away from material output to intangible sources of value in its composition of output. This scenario also reflects self-actualization in Maslow's (1968) sense (since lower-order physical needs cede to higher social demands) along with the argument already made that longer horizons shift economic relations away from conflict to concerts of value (augmenting complementarity at the expense of substitution). If institutions cannot keep pace with these shifting concerns, by expanding cooperation and downgrading competition, then economic growth is stymied due to both output lags and horizon effects.

These horizon effects show up in the form of organizational stress (Jennings 1999: section III.C.7), suggesting at least one reason for the emergence of a myopic culture. Examples of short-horizon behavior include the nature of TV programming (compared to what it could and should be) as well as of our political process and the American news media: the relentless shortsightedness seen therein is spawned by errors in economics, by systems unfit to their realms of use, standing on substitution assumptions applied to complementary settings. Competition does not work constructively in the horizonal sphere. What has happened to honor, love and integrity in our society? They – along with many other remarkable human traits – are associated with long horizons, so are sadly unsustainable in narrow or insecure realms.

So many attributes central to peace stay out of reach with short horizons, some may be worthy of mention. Liberty is founded upon a common choice to do no harm and democracy cannot prevail in the absence of an informed electorate. There is no aspect of organization that does not demand intelligent choice and firm moral leadership practices to build trust and cohesion. Instead, dire reports of system collapse surround us in many areas: social, financial, political and ecological crises surface so often that we grow inured to their risk. Competition in complementary settings is serving us ill, so we ought to wake up and take notice.

7 Summary and conclusions

The aim of this chapter was to explore the relation of planning horizons and complementarity to the role of ethics in economic societies. Substitution assumptions – as supported by The Hicksian Getaway and The Hirshleifer Rescue – rely on nothing more than assertion of a decreasing return to production. Neoclassical doctrine displaces more realistic constructs with equilibrium models and partial analyses simply untenable in the presence of falling cost (increasing returns) and complementarity. The whole case for competition as an efficiency standard depends on a hard core of indefensible – but well-defended – traditions.

The Hicksian Getaway yielded an Age of Denial in economics, reinforced by a Chicago School endorsement of unrealistic constructs standing on an absurd definition of realism as descriptive completeness (instead of essentiality in the selective focus of theory).

As a result, the existence of increasing returns and its consequences for the whole framework of economic theory has been completely neglected.... Without a major act of demolition – without destroying the basic conceptual framework – it is impossible to make any real progress.

(Kaldor 1972: 1240–1242)

Friedman's case for unrealistic constructions has been disastrous for the relevance of economic guidance (through understanding) to action: the value of theory inheres in the truth of projections structuring choice.

Increasing returns – shunned in neoclassical economics – support a complementary interdependence as the characteristic and dominant form of economic connection. But if our relations are ruled by concerts and not conflicts of value, then traditional welfare recommendations – specifically institutional legacies showing competition efficient – demand further revision in favor of systemic cooperation. The interhorizonal complementarity of horizon effects supports a case for cooperation as more efficient than competition. This is shown by ecological, educational, informational and ethical losses due to rivalry in our economy. Indeed, if competition is keeping us stupid and immature, we are ingesting a poison for cure because of false substitution assumptions and our ignorance of horizon effects.

Some may argue, as Schumpeter (1942: 91) did with characteristic grace, that: "this is ... the tritest common sense. But it is being overlooked with a persistence so stubborn as sometimes to raise the question of sincerity." In this sense, horizonal theory takes a novel turn, and even that development is not new (Margolis 1960). The basic concepts of economics – solid though they may be – are wrongly applied outside their defining conditions. Elementary, you might say. Yet "the history of every science, including that of economics, teaches us that the elementary is the hotbed of the errors that count most" (Georgescu-Roegen 1970: 9).

Notes

1 The debates started with Clapham (1922), then progressed through Pigou (1927; 1928) and Young (1928) to Chamberlin (1933) and Robinson (1933), Keynes (1936) and many other important developments (Jennings 2009a).
2 Friedman (1953: 14) asserted that "in general, the more significant the theory, the more unrealistic the assumptions ... To be important, therefore, a hypothesis must be descriptively false in its assumptions."
3 Stigler (1951: 140–144) represented the process of firms' growth by baldly asserting separability and substitution of productive functions over their complementarity thus:

> For our purpose it is better to view the firm as engaging in a series of distinct operations.... Certain processes are subject to increasing returns ... other[s] ... to diminishing returns ... Our ... assumption, that ... the functions are independent, is ... important. Actually, many processes will be rival ... Other processes will be complementary ... If, on balance, the functions are rival, then usually the firm will increase its rate of output of the final product when it abandons a function; and I think that this is generally the case.

An alternative view was offered by Nelson (1981: 1053–1055):

> If factors are complements, growth is superadditive.... The growth of one input augments the marginal contribution of others. Where complementarity is important, it makes little sense to try to divide up the credit for growth, treating the factors as if they were not complements.... [It is like] dividing up the credit for a good cake to various inputs.... In short, there are not neatly separable sources of growth, but rather a package of elements all of which need to be there.

4 In my dissertation, I deconstructed The Hirshleifer Rescue to show that it "does not really follow from Alchian's statements ... Hirshleifer's argument is a *non sequitur* ... Its status reduces to simple assertion, which flies in the face of an evident fact: unbounded increasing returns" (Jennings 1985: 99–100).
5 This conclusion can be derived – if done properly – from Alchian's (1959) nine propositions on cost, despite the erroneous effort by Hirshleifer (1962) and its acceptance by Oi (1967) and Alchian (1968): cf. Jennings (1985: chapter 5; 2009a).
6 Cf. Argyris (1971), Burns (1971), McGregor (1971 [1960]), Whyte (1972), for just a few examples, or Jennings (1999: section III.C.7). One notable exception is the emergence and development of game theory in economics, although the models seem much more restrictive than needed to address or resolve the organizational issue of complementarity: cf., e.g. Simon (1976: 140–141).
7 As Polanyi (1958: 139–142) put it: "The ideal of strictly objective knowledge, paradigmatically formulated by Laplace, continues to sustain a universal tendency to enhance the observational accuracy and systematic precision of science, at the expense of its bearing on its subject matter." Georgescu-Roegen (1967: 104) remarked on this subject thus:

> Objectivity ... requires ... that a proper scientific description should not include man in any capacity ... True, the ideal of a man-less science is gradually losing ground even in physics ... However, for a science of man to exclude altogether man from the picture is a patent incongruity. Nevertheless, standard economics takes special pride in operating with a man-less picture.

References

Alchian, Armen A. (1959), "Costs and Outputs" in Moses Abramovitz (ed.) *The Allocation of Economic Resources*, Stanford: Stanford University Press: 23–40.
—— (1968), "Cost" in the *International Encyclopedia of the Social Sciences, volume 3*, New York: Macmillan and Free Press: 404–415; reprinted as chapter 12 of Alchian's *Economic Forces at Work*, Indianapolis: Liberty Press (1977): 301–323.
Argyris, Chris (1971), "The Impact of the Organization on the Individual," in D.S. Pugh (ed.) *Organization Theory*, New York: Penguin: 261–278.
Arrow, Kenneth J. (1969), "The Organization of Economic Activity: Issues Pertinent to the Choice of Market Versus Nonmarket Allocation," reprinted in Edwin Mansfield (ed.) *Microeconomics: Selected Readings, 4th edition*, New York: Norton (1982).
—— (1974), *The Limits of Organization*, New York: Norton.
Arrow, Kenneth J. and Debreu, Gerard (1954), "Existence of an Equilibrium for a Competitive Economy," *Econometrica*, 22: 265–290.
Boland, Lawrence A. (1984), "On the State of Economic Methodology," in Warren J. Samuels (ed.) *Research in the History of Economic Thought and Methodology*, Greenwich, CT: JAI Press.
Boulding, Kenneth E. (1962), "Some Questions on the Measurement and Evaluation of Organization," in Harland Cleveland and Harold D. Lasswell (eds.) *Ethics and Bigness:*

Scientific, Academic, Religious, Political, and Military, New York: Harper and Brothers: 385–95; reprinted in Boulding's *Beyond Economics: Essays on Society, Religion and Ethics*, Ann Arbor: University of Michigan Press (1968): 131–140.

—— (1966), "The Economics of Knowledge and the Knowledge of Economics," *American Economic Review, Papers and Proceedings*, 56(2) May; reprinted as chapter 1 of D.M. Lamberton (ed.) *Economics of Information and Knowledge*, Middlesex, UK: Penguin (1971).

Burns, T. (1971), "Mechanistic and Organismic Structures," in D.S. Pugh (ed. *Organization Theory*, New York: Penguin: 43–55.

Chamberlin, Edward H. (1927), *The Theory of Monopolistic Competition*, Harvard PhD dissertation.

—— (1933), *The Theory of Monopolistic Competition: A Reorientation of the Theory of Value, 8th edition*, Cambridge, MA: Harvard University Press.

—— (1961), "The Origin and Early Development of Monopolistic Competition Theory," *Quarterly Journal of Economics*, 75(4) November.

Clapham, John H. (1922), "Of Empty Economic Boxes," *Economic Journal*, 32, with "Comment" by A.C. Pigou and "Rejoinder" by Clapham; reprinted in George J. Stigler and Kenneth E. Boulding (eds.) *A.E.A. Readings in Price Theory*, Chicago: Irwin (1952).

Elsner, Wolfram (2004), "The 'New' Economy: Complexity, Coordination and a Hybrid Governance Approach," *International Journal of Social Economics*, 31(11/12): 1029–1049.

Foley, Duncan K. (2006), *Adam's Fallacy: A Guide to Economic Theology*, Cambridge, MA: Harvard University Press.

Friedman, Milton (1953), "The Methodology of Positive Economics," in *Essays in Positive Economics*, Chicago: University of Chicago Press.

Frisch, Ragnar (1950), "Alfred Marshall's Theory of Value," *Quarterly Journal of Economics*, 64: 495–524; reprinted as chapter 3 of H. Townsend (ed.) *Price Theory: Selected Readings*, Baltimore: Penguin (1971).

Georgescu-Roegen, Nicholas (1967), *Analytical Economics: Issues and Problems*, Cambridge, MA: Harvard University Press.

—— (1970), "The Economics of Production," *American Economic Review, Papers and Proceedings*, 60(2) May.

Hicks, John R. (1939), *Value and Capital, 2nd edition*, Oxford: Oxford University Press.

—— (1977), "Preface (and Survey)," in *Economic Perspectives: Further Essays on Money and Growth*, Oxford: Oxford University Press.

Hirshleifer, Jack (1962), "The Firm's Cost Function: A Successful Reconstruction?," in *Journal of Business*, 35(3) July: 235–255.

Jennings, Frederic B. Jr. (1968), *Competition Theory and the Welfare Optimum: A Methodological Analysis*, Harvard Department of Economics, undergraduate honors thesis.

—— (1985), *Public Policy, Planning Horizons and Organizational Breakdown: A Post-Mortem on British Canals and Their Failure*, Stanford University PhD dissertation.

—— (1999), *Scaring the Fish: A Critique of the National Research Council's Justification for Individual Transferable Quotas (ITQs) and A Systems Analysis of Their Likely Effects*, a joint publication of the Center for Ecological Economic and Ethical Education (CEEEE), Ipswich, MA and Greenpeace, Washington, DC.

—— (2003), "Ecology, Economics and Values," *Environmental Health*, 3(2) June.

—— (2006), "A Horizonal Challenge to Orthodox Theory: Competition and Cooperation in Transportation Networks," in Michael Pickhardt and Jordi Sarda Pons (eds.) *INFER*

Research Perspectives, volume 1: Perspectives on Competition in Transportation, Berlin: Lit Verlag.

—— (2007), "Hammers, Nails and New Constructions – Orthodoxy or Pluralism: An Institutional View," presented at the 2007 Conference of the International Association for Pluralism in Economics (ICAPE), Salt Lake City, UT.

—— (2008a), "A New Economics of Complementarity, Increasing Returns and Planning Horizons," in Wolfram Elsner and Hardy Hanappi (eds.) *Varieties of Capitalism and New Institutional Deals*, Cheltenham, UK: Edward Elgar.

—— (2008b), "A Horizonal Theory of Pricing in the New Information Economy," in Christian Richter (ed.) *INFER Research Perspectives, volume 8: Bounded Rationality in Economics and Finance*, Berlin: Verlag.

—— (2009a), "'The Hicksian Getaway' and 'The Hirshleifer Rescue': Increasing Returns from Clapham to Kaldor," presented at the 2009 Conference of the Association For Institutional Thought (AFIT), Albuquerque, NM.

—— (2009b), "Six Choice Metaphors and Their Economic Implications," *Journal of Philosophical Economics*, 2(2) May.

Kaldor, Nicholas (1972), "The Irrelevance of Equilibrium Economics," *Economic Journal*, 82(327) December: 1237–1255.

—— (1975), "What is Wrong with Economic Theory," *Quarterly Journal of Economics*, 89(3) August: 347–357.

Keynes, John M. (1936), *The General Theory of Employment, Interest and Money*, Cambridge, UK: Macmillan and Cambridge University Press.

Kohn, Alfie (1986), *No Contest: The Case against Competition*, Boston: Houghton Mifflin.

Leontief, Wassily (1982), "Academic Economics," *Science*, 217 July; reprinted as "Foreword" to Alfred S. Eichner (ed.) *Why Economics is Not Yet a Science*, Armonk, NY: M.E. Sharpe (1983).

Lux, Kenneth (1990), *Adam Smith's Mistake: How a Moral Philosopher Invented Economics and Ended Morality*, Boston: Shambhala Publications.

McCloskey, Donald N. (1994), *Knowledge and Persuasion in Economics*, Cambridge, UK: Cambridge University Press.

McGregor, Douglas (1971 [1960]), "Theory X and Theory Y," in D.S. Pugh (ed.) *Organization Theory*, New York: Penguin.

Margolis, Julius (1960), "Sequential Decision Making in the Firm," *American Economic Review, Papers and Proceedings*, 50(2): 526–533.

Maslow, Abraham (1968), *Toward a Psychology of Being*, New York: Van Nostrand.

Matthew, Angus (2001), "The New Economy – Truth or Fallacy?," in *Pool: Business and Marketing Strategy* (13) Winter. Online, available at: www.poolonline.com/archive/issue13/iss13fea4.html.

Myrdal, Gunnar (1978), "Institutional Economics," *Journal of Economic Issues*, 12(4): 771–783.

Nelson, Richard R. (1981), "Research on Productivity Growth and Productivity Differences: Dead Ends and New Departures," *Journal of Economic Literature*, 19(3) September: 1029–1064.

Oi, Walter Y. (1967), "The Neoclassical Foundations of Progress Functions," *Economic Journal*, 77 September: 579–954.

Pigou, Alfred C. (1927), "The Laws of Diminishing and Increasing Cost," *Economic Journal*, 37(146) June: 188–197.

—— 1928, "An Analysis of Supply," *Economic Journal*, 38(150) June: 238–257.

Polanyi, Michael (1958), *Personal Knowledge: Towards a Post-critical Philosophy*, Chicago: University of Chicago Press.

Reder, Melvin W. (1982), "Chicago Economics: Permanence and Change," *Journal of Economic Literature*, 20(1) March: 1–38.

Robinson, Joan (1933), *The Economics of Imperfect Competition*, London: Macmillan.

Samuelson, Paul (1947), *Foundations of Economic Analysis*, Cambridge, MA: Harvard University Press.

Schumpeter, Joseph A. (1942), *Capitalism, Socialism and Democracy*, New York: Harper & Row.

Senge, Peter M. (1990), *The Fifth Discipline: The Art and Practice of the Learning Organization*, New York: Doubleday-Currency.

Shackle, George L.S. (1965), *A Scheme of Economic Theory*, Cambridge, UK: Cambridge University Press.

Simon, Herbert A. (1963), "Discussion" of Nagel, *American Economic Review, Papers and Proceedings*, 53(2) May: 229–231.

—— (1976), "From Substantive to Procedural Rationality" in Spiro J. Latsis (ed.) *Method and Appraisal in Economics*, Cambridge, UK: Cambridge University Press.

Smith, A. (1937 [1776]), *An Inquiry into the Nature and Causes of the Wealth of Nations*, New York: Modern Library.

Stigler, George J. (1951), "The Division of Labor is Limited by the Extent of the Market," *Journal of Political Economy*, 59 June: 185–193; also chapter 10 in William Breit and Harold M. Hochman (ed.) *Readings in Microeconomics, 2nd edition*, New York: Holt, Rinehart and Winston (1971): 140–148.

Waldrop, M. Mitchell (1992), *Complexity: The Emerging Science at the Edge of Order and Chaos*, New York: Simon & Schuster.

Whyte, W.F. (1972), "Models for Building and Changing Organizations," chapter 8 in J.M. Thomas and W.G. Bennis (eds.) *Management of Change and Conflict*, New York: Penguin: 227–238.

Young, Allyn A. (1928), "Increasing Returns and Economic Progress," *Economic Journal*, 38(152) December: 527–542.

Index

Note: **Bold** page numbers refer to tables and *italic* to figures

abundance paradox 115–17
Accra, declaration of faith 8, 213
activism 26–7
adult worker model 149–63; childcare
  services 154–8, *155–6*; employment
  rates 150–4, *151–4*; employment rates,
  gender differences 153–4; gender
  equality 161–2; leave facilities 158–60,
  159; negative employment effects 160
Africa: imposition of capitalist ideology
  18; poverty levels 223
Age of Denial 276–7
age and overwork 6, 97–114, 24/7
  economy 98–100; age effects and anger
  107; age effects and stress **108**; life
  course theory 103–4; negative effects
  100–1; normative contract theory and
  age 102–3; overwork 97–100; research
  design 105–8; research design, analysis
  106–7; research design, data 105;
  research design, measures 105–6;
  research design, results 107–8
algocracy 139
anger: and age effects **107**
Argentina 44–5, 48–50; El Puerto
  (example) 44–5; spectacular corruption
  45
Asian Crisis (1998) 2
Aubry laws: time sovereignty 81, 83–4

biblical evidence: need for distributive
  justice 217–21; utilitarianism and
  difference principle 221

capability theory of Sen 24, 35, 220
capitalism 4–5, 13–41; allocation of net
  surplus 16; capitalist accounting
  categories 33–5; capture of the state
  17–18; concept 15; debates 13–18;
  defenses 13; defined 15–18; desirabiity
  18–21; Easterbrook paradox 24; Easterlin
  paradox 23–4; human flourishing 13–15,
  22–6, 35–6; McCloskey, D 13–22;
  obsolescence lunacies 27–8, 33; thrust
  for profits/growth 31
capitalist society 16, 23
capitalistic justice 218–19
Catholic social thought, corporate social
  responsibility (CSR) 235–6, 237
Chicago School 276, 279
child labor 240
childcare services 154–8, *155–6*
Chile: PPH program 33–4
China: poverty levels 223
choice 256–74; motivated desires and
  motivating reasons 265–9; rational
  choice theory 269; symbolic utility 263;
  valuation and naturalistic fallacy 260–3;
  value of preferences 258–60
cognitivism 257–60
communism: and distributive justice
  215–16
competition 282–6; ecological impact
  283–4; educational system 284;
  information economy 284–5; social
  losses 283–4; welfare-reducing impact
  on socioeconomic culture 285–6
complementarity, and increasing returns
  275–6, 278–9; interhorizonal 281
computable general equilibrium models
  223; Global Trade Analysis project
  (GTAP) 223; LINKAGE model 223
consumption 125; position in society 88;
  use of time 83; working hours and
  environmental degradation 90
cooperation: versus competition 282

corporate social responsibility (CSR) 234–55; business life ethics 235–42; Catholic social thought 235–6; environmental consequences of companies' actions 236–7; fairness and unfairness behavior 239–41; information and communication technologies (ICTs), effects on irresponsible corporate behavior 241–2; No Dirty Gold (NDG) campaign 242–9; revenue-related pressures 239–40; socially responsible investment (SRI) 238; sweatshop and child labor 240; *see also* ethics
cultural influences: and happiness 119–20
culture, socioeconomic 285–6

democratic globalization, Argentine case study 44–5, 48–50; Nicaragua case study 47; and United Nations 42–57
democratic governance versus "foolish majority rule" 52–3
depression 123–4
descriptive completeness 276–7
developing countries: and globalization 225–6
diminishing returns: and substitution 275–6, 278–9
discounting 33
distributive justice 213–33; alternative standards 215; biblical evidence 217–18; distribution according to moral desert 217; entitlement theory 217; principle of 215

Easterbrook paradox: capitalism 24
Easterlin paradox: capitalism 23–4
ecological impact *see* environmental degradation
economic development processes 44–8; governance 44–6; knowledge and learning 46–8
economic growth, and happiness 116, 123; trade liberalization **229**
economic system: poverty, and Accra declaration of faith 213–33
education and happiness 117
educational system: competition 284
embeddedness, time sovereignty 140–1
employment, adult worker model 150–4, *151–4*; and happiness 120; *see also* work
environmental degradation, consequences of companies' actions 236–7; consumption and working hours 90; ecological impact of competition 283–4

equal rights, United Nations Charter preamble 50
ethical economics 8–9, 275–91; and cognitivism 257; cooperation versus competition 282; corporate social responsibility (CSR) 234–55; examples and applications 283–6; planning horizons 281–2; trust 282; violations of fairness 240
eudaimonia 14
Europe, EEA countries 150; financial wealth net of pension funds **203**; household wealth 1995–2004 **202**, **204**; income distribution, government share and economic freedom index **227**; main pension reforms 187–90, **190–7**
European Union, adult worker model 149–63; childcare services 154–8, *155–6*; employment rates 150–4, *151–4*; gender in workplace, adult worker model 149–63; Lisbon Council (2000) 149; Working Time Directive 84
evaluative judgments 256

fairness: violations 240
Families and Work Institute report 97–100
Fordist working time regime 81–2; post Fordist worker and new workplace structure 82–3
France: financial wealth net of pension funds **203**; household wealth 1995–2004 **202**, **204**; share ownership as percentage of total household wealth **200–1**; time sovereignty 81, 83–4
Fraser Institute, aspects of economic freedom **222**

gender in workplace 149–63; gender equality 161–2
Generalized Entropy inequality measure *GE (*2) 168–9, 171–2
German Socioeconomic Panel 166
Germany: determinants of intergenerational poverty, transmission **179**; determinants of intergenerational poverty (*see also* poverty); financial wealth net of pension funds **203**; household wealth 1995–2004 **202**, **204**; housing space 117; intergenerational income transitions 170–1, **177**; RTT laws 84; share ownership as percentage of total household wealth **200–1**; and United States, poverty study 164–81
gift exchange 59, 67–71

Gini coefficient 168, 171–2

Gini index 226, 227

Globalization: Annan 50–1; democracy within United Nations 42–57; and developing countries 225–6; inclusive 51; post-war, origin 2

gold industry: Golden Rules code of conduct 243–9; Golden Rules code of conduct, gold mining companies, effects on stock prices **248**; Golden Rules code of conduct, retail jewelers **245**, **247**; No Dirty Gold (NDG) campaign 242–9; No Dirty Gold (NDG) campaign, cyanide and mercury toxic waste 242; No Dirty Gold (NDG) campaign, GARCH model 246; No Dirty Gold (NDG) campaign, stakeholders in world gold industry *243*; No Dirty Gold (NDG) campaign, Valentines Day tactics 243

Golden Straitjacket (Friedman) 222

governance: economic development process 44–6

happiness 6, 115–35; abundance paradox 115–17; abundance paradox, overweight versus undernourished 116–17; consumption 125; cultural influences 119–20; depression 123–4; economic growth 116, 123; education 117; employment 120; housing 117; income and happiness 119, 121–2; long working hours and social costs 127–8; material abundance 115; materialism 122–3; policy prescription 128–30; renewed interest 115; role 118; social relationships 126–7; suicide 123–4; taxation effects 128–30; wealthier individuals 120–3; wealthy countries 118–20; windfall changes in wealth 121; work time reform 124–8; *see also* human flourishing

hedonistic disconnect 36

Hicksian Getaway 275–7, 279, 284

hierarchies of knowledge cooperation 58, 61–3

horizon effects 286

horizonal theory 280–1

household wealth 182–210, **202**, **204**, **205–6**; share ownership as percentage **200–1**

housing 117

Human Development Index (HDI) 224

human flourishing, and capitalism 13–15, 22–6, 35–6; conception 13–14, 22–6; conception, defined 14–15; conception,

objective and subjective 23, *24*; income 23; markets 15–16, 18–21; and property rights 17; rethinking work 35–6; Sen paradox 24, 35; volunteer time 33–4; and work 26–36; *see also* happiness

Humean theory, motivated desires and motivating reasons 265–9

income distribution: and capitalism 23; government share and economic freedom index, Europe **227**; intergenerational inequality and poverty transmission 164–81; worldwide trends **228**; *see also* poverty

income and happiness 119, 121–2; individual income benefits 121; relative income 121–2, 125–6; windfall changes 121

increasing returns and complementarity 275–6, 278–9

information and communication technologies (ICTs): effects on irresponsible corporate behavior 241–2; information economy, competition 284–5; interpretive flexibility of technology 142; social time in digital work places 136, 137–40; *see also* time sovereignty

innovation: motivation 70; *see also* knowledge cooperation

intellectual property rights (IPRs) 60

international work settings: time sovereignty 140–4, **141**

investment, socially responsible investment (SRI) 238

Italy, financial wealth net of pension funds **203**; household wealth 1995–2004 **202**, **204**; share ownership as percentage of total household wealth **200–1**

ITIL 139

Japan: financial wealth net of pension funds **203**; household wealth 1995–2004 **202**, **204**; pension reform 189–90; Japanese wellbeing 119

knowledge cooperation 58–78; access to knowledge 70–1; coordination 3 mechanisms 58, **65**; dissected coordination **66**; economic development process 46–8; gift exchange 59, 67–71; hierarchies 61–3, **65**; markets 59–61, **65**; monitoring 69; motivation 70; social relations and gifts 58–9, 63–71

Kuznets curve, poverty 225, 226

life course theory, age and overwork
103–4
life insurance 190, 199–206
life-support services 283–4

market operation: basic needs 223–4;
distributive justice 213; Gini index 226,
227; income equality between countries
227–9; income equality within countries
224–7; long term trends 226; socialist
justice 221–9; socialist justice,
indicators 221–2
markets 18–21; arguments for and against
21; distributive equity 19; free choice
19; and knowledge cooperation 59–61;
as liberal institutions 19; pro-market
economics 18–21; sociology 19–20
material abundance 115
materialism, and happiness 122–3
maternity/paternity leave **159**
morality 257, 263–4; symbolic utility 264;
valuation and naturalistic fallacy 260–3;
versus prudence 264
motivated desires and motivating reasons
265–9; Humean theory 265–9

National Time Regimes 141–3
naturalistic fallacy 260–3
needs principle 216; Human Development
Index (HDI) 224
negative feedback (substitution) 275–6,
278–9
network society 138
Nicaragua, Ocotal, democratic
globalization 47
Nike 240, 242

obsolescence lunacies 27–8, 33
overweight versus undernourishment
116–17

pension funds, contribution to shareholder
society 199; and life insurance,
differentiation for household assets
199–206; net acquisition **198**
pension reform 184–210; citizens'
financial position 185–6; continental
countries (corporative Bismarckian
welfare states) 187–8; Europe 187–90,
190–7; financial wealth net of pension
funds **203**; general governance of
production system 186; household assets
205–6; household debts *204*; household
wealth 182–210, **202**, **204**, **205–6**;

household wealth, share ownership as
percentage **200–1**; Japan 189–90; life
insurance, contribution to capital
increase 190, 199; PAYG (pay as you
go) pension systems 182–210;
Scandinavian countries 188–9; social
insurance function 185; stability of the
economy 186–7; UK and USA 189–90
pension system reforms 184–7
planning horizons 279–86; ethics 281–2;
learning 281–2; pricing implications
280–1
Pontifical Council of Peace and Justice
Social Agenda 236–7
positive feedback (complementarity)
275–6, 278–9
positivism 256
poverty 164–81; Accra declaration of faith
213–33; by world regions (1990, 1999,
2004) **223**; case study (USA and
Germany) 164–81; case study (USA and
Germany), contribution of income
sources to total inequality 169; case
study (USA and Germany), database
166–7; case study (USA and Germany),
determinants of intergenerational
poverty persistence 171–6; case study
(USA and Germany), determinants of
intergenerational poverty transmission
179; case study (USA and Germany),
empirical results 171–6; case study
(USA and Germany), Generalized
Entropy inequality measure *GE (*2)
168–9, 171–2; case study (USA and
Germany), Gini coefficient 168, 171–2;
case study (USA and Germany), income
inequality *172–3*; case study (USA and
Germany), intergenerational income
elasticity 169–70; case study (USA and
Germany), intergenerational income
inequality and poverty measures 168–9;
case study (USA and Germany),
intergenerational income mobility **175**;
case study (USA and Germany),
intergenerational income transitions
170–1, **177–8**; case study (USA and
Germany), methodology 168–71; case
study (USA and Germany), sample
organization 167; and globalization
225–6; Kuznets curve 225, 226; poverty
intensity *174*; trade liberalization 223,
225; *see also* distributive justice; income
distribution
preferences 258–60; value, defined 259

procedural justice 218–19
property rights, and capitalism 17
prudence, versus morality 264

rational choice theory 269
Rawlsian difference principle 216
Rawlsian principle of equal opportunities 216–17
redistribution: intergenerational inequality and poverty transmission 164–81
Reebok 242
Roosevelt, T. 28–9

Sarkozy, Nicolas 81
Scandinavian countries: financial wealth net of pension funds **203**; household wealth 1995–2004 **202, 204**; pension reform 188–9; share ownership as percentage of total household wealth **200–1**
science: and evaluative judgments 256
self determination: United Nations Charter preamble 50
Sen: capability theory 220
Sen paradox: capitalism 24, 35
share ownership **200–1**, 237–9; and CSR 237–9
Social Agenda: Pontifical Council of Peace and Justice 236–7
social relationships: gift exchange 59, 67–71; and happiness 126–7
social time *see* time sovereignty
socially responsible investment (SRI) 238
Sorel, G. 30
stress: age effects and stress **108**
substitution, case for 275–6; and diminishing returns 275–6, 278–9
suicide 123–4
sweatshop and child labor 240
symbolic utility 263; morality 264; substantive utility 263–4
systems theory 3 elements 279

taxation effects 128–30
time sovereignty 5–6, 81–96, 136–46; compromises 83–5; digital work places 137–40; externalities 89–92; Fordist working time regime 81–2; international work settings 140–4, **141**; international work settings, cyclic versus self time 140, **143**; international work settings, embeddedness 140–1; international work settings, synchronization 141; international work settings, time

stratification 141; interpretive flexibility of technology 142; labor control 139; labor integration 139; long working hours 86–92, **87**, 138; long working hours, environmental costs 89–90; long working hours, family relations 91–2; long working hours, flexibility 82–92; long working hours, medical argument 89; long working hours, overtime 84–5; long working hours, and situation of colleagues **87**; long working hours, social costs 90–1; National Time Regimes 141–3; network society 138; post Fordist worker and new workplace structure 82–3; wage-earners 85–9
trade liberalization, economic growth **229**; and poverty 223, 225
transaction cost theory 61
transportation networks 280
trust 282

UK: financial wealth net of pension funds **203**; household wealth 1995–2004 **202, 204**; income distribution, government share and economic freedom index **227**; pension reform 189–90
United Nations Charter 52; preamble 50
United Nations and democratic globalization 42–57; active citizenship benefits 47; democratic outcomes, achievement 51–3; economic development 44–8; elite or democratic globalization 48; governance 44–6; international institutions 48–53; knowledge and learning 46–8; Ocotal, Nicaragua (example) 47; principles and aims 50–3; transnational corporations 45
USA: depression incidence 123–4; determinants of intergenerational poverty, transmission **179**; determinants of intergenerational poverty *see also* poverty education 117; *Families and Work Institute* report 97–100; financial wealth net of pension funds **203**; household wealth 1995–2004 **202, 204**; housing space 117; income distribution, government share and economic freedom index **227**; intergenerational income transitions 170–1, **178**; Panel Study of Income Dynamics (PSID) 166; pension reform 189–90; Washington institutions, and globalization 49
utilitarianism 216
utility, symbolic 263–4

valuation and naturalistic fallacy 260–3; goodness 260–3; interpretations 260–2
value of preferences 259–60
Veblen effect 115, 125
volunteer time 33–4

work: alternative concepts 35–6; and costs, defined 32–3; idolatry 120; overwork, dual-earner families 99; overwork, negative effects 100–1; paradoxes 32–6; rethinking 35–6; versus leisure 26–31; work time reform, and happiness 124–8

workers model of gender equality 149–63; working hours *see* time sovereignty; adult worker model
Working Time Directive European Union 84
World Alliance of Reformed Churches (WRAC), declaration of faith 213; integrity of faith questioned 214
World Bank and IMF 53; effects on Argentina 48–9